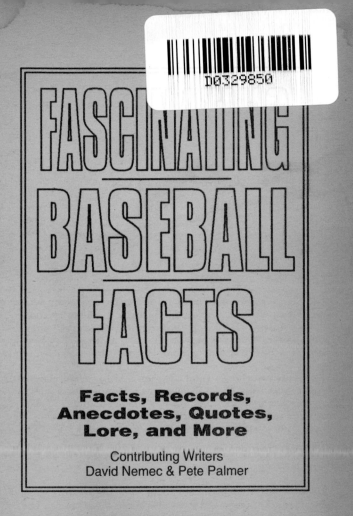

FASCINATING

BASEBALL

FACTS

Facts, Records, Anecdotes, Quotes, Lore, and More

Contributing Writers
David Nemec & Pete Palmer

**Publications
International, Ltd.**

David Nemec is a baseball historian and author. He is the author of *Great Baseball Feats, Facts & Firsts* and a co-author of *The Ultimate Baseball Book* and *20th Century Baseball Chronicle*. He has written numerous history, quiz, and memorabilia books as well as franchise histories for major league team yearbooks.

Pete Palmer edited both *Total Baseball* and *The Hidden Game of Baseball* with John Thorn. Palmer was the statistician for *1994 Baseball Almanac* and *1992-93 Basketball Almanac*. Palmer, a renowned sports statistician, is a member of the Society for American Baseball Research (SABR).

Photo Credits: National Baseball Library, Cooperstown, N.Y.; T.V. Sports Mailbag.

Contents

Details of the Game

Since baseball's legacy is made up of thousands of details, only a book that sorts the game's components can complete the picture. With *Fascinating Baseball Facts,* you get these particulars in the order that they happened, giving you a diehard's understanding of baseball's essence.

Some of the facts that you will find reveal a little about the time in which the game was played. For example, the world champion St. Louis Cardinals in 1934 drew only 350,000 fans in home attendance. In 1924, Freddy Lindstrom of the New York Giants, at age 18, was the youngest participant in World Series history. The song "Take Me Out to the Ball Game" was first introduced to the public in 1908.

The only player to collect 400 total bases in a season during the 1950s was Hank Aaron, who had exactly 400 in 1959. As this fact and others reveal, there are many things to discover about the legends who played the game. Did you know that the first World Series pinch homer was slugged by a Yankee rookie named Yogi Berra in 1947? Babe Ruth led the decade of the 1920s with 1,331 RBI. After pounding out 1,153 RBI, Rogers Hornsby was second during that decade only to Ruth.

Quotes from some of the men who played the game help enliven and illustrate any baseball discussion. Dizzy Dean, famed good ol' boy, once commented on his mangled English: "A lot of folks that ain't saying 'ain't' ain't eating." Manager Dave Bristol addressed his Giants team after a loss: "There'll be two buses leaving the hotel for the park tomorrow. The 2 o'clock bus will be for those of you who need a little extra work. The empty bus will leave at 5 o'clock." "Lots of people look up to Billy Martin," according to Jim Bouton. "That's because he just knocked them down."

Each chapter is jammed with decade-long (or era-long) batting, pitching, fielding, and managing and team leaders. The leader boxes reveal some surprising things. Harmon Killebrew was the top home run hitter in the 1960s with 393 dingers. Who was the top home run hitter of the

1970s? Willie Stargell with 296. Which pitcher had the most shutouts in the 1920s? Walter Johnson with 24. Many fans could probably guess that Whitey Ford had the best winning percentage in the 1950s (.708). What they might not know is that Ford also compiled the best earned run average (2.66) in that decade. These inclusive, up-to-date records inform you of each era's top performers.

A few of the statistical categories included for the records, both in the decades and the all-time lists in the back of the book, may be unfamiliar to some fans. The categories for batters are games played, runs, hits, total bases, doubles, triples, homers, runs batted in, stolen bases, walks, strikeouts, batting average, slugging average, on-base average, on-base average plus slugging average, and extra-base hits. Slugging percentage is the total number of bases divided by at bats. On-base average is the total number of times a batter reaches safely divided by the total number of plate appearances. On-base average plus slugging average simply adds those two numbers together to measure the effectiveness of a batter each time he makes a plate appearance.

The categories for pitchers are games pitched, games started, complete games, saves, shutouts, wins, innings pitched, strikeouts, winning percentage, earned run average, fewest walks per nine innings, and ratio. Ratio is the number of hits and walks a pitcher allows in nine innings. For fielders, the categories are putouts, assists, chances accepted, and fielding average.

For batters, the minimum for decade-long averages is 700 games played; the minimum for all-time averages is 1,000 games played. The minimum for pitchers decade-long averages is 1,000 innings pitched, all-time is 1,500 innings pitched. Fielding minimums are 500 games or 700 innings pitched for a decade, 700 games or 1,000 innings all time. For managers, the decade-long minimum for winning percentage was 500 games, with 700 for the all-time records.

The records and highlights establish baseball's heritage. Packed with information, *Fascinating Baseball Facts* is a must for any sports library.

Chapter 1
The Early Years

Trying to Keep Up With the Joneses

On June 10, 1880, Charley Jones of the Boston Red Stockings became the first player in major league history to hammer two home runs in an inning. The previous year Jones had led the National League with nine circuit clouts. Jones's reward was to be blackballed from the game by Boston owner Arthur Soden. Soden held back Jones's paycheck in an effort to extract a pledge from Jones to give up drinking. When Jones objected, he was released for what Soden deemed conduct unbecoming to baseball. Because the NL owners had the final say as to whether players should be allowed to play in other pro leagues as well, Jones was unable to earn his living at the game until the rebel American Association was formed in 1882.

1871-1892 GAMES

1.	Cap Anson	1,993
2.	Jim O'Rourke	1,869
3.	Paul Hines	1,659
4.	Deacon White	1,560
5.	Monte Ward	1,554
6.	Jack Glasscock	1,493
7.	Roger Connor	1,490
8.	King Kelly	1,435
9.	Harry Stovey	1,430
10.	Dan Brouthers	1,385
11.	H. Richardson	1,331
12.	Bid McPhee	1,325
13.	George Gore	1,310
14.	Fred Pfeffer	1,300
15.	George Wood	1,280
16.	Ned Hanlon	1,267
17.	John Morrill	1,265
18.	C. Comiskey	1,265
19.	Ezra Sutton	1,263
20.	Tom Burns	1,251

Sam Thompson averaged 2.12 career home runs for every 100 at bats, making him the only 19th-century player to average over two home runs per 100 at bats.

Ned Williamson of the Chicago White Stockings set the single-season record for home runs in 1884 when he hit 27. Babe Ruth broke Williamson's mark in 1919 by knocking 29 homers.

Baseball's first home run king was George Hall, who hit five home runs in 1876, the National League's inaugural season; a year later Hall was banned from the game.

Above: The 1880 Troy Trojans finished fourth in the National League with a 41-42 record, despite having Hall of Fame hurlers Mickey Welch and Tim Keefe. Even though they threw most of Troy's innings, the Trojans had an ERA higher than the league's average.

1871-1892 RUNS

1.	Jim O'Rourke	1,657
2.	Cap Anson	1,618
3.	Harry Stovey	1,445
4.	King Kelly	1,348
5.	George Gore	1,327
6.	Dan Brouthers	1,272
7.	Roger Connor	1,254
8.	Paul Hines	1,218
9.	Monte Ward	1,179
10.	Arlie Latham	1,150
11.	Deacon White	1,140
12.	H. Richardson	1,120
13.	Bid McPhee	1,105
14.	Tom Brown	1,012
15.	Jack Glasscock	1,007
16.	Ezra Sutton	992
17.	George Wood	965
18.	Ned Hanlon	930
	Charlie Comiskey	930
20.	Pete Browning	914

Foulest Batting Champ: Ross Barnes

Most baseball historians consider the first major league season to have been 1876, when the National League was formed. That year the Chicago White Stockings, owned by loop president William Hulbert, romped to an easy pennant after pilfering several stars from other teams. Among them was second baseman Ross Barnes, who became the first NL batting champ when he stroked .429. Barnes took advantage of the rules at the time that counted any batted ball that struck first in fair territory as a fair ball regardless of where it ultimately settled. When the rule was changed the following year, Barnes was never again an offensive force.

In 1876, the Chicago White Stockings set a team record that still stands when they hit .337.

On May 30, 1884, third baseman Ned Williamson of the Chicago White Stockings became the first player to hit three home runs in a game.

Original Louisville Slugger

The Hillerich & Bradsby Company, makers of Louisville Slugger bats, long the staple of the vast majority of major league hitters, might never have gone into the business of bat manufacturing were it not for Pete Browning. In 1884, the company still specialized in wagon tongues and butter churns, but that spring Browning, a lifelong resident of Louisville and already recognized as the top hitter in the American Association, prevailed upon young Bud Hillerich to begin custom-making bats for him. In an era when most players used only one bat all season, Browning had several dozen. Each was given a name, usually after a Biblical character. Browning's bats worked such magic for him that he earned four hitting titles and posted a .341 career batting average.

1871-1892 HITS

1.	Cap Anson	2,743
2.	Jim O'Rourke	2,490
3.	Paul Hines	2,131
4.	Deacon White	2,067
5.	Dan Brouthers	1,908
6.	Roger Connor	1,878
7.	King Kelly	1,795
8.	Monte Ward	1,769
9.	Jack Glasscock	1,743
10.	Harry Stovey	1,721
11.	H. Richardson	1,688
12.	George Gore	1,612
13.	Ezra Sutton	1,575
14.	Pete Browning	1,565
15.	George Wood	1,467
16.	Jimmy Wolf	1,440
17.	Charlie Comiskey	1,416
18.	Joe Start	1,411
19.	Bid McPhee	1,397
20.	Tip O'Neill	1,386

After losing a record 48 games to go with his 12 wins for the Philadelphia Quakers in 1883 (a team that won only 17 games), John Coleman became an outfielder and a good one; he led Pittsburgh in hits and RBI in 1887.

Pete Browning was the uncle of filmmaker and director Tod Browning, creator of Freaks, the bleak cinema classic about life in a carnival sideshow.

The 1869 Cincinnati Red Stockings were run by the aptly named Aaron Champion.

Pete Browning led the American Association in batting average three times, in 1882, 1885, and 1886. He also led the Players' League in batting in its only year of existence, 1890.

8

The last player to hit four triples in a nine-inning game was Bill Joyce, who did it with the New York Giants on May 18, 1897.

Bill Kuehne retired in 1892 with a .232 career batting average but had 115 triples, at the time a record for third basemen.

When Guy Hecker hit three homers in one game in 1886, all were inside-the-park dingers.

"You can't tell the players without a scorecard." —Harry Stevens, the first ballpark concessionaire

1871-1892 TRIPLES

1. Roger Connor 181
2. Harry Stovey 168
3. Dan Brouthers 167
4. Jim O'Rourke 144
5. Buck Ewing 142
6. John Reilly 139
7. George Wood 132
8. H. Richardson 126
   Bid McPhee 126
   Cap Anson 126
11. Bill Kuehne 115
12. Henry Larkin 111
13. Jimmy Wolf 109
14. Dave Orr 108
15. Oyster Burns 103
16. King Kelly 102
    Charley Jones 102
    Tom Brown 102
19. Deacon White 99
20. Bill Phillips 98

1871-1892 DOUBLES

1. Cap Anson 472
2. Jim O'Rourke 445
3. Paul Hines 405
4. Dan Brouthers 375
5. King Kelly 358
6. Harry Stovey 339
7. Roger Connor 328
8. Hardy Richardson 303
9. Pete Browning 284
10. Jack Glasscock 283
11. Deacon White 270
12. George Gore 262
13. John Morrill 239
    Henry Larkin 239
15. Tom Burns 236
16. Ezra Sutton 229
17. George Wood 228
    Ned Williamson 228
19. Fred Dunlap 224
20. Tip O'Neill 222
    Jerry Denny 222

Low, Lower, Lowest Batting Averages

In 1885, while Roger Connor was hitting .371 for the New York Giants to lead the National League in batting, Giants second baseman "Move Up Joe" Gerhardt posted a batting average more than 200 points lower. Gerhardt's .155 figure is the all-time record low for a regular player other than a catcher. Shockingly low batting averages were common for several years in the mid-1880s, owing largely to a rule instituted in 1884 allowing pitchers to throw overhand. The increased velocity made possible by an overhand delivery also caused strikeout totals to jump astronomically during that period.

When Walks Equaled Hits

In 1887, for one season only, baseball officials decided to credit a batter with a hit each time he received a base on balls or was struck by a pitch. Their generosity enabled outfielder Tip O'Neill of the American Association champion St. Louis Browns to register a .492 batting average. Statisticians have since deducted O'Neill's free passes from his hit total that season, thereupon reducing his average to a mere .435. In addition, O'Neill led or tied for the Association lead in every significant batting department in 1887 except walks. Although O'Neill's RBI figures for the 1887 season are incomplete, it is almost an absolute certainty that he knocked home more than any other Association hitter. Most historians consequently award him a Triple Crown—for a number of years he was even regarded as the first Triple Crown winner in major league history. O'Neill never again had a season remotely close to his 1887 campaign but did finish with a .326 career batting average for his ten years of work.

When the Boston Red Stockings won the National League pennant in 1878, they had no players among the top five in any major batting department and had the second-lowest batting average in the loop at .241.

Long Game
King Kelly, asked by a reporter if he drank while playing, responded: "It depends on the length of the game."

In 1892, catcher Wilbert Robinson led the Baltimore Orioles in RBI with 57—with 11 of them coming in the June 10, 1892, game.

1871-1892 HOME RUNS

1.	Harry Stovey	121
2.	Roger Connor	99
3.	Dan Brouthers	92
4.	Cap Anson	86
5.	Fred Pfeffer	84
6.	Jimmy Ryan	73
	Jerry Denny	73
8.	Sam Thompson	72
9.	Hardy Richardson	70
10.	John Reilly	69
	King Kelly	69
12.	George Wood	68
13.	Ned Williamson	64
14.	Mike Tiernan	63
15.	Jim O'Rourke	60
16.	Paul Hines	58
17.	Buck Ewing	57
18.	Charley Jones	56*
19.	Tip O'Neill	52
	Oyster Burns	52

5

Guy Hecker was the only AA player to hit three homers in one game.

On June 10, 1892, catcher Wilbert Robinson of the last-place Baltimore Orioles went 7-for-7 and had 11 RBI in a nine-inning game against St. Louis.

Three years after he became the American Association's first home run champion in 1882, Oscar Walker was out of baseball and working as a groundskeeper.

Hines Wins First Triple Crown

Upon the finish of the 1878 season, the National League batting crown was awarded to rookie Abner Dalrymple of Milwaukee. Not until nearly a century later did it emerge that calculation errors had been made in determining the NL bat leader in 1878. The true winner is now recognized to have been Paul Hines of Providence with a .358 mark, four points above Dalrymple's .354 figure. Dalrymple was originally credited with having outhit Hines .356 to .351. RBI totals for the 1878 season, another recent discovery, reveal that Hines also led in that department. Hines went to his grave in 1935 believing he had topped the NL only in home runs in 1878. Historians now know him to have been the first Triple Crown winner in major league history—and also the National League's first repeat batting champion. After allegedly finishing second to Dalrymple in 1878, Hines won the crown beyond all dispute the following year when he hit .357 for the pennant-winning Providence club.

The 1878 Providence Grays had an all-.300 hitting outfield, but had no infielders who could hit above .239.

1871-1892 RUNS BATTED IN

1. Cap Anson — 1,449
2. Dan Brouthers — 1,048
3. Roger Connor — 963
4. King Kelly — 935
5. Jim O'Rourke — 915
6. H. Richardson — 822
7. Fred Pfeffer — 813
8. Deacon White — 777
9. Paul Hines — 751
10. Sam Thompson — 746
11. Monte Ward — 713
12. Tom Burns — 683
13. Ned Williamson — 667
14. Jack Glasscock — 646
15. Jack Rowe — 644
16. John Morrill — 643
17. George Gore — 618
18. Jerry Denny — 613
19. Sam Wise — 595
20. Buck Ewing — 590

> **The *Cincinnati Enquirer*
> reported on Harry Wright: "He
> is a base ball Edison. He eats
> base ball, breathes base ball,
> thinks base ball, and
> incorporates base ball in his
> prayers."**

In 1894, Sam Thompson's .404 average wasn't even the best on his own team—Ed Delahanty hit .416.

The 1869 Cincinnati Red Stockings—the first openly professional team—had payroll expenses totaling about $9,400. That is about what the average contemporary player makes per game.

The first catcher with 500 at bats in a single season was Connie Mack in 1890.

1871-1892 STOLEN BASES

1. Arlie Latham	572
2. Harry Stovey	486
3. Monte Ward	455
4. Curt Welch	452
5. Tom Brown	427
6. Billy Hamilton	400
Charlie Comiskey	400
8. Bid McPhee	384
9. Hugh Nicol	383
10. King Kelly	365
11. T. McCarthy	339
12. Hub Collins	335
13. Ned Hanlon	329
14. Jim Fogarty	325
15. Mike Griffin	323
16. Darby O'Brien	321
17. Jack Glasscock	314
18. Paul Radford	290
Fred Pfeffer	290
20. George Pinkney	284

1869 Cincinnati Club Best Ever?

Ten years before he managed and shortstopped the Providence Grays to the National League flag in 1879, George Wright played under his brother Harry for arguably the most formidable team in history—the 1869 Cincinnati Red Stockings. The Queen City nine ran off a record 130 straight victories before being stopped on June 14, 1870, by the Atlantics of Brooklyn. So dominant was the Cincinnati outfit that its games seldom went a full nine innings. Frequently the opposition was blown out by over 100 runs. George Wright customarily did the brunt of the damage. His estimated batting average for all games in 1869 was around .629, and in a typical game he would score about five runs. As a team, the Red Stockings are believed to have hit well over .400 in 1869. Oddly, when the club's winning streak was finally derailed by the Atlantics, it was not a hitting failure but a muffed double-play ball that settled the issue.

"Pebbly" Dominates Early Shortstops

Fred Dunlap of the Union Association St. Louis Maroons set a record with a 1.58 runs per game average in 1884. Only a cut below Dunlap as both a fielder and a hitter in 1884 was Jack Glasscock. Nicknamed "Pebbly" because of his penchant for keeping his shortstop area free of small stones that might cause bad hops, Glasscock began the 1884 season with Cleveland of the National League but jumped in mid-campaign to the Cincinnati Outlaw Reds of the Union Association. In 38 games with the Cincinnati club, Glasscock hit .419 and first showed evidence that he was more than a deft fielder. Six years later, back in the National League with the New York Giants, Glasscock became the first shortstop in major league history to win a batting crown when he hit .336. Many analysts rate him the best shortstop of the game's first era.

1871-1892 STRIKEOUTS

1.	John Morrill	656
2.	Pud Galvin	630
3.	Sam Wise	616
4.	Jerry Denny	575
5.	George Wood	547
6.	Charlie Bennett	536
7.	Ned Williamson	532
8.	Joe Hornung	498
9.	Tom Brown	463
10.	Silver Flint	461
11.	Tom Burns	454
12.	H. Richardson	445
13.	Fred Pfeffer	442
14.	Emmett Seery	426
15.	King Kelly	412
16.	Tim Keefe	387
17.	Roger Connor	382
18.	Arthur Irwin	378
19.	A. Dalrymple	359
20.	Ned Hanlon	357

Above: Jack Glasscock led the NL in hits in 1889 with Indianapolis and in 1890 with New York. He replaced Monte Ward at shortstop for the '90 Giants after Ward formed the Players' League.

McTamany On Base

Only in recent years have players who are not particularly good hitters but are nonetheless proficient at the game's primary offensive task—getting on base and scoring runs—begun to receive their due. One such player in the game's early days was Jim McTamany, an outfielder who performed for seven years in the American Association. McTamany might be recognized as a star if he were playing now, but in his time he was so lightly regarded that he was squeezed out of the major leagues after the 1891 season at the early age of 28 when the American Association disbanded. Baseball moguls considered only McTamany's .239 batting average in 1891. What they failed to take into account were the 116 runs he scored and his 101 walks. McTamany's departure after what has since come to be viewed as a banner season left him the only player ever to collect both 100 or more walks and runs in his final big league campaign.

In 1887, playing in 127 games, Sam Thompson netted 166 RBI to set a pre-1893 record. Thompson also holds the mark for the second-most RBI in the last century—165 in 1895.

Ed Swartwood, who led the AA in 1883 with a .356 batting average, was the only Pittsburgh performer prior to Honus Wagner to be a batting leader.

Cap Anson was credited with being the originator of spring training. In 1886, he took his defending champion White Stockings to Hot Springs, Arkansas, to "boil out all the beer and booze they had swilled over the winter."

1871-1892 ON-BASE AVG.

1.	Dan Brouthers	.422
2.	Denny Lyons	.406
3.	Pete Browning	.399
4.	Roger Connor	.398
5.	Tip O'Neill	.392
6.	Cap Anson	.387
7.	George Gore	.386
8.	Mike Tiernan	.386
9.	Ed Swartwood	.378
10.	Henry Larkin	.377
11.	Yank Robinson	.375
12.	Jimmy Ryan	.375
13.	Jim McTamany	.373
14.	Tommy Tucker	.372
15.	Fred Carroll	.370
16.	Sam Thompson	.369
17.	King Kelly	.368
18.	Oyster Burns	.368
19.	Dave Orr	.366
20.	Mike Griffin	.364

The major league record for the most career at bats without an extra base hit is held by Herman Pitz, who collected just 47 singles in 284 at bats for two AA teams in 1890.

Monte Ward is the only player in major league history to win more than 150 games as a pitcher and accumulate more than 2,000 hits.

Worcester first baseman Chub Sullivan in 1880 failed to collect a single RBI all season in 166 at bats.

Lyons Early Offensive Threat at Third

Like Jim McTamany, Denny Lyons was an unrecognized offensive star from the pre-1893 period. Lyons was the leading hitter of his day at his position. The position was third base, a station that for reasons that are no longer entirely clear became the province in the last century of players with strong arms and weak bats. Lyons was one of the few exceptions. In his 13 big league campaigns he registered a .310 batting average, the highest of any third sacker who played prior to the advent of the lively ball era in 1920. He was often among league leaders in batting and fielding. Lyons's pinnacle came in 1887, his first full season, when he clubbed .367 for Philadelphia of the American Association and netted 209 hits; the latter figure for many years stood as a record for third basemen.

1871-1892 BATTING AVG.

1.	Dan Brouthers	.343
2.	Dave Orr	.342
3.	Pete Browning	.341
4.	Cap Anson	.333
5.	Tip O'Neill	.326
6.	Roger Connor	.321
7.	Denny Lyons	.316
8.	Jim O'Rourke	.313
9.	Sam Thompson	.312
10.	Deacon White	.312
11.	King Kelly	.308
12.	Jimmy Ryan	.306
13.	Mike Tiernan	.303
14.	Henry Larkin	.302
15.	Paul Hines	.302
16.	George Gore	.301
17.	Buck Ewing	.301
18.	Ed Swartwood	.299
19.	H. Richardson	.299
20.	Charley Jones	.298

On June 27, 1876, Davy Force of Philadelphia became the first player to make six hits in a nine-inning game.

In 1876, Mike McGeary of St. Louis in the NL set an all-time record when he fanned just once all season in 276 at bats.

15

On June 7, 1884, Charlie Sweeney of the Providence Grays struck out 19 batters during a game against the Boston Beaneaters. His single-game total of 19 was matched several times, but it was not broken until 1986.

On August 4, 1882, Pud Galvin pitched the most lopsided no-hitter in history when he beat Detroit 18-0.

In 1876, Pud Galvin (right) joined the Allegheny baseball club, which was in the International Association, the first minor league in history. Galvin was with Allegheny for two seasons.

Bad-Luck Year for Pitchers

The 1884 season featured bizarre occurrences and odd achievements. Pitching for the Baltimore Union Association entry, Bill Sweeney topped the UA in wins with 40. His 40 victories instead of meriting an encore appearance in the majors became the record for the most wins by a pitcher in his last season. Despite losing the lower half of his left arm in an explosion at the fireworks factory where he worked as a teenager, Hugh Daily fashioned a six-year career in the majors. He reached his apex in 1884, notching 28 wins and 483 strikeouts. After leaving the majors three years later, Daily dropped into oblivion. His whereabouts after baseball is a mystery that haunts present-day baseball researchers.

1871-1892 GAMES PITCHED

1.	Jim Galvin	705
2.	Bobby Mathews	578
	Tim Keefe	578
4.	Mickey Welch	564
5.	Charley Radbourn	528
6.	Jim McCormick	492
7.	Tony Mullane	481
8.	John Clarkson	473
9.	Tommy Bond	417
10.	Charlie Buffinton	414
11.	Jim Whitney	413
12.	Will White	403
13.	Al Spalding	347
	George Bradley	347
15.	Bob Caruthers	340
16.	Guy Hecker	334
17.	Silver King	329
18.	Adonis Terry	321
19.	Gus Weyhing	316
20.	Ed Morris	311

1871-1892 COMPLETE GAMES

1. Pud Galvin   646
2. Tim Keefe   537
3. Mickey Welch   525
   Bobby Mathews   525
5. C. Radbourn   489
6. Jim McCormick   466
7. John Clarkson   441
8. Tony Mullane   422
9. Will White   394
10. Tommy Bond   386
11. Jim Whitney   377
12. Charlie Buffinton 351
13. Guy Hecker   310
14. George Bradley 302
15. Bob Caruthers   298
16. Ed Morris   297
17. Silver King   293
18. Gus Weyhing   283
19. Al Spalding   281
20. Adonis Terry   280

Pud Galvin won a 19th-century record 361 games but was never a league leader in either wins, strikeouts, or ERA.

Beginning in 1890, Kid Nichols won 26 or more games for nine consecutive years. He was the top winning pitcher in any decade, winning 297 in the 1890s.

You Can Take the Boy Outta Jersey

During his 14-year career, Tim Keefe pitched in three major leagues and won games in an all-time record 47 different major league parks. One of Keefe's contemporaries went him one better. Between 1883 and 1891, Jersey Bakely toiled in four different major leagues and had at least one season in each of them in which he won in double figures. No other pitcher before or since has spread his work so widely. Bakely's trouble was that his work was seldom effective. He won just 76 of 201 decisions for a dismal .378 career winning percentage. The fault was not completely his, however, as only in his first season, when he appeared in a handful of games with the American Association champion Philadelphia Athletics, was he with a team that had a winning record. Bakely's best year was 1888 when he won 25 games for Cleveland, a sixth-place finisher in the American Association. His nickname, like those of many early day players, stemmed from the location where he was born.

When the American Association first allowed overhand pitching in 1885, batting averages throughout the circuit plummeted so sharply that Curt Welch, the top hitting regular for the pennant-winning St. Louis Browns batted just .271.

Caruthers Delivers Double Duty

The St. Louis Browns in 1887 showcased rookie sensation Silver King, and the club had two other fine hurlers, Bob Caruthers and Dave Foutz. The trio of 20-game winners gave the Browns the game's first outstanding three-man pitching rotation. King was the youngest at 19, but Caruthers was by far the exceptional all-around talent. In 1885, his first full season, Caruthers paced the American Association with 40 wins, a .755 winning percentage, and a 2.07 ERA. The following year he slipped to 30 victories, but part of the reason was because he was too busy elsewhere to devote full attention to his pitching. When not in the box Caruthers was playing right field for the Browns and leading the club in hitting. His .334 average was in fact the fourth-best in the AA that season. Caruthers continued to do double-duty until his pitching arm went in 1892, but not before he compiled a .688 career winning percentage, the highest by any hurler in the game's first era.

The 1882 Detroit Wolverines were the first major league team to have two 20-game losers.

Left: Tim Keefe racked up 342 wins between 1880 and 1893. The beloved "Sir Timothy" led his league in ERA three times and guided the New York Giants to their first pennant. His 1888 season, in which he led the NL in wins, ERA, strikeouts, and shutouts, made him the highest-paid Giant at a king-sized salary of $4,500.

1871-1892 WINS

1.	Pud Galvin	364
2.	Tim Keefe	332
3.	C. Radbourn	309
4.	Mickey Welch	307
5.	John Clarkson	304
6.	Bobby Mathews	297
7.	Jim McCormick	265
8.	Tony Mullane	259
9.	Al Spalding	253
10.	Tommy Bond	234
11.	Charlie Buffinton	233
12.	Will White	229
13.	Bob Caruthers	218
14.	Jim Whitney	191
15.	Silver King	180
16.	Gus Weyhing	177
	Larry Corcoran	177
18.	Guy Hecker	173
19.	Ed Morris	171
	George Bradley	171

After winning 24 games and topping the National League with an .800 winning percentage as a rookie in 1886, Jocko Flynn of Chicago never pitched another inning in the majors.

When he won 47 games for Chicago in 1876, Al Spalding logged just 39 strikeouts in 529 innings pitched.

The first southpaw in major league history was Bobby Mitchell, who had a 7-2 mark with the 1877 Cincinnati Red Stockings.

The first team to have two 30-game winners was the 1884 New York Metropolitans, which featured Tim Keefe (37-17) and Jack Lynch (37-15).

1871-1892 SHUTOUTS

1. Pud Galvin	57
2. Tommy Bond	42
3. Mickey Welch	41
4. Tim Keefe	39
5. Will White	36
John Clarkson	36
7. Charley Radbourn	35
8. Jim McCormick	33
9. George Bradley	32
10. Tony Mullane	30
Charlie Buffinton	30
12. Ed Morris	29
13. Jim Whitney	26
14. Monte Ward	24
Al Spalding	24
Bob Caruthers	24
17. Larry Corcoran	22
18. Gus Weyhing	21
19. Bobby Mathews	19
Candy Cummings	19

Hecker's Triple Threat: Hurling, Hitting, and Homers

A pitcher who took his regular turn in the box and hit .334 as an everyday player would stand as one of a kind in baseball history but for one small hitch. In 1886, Bob Caruthers was not the only hurler who was also a great hitter; he was not even the best of his time. That season, Guy Hecker of the Louisville Colonels won 26 games while working 420 innings and also led the American Association in hitting with a .341 mark. Hecker's arm was on the wane in 1886; two years earlier he had won 52 games for Louisville to establish an AA single-season record. In 1886, Hecker not only became the only pitcher ever to cop a batting crown, he also scored an all-time record seven runs in a game and in the same contest became the first pitcher to blast three home runs. Nicknamed "The Big Blond," Hecker finished with a .283 career batting average and 173 wins.

Cummings, Others Father New Deliveries

To Candy Cummings is attributed the invention of the curveball. Whether or not Cummings really did originate the curve will probably always be a matter of dispute. The early game offered a panoply of bizarre and contrasting pitching styles. Among the more interesting were the deliveries employed by Stooping Jack Gorman, so-called because he bent so low that his knuckles often scraped the ground when he released the ball. Another who collected a nickname for his unusual pitching style was Peek-a-Boo Veach, who reportedly kept his back to the batter and did not allow him even a peek at the ball until it actually left his hand. Gorman and Veach were never more than sporadically effective hurlers, however, nor was Billy Hart, who brought another dimension to the pitching art in the late 1890s when he began employing a spitball. Hart's spitter in 1897 got him just nine wins to go with his 27 losses for the last-place St. Louis Browns.

In 1889, John Clarkson of Boston won 21 more games and hurled 200 more innings than any other pitcher in the National League.

In 1886, Matty Kilroy, a rookie lefthander with the Baltimore Orioles of the American Association, fanned an all-time record 513 batters. He never again struck out more than 217 in a season.

1871-1892 INNINGS

1.	Pud Galvin	6,003.1
2.	Bobby Mathews	4,956.0
3.	Tim Keefe	4,883.1
4.	Mickey Welch	4,802.0
5.	C.Radbourn	4,535.1
6.	J. McCormick	4,275.2
7.	John Clarkson	4,090.2
8.	Tony Mullane	4,008.2
9.	Tommy Bond	3,628.2
10.	Will White	3,542.2
11.	Jim Whitney	3,496.1
12.	C. Buffinton	3,404.0
13.	George Bradley	2,940.0
14.	Guy Hecker	2,906.0
15.	Al Spalding	2,893.2
16.	Bob Caruthers	2,828.2
17.	Silver King	2,737.1
18.	Ed Morris	2,678.0
19.	Gus Weyhing	2,629.0
20.	Adonis Terry	2,625.1

First Curve

Candy Cummings described how he invented the curve: "A number of my chums and I were throwing shells one day in Brooklyn. When seeing a shell take a wide curve I said, 'Now if only I could make a ball do that I think the other clubs won't be in it.'"

Old Hoss Radbourn of National League Providence set an all-time record in 1884 when he won 60 games; that same year Guy Hecker won 52 for Louisville to break the American Association record, and Bill Sweeney won 40 for Baltimore to set the Union Association mark.

Francis Richter, in a eulogy to John Clarkson upon the great pitcher's death, said: "On all counts the deceased will always rank in history as one of the few great masters of the art of pitching."

In 1890, George Haddock led the Players' League with 26 losses; the following season his 34 wins topped the American Association.

1871-1892 STRIKEOUTS

1.	Tim Keefe	2,474
2.	John Clarkson	1,888
3.	Mickey Welch	1,850
4.	C. Radbourn	1,830
5.	Pud Galvin	1,799
6.	Jim McCormick	1,704
7.	C. Buffinton	1,700
8.	Tony Mullane	1,662
9.	Jim Whitney	1,571
10.	Toad Ramsey	1,515
11.	Adonis Terry	1,298
12.	Mark Baldwin	1,254
13.	Ed Morris	1,217
14.	Bobby Mathews	1,216
15.	Gus Weyhing	1,208
16.	Matt Kilroy	1,137
17.	Silver King	1,119
18.	Larry Corcoran	1,103
19.	Guy Hecker	1,099
20.	Amos Rusie	1,075

Whitney Tops and Bottoms

When Phil Niekro led National League pitchers in both wins and losses in 1979, statisticians had to go back 98 years to find a comparable achievement. In 1881, rookie Jim Whitney of the Boston Red Stockings posted a 31-33 mark to pace the National League in both victories and defeats. He also led the loop with 552 1/3 innings pitched. Two years later, Whitney had his best season when he logged 37 triumphs for the champion Bostons, but the club released him after he registered 32 setbacks in 1885. Whitney was nicknamed "Grasshopper" because he had a small head and an elongated body. In addition to being a fine pitcher for a few years, he was an outstanding hitter and the first hurler ever to lead his team in home runs. In 1882, he became the first pitcher ever to finish among his league's top five hitters when he batted .323. The following season Whitney collected 115 hits and 177 total bases along with winning 37 games.

Tony Mullane won 202 games in the American Association, making him the only pitcher to win 200 games in a loop other than the National League or the American League.

The NL record for the most wins in a season by a southpaw is held by Lady Baldwin of the Detroit Wolverines, who notched 42 victories in 1886.

Frequent Mound Climbers

Even poor teams in baseball's first era would sometimes stumble on a potentially great pitcher. If the hurler was lucky, he would be passed on to a quality organization early in his career. Take the case of Larry McKeon, an 18-year-old rookie with Indianapolis of the American Association in 1884 who set a frosh record when he went down to defeat 41 times. He started 60 games, completed 59, and hurled 512 innings. A scant two years later McKeon's wing was shot. But even as McKeon was departing the scene the lowly Baltimore Orioles of the American Association were unveiling another amazing rookie workhorse in Matt Kilroy. Kilroy celebrated his yearling season in 1886 by notching an all-time record 513 strikeouts for the last-place Orioles and working a total of 583 innings. After being similarly abused by the Orioles for four years, Kilroy had 121 career wins. He collected only 20 more victories before his arm collapsed from overwork.

1871-1892 WINNING PERCENTAGE	
1. Al Spalding	.796
2. Dave Foutz	.690
3. Bob Caruthers	.688
4. John Clarkson	.668
5. Larry Corcoran	.665
6. Dick McBride	.656
7. Lady Baldwin	.640
8. Kid Nichols	.639
9. Cy Young	.637
10. Fred Goldsmith	.622
11. Jack Stivetts	.618
12. Monte Ward	.617
13. Tom Lovett	.616
14. C. Radbourn	.613
15. Charlie Ferguson	.607
16. Candy Cummings	.607
17. Charlie Buffinton	.605
18. Tim Keefe	.604
19. Mickey Welch	.594
20. Tommy Bond	.589

The first pitcher to win 20 games for a last-place team was Lee Richmond, who notched 25 victories with Worcester in 1881.

In 1892, Bill Hutchinson of Chicago became the last hurler to work over 600 innings when he logged 627 frames.

Pitching Rotations Take Root

In 1879, the Chicago White Stockings, under manager Cap Anson, became the first major league team to try to develop a pitching rotation of sorts. Chicago's experiment was a success, but it took a year to pay dividends. In 1880, the White Stockings replaced their two boxmen from the previous season, Terry Larkin and Frank Hankinson, with a pair of rookies, Larry Corcoran and Fred Goldsmith. Corcoran proceeded to bag 43 wins and Goldsmith 21 to make the White Stockings the first team in history with two 20-game winners. By 1884, however, both had fallen prey to arm trouble, making it apparent that even a two-man rotation could create problems. That same season the Cincinnati Outlaw Reds of the Union Association found a partial solution when they spread the work among three pitchers. The Outlaw Reds became the first team in history with three 20-game winners—Dick Burns, George Bradley, and Jim McCormick.

"The only thing Abner Doubleday ever started was the Civil War."
—Branch Rickey

In 1892, Baltimore finished last in the National League with a 4.28 team ERA; two years later, with the mound now at 60'6", Baltimore won the NL pennant with a 5.00 ERA.

1871-1892 PITCHER FIELDING AVERAGE

1. Harry Staley	.942
2. Jim Devlin	.937
3. Pat Luby	.937
4. Guy Hecker	.935
5. John Ewing	.935

When the Boston Red Stockings cruised to the NL pennant in 1878, right-hander Tommy Bond had 40 of the club's 41 wins.

1871-1892 EARNED RUN AVERAGE

1.	Jim Devlin	2.05
2.	Monte Ward	2.10
3.	Al Spalding	2.22
4.	Will White	2.28
5.	Tommy Bond	2.31
6.	Larry Corcoran	2.36
7.	George Bradley	2.42
8.	Jim McCormick	2.43
9.	Terry Larkin	2.43
10.	Kid Nichols	2.49
11.	C. Cummings	2.51
12.	Cy Young	2.53
13.	Tim Keefe	2.56
14.	John Clarkson	2.63
15.	Charlie Ferguson	2.67
16.	C. Radbourn	2.67
17.	Mickey Welch	2.71
18.	Fred Goldsmith	2.73
19.	Tony Mullane	2.79
20.	Dave Foutz	2.79

Walking Arbiter

In the early days of baseball the man appointed to umpire a game was so much a gentleman that he would not even consider taking payment for his services. When baseball became a business and players began commanding regular salaries, however, umpires too thought to create a profession of their avocation. The first to make a full-time job of umpiring was probably Billy McLean, a former prizefighter. McLean earned the nickname "The King of Umpires" for the assertive way in which he took charge of games while officiating in the National Association in the early 1870s. A resident of Providence, he would sometimes rise at 4:00 A.M. and walk from his home in the Rhode Island city to Boston, where he would officiate a game that afternoon. McLean served as a National League umpire until 1884.

1871-1892 CATCHER GAMES

1. Charlie Bennett   894
2. Pop Snyder   876
3. Silver Flint   742
4. Doc Bushong   668
5. Jack Clements   646

1871-1892 CATCHER FIELDING AVERAGE

1. Charlie Bennett   .942
2. Buck Ewing   .931
3. Chief Zimmer   .931
4. Jocko Milligan   .930
5. Wilbert Robinson   .928

1871-1892 CATCHER ASSISTS

1. Pop Snyder   1,295
2. Silver Flint   1,052
3. Buck Ewing   1,017
4. Bill Holbert   1,013
5. Charlie Bennett   1,008

On May 10, 1884, catcher Alex Gardner of Washington in the American Association committed a major league record 12 passed balls while playing in his only major league game.

Charlie Bennett, considered by many to have been the game's finest defensive catcher during the 1880s, lost both legs when he slipped under the wheels of a moving train after the 1893 season.

"Baseball is a peculiar profession, perhaps the only one which capitalized a boyhood pleasure, unfits the athlete for any other career, keeps him young in mind and spirit, and then rejects him as too old before he has yet attained the prime of life."
—Gerald Beaumont, writer

1871-1892 FIRST BASE GAMES

1. Cap Anson	1,642
2. Dan Brouthers	1,346
3. Roger Connor	1,252
4. Charlie Comiskey	1,239
5. John Reilly	1,075

1871-1892 FIRST BASE FIELDING AVERAGE

1. Jake Beckley	.979
2. Roger Connor	.977
3. Sid Farrar	.974
4. Tommy Tucker	.974
5. Dave Orr	.973

In 1887, the New York Metropolitans of the AA made a record 643 errors.

The 1892 Boston Beaneaters, at 102-48, were the first major league team to win 100 games in a season.

The Chicago Cubs hold the major league record for the highest, the second-highest, the third-highest, and the fourth highest single-season winning percentages; the Cubs' four golden years came in 1880, 1876, 1885, and 1906.

In 1883, their first year of existence, the Philadelphia Quakers, ancestors of the present-day Phillies, made 639 errors in just 98 games, an average of more than six per contest.

American Association Pushes Umpiring as a Profession

Among the many innovations the American Association brought to the game during its ten-year sojourn as a major league was to make umpiring a reasonably well-paid and respectable profession. Whereas the stodgy National League had only one official working a game, the AA sometimes used as many as three. The loop's most famous arbiter was Ben Young, who was instrumental in forming a code of ethics for umpires before he was killed in a railway accident en route to work an AA game. Young also helped his fellow AA umpires to receive a regular salary during the baseball season, plus a per diem payment for travel expenses. While umpires in other circuits continued to officiate in street clothes, AA arbiters by the mid-1880s wore blue coats and caps issued them by the league office. The National League, the AA's rival major league, meanwhile continued to use only one umpire in a game until the early part of the 20th century.

Fleet Walker and pitcher George Stovey formed baseball's first black battery, playing for Newark in 1887.

1871-1892 SECOND BASE FIELDING AVERAGE

1. Danny Richardson	.939
2. Bid McPhee	.938
3. Charley Bassett	.932
4. Lou Bierbauer	.929
5. Sam Barkley	.929

Above: It is impossible to predict what kind of career Fleet Walker could have assembled if given the chance, but he did leave a legacy of another kind. The well-educated Walker published Our Home Colony *in 1908, an early call for black emigration to Africa as a response to American racial intolerance.*

Disgrace

Fleet Walker's brother Welday, in a letter to president George McDermott of the Tri-State League after the loop adopted a color ban, wrote: "The rule that you have passed is a public disgrace."

Moses and Welday Walker

To Moses Fleetwood Walker is accorded the honor of being the first American black player in major league history. A graduate of Oberlin College, "Fleet" joined the Toledo Blue Stockings in 1883 as a catcher. His brother Welday also played a few games for the club. Following the 1884 season, the Walkers were clandestinely barred from the majors when the owners bowed to a threatened rebellion by Cap Anson and several other leading white players if blacks were continued to be allowed to compete for major league jobs.

Other Blacks Who Played Early Pro Ball

Although the Walkers are considered now to have been the only black major leaguers prior to Jackie Robinson's arrival in 1947, the probability is strong that there were a number of other black players who broke the color barrier in the majors, particularly in the last century, by successfully passing as white. One may have been Sandy Nava, a backup catcher with the Providence Grays for three years in the early 1880s. Nava claimed to be Cuban to account for his dark complexion. Other great players of that time who were obviously black were barred from the majors but permitted to perform in the minors until the mid-1890s when the color ban was enforced throughout professional baseball. Perhaps the two best black performers of the last century were George Stovey, the top pitcher in the International League in the mid-1880s, and Frank Grant, a second baseman who was known as the "Black Fred Dunlap." In 1887, Grant hit .353 for Buffalo of the International League and led the loop in homers with 11 while Stovey set the IL record for wins when he posted 34 victories for Newark.

Ross Barnes not only won the first National League batting title in 1876, he also set a record for second basemen when he had a .910 fielding average.

1871-1892 THIRD BASE GAMES

1. Arlie Latham	1,201
2. Hick Carpenter	1,059
3. Jerry Denny	1,047
4. George Pinkney	943
5. Joe Mulvey	915

1871-1892 THIRD BASE FIELDING AVERAGE

1. George Pinkney	.894
2. Art Whitney	.888
3. Billy Nash	.887
4. Tom Burns	.886
5. Billy Shindle	.882

In 1882, a second major league, the American Association, was established to offer baseball fans lower admission prices (25 cents instead of 50 cents), beer and whiskey sales, and Sunday baseball.

The Pittsburgh NL team first became known as the Pirates in 1891 when the club "pirated" second baseman Lou Bierbauer from Philadelphia of the AA.

The 1889 season in the National League was the first time in history that a major league pennant race was decided on the final day of the campaign.

The 1885 to 1888 St. Louis Browns of the AA were the first team to win four straight major league pennants.

Shortstop Frank Fennelly of Cincinnati in 1886 became the first player to make 100 errors in a season when he committed 117 miscues. In 1889, rookie shortstop Herman Long tied the record 117 errors while playing for Kansas City of the American Association.

Joe Tinker called Monte Ward, "a star outfielder, a brilliant infielder, and a better pitcher than Radbourn. And he was one of the best baserunners who ever lived."

1871-1892 SHORTSTOP GAMES

1. Jack Glasscock	1,391
2. Germany Smith	998
3. Arthur Irwin	946
4. Monte Ward	826
5. Bill Gleason	796

1871-1892 SHORTSTOP FIELDING AVERAGE

1. Jack Glasscock	.908
2. Davy Force	.908
3. Germany Smith	.891
4. Herman Long	.890
5. Ed McKean	.885

In 1888, the total number of strikes allowed a batter before he was out was reduced from four to three, the present number.

Chicago White Stockings Are NL's First Powerhouse

The first team to claim three consecutive pennants after the National League opened its doors (in 1876) was the 1880 to 1882 Chicago White Stockings. In those three years, the White Stockings won more than 70 percent of their games. The club featured manager-first baseman Cap Anson, shortstop Fred Pfeffer, third baseman Ned Williamson, outfielders George Gore and Abner Dalrymple, and utility star King Kelly. When arm woes beset the team's twin pitching aces, Larry Corcoran and Fred Goldsmith, Chicago slipped to second place in 1883 and fourth in '84. The acquisition of hurler John Clarkson, though, rocketed the club back to the top in 1885. When the White Stockings triumphed again in 1886, it gave them five pennants in seven seasons.

Von der Ahe Assembles, Dismantles Browns Dynasty

Even as the White Stockings' dynasty was winding down in the mid-1880s, the St. Louis Browns were emerging as the most powerful dynasty in the last century. Between 1885 and 1888 the Browns swept four consecutive American Association pennants under beer-baron owner Chris Von der Ahe and manager-first baseman Charlie Comiskey. Von der Ahe built his juggernaut by paying his players well, outfitting them in tailor-made uniforms, and organizing parades and other gala events to fete them. When the Browns lost the 1887 World Series between the National League and the AA to the Detroit Wolverines, Von der Ahe angrily began to dismantle his team. Prior to the 1888 season the club's two highest paid pitchers, Dave Foutz and Bob Caruthers, were shipped to Brooklyn. The Browns held on to their throne for one last hurrah in 1888 but then gave way to Brooklyn the following year and never again regained the top spot. Von der Ahe too fell on hard times, dying impoverished and forgotten.

Above: The first man to record a hit in the National League, Jim O'Rourke served as a player, manager, umpire, and minor league prresident in addition to his 22 years of playing time in the National Association, National League, and Players' League. "Orator" Jim hit .300 13 times.

1871-1892 OUTFIELD GAMES

1.	Paul Hines	1,374
2.	Jim O'Rourke	1,355
3.	George Gore	1,297
4.	Ned Hanlon	1,251
5.	George Wood	1,232
6.	Tom Brown	1,169
7.	Curt Welch	1,061
8.	Joe Hornung	1,054
9.	Jimmy Wolf	1,042
10.	Pop Corkhill	1,041
11.	Tip O'Neill	1,024
12.	Blondie Purcell	995
13.	Tom York	959
14.	Abner Dalrymple	951
15.	Pete Browning	938

Fans Beware

Many of the major injuries incurred during a baseball game when the sport was in its infancy did not take place on the field of play. Being a spectator at that time could be a risky business. Until Providence of the National League installed a wire screen behind home plate in its park in the late 1870s, an innovation that other clubs quickly adopted, the stands back of the plate were known as "The Slaughter Pens" because so many fans who sat there were felled by foul balls. Fires and shoddy workmanship of the old wooden stands were other dangers that confronted early spectators. On Opening Day in 1884, in the very first official game the American Association Cincinnati Red Stockings played in their new American Park, a section of the right field grandstand collapsed as fans were hastening out of the park moments after the last out was made. One man in attendance was killed and scores more were badly hurt. Improvements in park construction and design eventually eliminated similar mishaps. Fire remained an ever-present peril until 1920, however, when the St. Louis Cardinals abandoned Robison Field, the last all-wood park in the majors.

Alexander Cartwright's Knickerbocker club abolished the established practice of throwing a hit ball at a runner to retire him. This meant that a harder, faster-traveling baseball could be used.

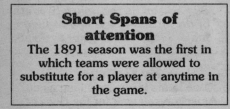

Short Spans of attention

The 1891 season was the first in which teams were allowed to substitute for a player at anytime in the game.

1871-1892 MANAGER WINS

1. Harry Wright	1,153
2. Cap Anson	972
3. Charlie Comiskey	719
4. Jim Mutrie	658
5. Billy Barnie	470
6. Gus Schmelz	469
7. Bob Ferguson	417
8. Frank Bancroft	366
9. Jack Chapman	351
10. John Morrill	348

First Famous Fans

Baseball spectators were originally called kranks. Around 1883, St. Louis Browns manager Ted Sullivan coined the term "fan" when team owner Chris Von der Ahe referred to the Browns rooters as fanatics. The most well-known fan at the time was Arthur Dixwell of Boston. Dixwell was nicknamed "Hi! Hi!" because he shouted, "Hi! Hi!" whenever he was stirred by the action on the field. Another early fan, Harry Stevens, spotted an unfilled need at ballparks and began hawking scorecards and eventually food to fellow fans. Known as "The Scorecard Man," Stevens soon nailed down exclusive concession rights at most major league parks, a privilege that his heirs still hold. To promote the sale of his scorecards, Stevens encouraged club owners to assign their players uniform numbers, but his plea fell on deaf ears. Not until the early 1930s would players begin wearing numbered uniforms.

The St. Paul White Caps, of the Union Association in 1884 for just eight contests, are the only major league team that never played a home game.

The smallest city to have a major league team is Altoona, Pennsylvania, a member of the Union Association in 1884.

When Boston paid Chicago $10,000 to obtain King Kelly prior to the 1887 season, it was the first five-figure transaction.

Richmond, of the American Association for the last half of the 1884 season, is the only city south of the Mason-Dixon line to field a major league team prior to 1966.

1871-1892 MANAGER WINNING PERCENTAGE

1.	Charlie Comiskey	.640
2.	Cap Anson	.618
3.	Jim Mutrie	.611
4.	Harry Wright	.582
5.	Bill Watkins	.532
6.	Frank Bancroft	.529
7.	Gus Schmelz	.520
8.	John Morrill	.510
9.	Billy Barnie	.461
10.	Horace Phillips	.449

By George

"Two hours is about as long as an American can wait for the close of a baseball game—or anything else, for that matter."
—Albert Spalding

Chapter 2
The Turn of the Century

The record for the highest season batting average belongs to Hugh Duffy who hit .438 for Boston in 1894.

NL Moves Pitcher's Mound to 60'6"

Following the 1891 season, the American Association gave up its struggle to compete with the entrenched National League for major league status and allowed four of its teams to be absorbed by the older circuit. Where there had been 24 major league teams just two years earlier, there were but half that number in 1892. The cutback enabled the 12 still-existing clubs to weed out the weaker pitchers and resulted in a sharp drop in hitting. Alarmed when the NL as a whole batted just .245 in 1892, loop moguls ordered the distance from the pitcher's box to home plate to be lengthened 10 feet and the box to be made circular and elevated. Reportedly a printer's error caused the new pitcher's mounds to be installed at a 60'6" distance rather than the proscribed 60 feet, but in any case the conversion immediately had the desired effect on the game. In 1893, NL hitters averaged .280 and the next season the loop batting mark climbed to an all-time record .309 as hitters feasted.

Long after his stellar career, Hugh Duffy was a batting coach with the Boston Red Sox in the 1940s. His top student was a young outfielder whom Duffy promised would be a legend. The protégé's name was Ted Williams.

Perry Werden First Fence Buster

As has happened throughout the game's history, trends in the majors were almost exactly paralleled in the minors during the mid-1890s. In 1895, the Western League, the forerunner of the present-day American League, saw all eight of its teams top the .300 mark, led by the champion Indianapolis Hoosiers with a .354 batting average. Second to the Indiana club was Minneapolis, which hit .350 and scored a loop-leading 1,282 runs in 123 games, an average of more than 10 runs per contest. Minneapolis was spearheaded by first baseman Perry Werden, who paced the WL in batting with a .438 mark and clouted 45 home runs, the pre-Babe Ruth professional record. Werden preferred life in the minors, particularly when he was allowed to wield his bat in a tiny park like the one in Minneapolis, but he also left his mark on the major league game. Just two years before he embarked on his slugging spree in the WL, Werden clubbed 29 triples for St. Louis of the National League to establish a senior loop record.

Perry Werden might never have hit 45 home runs if not for an arm injury. Originally a pitcher, he compiled a 12-1 record in 1884. Fortunately for opposing batters, Werden's wing went bad, and he shifted to first base.

1893-1899 RUNS	
1. Jesse Burkett	955
2. Billy Hamilton	945
3. Ed Delahanty	931
4. Willie Keeler	910
5. Joe Kelley	873
6. George VanHaltren	850
7. Hugh Duffy	844
8. John McGraw	782
9. Herman Long	778
10. Patsy Donovan	762
11. Cupid Childs	758
12. Bill Dahlen	755
13. Hughie Jennings	742
14. Dummy Hoy	740
15. Elmer Smith	701
16. George Davis	698
17. Jimmy Ryan	696
18. Bill Lange	689
19. Mike Tiernan	687
20. Bobby Lowe	681

1893-1899 HITS	
1. Jesse Burkett	1,462
2. Ed Delahanty	1,431
3. Willie Keeler	1,346
4. Hugh Duffy	1,305
5. George VanHaltren	1,297
6. Joe Kelley	1,237
7. Patsy Donovan	1,169
8. Billy Hamilton	1,167
9. Ed McKean	1,140
10. George Davis	1,139
11. Herman Long	1,108
12. Elmer Smith	1,085
13. Jake Beckley	1,080
14. Steve Brodie	1,074
15. Tommy Dowd	1,070
16. Jimmy Ryan	1,060
17. Bill Lange	1,055
18. Dummy Hoy	1,053
19. Bobby Lowe	1,047
20. Fred Clarke	1,034

Major Talents in Minor Leagues

Perry Werden was by no means the only minor league star who was content to perform at a lower competitive level than his talents seemingly would have warranted. Count Campau, a native of Detroit, dropped down to the minors in 1889 after Detroit was jettisoned from the NL. He compiled 2,286 hits and 136 home runs in a string of lower leagues before retiring in 1905. Connecticut-born Hi Ladd played only two games in the majors in a career that spanned 20 seasons, the last 10 of them with Bridgeport of the Connecticut League. Ladd twice led the circuit in batting, in 1900 and again in 1905.

1893-1899 TRIPLES

1.	Joe Kelley	112
2.	Jake Beckley	105
3.	Elmer Smith	101
4.	Ed Delahanty	96
5.	Kip Selbach	90
6.	George Davis	87
7.	Ed McKean	86
	Willie Keeler	86
9.	Mike Tiernan	85
10.	George VanHaltren	83
11.	Jesse Burkett	82
12.	Bill Dahlen	81
13.	Bill Lange	80
14.	Tommy Corcoran	75
	John Anderson	75
16.	Dummy Hoy	73
17.	Sam Thompson	72
	Jimmy Ryan	72
19.	Jake Stenzel	71
20.	Heinie Reitz	65

1893-1899 DOUBLES

1.	Ed Delahanty	298
2.	Joe Kelley	202
3.	Jake Stenzel	189
	Jimmy Ryan	189
5.	Hugh Duffy	187
6.	Bill Dahlen	184
7.	Herman Long	182
8.	George Davis	181
9.	Jake Beckley	180
10.	Ed McKean	171
11.	Jesse Burkett	168
12.	Lave Cross	164
13.	Jack Doyle	158
14.	Mike Griffin	157
15.	Hughie Jennings	153
16.	George VanHaltren	148
17.	Elmer Smith	147
18.	Sam Thompson	144
19.	Kip Selbach	139
20.	Tommy Tucker	138

Sam Crawford commented on Wee Willie Keeler: "He choked up on the bat so far he only used about half of it, and then he'd just peck at the ball. Just a little snap swing and he'd punch the ball over the infield."

Willie Keeler tied a record when he amassed 17 hits over a four-game span in 1897.

Bill Dahlen held the consecutive hitting streak record before Wee Willie Keeler broke it. In 1894, Dahlen had a 42-game hitting streak. The day after it was snapped, he started a 28-game hitting streak.

Joyce Victimized by Contract Disputes

In all of major league history precious few rookies have ever led a league in walks. Ted Williams was one who did. Another was Bill Joyce, whose 123 free passes paced the Players' League in 1890. Joyce was not on a par with Williams as an all-around hitter, but he may not have been far from it. In a career marred by injuries and bitter holdout battles, Joyce was nevertheless one of the game's top offensive performers in the 1890s. His high mark came in 1894 when he batted .355 for Washington and knocked home 89 runs in just 99 games. Two years later Joyce tied for the National League lead in home runs with 13 and was second with 101 walks. Playing by then for the New York Giants, Joyce quit after the 1898 season rather than continue to deal with Andrew Freedman, the club's universally despised owner.

Above: *Although only 5'4", Willie Keeler was well respected as a stellar bunter and contact hitter during his 19-year career. As leadoff man and right fielder on the rough-and-tumble Oriole squads of the 1890s, Keeler won back-to-back batting titles and scored 150 runs four consecutive times. His lifetime .343 batting mark is ninth best on the all-time list.*

1893-1899 HOME RUNS

1.	Ed Delahanty	65
2.	Hugh Duffy	62
3.	Bill Joyce	60
4.	Sam Thompson	55
5.	Bobby Lowe	53
6.	Herman Long	48
7.	Jack Clements	47
	Bill Dahlen	47
9.	Joe Kelley	46
10.	Mike Tiernan	43
	George Davis	43
12.	Ed McKean	41
13.	Jake Beckley	40
14.	Bill Lange	39
	Roger Connor	39
16.	Jimmy Collins	34
	Fred Clarke	34
	Jesse Burkett	34
19.	Jake Stenzel	32
20.	Billy Nash	31

1893-1899 RBI

1. Ed Delahanty	834
2. Hugh Duffy	815
3. Joe Kelley	742
4. Ed McKean	704
5. George Davis	689
6. Jake Beckley	664
7. Steve Brodie	612
8. Bobby Lowe	602
9. Lave Cross	591
10. Herman Long	580
11. Bill Lange	578
Hughie Jennings	578
13. Sam Thompson	550
George VanHaltren	550
Jack Doyle	550
16. Jake Stenzel	530
17. Tommy Corcoran	517
18. Jesse Burkett	504
19. Bill Dahlen	502
20. Tommy Tucker	495

On July 13, 1896, Ed Delahanty of Philadelphia became the only player other than Atlanta's Bob Horner to hit four home runs in a losing cause.

On the science of batting, Wee Willie Keeler explained, "Keep your eye on the ball and hit 'em where they ain't."

Despite a reputation as a poor hitter infielder Bobby Wallace led the Spiders in 1898 with 99 RBI.

In 1897, Jesse Burkett poked 240 hits in just 133 games to claim his second straight batting title with a .410 average.

Jake Stenzel Typifies Shooting Star '90s

The decade of the 1890s was rife with players who had one or two great seasons and then rapidly, and in some cases inexplicably, descended to mediocrity. Among them was Tuck Turner, one of only two players in history with a .380-plus career batting average after their first 700 at bats in the majors (the other was Shoeless Joe Jackson). Considerably more enduring than Turner, who played only 377 games in the majors, was Jake Stenzel. After flopping in two brief earlier trials, Stenzel cracked .362 for Pittsburgh in 1893 when the Pirates gave him a late-season look. Stenzel followed his first prolonged test by hitting .354, .374, .361, and .353 over the next four seasons and also ranking among the National League's RBI and slugging leaders. In 1898, Stenzel slumped to .275. When he started slowly again in 1899, he was traded to his home-town team, the Cincinnati Reds, and then released after getting into just nine games with the Queen City entrant.

1893-1899 STOLEN BASES

1. Billy Hamilton — 460
2. Bill Lange — 399
3. John McGraw — 350
4. Joe Kelley — 319
5. Jack Doyle — 310
6. George Davis — 298
7. Jake Stenzel — 291
8. Willie Keeler — 288
9. Dummy Hoy — 281
10. Patsy Donovan — 272
11. Hugh Duffy — 269
12. George VanHaltren — 268
13. Hughie Jennings — 266
14. Ed Delahanty — 255
15. Tommy Dowd — 245
    Fred Clarke — 245
17. Bill Dahlen — 233
18. Tom Brown — 230
19. Jesse Burkett — 214
20. Kip Selbach — 210

In 1894, the Baltimore Orioles hit just 33 home runs but collected a record 150 triples.

Who's On First?

During the 1890s—while George Davis was setting RBI marks for shortstops, second baseman Heinie Reitz hammered 31 triples, and the Phillies had a .400-hitting outfield and a .394-hitting catcher, Jack Clements—the lone position that was notably lacking in outstanding offensive performers was first base. Part of the reason for the sudden dearth in talented first basemen could be contributed to the disdain with which the position was viewed by analysts of the time. No player who possessed solid overall skills wanted to be stationed there. By 1897, however, the position was on the upswing again with the arrival of Fred Tenney, one of the most graceful first sackers ever, and Nap Lajoie, who was placed at the initial hassock by the Phillies in his first full major league season. Lajoie promptly set several period batting records for first basemen when he collected 127 RBI and topped the National League with a .578 slugging average.

Nap Lajoie, later one of the greatest second basemen ever, set an era record for first basemen in 1897 when he hit .361 for Philadelphia.

Count Campau led the American Association in home runs in 1890 with 10.

In 1894, the Boston Beaneaters hit 103 home runs to become the first team other than the 1884 Chicago White Stockings to reach triple figures in four-baggers.

1893-1899 BATTING AVERAGE

1. Willie Keeler .385
2. Ed Delahanty .384
3. Jesse Burkett .378
4. Billy Hamilton .369
5. Joe Kelley .348
6. Hughie Jennings .348
7. John McGraw .346
8. Jake Stenzel .341
9. George Davis .338
10. Hugh Duffy .338
11. Fred Clarke .334
12. Elmer Smith .333
13. Bill Lange .330
14. George VanHaltren .328
15. Jack Doyle .327
16. Steve Brodie .322
17. Mike Tiernan .318
18. Cupid Childs .317
19. Mike Griffin .317
20. Jake Beckley .317

On April 21, 1898, Phillies hurler Bill Duggleby became the only player ever to hit a grand slam home run in his first major league at bat.

Hugh Duffy was the only player to win two NL home run crowns between 1893 and 1899 (he did it in '94 and '97).

George Davis Hammers from Both Sides of Plate

Switch-hitters are relatively common now, but for many years they were something of a rarity. Before Mickey Mantle, in fact, only one player who hit from both sides of the plate, Tommy Tucker of the 1889 Baltimore Orioles, had ever copped a batting title. The game's first great switch-hitter was not Tucker, however, but George Davis. In addition, Davis was the most potent offensive force among the infielders of his time. Operating at third base and then moving to shortstop, he compiled 2,660 career hits, a record for switch-stickers that lasted until Pete Rose came along. Davis also set a single-season RBI record for National League shortstops that still stands when he brought home 136 New York Giants teammates in 1897. At the time, he was regarded as not only the NL's best-hitting shortstop but also as the finest fielder at the position and perhaps the best all-around player in the game.

George Davis has offensive numbers better than most Hall of Fame shortstops. He had a 6-for-6 game and two extra-inning games in which he hit three triples. Davis hit 47 triples in a two-year period.

While not collecting as many hits as some other players of the era, "Sliding" Billy Hamilton stole 915 bases in his career, which helped him score 945 runs in seven years.

38

Clements Left Other Backstoppers Behind

When Mike Squires went behind the bat for the Chicago White Sox in 1980, it marked the first time in many years that a lefthander had caught in a major league game. Until the early part of the 20th century, southpaw backstoppers were not uncommon. None had a career of much distinction, however, except for Jack Clements. In a 17-year career spanning from 1884 to 1900, Clements not only established the record for the most games caught by a lefthander (1,073), but he posted the highest single-season batting average by a major league receiver when he hit .394 in 1895 for the Philadelphia Phillies. That same season, Clements tagged 13 circuit clouts in 322 at bats to pace the National League in home-run percentage. A short (5'8"), powerfully built man (205 pounds), he retired with a .421 slugging percentage. During his career Clements also on occasion played shortstop and third base, two other positions that are now regarded as anathema to lefthanders.

Besides being a lefthanded backstop, Jack Clements also has claim to preserving every modern catcher's safety. Early in his career, Clements began to wear a chest protector while behind the plate. His "sheep-skin" was mocked, but it soon became common equipment.

In 1894, Louisville was the only NL team that failed to hit at least .286, finishing at .269.

Billy Hamilton set the single-season record for runs scored when he totaled 196 in 1894; he totaled 19 more than Tom Brown's record 177 set in 1891.

In 1894, Billy Hamilton scored at least one run in an all-time record 24 consecutive games.

Billy Hamilton, who led the National League in walks six times, only drew four bases on balls in 35 games in his rookie season with Kansas City in 1888. The next year, he walked 87 times and scored 144 runs.

Beaneaters Almost Have Four 20-Game Winners

Moving the pitching mound $10\frac{1}{2}$ feet farther from the plate in 1893 put an immediate end to the days when a team could get by for a full season with just two strong hurlers. By the middle of the decade most clubs had gone to a three-man rotation, and several even used four starters on a regular basis. In 1898, the Boston Beaneaters, en route to their second consecutive National League flag, nearly became the first team in history to have four 20-game winners. Staff leader Kid Nichols posted 31 wins, Ted Lewis followed with 26 victories, and rookie ace Vic Willis kicked in 25 wins. Fred Klobedanz, the previous year's rookie star, narrowly missed joining the charmed circle when he finished with 19 triumphs. The four stalwarts accounted for all but one of Boston's 102 victories. Win No. 102 was claimed by Piano Legs Hickman, who took some turns on the mound before he became a slugging utility player. In 1899, the Brooklyn Superbas also just missed having four 20-game winners as three members of the club's staff reached the charmed circle and Doc McJames fell one victory short of it.

The only rookie to debut with 30 or more wins since the mound was moved to its present distance from home plate in 1893 was Bill Hoffer of the 1895 Orioles.

Above: *Kid Nichols pitched with Boston from 1890 to 1901. He led the NL in wins from 1896 to 1898 as the Beaneaters won two NL crowns. In 1900, Nichols became the youngest pitcher ever to win 300 games.*

1893-1899 GAMES PITCHED

1.	Cy Young	339
2.	Kid Nichols	336
3.	Ted Breitenstein	307
4.	Pink Hawley	306
5.	Brickyard Kennedy	299
6.	Jack Taylor	266
7.	Jouett Meekin	260
8.	Frank Killen	244
9.	Win Mercer	240
10.	Clark Griffith	235
11.	Amos Rusie	234
12.	Frank Dwyer	228
13.	Nig Cuppy	225
14.	Gus Weyhing	204
15.	Red Ehret	202
16.	Kid Carsey	195
17.	Jack Stivetts	190
18.	Bert Cunningham	170
19.	Doc McJames	165
20.	Red Donahue	151

Spiders Use Cuppy as a Reliever

In the 1890s starting pitchers were expected to finish what they began. Many teams, regardless of the score, stubbornly refused to lift a starter, and in consequence relief pitching was still for the most part an undiscovered art. The Cleveland Spiders were one of the few clubs that broke precedent after manager Patsy Tebeau realized he had something of a find in Nig Cuppy. In 1894, Cuppy won 24 games altogether but only 16 came as a starter. The remaining eight victories were the result of relief stints. Cuppy's eight wins as a fireman set a post-1893 record for relief triumphs that lasted until 1925 when Elam Vangilder of the St. Louis Browns bagged 11 verdicts while working out of the bullpen. What made Cuppy's feat even more spectacular is that he was unbeaten as a reliever in 1894 and at one point in his career was a perfect 14-0 in mop-up roles.

1893-1899 COMPLETE GAMES	
1. Cy Young	279
2. Kid Nichols	276
3. Ted Breitenstein	252
4. Brickyard Kennedy	229
5. Pink Hawley	228
6. Jouett Meekin	214
7. Clark Griffith	213
8. Jack Taylor	205
Amos Rusie	205
10. Frank Killen	190
11. Win Mercer	179
12. Nig Cuppy	168
13. Frank Dwyer	163
14. Gus Weyhing	158
15. Kid Carsey	142
16. Bert Cunningham	140
17. Jack Stivetts	134
18. Doc McJames	131
19. Red Ehret	130
20. Red Donahue	127

Nig Cuppy of Cleveland set a National League record for pitchers when he tallied five runs in a game on August 9, 1895.

Frank Bates was the only pitcher to register a win for the Cleveland Spiders in both 1898 and 1899.

Frank Bates, Crazy Schmit, and Harry Colliflower, three second-line pitchers for the Cleveland Spiders in 1899, had a composite 4-46 record.

In 1895, Washington pitcher Win Mercer tied for the NL lead in pinch hits with two.

In 1899, rookie lefthander Noodles Hahn debuted with a 23-7 record for Cincinnati and topped the NL with 145 stikeouts.

Seymour Collects Strikeout and Batting Crowns

Even casual students of the game in the 1890s naturally assume that all the period single-season strikeout records were set by Amos Rusie. Nicknamed "The Hoosier Thunderbolt," Rusie indeed was the most prolific K artist during the game's second era. The era's highest season strikeout total, however, was registered by a teammate of Rusie's on the New York Giants. In 1898 southpaw Cy Seymour mowed down 244 National League hitters. After notching 142 whiffs in 1899, Seymour fell prey to arm problems, but his career was far from over. By 1901, he had completed the transition from the mound to an every-day player and emerged as one of the game's premier hitters—so good that he remains to this day the only player since 1893 to claim a pitching strikeout crown and a batting title.

Cy Seymour in 1898 led the NL with 239 strikeouts pitching; after his pitching career was over, he went on to become an outfielder. Cy almost won the NL's batting Triple Crown in 1905.

When Ted Breitenstein of Cincinnati and Jim Hughes of Baltimore both hurled no-hitters on April 22, 1898, it was the first time two no-nos had occurred on the same day.

O.P. Caylor of the *New York Herald* wrote about Amos Rusie: "The Giants without Rusie would be like *Hamlet* without the melancholy Dane."

1893-1899 SHUTOUTS

1.	Cy Young	19
	Kid Nichols	19
3.	Amos Rusie	17
4.	Jack Powell	10
	Bill Hoffer	10
6.	Jesse Tannehill	9
	Frank Killen	9
	Brickyard Kennedy	9
	Pink Hawley	9
	Ted Breitenstein	9
11.	Jim Hughes	8
	Wiley Piatt	8
	Nig Cuppy	8
14.	Gus Weyhing	7
	Jack Taylor	7
	Red Ehret	7
	Frank Dwyer	7
18.	Vic Willis	6
	Cy Seymour	6
	Billy Rhines	6
	Al Orth	6
	Jouett Meekin	6
	Doc McJames	6
	George Hemming	6
	Red Donahue	6
	Nixey Callahan	6

Put It In the 'L' Column

For a pitcher the quality of the team behind him can mean nearly everything. When Bill Hoffer logged a rookie-record 31 wins in 1895, he was hurling for the National League champion Baltimore Orioles. In 1896, another rookie named Bill—Still Bill Hill—set the reverse frosh record when he was beaten 28 times while working for the cellar-dwelling Louisville Colonels. That same season Billy Hart set a post-1893 record by suffering 29 defeats with St. Louis, which finished a notch above Louisville in 11th place. In 1897, Louisville swapped places with St. Louis in the standings, helping Hill to cut his losses to just 17. Hart meanwhile lost 27 more games for St. Louis in 1897, but his moundmate Red Donahue fared even worse. With his St. Louis club able to win only 29 of 131 contests, Donahue dropped a post-1893 record 35 games. Traded to Philadelphia in 1898, Donahue went on to fashion a productive career, but Hill and Hart never recovered from their early stints with abysmal teams.

On June 14, 1893, Bill Rhodes of the Louisville Colonels, making his second major league start, was allowed to go the route by manager Billy Barnie despite surrendering an all-time record 55 total bases.

1893-1899 WINS			1893-1899 INNINGS	
1. Kid Nichols	205		1. Cy Young	2,696.2
2. Cy Young	195		2. Kid Nichols	2,683.1
3. Brickyard Kennedy	141		3. Ted Breitenstein	2,446.0
4. Amos Rusie	140		4. Pink Hawley	2,334.2
5. Ted Breitenstein	139		5. B. Kennedy	2,288.2
6. Clark Griffith	138		6. Jouett Meekin	2,094.0
7. Pink Hawley	136		7. Jack Taylor	2,045.0
8. Jouett Meekin	133		8. Amos Rusie	1,941.2
9. Frank Killen	125		9. Clark Griffith	1,940.2
10. Nig Cuppy	122		10. Frank Killen	1,901.0
11. Jack Taylor	119		11. Win Mercer	1,763.0
12. Frank Dwyer	113		12. Frank Dwyer	1,724.1
13. Jack Stivetts	96		13. Nig Cuppy	1,709.2
14. Win Mercer	94		14. Gus Weyhing	1,580.1
15. Bill Hoffer	89		15. Kid Carsey	1,482.1
16. Kid Carsey	82		16. Red Ehret	1,442.2
17. Gus Weyhing	81		17. Jack Stivetts	1,421.0
18. Bert Cunningham	77		18. B. Cunningham	1,340.2
19. Doc McJames	74		19. Doc McJames	1,270.1
20. George Hemming	73		20. G. Hemming	1,203.0

Cy Young was the staff ace and leading winner for the Cleveland Spiders each year from 1891 to 1898. During that span, Young led the NL in such diverse categories as wins, strikeouts, ERA, saves, and relief wins.

Colonel Bert Saves Louisville Baseball

Accepted into the National League when the American Association collapsed after the 1891 season, the Louisville Colonels finished ninth in 1892, their first campaign in the new 12-team circuit, but then became the loop's perennial doormat, finishing either last or next to last for each of the next five seasons. The club's most glaring weakness was pitching. While most of the other NL clubs had at least one 20-game winner, Louisville entered the 1898 season not having had a hurler attain the charmed circle since Scott Stratton won 21 games in 1892. Among the club's mound hopefuls that spring was Bert Cunningham, then 32 years old and the owner of a lackluster career record of 93 wins and 131 defeats. To the dismay of the entire baseball community, Cunningham snared 28 victories in 1898 and helped save the Louisville franchise from extinction. Part-owner Barney Dreyfus had been ready to dispose of his interest in the team before Cunningham brought it credibility. Dreyfus instead held on to his piece of the club until the finish of the 1899 season when he took its best players to Pittsburgh, which he also owned, and formed the team that would soon become the NL's best.

Rookie hurler Frank Donnelly in 1893 had a 3-1 record for Chicago, hit .444, and led the National League in saves but never again played in the majors.

1893-1899 STRIKEOUTS

1.	Amos Rusie	853
2.	Kid Nichols	822
3.	Cy Young	771
4.	Ted Breitenstein	708
5.	Pink Hawley	675
6.	Jouett Meekin	628
7.	Cy Seymour	563
8.	Doc McJames	551
9.	Brickyard Kennedy	538
10.	Frank Killen	536
11.	Jack Taylor	518
12.	Clark Griffith	512
13.	Gus Weyhing	440
14.	Win Mercer	415
15.	Nig Cuppy	356
16.	Jack Stivetts	352
17.	Red Ehret	350
18.	Chick Fraser	306
19.	Ed Doheny	296
20.	Bill Hoffer	295

Stay West

Between 1892 and 1900 the National League was considered to be the only major league in operation—by those who lived east of the Mississippi anyway. Baseball players in the far West thought the caliber of competition on the Pacific Coast was every bit as strong as the NL offered. Since the weather there was considerably better, making it possible to play year around, and railway travel was still hazardous, many chose to play close to the Pacific. Among them were two pitchers of considerable skill: Joe Corbett and Jim Hughes. The brother of heavyweight champion Gentleman Jim, Joe Corbett balked at returning to Baltimore after posting 24 wins for the Orioles in 1897 and, except for a brief spell with St. Louis in 1904, remained on the West Coast for the rest of his career. Hughes lasted four seasons in the National League and bagged 83 wins before moving his game to the West Coast after his new bride refused to go East with him. In 1924, his body was found below a railroad bridge in Sacramento, California; it was never established whether he fell from the bridge or was pushed to his death.

1893-1899 EARNED RUN AVERAGE	
1. Amos Rusie	3.08
2. Kid Nichols	3.21
3. Cy Young	3.25
4. Doc McJames	3.34
5. Clark Griffith	3.44
6. Bill Hoffer	3.68
7. Nig Cuppy	3.68
8. Frank Killen	3.97
9. Frank Dwyer	4.00
10. Ted Breitenstein	4.00
11. Pink Hawley	4.03
12. B. Kennedy	4.03
13. Bert Cunningham	4.04
14. Jouett Meekin	4.06
15. Win Mercer	4.09
16. Billy Rhines	4.14
17. Jack Taylor	4.27
18. Ed Stein	4.41
19. Chick Fraser	4.42
20. Jack Stivetts	4.48

Despite leading the National League only once in triples, Jake Beckley's 243 three-base hits rank fourth on the all-time list.

In 1898, the Beaneaters won 102 games while cruising to the NL pennant.

Jake Beckley scored over 100 runs five times during the 1890s, including a high of 121 in 1894.

The last southpaw to win 30 games for an NL team was Frank Killen, who bagged exactly 30 victories for the 1896 Pittsburgh Pirates.

Crooks Robbed of Career

Beginning in 1893, when the pitcher's mound was stationed at its present distance and batting averages jumped by some 50 points, even middle infielders were expected to hit close to .300. The St. Louis Browns released Jack Crooks after he batted a meager .237 that season, disregarding his .408 on-base percentage and National League leading total of 121 walks (the third consecutive seasons he had more than 100 walks in a season). Crooks returned to the NL with Washington in 1895 but was soon jettisoned again, as much a victim of his times as outfielder Jim McTamany had been in the game's previous era. His low batting averages notwithstanding, Crooks was possibly the best pure leadoff hitter of his day, skilled both at coaxing walks and moving runners along with sacrifice bunts. Crooks also ranked among the top defensive second basemen of his era. In 1891 he set a new standard for the position when he posted a .957 fielding average. He died in a St. Louis mental hospital in 1918.

Cheaters Sometimes Prosper

Heywood Broun wrote about the old Baltimore Orioles: "The tradition of professional baseball always has been agreeably free of chivalry. The rule is: Do anything you can get away with."

In 1896, the Phillies featured both the last southpaw to be a regular catcher, Jack Clements, and the last lefthander to be a regular shortstop, Billy Hulen.

To curb pesky hitters like Willie Keeler, who kept bunting pitches foul until they got one they liked, in 1894 a rule was put in making a foul bunt a strike.

1893-1899 CATCHER GAMES

1.	Deacon McGuire	652
2.	Wilbert Robinson	574
3.	Heinie Peitz	514
4.	Duke Farrell	505
5.	Chief Zimmer	501

The current infield fly rule was first adopted by the National League in 1895.

1893-1899 FIRST BASE GAMES

1.	Tommy Tucker	860
2.	Jake Beckley	858
3.	Candy LaChance	595
4.	Patsy Tebeau	591
5.	Jack Doyle	565

Phillies Lose Allen, 1894 Pennant

Another middle infielder whose skills were undervalued during the 1890s was Bob Allen. As a rookie with the Philadelphia Phillies in 1890, Allen quickly made a case that he was the best defensive shortstop in the game at the time. Despite batting averages that generally hovered in the .220s, Allen provided the glue for the Phillies infield during the next four seasons. Loaded with offensive talent in its three future Hall of Fame outfielders—Billy Hamilton, Sam Thompson, and Ed Delahanty—Philadelphia seemed poised to make its first serious pennant bid in 1894, only to have its chances short-circuited when Allen was sidelined early in the season by a beaning. Without Allen the club sagged from the NL's top fielding unit in 1893 to no better than average and wound up a distant fourth. Allen's head injury prevented him from playing in the majors again until 1897, and even then he never fully recovered his early form.

Hall of Fame first baseman Jake Beckley was released by the New York Giants early in the 1897 season but went on to play 10 more years after he was picked up by Cincinnati.

1893-1899 SECOND BASE GAMES

1. Cupid Childs	841
2. Bobby Lowe	839
3. Bid McPhee	801
4. Bill Hallman	713
5. Heinie Reitz	687

In 1893, three Spiders had 100 RBI with six or fewer homers each.

The 1897 Boston Beaneaters were the last team prior to 1930 to top 1,000 runs.

Gotta Be Tough to Play in Cleveland

Cleveland player-manager Patsy Tebeau said about his band of Spiders: "A milk-and-water goody-goody player can't wear a Cleveland uniform."

Cleveland's Jesse Burkett led the NL in 1896 with 160 runs scored, 240 hits, and a .410 batting average.

Mike Griffin of Brooklyn led all National League outfielders in fielding average three times between 1893 and 1899.

The 1894 to 1897 Orioles are the only team to win more than two-thirds of its games for four consecutive years.

The Washington Nationals and the Philadelphia Phillies combined to collect an all-time record 73 hits in a doubleheader on Independence Day in 1896.

Pictured above, clockwise from far left, are: Willie Keeler, John McGraw, Hughie Jennings, and Joe Kelley. These four key members of the 1890s Orioles helped to bring winning baseball to the Chesapeake Bay under manager Ned Hanlon.

Hanlon Teaches Orioles Winning Rowdy Style

To alter its fortunes after finishing last in the 12-team National League in 1892, the Baltimore club hired Ned Hanlon as manager. Hanlon steered the Orioles to an eighth-place finish in 1893, then lifted Baltimore to three straight pennants. A series of shrewd trades that brought Hall of Famers Joe Kelley, Wee Willie Keeler, and Hughie Jennings to Baltimore helped put the club over the top, but equally instrumental were two members of the Orioles' original NL cast in 1892: third baseman John McGraw and catcher Wilbert Robinson. Perhaps more than any other player, McGraw exemplified the guileful, spikes-flying brand of play that proliferated during the 1890s.

A *New York World-Telegram* reader, informing reporter Joe Williams in the 1920s, wrote: "Individually, you haven't lost much in having missed seeing the Old Orioles. But collectively, oh, my dear scribbler, could you have seen them, your whole life might have been different."

Selee Directs 1890s' Best Club

1893-1899 OUTFIELD GAMES

1. George VanHaltren — 948
2. Hugh Duffy — 933
3. Jesse Burkett — 931
4. Dummy Hoy — 913
5. Joe Kelley — 911
6. Patsy Donovan — 888
7. Elmer Smith — 831
8. Steve Brodie — 826
9. Ed Delahanty — 823
10. Jimmy Ryan — 822
11. Willie Keeler — 794
12. Tommy Dowd — 791
13. Billy Hamilton — 782
14. Fred Clarke — 758
15. Mike Tiernan — 753

The 1899 Cleveland Spiders won only 20 of 154.

1893-1899 THIRD BASE GAMES

1. Billy Shindle — 742
2. Lave Cross — 653
3. Jimmy Collins — 594
4. John McGraw — 590
5. Billy Nash — 556

Although the Baltimore Orioles emerged as the most famous team of the 1890s, they were not the era's best club. The Boston Beaneaters, under manager Frank Selee, had a better overall record during the decade than the Orioles. Selee's forte was recognizing, signing, and nurturing young talent. Among Selee's finds were Hall of Famers Kid Nichols and Jimmy Collins, and Vic Willis, regarded by many as the best pitcher not in the Hall of Fame. He managed the Boston NL club from 1890 to 1901, going 1,004-649 and winning five pennants. When his Boston dynasty began to falter in the early 1900s, Selee took over the operation of the Chicago Cubs in 1902. A franchise in disarray, the Cubs had not been a contender since the late 1880s. With Selee at the helm, Chicago quickly rebounded and was only a year away from its first pennant since 1886 when tuberculosis forced Selee to surrender control of the team to Frank Chance.

In their season finale against the Cincinnati Reds, the hapless 1899 Cleveland Spiders named Eddie Kolb, a Cincinnati cigar store clerk, their starting pitcher.

In a game on May 9, 1896, Washington and Pittsburgh pitchers combined to hit an all-time record eight batters.

1893-1899 SHORTSTOP GAMES

1. Herman Long — 855
2. Tommy Corcoran — 842
3. Ed McKean — 837
4. Bones Ely — 828
5. Bill Dahlen — 735

Soden's Stubbornness Surrenders Beaneaters Reign

A large part of the reason that Frank Selee abandoned Boston for Chicago was Beaneaters owner Arthur Soden. Always intransigent, reactionary, and tight-fisted in his mode of operation, Soden by the early 1900s had become so aloof from his players that he did not even know the names of many of them. During the 1890s when there was only one major league and his players were bound to him like chattels, Soden's intractability had been masked by Selee's genius as a manager. After the American League formed in 1901 as a rival major circuit, though, Soden swiftly began to lose most of his star players to aggressive owners from the other loop who were willing and ready to pay them what they were worth. From the best team in the 1890s, Soden's club descended so far in the following decade that it ranked as the game's worst at its end.

In 1895, the New York Giants came in ninth in the 12-club NL with a .504 winning percentage, the lowest finish ever by a team able to win more than half its games.

Tommy Leach remembered Dummy Hoy, the deaf-mute outfielder: "He was a real fine ballplayer. When you played with him in the outfield, the thing was you never called for a ball. You listened for him, and if he made this little squeaky sound, that meant he was going to take it."

To convey ball-and-strike calls to the deaf Dummy Hoy, 1890s plate umpires began using hand signals.

In 1894, the pitching staff of the Washington Senators, then in the NL, struck out just 190 batters in 132 games and allowed opponents to hit a pre-1930 major league record .331.

In 1896, a Princeton professor named Hinton invented the first mechanical pitching machine.

In 1894, the Philadelphia Phillies hit .349 as a team, had three outfielders who batted over .400 and another who hit .399, and finished in fourth place, 18 games off the pace.

1893-1899 MANAGER WINS

1. Ned Hanlon — 613
2. Frank Selee — 604
3. Patsy Tebeau — 539
4. Buck Ewing — 394
5. Cap Anson — 324
6. Dave Foutz — 264
7. Arthur Irwin — 249
8. Fred Clarke — 180
9. Bill Joyce — 179
10. Billy Barnie — 162

1893-1899 TEAM WINS

	W	L
1. Boston-NL	604	352
2. Baltimore-NL	598	346
3. Cincinnati-NL	514	435
4. Philadelphia-NL	510	441
5. New York-NL	506	451
6. Pittsburgh-NL	491	457
7. Brooklyn-NL	480	466
8. Chicago-NL	475	472
Cleveland-NL	475	474
10. Louisville-NL	356	594
11. Wash.-NL	352	604
12. St.Louis-NL	344	613

In 1894, Washington pitchers fanned only 190 enemy hitters and were led by rookie Win Mercer with 69 Ks.

All seven National League pennants between 1893 and 1899 were claimed by two managers, Ned Hanlon and Frank Selee.

Handsome Tony Mullane Helps Create 'Ladies Day'

Times were hard in the 1890s. Throughout most of the decade the country was suffering from an economic depression, and baseball was not spared the effects of it. In an effort to spark dwindling attendance National League club owners turned to several ploys devised by the American Association in the 1880s after previously being disdainful of them. One of the most popular was "Ladies Day" games in which females were allowed into the park for free. Among the first AA moguls to institute Ladies Days was Cincinnati owner Aaron Stern, who observed that women would flock to his club's games on days that handsome Tony Mullane was slated to pitch. From then on, whenever Mullane worked against weak teams that normally drew poorly, Stern advertised the contest as a special "Ladies Day" event. Other AA owners, like Brooklyn's Charles Byrne, soon adopted the innovation. With the help of Ladies Days, Byrne's 1889 Brooklyn Bridegrooms set a 19th century season attendance record.

Chapter 3
The 1900s

Dahlen, Other Loop Leaders Low

In 1894, Bill Dahlen collected 107 runs batted in, a total that barely placed him among the top 20 RBI men in the National League. Exactly a decade later Dahlen notched 80 RBI, seemingly an indication that his offensive production had declined. In actuality, however, it was not Dahlen that declined but offensive production in general. By 1904, the game was so deeply in the throes of the dead-ball era that Dahlen's modest total of 80 RBI topped the National League.

1900s RUNS

1. Honus Wagner	1,014
2. Fred Clarke	885
3. Roy Thomas	862
4. Ginger Beaumont	835
5. Tommy Leach	828
6. Sam Crawford	813
7. Jimmy Sheckard	807
8. Nap Lajoie	806
9. Fielder Jones	799
10. Willie Keeler	797
11. Elmer Flick	761
12. Fred Tenney	758
13. Topsy Hartsel	754
14. Harry Davis	721
15. Bill Bradley	700
16. Jimmy Slagle	687
17. Jimmy Williams	655
18. Frank Chance	646
19. Jimmy Collins	624
20. Cy Seymour	622

1900s GAMES PLAYED

1. Sam Crawford	1,410
2. Honus Wagner	1,391
3. Bobby Wallace	1,362
4. Bill Dahlen	1,332
5. Fred Tenney	1,329
6. Jimmy Sheckard	1,312
7. Jimmy Williams	1,304
8. Harry Steinfeldt	1,303
9. Bill Bradley	1,292
10. Fielder Jones	1,289
11. Hobe Ferris	1,287
12. Willie Keeler	1,278
13. Roy Thomas	1,276
G. Beaumont	1,276
15. Tommy Leach	1,273
16. Claude Ritchey	1,272
17. Freddy Parent	1,241
18. Fred Clarke	1,234
19. Cy Seymour	1,224
Nap Lajoie	1,224

Bill Dahlen played an NL record 20 years at shortstop, collected a major league record 13,325 total chances and an NL record 7,500 assists, and made 972 errors, the most by a player at any position in a single league.

In 1906, rookie catcher Branch Rickey became the first player from the St. Louis Browns to hit two dingers in one game.

In 1909, Brooklyn catcher Bill Bergen hit .139, the lowest average in history by a regular.

Dead-Ball Clobbers Minors

The dead-ball era impacted not just on the two major leagues. In some ways it had an even more pervasive effect on the game in the minors. In 1906, a year after Elmer Flick had won the AL title with a .306 average, George Whiteman of Cleburne led the Texas League with a .281 figure. A year earlier, Scott Ragsdale of Waco had reigned as the Texas League batting king with a .292 mark. Ragsdale and Whiteman were far from the only minor league leaders to post sub-.300 batting averages during that era. In 1906, Jack Thoney topped the International League with a .294 average. Three years later, both the Southern Association and the American Association lacked a .300 hitter. In 1909, Bill McGilvray's .291 batting average led the Southern Association, while Minneapolis's Mike O'Neill topped the American Association by hitting .296.

Pittsburgh's Tommy Leach led the NL with six homers in 1902, the fewest by a loop leader in the 20th century.

Cincinnati's Fred Odwell led the NL with nine homers in 1905.

1900s HITS

1.	Honus Wagner	1,847
2.	Sam Crawford	1,677
3.	Nap Lajoie	1,660
4.	Willie Keeler	1,566
5.	Ginger Beaumont	1,559
6.	Cy Seymour	1,460
7.	Elmer Flick	1,431
8.	Fred Clarke	1,396
9.	Fred Tenney	1,387
10.	Bobby Wallace	1,373
11.	Bill Bradley	1,348
12.	Jimmy Sheckard	1,343
13.	Roy Thomas	1,341
14.	Harry Davis	1,332
15.	Tommy Leach	1,325
16.	Fielder Jones	1,322
17.	Jimmy Williams	1,288
18.	Harry Steinfeldt	1,262
19.	Freddy Parent	1,255
20.	Jimmy Collins	1,253

Cub Jimmy Sheckard collected an NL record 46 sacrifice hits in 1909.

On May 23, 1901, Nap Lajoie was the first player to be intentionally walked with the bases full.

Tommy Leach, who once won a home-run crown largely by hitting inside-the-park homers, remarked: "Today they seem to think that the most exciting play in baseball is the home run. But in my book the most exciting play in baseball is a three-bagger, or an inside-the-park home run."

Drought Grips West Coast

Nowhere in organized baseball was the offensive drought more deeply felt during the dead-ball era than in the Pacific Coast League. While all of the other top minor circuits of that time experienced at least one season without a .300 hitter, the Pacific Coast League lacked a .300 average by a regular player a record three years in a row. In 1908, Babe Danzig of Los Angeles paced the PCL with a .298 mark, and the following year San Francisco's Harry Melchior hit a slightly lower .298 to take the bat crown. In 1910, Hunky Shaw of San Francisco won the honor by finishing with a .281 figure. By 1910, hits and runs were so hard to come by in the Coast loop that the Portland Beavers pitching staff was able to compile a record 88 consecutive shutout innings at one point in the season, and Kid Mohler was voted to the circuit's All-Star Team at second base despite hitting a paltry .191.

Sam Crawford, an outfielder for the Reds and the Tigers from 1899 to 1917, was the first player to be both an NL and an AL leader in home runs.

A former barber from Nebraska, "Wahoo Sam" Crawford tallied an all time-best 312 triples in his 19-year career, 15 more than former teammate Ty Cobb, who collected 297 three-baggers.

Philadelphia Athletic Socks Seybold led the AL with 16 homers in 1902, tying Sam Crawford's 20th century record.

1900s DOUBLES

1.	Honus Wagner	372
2.	Nap Lajoie	361
3.	Harry Davis	291
4.	Sam Crawford	263
5.	Bill Bradley	256
6.	Bobby Wallace	243
7.	Jimmy Sheckard	238
8.	Jimmy Collins	232
9.	Elmer Flick	228
10.	Harry Steinfeldt	225
11.	Jimmy Williams	214
	Danny Murphy	214
	John Anderson	214
14.	Socks Seybold	213
	Charlie Hickman	213
16.	Cy Seymour	205
	Kitty Bransfield	205
18.	Hobe Ferris	192
19.	Fred Clarke	189
20.	Bill Dahlen	188

The pennant-winning Detroit Tigers had just 11 home runs in 1907 as six of the team's regulars failed to hit a single four-bagger.

54

Jimmy Sebring of Pittsburgh hit the first home run in a modern World Series, taking Boston's Cy Young deep in the opening contest of the 1903 fall classic.

After leading the National League with 10 home runs in 1907, Boston third baseman Dave Brain never hit another four-bagger in the majors.

Cincinnati's Fred Odwell led the National League with nine homers in 1905, and never hit another homer in the majors.

White Sox shortstop George Davis in 1902 became the first switch-hitter in baseball history to collect 2,000 hits.

1900s TRIPLES

1.	Sam Crawford	167
2.	Honus Wagner	148
3.	Elmer Flick	139
4.	Fred Clarke	134
5.	Tommy Leach	123
6.	Jimmy Williams	111
7.	Buck Freeman	103
8.	Hobe Ferris	89
9.	Topsy Hartsel	88
10.	Cy Seymour	87
	Nap Lajoie	87
12.	Charlie Hickman	85
13.	Jimmy Sheckard	84
14.	Bill Bradley	82
15.	Mike Donlin	81
16.	Sam Mertes	80
17.	Sherry Magee	79
18.	Chick Stahl	78
19.	Harry Davis	77
20.	Harry Steinfeldt	75

Cobb Cloaks Dead-Ball Scoring Dearth

The first half of the century's initial decade was the only period when the dominant hitter in each league was a middle infielder. The AL's top performer was second baseman Nap Lajoie, while shortstop Honus Wagner copped the majority of the hitting honors in the NL. Wagner's dominance continued until the end of the decade, but Lajoie by 1907 had given way to Detroit outfielder Ty Cobb. Then in his third season, the rising Tigers star won his first of 11 batting titles (some books still say 12, crediting him with the controversial 1910 AL hitting crown) as he hit .350—103 points above the AL average. In 1908, Cobb slipped to .324 but still led the AL by a comfortable 13-point margin. With the exception of the 1910 season, Cobb not only paced the AL in batting every year between 1907 and 1916, but he customarily topped the average hitter in the game by between 120 and 140 points. Cobb's phenomenal offensive feats obscured how little offense most other players in the dead-ball era were able to generate.

1900s HOME RUNS

1.	Harry Davis	67
2.	Charlie Hickman	58
3.	Sam Crawford	57
4.	Buck Freeman	54
5.	Honus Wagner	51
	Socks Seybold	51
7.	Nap Lajoie	48
8.	Cy Seymour	43
9.	Jimmy Williams	40
	Hobe Ferris	40
11.	Mike Donlin	39
12.	Harry Lumley	38
13.	Elmer Flick	37
14.	Tommy Leach	36
15.	Jimmy Sheckard	34
	Ginger Beaumont	34
17.	Tim Jordan	31
	Jimmy Collins	31
	Jesse Burkett	31
	Bill Bradley	31

Nig Clarke of the Texas League's Corsicana went 8-for-8 with eight homers during a game in 1902.

Boston's Jimmy Collins led NL third sackers in putouts five times, in assists four times, and in double plays twice.

Before pounding pitchers with his heavy hitting, Cy Seymour was a hard throwing southpaw with the Giants, notching 20 and 25 wins in 1897 and '98 as well as pacing the NL in strikeouts and walks.

Seymour Misses Hat Trick by Homer

Since 1967, when Carl Yastrzemski led the American League in batting and RBI and tied for the top spot in homers, no one has come close to claiming a Triple Crown. Prior to 1967, no player came closer to winning a Triple Crown without achieving it than Cy Seymour. After converting to the outfield when his pitching arm failed him, Seymour bounced around for several years in the early 1900s before landing in Cincinnati, where he soon began to challenge Honus Wagner for National League hitting honors. The 1905 season was Seymour's apex; he paced the senior circuit in batting average, RBI, hits, total bases, doubles, triples, and slugging average. Missing, however, from his trophy case at the end of the season was the loop home run crown, which was won by his Cincinnati teammate Fred Odwell. In 1905, Odwell tagged nine round-trippers and Seymour finished as the loop runner-up with eight. One more circuit clout would have tied Seymour for the lead and meant a Triple Crown. Ironically, Fred Odwell never hit another home run in the majors after the 1905 season.

Donlin Makes Dramatic Exit

In 1905, outfielder Mike Donlin of the New York Giants ranked right behind Cy Seymour and Honus Wagner among the National League's premier offensive performers. That season Donlin paced the majors with 124 runs and was second only to Seymour in total bases and hits. Donlin was 27 years old and had put together four strong offensive seasons, broken only by a jail stint in the summer of 1902 stemming from an altercation he precipitated with the police while playing for Baltimore of the AL. After the 1905 campaign, he played regularly in the majors only one more season. That came in 1908, when "Turkey Mike" returned to the Giants after missing all but a fraction of the previous two seasons and promptly hit .334 to lead the club in batting. His protracted absences from the game were the result of suspensions owing to alcoholism or holdouts and his dramatic ambitions. Early in his career, Donlin married Mabel Hite, an actress, and the two starred together in several stage and vaudeville productions.

Phillies center fielder Roy Thomas collected 100 or more walks six times between 1900 and 1909, something no other NL player could do more than once during that period.

The leading hitter for the first AL flag winner, the 1901 Chicago White Sox, was third baseman Fred Hartman at .309.

The New York Giants collected a record 31 hits on June 9, 1901; six of them were notched by Kip Selbach.

Wee Willie Keeler collected at least 200 hits for eight straight years from 1894 to 1901 to set the National League record.

1900s RUNS BATTED IN

1.	Honus Wagner	956
2.	Sam Crawford	808
3.	Nap Lajoie	793
4.	Harry Davis	688
5.	Cy Seymour	685
6.	Jimmy Williams	680
7.	Bobby Wallace	638
8.	Harry Steinfeldt	610
9.	Bill Dahlen	597
10.	Charlie Hickman	590
11.	Kitty Bransfield	581
12.	Sam Mertes	579
13.	Elmer Flick	570
14.	Buck Freeman	569
15.	Ginger Beaumont	557
	John Anderson	557
17.	Hobe Ferris	550
18.	Socks Seybold	548
	Lave Cross	548
20.	Jimmy Collins	545

Nap Lajoie (above) used a split-hands grip on the bat in order to maintain outstanding bat control. The lower portion of Lajoie's bat was specially designed by the J.F. Hillerich Company with two knobs, so he could still generate some power.

Sherry Magee Outshines Top NL Outfielders

For the 10-year period between 1905 and 1914, Sherry Magee was the National League's most potent offensive force apart from Honus Wagner. Magee led the NL three times during that span in RBI, twice in slugging average, and once in batting. After serving the Phillies for 11 seasons without yet being on a pennant winner, Magee was traded after the 1914 campaign to the reigning National League champion Boston Braves. It seemed a great break for him at first but proved otherwise when the Phillies captured their first pennant in franchise history in 1915.

In 1901, Philadelphia's Nap Lajoie set a 20th century record when he hit .426 to lead the AL; he also won the Triple Crown.

In 1901, Jimmy Sheckard of Brooklyn became the first major league player to hit a grand slam home run in two consecutive games.

Ed Walsh said about Nap Lajoie: "If you pitched inside to him, he'd tear the hand off the third baseman, and if you pitched outside he'd knock down the second baseman."

The 1901 Phillies keystone combo of Bill Hallman and Monte Cross hit .184 and .197.

Had Mike Donlin collected the 146 more at bats needed to reach the qualifying 4,000, his lifetime .333 batting average would have placed him with the 21st highest average.

Jim Dunleavy of Pacific Coast League Oakland in 1905 played in an organized baseball record 227 games.

When Ty Cobb won his first hitting title in 1907 with a .350 batting average, he collected just 24 walks.

1900s STOLEN BASES

1. Honus Wagner	487
2. Frank Chance	357
3. Sam Mertes	305
4. Jimmy Sheckard	295
5. Elmer Flick	275
6. Jimmy Slagle	251
7. Frank Isbell	250
8. Fielder Jones	239
Wid Conroy	239
Fred Clarke	239
11. Sherry Magee	238
12. Topsy Hartsel	233
Bill Dahlen	233
14. Johnny Evers	230
15. Joe Tinker	229
Art Devlin	229
17. Tommy Leach	226
18. Dan McGann	220
Patsy Dougherty	220
20. Ginger Beaumont	219

1900s BATTING AVERAGE

1. Honus Wagner	.352
2. Nap Lajoie	.346
3. Mike Donlin	.338
4. Elmer Flick	.312
5. Jesse Burkett	.312
6. Willie Keeler	.311
7. Cy Seymour	.311
8. Jake Beckley	.309
9. Ginger Beaumont	.309
10. Sam Crawford	.307
11. Fred Clarke	.301
12. Frank Chance	.299
13. Socks Seybold	.296
14. Charlie Hickman	.294
15. Danny Green	.291
16. Lave Cross	.291
17. Chick Stahl	.291
18. Sherry Magee	.291
19. Joe Kelley	.289
20. Jimmy Barrett	.289

Davis Wins Four Straight Homer Crowns

Improbable as it might seem, the first player to claim four consecutive league home run crowns is not in the Hall of Fame. Much of the reason is that during the span when he reigned as the AL four-bagger king (1904 to 1907), Harry Davis collected just 38 home runs, an average of less than 10 per season. While many observers took no particular notice of Davis's home run stats, they did recognize the Philadelphia first baseman's stature as an all-around slugger and run producer. He also paced the American League twice in RBI and three times in doubles.

Only Seven Bat Over .300 in 1908

In 1898, some 33 regular players in the National League hit above .300. Ten years later the game had changed so much that just seven regulars in the major leagues were able to bat .300, and a mere four managed to hit above .308. Offensive production was so dismal that the National League and the American League each hit a composite .239, a figure that still stands as the record low for the senior loop and has been topped only in 1968 by the AL. In 1908, just two teams, one in each league, succeeded in hitting above .250. Detroit topped the AL with a .263 mark, thanks in large part to Ty Cobb and Sam Crawford, the loop's two top hitters that season, while the New York Giants rapped .267 to lead the majors. The Giants had just one hitter among the top five in the NL, the .334-batting Mike Donlin, but were also blessed with two part-time regulars, Larry Doyle and Moose McCormick, who cracked the .300 barrier. This trio combined with shortstop Al Bridwell, center fielder Cy Seymour, and catcher Roger Bresnahan to give the Giants an offense that led the majors with 652 runs, produced in 157 games.

In 1908, the New York Giants led the majors in runs with 652 and in hitting with a .267 batting average as offense was so skimpy that both loops averaged an identical .239.

Bobby Byrne of the St. Louis Cardinals had just 14 RBI in 1908, the all-time record low by a third baseman in 400 or more at bats.

Cub Frank Chance was hit by pitches a record five times in a 1905 doubleheader.

Swing, Batter, Swing

Bill Byron, the singing umpire, serenaded a batter who took a called third strike: "Let me tell you something, son/ Before you get much older/ You cannot hit the ball, my friend/ With the bat upon your shoulder."

On April 12, 1906, Johnny Bates became the first player in the century to homer in his first major league at bat.

Future Hall of Famer Ed Delahanty (above) was swept over Niagara Falls to his death after getting kicked off a train for being disorderly, leaving his .346 lifetime average the fourth highest ever.

Ed Delahanty in 1902 became the first player to win batting titles in both the National League and the American League. He won the NL title in 1899 with a .410 average and won the AL batting title in 1902 with a .376 average.

Cards, Others Average Deuce Per Game

While the New York Giants were scoring runs at the "heady" rate of over four a game in 1908, the Brooklyn Superbas and the St. Louis Cardinals averaged little more than two tallies per contest. In 1908, the Cardinals crossed the plate just 371 times in 154 games and Brooklyn collected a mere 377 tallies. Brooklyn moreover had only one player, Tim Jordan, who notched more than 41 RBI. Jordan not only led the club in ribbies with 60 but his .247 average paced it in batting as the club posted 20th century National League record lows for both batting average and slugging average with figures of .213 and .277 respectively. With all that, Brooklyn avoided the cellar, leaving that ignominy to the Cardinals. Two years later the Chicago White Sox also dodged the American League basement when they registered 20th century record lows with a .211 batting average and a .261 slugging average. Pitching was much of the reason that Brooklyn and Chicago survived with so little firepower. The Superbas had a 2.47 staff ERA in 1908 while the White Sox in 1910 posted a 2.01 staff ERA and allowed the second-fewest runs in the majors.

Big Ed Supplies Own Attack

No pitcher profited more from the style of play during the dead-ball era than Big Ed Walsh. At the same time no pitcher suffered more as a result of it. Allowed to throw a spitball, Walsh became the reigning master of the wet delivery. What made the pitch even more effective was the fact that when he was on the mound the same ball was sometimes used for the entire game. By the late innings, the sphere was so soggy and lopsided that batters found it virtually impossible to hit out of the infield. But the benefits Walsh accrued during the dead-ball era were on occasion severely outweighed by the impact it had on his own team, the Chicago White Sox. Labeled "The Hitless Wonders" in 1906, they won their only pennant while Walsh was with the club despite posting the lowest team batting average in the American League. In 1908, while becoming the last pitcher to win 40 games in a season, Walsh was supported by a crew that hit .224 and scored just 537 runs.

Ed Walsh's 464 innings in 1908 set a 20th century record, breaking Jack Chesbro's old mark.

1900s GAMES PITCHED

1.	Joe McGinnity	417
2.	Cy Young	403
3.	Vic Willis	398
4.	Christy Mathewson	388
5.	Rube Waddell	385
6.	Jack Powell	377
7.	Jack Chesbro	373
8.	Eddie Plank	334
9.	George Mullin	330
10.	Bill Dinneen	325
11.	Al Orth	315
12.	Doc White	309
	Harry Howell	309
14.	Sam Leever	306
15.	Tom Hughes	298
16.	Deacon Phillippe	296
17.	Bill Donovan	295
18.	Chick Fraser	288
19.	Tully Sparks	281
20.	Dummy Taylor	274

Lefty Tex Neuer won four of six for the New York Yankees in the last month of the 1907 season. He never pitched again in the majors.

What Did You Expectorate?

About Ed Walsh's spitter, Sam Crawford said: "I think that the ball disintegrated on the way to the plate and the catcher put it back together again. I swear, when it went past the plate it was just the spit that went by."

Hub Quartet Drops Score

In 1905, Vic Willis's final season with the Boston Braves, the Beantown club became the first in major league history with four pitchers who lost 20 or more games. In addition to Willis, who was tagged with a record 29 defeats, Chick Fraser and Kaiser Wilhelm both sustained 22 setbacks and rookie Irv Young was bested 21 times. Young that season became the only modern hurler both to win and lose 20 games in his yearling season as he also collected 20 victories. In 1906, the Braves again had four 20-game losers as they finished a 20th century major league record 66½ games out of first place. Leading the club in losses were Young and Gus Dorner with 25 apiece, while Viv Lindaman absorbed 23 setbacks, and Jeff Pfeffer 22. Bad as the quartet was, it was just about all the Braves had. The foursome accounted for all 49 of the Braves victories and for 95 of the team's 102 defeats.

Henry Schmidt snagged 22 wins as a rookie with Brooklyn in 1903 but then never pitched another game in the major leagues.

Dode Criss, a rookie hurler with the St. Louis Browns, collected 12 pinch hits in 1908 to break Howard Wakefield's old major league mark.

Boston's Vic Willis notched an NL record 45 complete games in 1902.

Brooklyn's Joe McGinnity led the NL with 28 wins in 1900, while no other pitcher won more than 20.

1900s COMPLETE GAMES

1.	Cy Young	337
2.	Vic Willis	312
3.	Christy Mathewson	281
4.	Jack Powell	277
5.	Joe McGinnity	276
6.	Eddie Plank	263
7.	George Mullin	258
8.	Bill Dinneen	254
9.	Rube Waddell	251
10.	Bill Donovan	246
	Jack Chesbro	246
12.	Jack Taylor	234
13.	Al Orth	229
14.	Addie Joss	225
15.	Harry Howell	221
16.	Chick Fraser	219
17.	Doc White	215
18.	Case Patten	206
19.	Deacon Phillippe	204
20.	Sam Leever	200

Cy Young pitched the first perfect game of the 20th century on May 5, 1904, notching a 3-0 win over the Philadelphia A's and Rube Waddell.

1900s SHUTOUTS

1. Christy Mathewson	61
2. Rube Waddell	49
3. Cy Young	45
4. Addie Joss	44
5. Vic Willis	43
6. Mordecai Brown	41
7. Doc White	38
8. Ed Walsh	36
Eddie Plank	36
10. Sam Leever	35
Jack Chesbro	35
12. Jack Powell	32
13. Bill Donovan	31
14. Ed Reulbach	28
Joe McGinnity	28
16. Jesse Tannehill	25
Orval Overall	25
Al Orth	25
George Mullin	25
20. Deacon Phillippe	24

In game five of the 1908 World Series, Cub hurler Orval Overall struck out four Detroit batters in one inning.

1906 Cub Staff Best Ever?

At the opposite end of the spectrum from the 1906 Boston Braves' four 20-game losers was the Chicago Cubs' hill staff, which laid claim to being the deepest of its time and arguably the best in history. Led by Three Finger Brown's loop-leading 26 wins and 1.04 ERA, the Cubs that season bagged a record 116 victories and posted a record 1.75 staff ERA. Brown's supporting cast numbered Jack Pfiester, Ed Reulbach, Carl Lundren, Jack Taylor, and Orval Overall. The six Bruins hurlers combined for 106 wins and just 30 defeats. All but Lundgren had an ERA of 1.88 or less, and Pfiester was the only staff member to lose as many as eight games. In 1906, the Cubs led the majors in runs with 704 while surrendering the fewest tallies, 381. Nevertheless, the Bruins lost the first inter-city World Series in history four games to two to the crosstown Chicago White Sox in the biggest sports upset to that time and were made to wait until the following autumn to garner their first 20th century world championship.

Cub pitcher Three Finger Brown was 13-9 in head-to-head matchups against Giants hurler Christy Mathewson.

In 1904, McGinnity and Mathewson won 68 games for the Giants.

In 1909, Walter Johnson lost an AL record 10 games in which his team (the Washington Senators) was shut out—five of them to Chicago.

After tallying 31 wins in the regular season, Giants hurler Christy Mathewson (above) shut out the Philadelphia Athletics in games one, three, and five of the 1905 World Series, allowing only 14 hits and leading New York to the Series crown.

Philly Gets Straight A's

In 1906, the Philadelphia Athletics collected the last key ingredient to the mound staff that would set the American League ERA record four years later when Jack Coombs joined the club. In 1910, Coombs led all hurlers in the game with 31 wins and chipped in a 1.30 ERA. As a unit, the A's registered a 1.79 ERA, shattering their own year-old loop mark of 1.92. Teaming with Coombs for the record-breaking A's were Hall of Famers Chief Bender and Eddie Plank.

1900s WINS

1.	Christy Mathewson	236
2.	Cy Young	230
3.	Joe McGinnity	218
4.	Jack Chesbro	192
5.	Vic Willis	188
6.	Eddie Plank	186
7.	Rube Waddell	183
8.	Sam Leever	166
9.	Jack Powell	160
10.	George Mullin	157
11.	Addie Joss	155
	Bill Donovan	155
13.	Doc White	154
	Deacon Phillippe	154
15.	Bill Dinneen	147
16.	Mordecai Brown	144
17.	Jesse Tannehill	138
	Al Orth	138
19.	Jack Taylor	129
20.	Chick Fraser	118

Judge Landis, said of Christy Mathewson: "Why should God wish to take a thoroughbred like Matty and leave some others down here that could well be spared?"

Easy Livin'

Roger Bresnahan remarked about Christy Mathewson: "I could have caught him sitting in a rocking chair."

ChiSox Find Cleveland 'Joss Perfect'

When the Chicago White Sox arrived at Cleveland's League Park on Friday afternoon, October 2, 1908, to begin a do-or-die series for the American League pennant, a crowd of 10,598 was on hand. No ballpark in the world, however, would have been large enough had the baseball-going public known what was in the offing. That day in Cleveland, Addie Joss dueled Ed Walsh in the greatest pitchers' battle in history considering the stakes and the outcome. Walsh allowed just one unearned run in the contest, it coming on a third-inning wild pitch, but Joss was even more brilliant. Not a single White Sox batter reached first base safely the entire game, as Cleveland prevailed 1-0 and moved into first place. Cleveland ultimately lost the pennant to Detroit by a half-game margin, but it was no fault of Joss's. Working against one of the greatest pitchers of his time in a game that potentially could mean everything, Joss authored the only perfect game in major league history under such auspicious circumstances.

Chick Fraser lost 20 or more games for three consecutive seasons with three different National League teams between 1904 and 1906.

1900s STRIKEOUTS

1.	Rube Waddell	2,251
2.	C. Mathewson	1,794
3.	Cy Young	1,565
4.	Eddie Plank	1,342
5.	Vic Willis	1,304
6.	Bill Donovan	1,293
7.	Jack Chesbro	1,237
8.	Jack Powell	1,209
9.	Tom Hughes	1,115
10.	Doc White	1,105
11.	George Mullin	1,091
12.	Joe McGinnity	994
13.	Bill Dinneen	953
14.	Chief Bender	935
15.	Harry Howell	925
16.	Ed Walsh	901
17.	Bob Ewing	884
18.	Addie Joss	871
19.	Red Ames	844
20.	Earl Moore	833

Between June 20, 1901, and August 9, 1906, Jack Taylor started 187 games in the NL and completed every one of them.

Cub Three Finger Brown in 1906 led the NL with a 1.04 ERA.

In 1906, en route to a 2-21 record, Joe Harris of the Boston Red Sox hurled the longest complete-game loss in American League history, a 24-inning setback at the hands of Philadelphia.

Two Shutouts All in Day's Work For Reulbach

The 1908 season was made for pitchers. With scoring at an all-time low and both pennant races destined to go down to the wire, conditions were ideal for monumental hill feats. Ed Walsh's 40 wins and Addie Joss's perfect game were the two most enduringly famous achievements, but Ed Reulbach's performance on September 26 of that season was only a notch behind. That day, Reulbach pitched two complete-game victories for the Chicago Cubs over Brooklyn. Many other hurlers have posted doubleheader wins, but none have matched his excellence. Reulbach not only logged two complete-game triumphs in the thick of the 1908 pennant race—he hurled two shutouts, winning the first game 5-0 and the second contest 3-0—but he allowed just eight Brooklyn safeties in the twin-bill. For the season, Reulbach posted a 24-7 record and topped the National League with a .774 winning percentage.

Three Finger Brown, asked if his curve was helped by his missing index finger, responded: "To know for sure, I'd have to throw with a normal hand, and I've never tried it."

Harry "Rube" Vickers in 1906 pitched an organized baseball record 526 innings with Seattle in the Pacific Coast League.

On September 26, 1908, Ed Reulbach of the Cubs notched two shutouts in one day.

**Ogden Nash penned this poem:
Y is for Young
The Magnificent Cy
People batted against him
But I never knew why.**

1900s INNINGS

1.	Cy Young	3,344.2
2.	Vic Willis	3,130.1
3.	Joe McGinnity	3,074.2
4.	C. Mathewson	2,967.0
5.	Jack Powell	2,876.2
6.	Rube Waddell	2,835.1
7.	Jack Chesbro	2,748.0
8.	Eddie Plank	2,666.0
9.	George Mullin	2,592.1
10.	Bill Dinneen	2,565.1
11.	Bill Donovan	2,426.0
12.	Al Orth	2,393.2
13.	Harry Howell	2,337.0
14.	Doc White	2,315.0
15.	Jack Taylor	2,221.1
16.	Addie Joss	2,219.2
17.	Chick Fraser	2,204.1
18.	D. Phillippe	2,158.1
19.	Tully Sparks	2,143.0
20.	Sam Leever	2,138.0

The 1900s

Rube Waddell of the Athletics fanned 349 batters in 1904, breaking his one-year-old record of 302 strikeouts.

When Eddie Plank and Rube Waddell won 51 games between them in 1904, they made the Philadelphia A's the only team in this century to have two southpaw 25-game winners.

Branch Rickey, who played against Rube Waddell, recalled: "When Waddell had control—and some sleep—he was unbeatable."

When he bagged 27 wins in 1907, Doc White of the White Sox set a 20th century southpaw record that stood until 1930.

In his lone game with the Red Sox, King Brady flipped a complete-game shutout in 1908.

Early Aces Render Relief

In the early 1900s, starting pitchers still were seldom relieved no matter how one-sided the game. As late as 1906, the Boston Braves notched 137 complete games even though the club claimed only 49 victories. By the end of the decade, however, a change in philosophy was occurring. In 1909, the Boston Red Sox finished third in the American League despite registering only 75 complete games. The Red Sox featured a combination starter-reliever in Frank Arellanes, who headed the majors with eight saves, but most clubs preferred to use their ace starter in a fireman role if the game was on the line. The National League save leader in 1909 hence was Cubs star Three Finger Brown, who also topped the loop that year in wins and innings pitched.

1900s WINNING PERCENTAGE

1.	Ed Reulbach	.713
2.	Sam Leever	.697
3.	Mordecai Brown	.689
4.	Christy Mathewson	.678
5.	Hooks Wiltse	.637
6.	Ed Walsh	.636
7.	Joe McGinnity	.634
8.	Jesse Tannehill	.633
9.	Deacon Phillippe	.631
10.	Addie Joss	.628
11.	Carl Lundgren	.623
12.	Cy Young	.612
13.	Clark Griffith	.612
14.	Jack Chesbro	.610
15.	Eddie Plank	.606
16.	Orval Overall	.605
17.	Frank Smith	.594
18.	Lefty Leifield	.592
19.	Bill Bernhard	.591
20.	Red Ames	.590

Crandall Forerunner to Relief Specialists

Saves by relief pitchers were not kept in the early part of the century. Team and individual save totals during the days of Three Finger Brown, Christy Mathewson, and Ed Walsh are therefore the result of recent research efforts and are still the subject of some controversy. What has been clearly established, however, is that John McGraw was probably the first manager who played with the notion of developing relief specialists. In 1908, McGraw stumbled on Doc Crandall, a rookie righthander whom he soon decided was perfectly suited to relief roles. When the Federal League formed as a rival major league, though, Crandall jumped to the St. Louis Terriers in 1914 on the promise that he would be given a crack at a starting job.

In 1901, Noodles Hahn won a 20th-century record 22 games for a last-place team—the 52-87 Reds. He was the last lefthander to have won 20 for a last-place club until Steve Carlton did it in 1972.

1900s EARNED RUN AVERAGE

1.	Mordecai Brown	1.63
2.	Ed Walsh	1.68
3.	Ed Reulbach	1.72
4.	Addie Joss	1.87
5.	Christy Mathewson	1.98
6.	Rube Waddell	2.11
7.	Cy Young	2.12
8.	Orval Overall	2.13
9.	Frank Smith	2.19
10.	Doc White	2.20
11.	Lefty Leifield	2.20
12.	Jake Weimer	2.23
13.	Hooks Wiltse	2.29
14.	Andy Coakley	2.32
15.	Sam Leever	2.33
16.	Ed Killian	2.35
17.	Bob Ewing	2.37
18.	Barney Pelty	2.39
19.	Eddie Plank	2.42
20.	Carl Lundgren	2.42

Henry Schmidt, a Californian who went 22-13 as a rookie pitcher with Brooklyn in 1903, returned his unsigned contract the following spring with this comment: "I do not like playing in the East and will not report." Schmidt never again pitched in the major leagues.

On April 28, 1901, rookie Bock Baker, making his first and only start for Cleveland, was touched for 23 hits, all of them singles.

Tigers Take Title by One-Half Game

The tightest finish in AL or NL history occurred in 1908 when the Detroit Tigers claimed the AL flag by a mere four percentage points, finishing half a game ahead of Cleveland. Going into the season's final day on October 6, Cleveland was mathematically eliminated from the race, having split a doubleheader with St. Louis the previous afternoon. The White Sox and Tigers meanwhile squared off in Detroit with the Sox just half a game back and the pennant slated to go to the winner. When Detroit beat Chicago ace Ed Walsh, it vaulted Cleveland ahead of Chicago into second place and gave the Motor City club the flag. Anger in Cleveland over the fact that the local team might have tied for the pennant if the Tigers had been forced to make up a postponed game resulted in a rule change that required all unplayed games to be rescheduled if they had a potential bearing on a pennant race.

"It was more fun to play ball then. The players were more colorful, you know, drawn from every walk of life, and the whole thing was sort of chaotic most of the time, not highly organized in every detail like it is nowadays."
—Davy Jones, on the game in the early 1900s

1900s CATCHER FIELDING AVERAGE

1. Billy Sullivan		.976
2. John Warner		.975
3. George Gibson		.974
4. Lou Criger		.974
5. Pat Moran		.974

The Tigers committed an AL record 12 errors in one game on May 1, 1901. Two years later, the White Sox tied the AL single-game record with 12 errors on May 6; in the same game, the Tigers made six errors.

1900s CATCHER GAMES

1. Billy Sullivan	923
2. Johnny Kling	849
3. Red Dooin	811
4. Bill Bergen	768
5. Lou Criger	761

In 1904, Jack Chesbro and Jack Powell between them started 97 of the 155 games played by the New York Highlanders and completed 86 of them. Chesbro set the major league record with 454⅔ innings pitched.

Cobb In Cleveland? Thought Flick-ers Out

The most significant trade during the first decade of the century was one that was not made. Cleveland consistently contended for the pennant but had yet to win one and Detroit manager Hugh Jennings was tired of having to cope with his fiery new star, Ty Cobb. Jennings offered Cobb to Cleveland for outfielder Elmer Flick, even up, but the Naps opted to keep Flick. Illness idled Flick for most of the 1908 campaign, and he was never again able to play regularly. Cobb went on to play for two more decades at a level that undoubtedly would have meant several pennants for Cleveland.

Honus Wagner (above left) and Ty Cobb (above right) were the two greatest players of the early 1900s, and they faced off in the 1909 World Series. From 1907 to 1909, each player led his respective league in batting average and RBI.

The modern infield fly rule was adopted in 1901. The rule was developed to thwart the fly-ball trap play, during which a fielder would trap pop-ups instead of catching them to throw out the lead runner of a double play.

"Baseball is in its infancy." —Brooklyn owner Charlie Ebbets in 1909

1900s FIRST BASE GAMES

1. Fred Tenney	1,318
2. Harry Davis	1,191
3. Kitty Bransfield	1,169
4. Dan McGann	1,094
5. Jake Beckley	921

Pirates Swap, Shuffle Deck

Prior to the turn of the century, player deals were relatively uncommon, but in the early 1900s a number of teams suddenly became quite active in the trade mart. At the forefront was Pittsburgh. On December 15, 1905, the Pirates swapped three players to the Boston Braves for mound ace Vic Willis. Almost exactly a year later Pittsburgh dealt three more players, including former batting king Ginger Beaumont, to the Braves for infielder Ed Abbaticchio. Both trades ultimately helped the Pirates in their bid to dethrone the Chicago Cubs as the reigning National League champion, but a swap engineered with the Philadelphia Phillies a year before the Willis trade made Pittsburgh's task considerably harder. On December 20, 1904, the Pirates sent first baseman Kitty Bransfield and two other players to the Quaker City entry for first sacker Del Howard. Howard played just one season for the Pirates before going to Boston in the Willis deal.

1900s SECOND BASE GAMES

1. Claude Ritchey	1,262
2. Jimmy Williams	1,176
3. Nap Lajoie	1,118
4. Hobe Ferris	1,019
5. Kid Gleason	935

Hugh Fullerton, sportswriter, called Johnny Evers "a bundle of nerves with the best brain in baseball."

1900s SHORTSTOP FIELDING AVERAGE

1. Terry Turner	.950
2. George Davis	.944
3. Bobby Wallace	.940
4. Bill Dahlen	.937
5. Tommy Corcoran	.936

Franklin P. Adams, a journalist for the *New York World*, penned this poem in 1908:

These are the saddest of possible words:
"Tinker to Evers to Chance."
Trio of bear cubs, and fleeter than birds,
Tinker and Evers and Chance.
Ruthlessly pricking our gonfalon bubble,
Making a Giant hit into a double—
Words that are heavy with nothing but trouble:
"Tinker to Evers to Chance."

In 1902, the Pittsburgh Pirates won the National League pennant by a record 27½ games. The Pirates compiled a 56-15 home record, the best home record ever in the NL.

1900s THIRD BASE GAMES

1. Bill Bradley   1,238
2. Harry Steinfeldt 1,158
3. Jimmy Collins   1,089
4. Lave Cross   979
5. Bill Coughlin   977

After a spring training game in 1904, New York Giants players, fomented by manager John McGraw, beat an umpire unconscious. McGraw was suspended in 1905 for 15 days and fined $150 by the NL for abusing umpires, then in 1906, he got into a savage fight with Phils rookie infielder Paul Sentell.

Gloves Preserve McBride and Wallace

The dead-ball era put runs at such a premium that most teams relied on a strong defense to keep them in the game. Accordingly, there was always a place on the major league scene for a good-field no-hit middle infielder or catcher. In 1906, Brooklyn backstopper Bill Bergen hit .159 while working 103 games but nonetheless held his job. That season, the St. Louis Cardinals released shortstop George McBride after he batted .169 in 90 contests, but McBride's glovework was so sturdy that the Washington Senators handed him their shortstop post two years later. Hall of Fame shortstop Bobby Wallace was another whose defensive skill kept him in the game long after the dead-ball era had undermined his offensive talent. Early in his career, Wallace customarily hit around .300, but after batting .324 for the St. Louis Cardinals in 1901, he jumped to the American League St. Louis Browns and played 17 more seasons while just once hitting above .280.

Alibi Ike

"You must have an alibi to show why you lost. If you haven't one, you must fake one. Your self-confidence must be maintained. Always have that alibi. But keep it to yourself. That's where it belongs."
—Christy Mathewson

Washington's George McBride led AL shortstops in fielding percentage every year from 1912 to 1915.

1900s Hurlers Truly Fifth Infielders

A typical big inning in the dead-ball era consisted of a bunt single, a stolen base, a sacrifice bunt to put the runner on third, and a wild pitch or a passed ball that enabled him to score. Owing to the frequency of bunt attempts, a pitcher in the early 1900s truly did function as a fifth infielder, and as a result the vast majority of single-season records for fielding chances handled by a moundsman were set between 1901 and 1910. In 1904, for instance, southpaw Nick Altrock of the Chicago White Sox registered a 20th century record 49 putouts by a pitcher. That season, Vic Willis logged 39 putouts to set the modern National League record. Three years later, White Sox ace Ed Walsh established all-time major league single-season marks for both assists (227) and total chances (262). In 1905, Harry Howell, good enough with a glove to play second base on days when he wasn't on the mound, set the all-time hurlers mark for the most chances handled per game when he averaged 5.24 chances each time he toed the rubber for the St. Louis Browns.

Cleveland shortstop John Gochnauer in 1903 made a 20th century record 98 errors, and he batted only .185.

Outfielder Jack McCarthy of the Chicago Cubs threw a record three runners out at the plate during a game against Pittsburgh on April 26, 1905.

1900s SHORTSTOP GAMES	
1. Bobby Wallace	1,330
2. Bill Dahlen	1,309
3. Freddy Parent	1,125
4. Joe Tinker	1,080
5. Honus Wagner	1,044

"You can learn little from victory. You can learn everything from defeat." —Christy Mathewson

The 1906 Cubs won the NL pennant and may have been the best club of all time. Manager and first baseman Frank Chance's team won 116 games, still a record, and lost only 36 for a record .763 winning percentage. The Cubs had a record 60-15 road mark. A 50-7 stretch drive included a 26-3 run in August.

1900s OUTFIELD GAMES

1.	Jimmy Sheckard	1,289
	Fielder Jones	1,289
3.	Sam Crawford	1,285
4.	Roy Thomas	1,268
5.	Ginger Beaumont	1,251
6.	Willie Keeler	1,243
7.	Fred Clarke	1,209
8.	Cy Seymour	1,189
9.	Elmer Flick	1,180
10.	Topsy Hartsel	1,177
11.	Jimmy Slagle	1,146
12.	George Browne	1,041
13.	Patsy Dougherty	1,004
14.	Charlie Hemphill	962
15.	John Titus	941

In the 1900s, only two umpires, instead of today's four, were assigned to oversee each game.

The Cardinals made a record 17 errors in a doubleheader on July 3, 1909.

Umpire O'Day Makes Tough Call on Merkle

To plate umpire Hank O'Day fell the responsibility of calling Fred Merkle out for failing to touch second base when base arbiter Bob Emslie claimed he had not seen the play in the historic 1908 game at the Polo Grounds. O'Day had been watching for the play after having been alerted to its potential significance several days earlier by Cubs second baseman Johnny Evers in a game with Pittsburgh. Belatedly, O'Day realized Evers had been correct in asserting that Warren Gill of the Pirates should be declared out for neglecting to tag second base as another Pirate scored the game-winning run. O'Day's decision in the Merkle game earned the eternal wrath of Giants manager John McGraw but made him one of the most well-known umpires of his time. A former big league pitcher, O'Day had first turned to umpiring back in the late 1880s while still an active player. Emslie, O'Day's co-worker in the Merkle game, also had pitched in the majors.

Take That

When threatened by John McGraw that McGraw would have umpire Bill Klem stripped of his job after he rendered an unpopular decision against the Giants, Klem responded: "Mr. Manager, if it's possible for you to take my job away from me, I don't want it."

Wildfire Schulte of the Chicago Cubs set a record for outfielders that stood until 1928 when he had a .994 fielding average in 1908.

Pennsylvania Launches Two Parks

In 1909, Shibe Park and Forbes Field, the first two all concrete-and-steel major league baseball stadiums, first opened their doors. Shibe was home to the Philadelphia Athletics, while Forbes housed the Pittsburgh Pirates. Forbes had triple-decker stands, elevators, electric lights, telephones, inclined ramps instead of stairs, and maids in the ladies' restrooms. It also shared with Shibe the distinction of having the first visitors' dressing room. Shibe Park continued through the 1970 season. Forbes Field also closed in 1970 after the Pirates moved to Three Rivers Stadium.

Both the Philadelphia Phillies and Athletics played at Shibe Park, named for Athletics stockholder Ben Shibe. In the new stadium's first seven seasons, five Philadelphia teams played World Series games there.

New York Giant backstop Roger Bresnahan experimented with the first "batting helmet" after being beaned in a game in 1905.

1900s MANAGER WINS	
1. Fred Clarke	938
2. John McGraw	782
3. Connie Mack	734
4. Clark Griffith	653
5. Jimmy McAleer	606
6. Ned Hanlon	540
7. Frank Chance	481
8. Jimmy Collins	455
9. Fielder Jones	426
10. Frank Selee	415

In 1903, the American league joined the National League in counting foul balls as strikes.

Winning Is Everything

"In playing or managing, the game of ball is only fun for me when I'm out in front and winning. I don't care a bag of peanuts for the rest of the game."
—John McGraw

Mike Donlin, on hearing night baseball was now played in the minors, exclaimed: "Jesus! Think of taking a ballplayer's nights away from him."

1900s TEAM WINS

	W	L
1. Pittsburgh-NL	938	538
2. Chicago-NL	879	592
3. New York-NL	823	645
4. Chicago-AL	744	575
5. Phila.-AL	734	568
6. Phila.-AL	709	752
7. Cincinnati-NL	705	769
8. Cleveland-AL	698	632
9. Boston-AL	691	634
10. Detroit-AL	683	632
11. Brooklyn-NL	649	809
12. Boston-NL	587	877
13. St.Louis-NL	580	888
14. St.Louis-AL	551	632
15. New York-AL	520	518
16. Wash.-AL	480	834
17. Baltimore-AL	118	153
18. Milwaukee-AL	48	89

Cardinals Jack and Mike O'Neill formed the NL's first brother battery in 1902.

First Modern Series— Phillippe Completes Five Games

During the 1903 season, flag-winners Pittsburgh of the NL and Boston of the AL agreed to play a best five-of-nine postseason series. Pittsburgh was 91-49 in 1903, while Boston was 91-47 that year. There were a number of late-season injuries to two of the Pirate pitchers, including Sam Leever, who had hurt his shoulder. Nevertheless, the Pirates beat Boston 7-3 in game one, as Deacon Phillippe struck out 10 and walked none on a six-hitter. After Boston evened matters behind Bill Dinneen in game two, Phillippe returned on a day's rest to win again in game three, 4-2. Phillippe started again in game four, played three days later. Though his arm was showing signs of strain (he struck out only one), he won again, beating Dinneen 5-4. The Series stood at Boston one game, Phillippe three. The tide turned in games five and six; Cy Young shut down the Pirates 11-2 and Dinneen beat Leever 6-3. Young then beat Phillippe 7-3 in game seven, and Dinneen beat Phillippe 3-0 in game eight. The Bucs won four straight to win the first modern World Series, although Phillippe hurled five complete games in eight contests.

In 1901, John McGraw tried to sign Charlie Grant, a black second baseman, by claiming that Grant was a Cherokee Indian.

Chapter 4
The 1910s

Oldster Cravath Masters 1910s

Gavvy Cravath was nearly as dominant a slugger during the 1910s as Babe Ruth would be in the following decade. Beginning in 1913, Cravath won six National League home run crowns over the next seven seasons and twice led the circuit in RBI and slugging average. Cravath's slugging peak came in 1915 when he hammered 24 home runs to spark the Phillies to their first pennant and set a post-1900 major league record. His two finest all-around seasons, though, were probably his first and last as the NL four-bagger champ. In 1913, Cravath pounded home 128 teammates to go with his 19 home runs and .341 batting average. Six years later, reduced by age to part-time status, he nonetheless topped the NL with 12 round-trippers despite accumulating only 214 at bats. Cravath's performance was made all the more extraordinary by the fact that he did not arrive in the majors to stay until he was past 32 years old.

1910s GAMES

1.	Donie Bush	1,450
2.	Eddie Collins	1,441
3.	Tris Speaker	1,438
4.	Ed Konetchy	1,430
5.	Harry Hooper	1,427
6.	Fred Merkle	1,406
7.	Clyde Milan	1,393
8.	Larry Gardner	1,367
9.	Jake Daubert	1,353
10.	Zack Wheat	1,348
11.	H. Zimmerman	1,340
12.	Ty Cobb	1,334
13.	Duffy Lewis	1,325
14.	Fred Luderus	1,319
15.	Jimmy Austin	1,315
16.	Dode Paskert	1,312
17.	Larry Doyle	1,309
18.	Buck Herzog	1,296
19.	Hal Chase	1,291
20.	Stuffy McInnis	1,260

Ed Walsh in 1910 topped the AL with a 1.26 ERA, nonetheless he lost 20 games, as the Sox hit a record-low .211 as a team. The 1910 White Sox compiled a major league record-low .261 slugging percentage.

Fear

"Every great batter works on the theory that the pitcher is more afraid of him than he is of the pitcher."
—Ty Cobb

New Ball Core Uncorks Offense

Cleveland's Shoeless Joe Jackson gathered a .408 batting average in 1911 to set a major league rookie record.

1910s RUNS

1. Ty Cobb	1,050
2. Eddie Collins	991
3. Tris Speaker	967
4. Donie Bush	958
5. Harry Hooper	868
6. Joe Jackson	765
7. Clyde Milan	758
8. Larry Doyle	745
9. Frank Baker	733
10. Jake Daubert	727
Max Carey	727
12. Dode Paskert	704
13. Burt Shotton	698
14. Ed Konetchy	679
15. Sherry Magee	670
16. Fred Merkle	662
17. Bob Bescher	660
18. H. Zimmerman	655
19. Hal Chase	654
20. George Burns	651

Following the 1910 season, the increasing imbalance between pitchers and hitters finally induced baseball moguls to take steps to pep up the game. In 1911, a cork-and-rubber center ball replaced the dead-as-duck-feathers rubber-core ball, and the results were immediately heartening. Joe Jackson of Cleveland hit a rookie-record .408 but failed to win the American League batting title. Ty Cobb batted .420, collected 248 hits and 367 total bases, and posted a .621 slugging average. All of Cobb's figures were major league records since the adoption of a 154-game schedule in 1904. But Cobb's totals, astonishing as they were, could have been more or less anticipated. The real surprise was the 21 home runs Wildfire Schulte slammed to lead the National League and set a 20th century record. Adding juice to the ball pumped up offensive stats across the board. The American League as a whole tallied 5,658 runs, a whopping 20-percent increase over its 1910 total, and the National League run total jumped 10 percent.

Shoeless Joe Jackson led all batters in the 1919 World Series with 12 hits and a .375 batting average. He was later thrown out of baseball by commissioner Kenesaw Mountain Landis for conspiring to throw the Series.

Gavvy Cravath of the Philadelphia Phillies slugged 24 homers in 1915, a 20th century major league record.

New York Giants second baseman Larry Doyle (above) quickly became one of manager John McGraw's favorites due to his quick bat, strong defense, and baserunning speed. Doyle hit .300 five times.

1910s HITS	
1. Ty Cobb	1,949
2. Tris Speaker	1,821
3. Eddie Collins	1,682
4. Clyde Milan	1,556
5. Joe Jackson	1,548
6. Jake Daubert	1,535
7. Zack Wheat	1,516
8. Frank Baker	1,502
9. H. Zimmerman	1,481
10. Ed Konetchy	1,475
11. Harry Hooper	1,468
Hal Chase	1,468
13. Stuffy McInnis	1,430
14. Fred Merkle	1,413
15. Larry Doyle	1,406
16. Duffy Lewis	1,400
17. Larry Gardner	1,381
18. Donie Bush	1,334
19. Fred Luderus	1,328
20. Max Carey	1,284

Doyle At Second Is First in Batting

In 1915, the New York Giants finished in the cellar for the only time under manager John McGraw, but the club was far from a typical last-place team. First and foremost, it posted a .454 winning percentage and finished just 21 games behind the pennant-winning Phillies; both figures are record highs for a basement dweller. Furthermore, the NL teams were so tightly packed that the Giants would have finished in the first division if they had lost just four fewer games. Finally, McGraw's 1915 Giants were the first cellar-finisher in major league history to showcase a batting titlist. New York second sacker Larry Doyle paced all senior loop hitters, albeit with a .320 average, the lowest prior to 1988 by an NL leader. Doyle was also in the top five in runs, hits, doubles, total bases, on-base percentage, and slugging percentage. Doyle became the first second sacker since 1876 to cop a senior loop batting title.

Ernie "Crazy Snake" Calbert set a new baseball record in 1917 when he slugged 43 home runs for Muskogee of the Western Association.

1910s DOUBLES

1. Tris Speaker	367
2. Ty Cobb	313
3. Duffy Lewis	277
4. Joe Jackson	265
5. Heinie Zimmerman	261
6. Sherry Magee	259
7. Fred Merkle	257
Frank Baker	257
9. Fred Luderus	248
10. Ed Konetchy	246
11. Zack Wheat	244
12. Larry Doyle	232
Hal Chase	232
14. Dode Paskert	231
15. Del Pratt	225
16. Gavvy Cravath	217
17. Bobby Veach	216
18. Harry Hooper	213
19. Shano Collins	209
20. Red Smith	208

In Two Stretches, Giants Go 43-0

Incensed by his Giants' last-place finish in 1915, John McGraw made two key lineup changes the following season, replacing aging Fred Snodgrass in center field with Federal League star Benny Kauff and installing another Federal League refugee, Bill McKechnie, at third base in place of Hans Lobert. McGraw's Giants responded by rattling off a record 17 consecutive victories on the road in May. In September, McGraw's crew embarked on a 26-game winning streak, the longest victory skein since the National League was formed in 1876. For nearly two full months of the 1916 season, then, the New York Giants had an incredible 43-0 record. During the other five months of the campaign, however, McGraw's team also won 43 games—but against 66 losses. Overall, the Giants ended with an 86-66 mark, good only for fourth place.

Shortly after Fenway Park first opened in 1912, Red Sox first baseman Hugh Bradley hit the first home run over Fenway's "Green Monster" (short but towering left field wall).

Thou Shalt Not Steal
Sportswriter Bugs Baer, commenting on slowfooted Ping Bodie, wrote: "He had larceny in his heart but his feet were honest."

On June 9, 1914, Honus Wagner became the first player in history to collect 3,000 hits.

Ex-Fed Star Kauff Romps in National League

Rival National League owners and managers winced at first when the New York Giants signed center fielder Benny Kauff prior to the 1916 season. In each of his two previous campaigns, he had led the rebel Federal League in both batting and stolen bases and became known as "The Ty Cobb of the Feds." Most observers felt that Kauff was no more than an average player whose stats were inflated by the uneven quality of play in the Federal League. Kauff's first season with the Giants seemed to confirm this gloomy assessment when he hit just .264. In 1917, however, he hiked his average to .308 and finished fourth in the National League in batting and third in runs. Although he never approached his towering achievements in the Federal League, Kauff proved to be a much more productive player than Federal League critics had predicted. He was still in his prime when he was banned from the game by Commissioner Kenesaw Mountain Landis in 1920 after he was implicated in a stolen-car ring.

In 1911, the Chalmers Award was established as the first modern Most Valuable Player honor. That year, Cub Wildfire Schulte won the NL's Chalmers Award, while Ty Cobb received the AL Chalmers.

1910s HOME RUNS

1.	Gavvy Cravath	116
2.	Fred Luderus	83
3.	Frank Baker	76
4.	Frank Schulte	75
5.	Larry Doyle	64
6.	Sherry Magee	61
7.	Heinie Zimmerman	58
8.	Fred Merkle	56
9.	Vic Saier	55
10.	Chief Wilson	52
11.	Zack Wheat	51
12.	Babe Ruth	49
	Cy Williams	49
14.	Ed Konetchy	47
	Ty Cobb	47
	Hal Chase	47
17.	Benny Kauff	46
18.	Joe Jackson	42
19.	Tilly Walker	39
	Sam Crawford	39
	Beals Becker	39

"I was like a steel spring with a growing and dangerous flaw in it. If it is wound too tight or has the slightest weak point, the spring will fly apart and then it is done for."
—Ty Cobb

1910s TRIPLES

1. Ty Cobb		161
2. Joe Jackson		148
3. Sam Crawford		135
4. Tris Speaker		133
5. Ed Konetchy		126
6. Eddie Collins		114
7. Harry Hooper		109
8. Zack Wheat		104
9. Heinie Zimmerman		102
10. Larry Doyle		101
11. Jake Daubert		99
Hal Chase		99
13. Larry Gardner		98
14. Chief Wilson		95
15. Shano Collins		94
16. Bobby Veach		92
17. Dots Miller		90
18. Sherry Magee		87
19. Del Pratt		86
20. Honus Wagner		84

In 1910, the American League had a composite .243 batting average; the following year, after the ball was juiced up, the St. Louis Browns were the only AL team to hit below .250.

Marty Kavanagh of Cleveland hit the first pinch grand slam in American League history on September 24, 1916, when his blow skipped through a hole in the fence.

The only Chalmers Award recipient to be a unanimous selection was Ty Cobb, who received all 64 first-place votes in 1911.

Edd Roush Best Ex-Fed

Benny Kauff was far and away the most coveted Federal League star when the Feds closed up shop after 1915. Several other players who first cut their major league teeth in the outlaw circuit, however, had a much greater impact on the game over the fullness of time. Easily the most famous Federal League alumnus was Edd Roush. A .298 hitter for the Newark Feds in 1915, Roush, like Kauff, was signed by the New York Giants for the 1916 season. But since both of them played center field, Roush saw little action in New York and was included as a throw-in player in a midseason trade that sent Christy Mathewson to Cincinnati to manage the Reds. It was the deal that Giants manager John McGraw would live to regret above all others. For the next decade, while Roush twice led the National League in batting and was the loop's best all-around center fielder, McGraw worked to reacquire him. Finally, in 1927 McGraw met with success, but by then Roush was on the wane.

Tris Speaker pounded out an AL single-season record 53 doubles in 1912.

Athletics third baseman Frank Baker received the nickname "Home Run" because of two clutch homers that he hit during the 1911 World Series against the Giants.

Zimmerman Sizzles At Bat, Hot Corner

In 1912, Heinie Zimmerman of the Chicago Cubs had the greatest offensive season to that point by a third baseman when he hit .372 and collected 14 home runs and 103 RBI. Since all three figures topped the National League, Zimmerman was voted the loop's most valuable player and awarded the Triple Crown. The MVP prize was entirely deserved, but the Triple Crown now seems to have been tainted. In recent years, a close scrutiny of 1912 box scores and game reports revealed that Zimmerman accumulated only 99 RBI that season and the real leader was Honus Wagner with 102. Baseball officials, preferring not to tamper with records that many feel have already been etched in stone, continue to recognize Zimmerman as a Triple Crown winner, but many current encyclopedias list Wagner as the 1912 RBI king. In any event, Zimmerman's 1912 season stands unchallenged in one very important respect. His .372 batting average made him the first third baseman in major league history to bag a hitting crown.

In 1915, Detroit's three regular outfielders—Bobby Veach, Sam Crawford, and Ty Cobb—finished 1-2-3 in the American League in RBI.

1910s RUNS BATTED IN

1.	Ty Cobb	828
2.	Frank Baker	793
3.	Heinie Zimmerman	765
4.	Sherry Magee	746
5.	Tris Speaker	718
	Duffy Lewis	718
7.	Sam Crawford	697
8.	Ed Konetchy	687
9.	Eddie Collins	682
10.	Gavvy Cravath	665
11.	Fred Merkle	662
12.	Joe Jackson	658
13.	Hal Chase	649
14.	Larry Doyle	645
15.	Stuffy McInnis	642
16.	Zack Wheat	636
	Bobby Veach	636
18.	Fred Luderus	629
19.	Larry Gardner	606
20.	Dots Miller	578

McGraw Wisens Up, Chase Zimmerman Out of Game

After his remarkable season in 1912, Heinie Zimmerman remained a potent offensive force until the end of the decade, although he never again challenged for a batting crown. It remains unclear, however, whether his hitting dropped off because pitchers got on to him or because he was not always giving his best. Zimmerman was a member of the game's unsavory element during the 1910s, a faction that included Lee Magee, Claude Hendrix, Hal Chase, and a number of other players who were strongly suspected of entering into collusion with gamblers to dump games when the price was right. In 1919, Zimmerman teamed with Chase on the New York Giants. By having substandard years, both helped cripple the club, a preseason favorite to win the National League pennant. Giants manager John McGraw then heeded rumors that certain team members were not always playing to win. Although never formally banned from the game, Zimmerman and Chase were released at the close of the 1919 season and never again given the opportunity to hold major league jobs.

Ty Cobb (above) led the AL in slugging percentage eight times (including six years consecutively) and won four RBI crowns.

Ty Cobb in 1911 had a base hit in 40 straight games, an AL record.

Gen. Douglas MacArthur commented about Ty Cobb: "This great athlete seems to have understood early in his professional career that in the competition of baseball, just as in war, defensive strategy never has produced ultimate victory, and as a consequence, he maintained an offensive posture to the end of his baseball days."

Jackson's Early Records
Would Have Been Shoo-Ins

Most record books do not recognize Joe Jackson's .408 batting average in 1911 as a record for the highest mark by a rookie, because Jackson was not considered a yearling player at the time, since he had played a handful of games in the majors prior to 1911. By today's rules, however, Jackson was still a rookie during the 1911 campaign. If the modern standard is accepted, then Jackson also set a second mark when he hit .395 in 1912, his second full big league season. No other player has ever averaged over .400 when his freshman and sophomore years are combined. Oddly, even though Jackson remained a steady .300 hitter throughout his career, his lifetime batting mark dipped every year after 1912 until his last season in 1920. That year Shoeless Joe cracked .386, hiking his overall average to .356. When he was banished from the game at the season's close, he took with him the highest career batting mark of any man to that point who was no longer an active player.

"I am honored to have John Lloyd called the Black Wagner. It is a privilege to have been compared with him."
—Honus Wagner

The record for the fewest career home runs by a first baseman in over 500 games belongs to Fritz Mollwitz, who hit just one four-bagger in 1,740 at bats during the 1910s.

When he paced the National League with 263 total bases in 1917, Rogers Hornsby of the St. Louis Cardinals became the first shortstop other than Honus Wagner to lead a major league in that department.

1910s BATTING AVERAGE

1.	Ty Cobb	.387
2.	Joe Jackson	.354
3.	Tris Speaker	.344
4.	Eddie Collins	.326
5.	Nap Lajoie	.321
6.	Edd Roush	.314
7.	Sam Crawford	.313
8.	Benny Kauff	.313
9.	Frank Baker	.310
10.	Stuffy McInnis	.309
11.	Bobby Veach	.304
12.	Jake Daubert	.302
13.	Zack Wheat	.299
14.	Honus Wagner	.296
15.	H. Zimmerman	.296
16.	Hal Chase	.295
17.	Heinie Groh	.294
18.	Clyde Milan	.293
19.	Chief Meyers	.293
20.	Sherry Magee	.292

Hollocher Leads NL in Total Bases as Rookie

In 1911, Chief Meyers of the Giants fell one hit short of being the first catcher to win a batting title.

The Philadelphia A's set a dead-ball era record in 1911 when they compiled a .296 team batting average.

1910s STOLEN BASES

1. Ty Cobb	576
2. Eddie Collins	489
3. Clyde Milan	434
4. Max Carey	392
5. Bob Bescher	363
6. Tris Speaker	336
7. Donie Bush	322
8. George Burns	293
9. Buck Herzog	286
10. Burt Shotton	285
11. Harry Hooper	269
12. Fred Merkle	260
13. Larry Doyle	236
14. Benny Kauff	231
15. Hal Chase	229
16. Dode Paskert	227
George Cutshaw	227
18. Rollie Zeider	223
19. Ray Chapman	220
20. Jimmy Austin	209

Joe Jackson was far from the only hitter during the 1910s to enjoy a great rookie season. In 1913, his first full season, second baseman Jim Viox hit .317 for the Pirates and finished third in the National League batting race. Viox soon proved to be a flash in the pan, but another National League rookie middle infield star later in the decade failed to match his superb frosh campaign for a very different reason. In 1918, Charlie Hollocher, the Cubs yearling shortstop, hit .316 and topped the senior loop in total bases. Unlike Viox, Hollocher subsequently had several other fine seasons, but mental problems kept him continually on the brink between having to quit the game and blossoming into a full-fledged star. Hollocher managed to stick it out until 1924 when his disturbances overcame him. Then just age 28, he returned to his home in Missouri, where he continued to struggle with his internal demons until he committed suicide in 1940.

Detroit catcher Oscar Stanage set a record for the fewest runs by a player in 400 or more at bats when he collected just 16 tallies in 1914.

In 1919, Brooklyn outfielder Hy Myers's 73 RBI topped the National League, which played an abbreviated 140-game schedule that year.

Wood Blazes to 30 Wins

> "Can I throw harder than Joe Wood? Listen, my friend, there's no man alive who can throw harder than Joe Wood."
> —Walter Johnson

Chicago Cub pitcher King Cole in 1910 compiled a 20-4 record, setting a National League rookie record with an .833 winning percentage.

Philadelphia's Jack Coombs in 1910 hurled an AL record 13 shutouts.

Smokey Joe Wood pitched his first game in the majors for the Boston Red Sox in 1908 when he was just 18 years old. The following year he stuck with the Sox, and at the finish of the 1911 season, although just 21 years old, he already had 47 career wins. Great as Wood's achievements at such a tender age were, they did little to prepare the baseball world for his 1912 campaign. That season Wood became the youngest 30-game winner since 1893. Wood fashioned a 34-5 mark that included 35 complete games, 10 shutouts, and an .872 winning percentage. In 1912, Wood topped the American League in every major mound category except strikeouts and, in addition, launched a loop-record 16-game winning streak. But Wood was not done. In the World Series that fall against the New York Giants, he won three more games, including the deciding 10-inning clash that is considered to have been the most exciting postseason game in the dead-ball era.

In 1914, Boston Red Sox lefthander Dutch Leonard posted a 20th-century record-low 0.96 ERA. He had seven shutouts in 25 starts.

Chief Bender of the Philadelphia Athletics in 1913 saved an American League record 13 games.

On August 1, 1918, Braves hurler Art Nehf pitched 20 scoreless innings before losing 2-0 in the 21st inning against the Pirates.

Smokey Joe Cultivates New Career as Gardener

The toast of the baseball world and a winner of 81 career games before he turned 23, Joe Wood was fated to win only 39 more games before his arm betrayed him. Unlike many other great pitchers whose careers were ended prematurely by arm and shoulder problems, though, Wood had an option. A pretty good hitter for a pitcher, he believed he could make a comeback as an outfielder. By 1918, Wood's conversion was so successful that he held down the regular left field post for Cleveland. He had a .366 batting average in 1921 in 194 at bats. At the close of the 1922 season, he retired to become a college coach after notching 92 RBI, prior to 1986 a record for a player in his final major league season who retired of his own volition. Interestingly, another converted pitcher had an equally noteworthy season in 1922. Reb Russell, a former 20-game winner with the White Sox, hit .368 and knocked home 75 runs in just 60 games as a utility outfielder with the Pittsburgh Pirates.

The 1910 Philadelphia A's pitching staff set an AL record when it compiled a 1.79 ERA. The principal members of that staff were Jack Coombs, Chief Bender, Cy Morgan, and Eddie Plank.

The 1917 Chicago White Sox are the only world championship team to be victimized twice during the season by no-hitters.

When he defeated the Red Sox in game three of the 1916 World Series, Jack Coombs became the first pitcher to win a game for both a National League and an American League club in the fall classic.

How Do You Spell Relief?
Eddie Collins described his pitching teammate Eddie Plank: "His motion was enough to give a batter nervous indigestion."

Perry Wins 20 in Abbreviated Campaign

Very few pitchers since 1900 have won 20 games while toiling for a last-place team, which makes Scott Perry's 20 victories in 1918 for the cellar-dwelling Philadelphia A's a remarkable feat. With the country involved in World War I, a "Work or Fight" order called a halt to the campaign on Labor Day. At that time the A's had played just 128 of their scheduled 154 games. Had the complete slate been played Perry was on course to make another seven or eight starts.

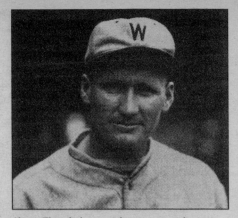

Above: *Thought by some the greatest pitcher ever, Walter Johnson was a durable and overpowering righthander who won 20 games in a season 12 times and is second all-time with 416 victories.*

Washington's Walter Johnson pitched a record fifth Opening Day shutout in 1919, winning 1-0 over the A's in 13 innings.

1910s COMPLETE GAMES

1.	Walter Johnson	327
2.	Pete Alexander	243
3.	Eddie Cicotte	193
4.	Hippo Vaughn	184
5.	Claude Hendrix	172
6.	Dick Rudolph	167
7.	Slim Sallee	163
8.	Lefty Tyler	160
	Ray Caldwell	160
10.	Hooks Dauss	156
11.	C. Mathewson	153
12.	Eddie Plank	147
13.	Rube Marquard	142
14.	Bob Groom	140
	Babe Adams	140
16.	Jack Coombs	136
17.	Jeff Pfeffer	135
18.	Bob Harmon	133
19.	Larry Cheney	132
20.	Wilbur Cooper	128

Blinded

Ping Bodie explained what it was like to bat against Walter Johnson by saying: "You can't hit what you can't see."

Nabors Goes 1-20 for A's

A letter-writer, informing the Washington club of Walter Johnson's talent as an Idaho semi-pro, reported: "He knows where he's throwing because if he didn't there would be dead bodies strewn all over the place."

Walter Johnson became the first Senator pitcher to win 20 in a season (25 in 1910).

Christy Mathewson in 1913 pitched an NL record 68 consecutive innings without giving up a walk.

After Connie Mack broke up his early 1910s Philadelphia Athletics dynasty, the team in the latter half of the 1910 decade provided a graveyard for promising young pitchers, like Scott Perry. Between 1915 and 1921 Connie Mack's club finished in the cellar a major league record seven straight seasons. Along the way, fireballer Elmer Myers set a rookie mark in 1916 when he issued 168 walks. Three years later Myers escaped the A's when he was traded to Cleveland, but other hurlers, such as Jack Nabors, were not so fortunate. After losing all five of his decisions in his 1915 debut with the A's, Nabors suffered the worst season ever by a pitcher the following season when he sustained 20 losses while garnering just one win. His ERA was 3.47, just 0.65 above the league average of 2.82. At one point, Nabors reportedly grew so frustrated with his team that he deliberately threw a wild pitch to allow the winning run to score in the ninth inning of a tie game, preferring to end the contest then and there rather than labor on to an almost certain defeat in overtime.

In 1913, Walter Johnson and Joe Boehling had a combined 53-14 record for Washington, but the Senators failed to win the American League pennant because their other hurlers were only 37-50.

Reb Russel of the White Sox tied the all-time rookie record when he bagged eight shutouts in 1913.

Larry Gardner reminiscing about Babe Ruth said: "That's the first thing I can remember about him—the sound when he'd get a hold of one. It was just different, that's all."

Eddie Plank became the first southpaw to win 300 career games in 1915.

The first pitcher to collect 300 wins in the 20th century was Christy Mathewson; Walter Johnson was the second.

Phillies righthander Pete Alexander hurled 16 shutouts in 1916, an all-time major league record.

1910s SHUTOUTS

1. Walter Johnson	74
2. Pete Alexander	70
3. Hippo Vaughn	37
4. Eddie Plank	33
5. Dutch Leonard	29
6. Lefty Tyler	28
Eddie Cicotte	28
8. Jeff Tesreau	27
Claude Hendrix	27
Babe Adams	27
11. Dick Rudolph	26
12. Reb Russell	24
Rube Marquard	24
14. Joe Wood	23
Slim Sallee	23
Jeff Pfeffer	23
Pol Perritt	23
18. Fred Toney	22
Jim Scott	22
Nap Rucker	22
Jack Coombs	22
Joe Bush	22

Ernie Shores Up Perfectly for Ruth

On June 23, 1917, the Boston Red Sox sent Babe Ruth to the mound in a game against the Washington Senators. After walking Ray Morgan, the Senators leadoff hitter, Ruth got into an argument with the home plate umpire and was heaved out of the game. His replacement in the box, Ernie Shore, watched as Morgan was thrown out trying to steal second base. Shore then retired the next two Senators to end the first inning. He proceeded to set down the side one-two-three for the next eight innings to earn a 4-0 verdict. Since, technically, he retired 27 Senators in a row, Shore was judged to have hurled a perfect game even though he was not the starting pitcher. Many analysts have since argued that Shore's effort cannot be considered perfect since he pitched neither a complete game nor one in which there were no enemy base runners. Sound as their complaints would seem, the contest is still listed in many record books as the lone perfect game in the majors between 1908 and 1922.

1910s WINS

1.	Walter Johnson	265
2.	Pete Alexander	208
3.	Eddie Cicotte	162
4.	Hippo Vaughn	156
5.	Slim Sallee	149
6.	Rube Marquard	144
7.	Eddie Plank	140
8.	Christy Mathewson	137
9.	Claude Hendrix	135
10.	Hooks Dauss	125
11.	Jack Coombs	123
12.	Babe Adams	119
13.	Dick Rudolph	117
14.	Larry Cheney	116
15.	Jeff Tesreau	115
16.	Lefty Tyler	113
17.	Bob Groom	112
18.	Red Ames	111
19.	Chief Bender	110
20.	Ray Caldwell	107

Cy Young, on why he retired in 1912, said: "I guess it was about time. I was 45 years old. I never had a trainer rub my arm the whole time I was in baseball."

Pitchers Lead BoSox to Four Crowns in Seven Seasons

After winning a World Championship in 1912, the Boston Red Sox surrendered the American League's top rung to the Philadelphia A's for the next two seasons when Joe Wood and several other young Hub pitchers stumbled. Babe Ruth's arrival in 1914, however, heralded a return to the head of the AL and the making of the game's leading dynasty during the 1910s. Between 1912 and 1918, the Red Sox snagged four pennants and on each occasion were victorious in the World Series. Ruth's pitching was an important reason for the Sox ascendancy, but the club also had several other moundsmen nearly as good. Among them were Bullet Joe Bush, Dutch Leonard, and Carl Mays. In 1918, when the Sox claimed their fourth world title during the decade, Mays led them with 21 victories. On September 11, he bested the Chicago Cubs 2-1 to win the sixth and final game of the World Series. No one could possibly have predicted then that Mays's triumph would be the last time to date that a Red Sox hurler ended a fall classic with a victory.

Jeff Tesreau's 1912 season is one of the best ever for a first-year pitcher. He won 17 games for the pennant-winning Giants, tossed a no-hitter, and won the league ERA crown with a 1.96 mark.

The majority of minor leagues shut down in 1918 due to World War I.

1910s INNINGS

1. Walter Johnson 3,434.0
2. Pete Alexander 2,752.1
3. Eddie Cicotte 2,535.0
4. Hippo Vaughn 2,317.1
5. Slim Sallee 2,244.2
6. Claude Hendrix 2,167.2
7. Rube Marquard 2,128.1
8. Bob Groom 2,075.2
9. Red Ames 2,011.1
10. Lefty Tyler 1,987.0
11. Dick Rudolph 1,923.1
12. Babe Adams 1,908.2
13. Bob Harmon 1,895.0
14. Larry Cheney 1,881.1
15. Hooks Dauss 1,869.0
16. Ray Caldwell 1,857.1
17. Eddie Plank 1,829.2
18. C. Mathewson 1,814.0
19. Rube Benton 1,723.2
20. Wilbur Cooper 1,687.0

Above: Perhaps the best of Connie Mack's Philadelphia Athletics mound stars, Charles "Chief" Bender led the American League three times in winning percentage. Relying on excellent control, Bender won 191 AL games in 12 seasons.

Cicotte Polishes Delivery, Shines as Pitcher

During the 1910s, the spitball continued to be the "out" pitch for many hurlers. None threw it more often than Bill Doak, thus explaining his nickname of "Spittin' Bill." Other pitchers became masters of trick deliveries like the shine ball or the emery ball. To Russ Ford is credited the invention of the latter. Ford would abrade a spot on a ball with an emery board he secreted in his glove, causing his pitches to dip unpredictably. The shine ball was the creation of Dave Danforth, but Eddie Cicotte became its most infamous practitioner. By rubbing powder on a portion of the dirty, spit-laden ball that was customarily in play when he was on the mound, Cicotte added both an extra bit of weight and a glint of shininess to the horsehide, making its path to the plate all the more difficult for a batter to follow. The shine ball and the emery ball were among the pitches that were banned when a rule was instituted barring the application of any foreign substance to a ball.

Hurlers Streak Wrong Way

More significant mound winning and losing streaks were manufactured during the 1910s than any other decade in the game's history. Not only did Rube Marquard establish the all-time record for most consecutive victories with 19 and Walter Johnson and Smokey Joe Wood both fashioned 16-game win skeins to set an AL record, but several monumental losing streaks also occurred during the period. In 1916, Jack Nabors of the A's dropped 19 straight games to tie the single season record. And in 1910, Boston Braves hurler Cliff Curtis embarked on a streak that carried over into the following season. Curtis dropped his last 18 verdicts in 1910 and his first five decisions in 1911, giving him 23 straight defeats, a record that stood until the Mets' Anthony Young dropped 24 during the 1992-93 seasons.

Despite debuting at age 21, Ed Cicotte never led the AL in any pitching category before he reached age 33.

1910s STRIKEOUTS

1.	Walter Johnson	2,219
2.	Pete Alexander	1,539
3.	Hippo Vaughn	1,253
4.	Rube Marquard	1,141
5.	Eddie Cicotte	1,104
6.	Bob Groom	1,028
7.	Claude Hendrix	1,020
8.	Lefty Tyler	938
9.	Larry Cheney	926
10.	Willie Mitchell	913
11.	Eddie Plank	904
12.	Joe Wood	889
13.	Jeff Tesreau	880
14.	Dutch Leonard	873
15.	Red Ames	858
16.	Ray Caldwell	850
17.	Ed Walsh	835
18.	Jim Scott	810
19.	Chief Bender	776
20.	Dick Rudolph	756

Walter Johnson of the Senators in 1912 won an AL single-season record 16 straight games. Smoky Joe Wood began his AL single-year record-tying skein of 16 straight wins even while Johnson's streak was still going.

Rube Marquard in 1912 set a single-season record by winning 19 straight games for the New York Giants.

Money

Connie Mack described Chief Bender: "If I had all the pitchers I ever handled, with one game coming up that I simply had to win, I would call on the Chief. He was my greatest money pitcher."

Leonard's Sub-1.00 ERA Dutch Treat

Earned run averages were first made an official statistic in 1912. Two years later, Dutch Leonard of the Boston Red Sox paced the American League with an ERA that was calculated at the time as being 1.01. When a decision was made during the 1980s to round off fractions of an inning pitched to the next full inning, either higher or lower, Leonard's 222⅔ innings worked became 223 and his ERA was altered to 1.00. Researchers have since determined that Leonard was charged with a run that ought to have been viewed as unearned, reducing his ERA to 0.96. The baseball powers have not yet officially accepted Leonard's 0.96 figure, but most historians now recognize his mark to be the best single-season ERA in history by a hurler since the early 1880s, when the schedule was first lengthened to over 100 games. Tim Keefe in 1880 had the best ERA with a 0.86 mark, which he accumulated in 105 innings (in 12 games).

John McGraw chose rookie Jeff Tesreau over Christy Mathewson and Rube Marquard to pitch game one of the 1912 World Series.

On May 2, 1917, neither Reds pitcher Fred Toney nor Cubs hurler Hippo Vaughn allowed a hit through nine innings. It was major league history's only double no-hit game. Cincinnati won on one hit in the 10th inning, 1-0.

New York Yankee hurler Russ Ford notched 26 wins in 1910, setting an AL rookie record. Ford introduced the "emery ball" delivery to the majors, and he beat the A's 1-0 in his debut.

Three Finger Brown of the Chicago Cubs notched 13 saves in 1911, setting a National League record.

Maybe Not
About Babe Ruth becoming an outfielder, Tris Speaker said: "Ruth made a grave mistake when he gave up pitching. Working once a week, he might have lasted a long time and become a great star."

Burleigh Grimes described Pete Alexander: "If anybody was ever a better pitcher than that guy, I wouldn't know what his name was. It was just a pleasure to watch him work, even though he was beating your brains out most of the time."

The Giants' 347 steals in 1911 set a 20th-century major league record for a team.

Gregg Beset by Tribe Luck

A good case can be made that the Cleveland American League franchise has been jinxed ever since its inception. Addie Joss, the club's first great pitcher, died of meningitis on the eve of the 1911 season. That same year Cleveland fans first thrilled to Joss's heir apparent, Vean Gregg. The rookie southpaw won 23 games in 1911 and paced the American League with a 1.81 ERA. Gregg followed his stunning debut by winning 20 games in 1912 and again reaching the charmed circle in 1913. He then fell prey to the ill luck that has been visited on so many Cleveland rookie stars over the years and in particular southpaw pitchers. After winning 63 games in his first three seasons, Gregg had only 28 more major league wins left in his arm. His final two triumphs came with Washington in 1925 when he was past age 40. Prior to that season, Gregg had labored for six years in the minors to receive his final big league chance.

1910s EARNED RUN AVERAGE	
1. Walter Johnson	1.60
2. Joe Wood	1.97
3. Ed Walsh	1.98
4. Pete Alexander	2.09
5. Carl Mays	2.15
6. Babe Ruth	2.19
7. Jeff Pfeffer	2.20
8. Dutch Leonard	2.22
9. Eddie Plank	2.25
10. Fred Toney	2.28
11. Eddie Cicotte	2.29
12. Jim Scott	2.30
13. Hippo Vaughn	2.31
14. Reb Russell	2.33
15. Stan Coveleski	2.37
16. C. Mathewson	2.39
17. Wilbur Cooper	2.40
18. Carl Weilman	2.42
19. Jeff Tesreau	2.43
20. Joe Benz	2.43

Babe Ruth made his major league debut on July 1, 1914, pitching seven innings for the Boston Red Sox to beat Cleveland.

First sacker Ed Konetchy posted the top fielding average in his league eight times between 1910 and 1919.

Czar Landis Cleans House

Many close to the game in the late 1910s felt the Black Sox Scandal was merely the tip of the iceberg and that there were a sizeable number of players who were not averse to dumping games for a cash inducement. Baseball moguls, without a clue how to clean their own house, hired United States District Judge Kenesaw Mountain Landis to be the game's first commissioner. Among his first acts as the new baseball czar, Landis barred the eight accused 1919 World Series fixers from the game even in the absence of conclusive evidence of their guilt. Few criticized Landis for this move or for any of his numerous subsequent lifetime expulsions over the next few years, for the game had entered the period of its greatest prosperity to date. Only years later did it emerge that several players barred by Landis, most notably pitcher Ray Fisher, were guilty of little more than insubordination.

The 1912 World Series was the first to go the limit and be won by a team in its final at bat in the final game.

On July 19, 1911, center fielder Walter Carlisle of the Vernon Villagers in the Pacific Coast League performed an unassisted triple play, the only one in history by an outfielder.

The majority of the minor leagues shut down in mid 1918 due to World War I.

Square Deal

"In the old days, you know, a shake of your hand was your word and your honor. In those days, if anything was honest and upright, we'd say it was 'on the square.' Nowadays, they've even turned that word around. Now it means you don't belong, you're nothing. You're a 'square.' Where do they get that stuff, anyhow?"
—Chief Meyers, Giants catcher

Tris Speaker in 1918 made a major league season record two unassisted double plays by an outfielder.

1910s CATCHER GAMES

1. Oscar Stanage	916
2. Ray Schalk	905
3. Bill Rariden	898
4. Bill Killefer	891
5. Chief Meyers	847

Eight is Too Many?

When the heavily favored Chicago White Sox lost the 1919 World Series to the Cincinnati Reds, many people smelled something foul in the air. Not until 1920 did it emerge that eight members of the Pale Hose had indeed taken money from gamblers to dump the Series. The eight were hurlers Eddie Cicotte and Lefty Williams, shortstop Swede Risberg, first sacker Chick Gandil, third baseman Buck Weaver, outfielders Joe Jackson and Happy Felsch, and utility player Fred McMullin. Their sell-out resulted in their wholesale expulsion from the game by Commissioner Landis and the team being dubbed the Black Sox.

Above, left to right: *Honus Wagner, Tommy Leach, and Fred Clarke came together with the 1900 Pittsburgh Pirates and remained a trio until 1911. Wagner was easily the game's greatest shortstop ever; Leach was a speedy jack-of-all trades; and Clarke was a .300-hitting player-manager.*

**"For over half a century I've had to live with the fact that I dropped a ball in the World Series. But nevertheless, those were wonderful years, and if I had the chance I'd gladly do it all over again, every bit of it."
—Fred Snodgrass**

Major League owners first encountered Judge Landis in 1915 when he disallowed the Federal League's antitrust lawsuit.

New York's Fritz Maisel led the 1914 AL with 74 steals, setting a record for third basemen.

1910s FIRST BASE GAMES
1. Ed Konetchy 1,421
2. Fred Merkle 1,360
3. Jake Daubert 1,347
4. Fred Luderus 1,308
5. Hal Chase 1,204

Magee Suspends RBI Title Fight

Billy Evans was not the only umpire in the early 1900s to engage in fisticuffs with a player, but he was among the last. By the time Judge Landis took office as baseball's first Commissioner in 1920, umpires were no longer fair game for irate players whenever they rendered an unpopular decision. Had Landis been made to review an incident like the one in July of 1911 involving Phillies outfielder Sherry Magee and rookie National League umpire Bill Finneran, he might well have banished Magee for life. Magee slugged Finneran after he was thrown out of the game for disputing a call. For what was described as his "brutal and unprovoked assault," Magee was suspended for the season and fined $200. However, league president Tom Lynch, himself a former umpire, lifted the suspension after Magee had been out of uniform just 36 days. Brief as the suspension was, however, considering the seriousness of Magee's offense, it probably cost him the NL RBI crown that year. He finished with 94 ribbies, just 13 behind the leader, Honus Wagner.

In 1914, Frank Crossin of the St. Louis Browns became the only catcher ever to perform two unassisted double plays in a season.

Twice in an 11-day period, Eddie Collins stole a major league single-game record six bases, on September 11 and again on September 22, 1912.

First sacker George Burns was dropped by Detroit after he hit .226 in 1917; the following year he batted .352 for Philadelphia to finish second in the American League in batting.

1910s SECOND BASE GAMES

1. Eddie Collins	1,440
2. Larry Doyle	1,280
3. Del Pratt	1,121
4. George Cutshaw	1,098
5. Otto Knabe	857

Giant Attitude

"Oh it's great to be young and a Giant."
—Larry Doyle, the Giants second baseman for more than 10 seasons

1910s THIRD BASE GAMES

1. Frank Baker   1,250
2. Jimmy Austin   1,231
3. Larry Gardner   1,184
4. Red Smith   1,050
5. Mike Mowrey   967

To produce more scoring, both leagues introduced a new "jack-rabbit" ball during the 1910 season.

John McGraw said to Connie Mack after 1911 Series: "You have one of the greatest teams I've ever seen. It must be. I have a great team too, but you beat us."

Cobb Trounces Umpire

Even though the rowdyism brought to the game by John McGraw and others of his type was curbed to a large extent in the 1910s, there were still isolated incidents. In 1912, Ty Cobb was suspended after he went into the stands in New York to fight with a fan. Cobb's pugnacious temperament got him into a multitude of fistfights with fellow players and on at least one occasion with an umpire. Billy Evans, the most fastidious and also generally the most mild-mannered arbiter of his day, nevertheless locked horns with Cobb during a contest he was officiating. The argument grew so heated that Cobb challenged Evans to meet him under the stands after the game. To Cobb's surprise and pleasure, Evans accepted. Witnesses later characterized it as quick and brutal, with Cobb as expected administering a sound thrashing to Evans. Following the custom of the times, Evans chose not to report the incident to the American League office.

On July 19, 1915, catcher Steve O'Neill of Cleveland suffered in silence as a record eight Washington Senators stole bases against him in the first inning. On July 7, 1919, Giant catcher Mike Gonzalez allowed eight stolen bases in a single inning.

After winning the AL pennant in 1918 for the third time in four seasons, the Boston Red Sox did not finish in the first division again until 1934.

Ty Cobb in 1915 stole 96 bases, the record for a 154-game season.

Babe Ruth, still a part-time pitcher, tied for the AL homer lead with 11 in 1918. In 1919, the Boston Red Sox finished sixth in Ruth's last year with the club as Ruth hit 29 of the team's 33 home runs.

Earl Mack of the A's in 1910 was the first son to play in the major leagues for his father (manager Connie Mack).

The 1911 Boston Braves posted a home record of 19-54, the worst in this century by an NL team.

Brooklyn owner Charlie Ebbets announced why he built Ebbets Field: "Brooklyn has supported a losing team better than any other city on Earth. Such a patronage deserves every convenience and comfort that can be provided at a baseball park, and that is what I hope to provide."

1910s SHORTSTOP GAMES

1. Donie Bush	1,448
2. Art Fletcher	1,177
3. George McBride	1,121
4. R. Peckinpaugh	1,010
5. Mickey Doolan	915

Early Black Stars Shine Against Major League Competition

Although the first organized black league, the Negro National League, was not founded until 1920, there were a number of loosely organized black federations during the early part of the century. In the main, though, black players and teams enjoyed most the head-to-head competition with their all-white major league peers. It was in these exhibition contests that black stars earned their greatest recognition. John Lloyd, for one, became known as "The Black Honus Wagner" after white audiences saw him perform at shortstop during the 1910s with the New York Lincoln Giants and the Chicago American Giants. In a like vein, Joe Rogan, a hard-throwing black righthander, was nicknamed "Bullet Joe" after Bullet Joe Bush, a hard-throwing white major league righthander. Other great black pitchers of the era, particularly those of Cuban heritage such as Cristobel Torriente, were seldom seen, however, by white fans.

1910s OUTFIELD GAMES

1. Tris Speaker   1,430
2. Harry Hooper   1,424
3. Clyde Milan   1,380
4. Zack Wheat   1,324
5. Ty Cobb   1,307
6. Duffy Lewis   1,306
7. Dode Paskert   1,258
8. Max Carey   1,217
9. Burt Shotton   1,198
10. Jack Graney   1,190
11. Joe Jackson   1,135
12. Frank Schulte   1,114
13. George Burns   1,053
14. Bob Bescher   1,039
15. Sherry Magee   1,034

Above: *The Philadelphia A's star "$100,000" infield of (left to right) Stuffy McInnis, Frank "Home Run" Baker, Jack Barry, and Eddie Collins. After winning three World Series between 1910 to 1914, Connie Mack traded or sold all but McInnis.*

Pirates Plunder Glove Mark

As late as 1911, it was a rare team that made fewer than 250 errors in a season. In 1911, the St. Louis Browns committed 358 bobbles, six other teams also topped 300 miscues, and the record for the fewest errors (194) and the best fielding average (.969) was held by the 1906 Chicago Cubs. But in 1912, the Pittsburgh Pirates shattered all then-existing team fielding marks when they collected just 169 errors and posted a .972 fielding average. As an illustration of just how much better the Pirates were defensively than the game's other 15 clubs, the New York Yankees made 382 errors in 1912, the Philadelphia A's led the American League in fewest miscues with 263, and only one team, the Philadelphia Phillies (.963), finished within 12 points of Pittsburgh in fielding average.

William Taft started the custom of the President of the United States throwing out the first ball at the 1910 Washington home opener.

Heywood Broun wrote in *The New York Times* in 1914 that "it may be true that a person can do only one thing at a time but this rule does not hold true for Larry Doyle on his good days."

Miscues Still Abound

The Pirates' watershed fielding performance in 1912 proved to be a quirk rather than a harbinger of a general improvement in fielding stats. For several years afterward teams regularly continued to make upwards of 300 errors a season. In 1914, the Cubs had not one but two infielders, shortstop Red Corriden and Heinie Zimmerman, who had fielding averages below .900. Two years earlier right fielder Guy Zinn of the Yankees registered an .893 fielding average, the last sub-.900 fielding average in history by a regular outfielder, and in 1916 A's third sacker Charlie Pick became the last regular until Butch Hobson in 1978 to fall below the .900 mark when he finished with an .899 fielding average. In 1916, Pick's club became the last to make over 300 errors in a season as improvements in the construction of gloves during the latter part of the decade resulted in a sharp drop in both runs and miscues as the dead-ball era wound to a close.

Cincinnati outfielder Edd Roush said about the 1919 World Series and the Black Sox: "One thing that's always overlooked in the whole mess is that we could have beaten them no matter what the circumstances!"

Helen Britton became the first woman to own a major league team when she took control of the St. Louis Cardinals in 1911.

By mutual agreement the Coveleski brothers, Stan and Harry, never pitched against each other in a major league game.

1910s MANAGER WINS

1. John McGraw	889
2. Hughie Jennings	790
3. Clark Griffith	770
4. Connie Mack	710
5. George Stallings	595
6. Miller Huggins	486
7. Fred Clarke	484
8. Wilbert Robinson	445
9. Pat Moran	419
10. Frank Chance	404

The 1912 New York Yankees featured the first brother battery, catcher Homer Thompson (who appeared in only one major league game) and his brother, hurler Tommy Thompson.

1910s TEAM WINS

	W	L
1. New York-NL	889	597
2. Boston-AL	857	624
3. Chicago-NL	826	668
4. Chicago-AL	798	692
5. Detroit-AL	790	704
6. Philadelphia-NL	762	717
7. Washington-AL	755	737
8. Cleveland-AL	742	747
9. Pittsburgh-NL	736	751
10. Cincinnati-NL	717	779
11. Phila.-AL	710	774
12. New York-AL	701	780
13. Brooklyn-NL	696	787
14. Boston-NL	666	815
15. St.Louis-NL	652	830
16. St.Louis-AL	597	892
17. Chicago-FL	173	133
18. Buffalo-FL	154	149
19. Pittsburgh-FL	150	153
20. St.Louis-FL	149	156
21. Kansas City-FL	148	156
22. Brooklyn-FL	147	159
23. Baltimore-FL	131	177
24. Indian.-FL	88	65
25. Newark-FL	80	72

A rule giving a runner three bases if a fielder stops a ball with a thrown glove or cap was adopted by organized baseball in 1914.

Above, left to right: *Ty Cobb, Joe Jackson, and Sam Crawford. Crawford hit more triples than any player in history (317); Cobb is second on the list with 297. Jackson ranks 26th with 168, though he did lead the AL three times in three-baggers.*

Comiskey Conducts Experiment Under Light

The first baseball game under artificial light was played on September 2, 1880, between two Boston department store teams barely a year after Thomas Edison invented the incandescent lamp, but the illumination was still too rudimentary for any major league team to consider adopting the idea of installing lights. By the early 1900s, however, George Cahill had devised a portable lighting system that was both good enough and economic enough to entice White Sox owner Charlie Comiskey to stage an exhibition game under artificial glare at his new stadium, Comiskey Park. Some 20,000 Chicagoans watched two local amateur teams play a full nine innings under 20 different 137,000-candlepower arc lights on a summer night in 1910.

Chapter 5
The 1920s

Williams Pulls Weight for Phillies

For the first decade of Babe Ruth's reign as the game's home run king his closest counterpart in the National League was Cy Williams, an outfielder with the Cubs and Phillies. Williams won his first NL four-bagger crown in 1916 and his fourth and last in 1927 when he was just two months shy of his 40th birthday. Three years later, he became the first player to retire with more than 250 career home runs. A sinewy lefthanded pull-hitter, Williams benefited from playing in the Baker Bowl for much of his career. The Phillies' home park had the shortest right field porch in the majors. For at least half his games every year, Williams had a target that was only 280 feet from the plate.

In 1927, Phillies outfielder Cy Williams had 30 homers but just 98 ribbies to become the first 30-homer man to notch fewer than 100 RBI.

Lee Allen explained Rogers Hornsby: "He was frank to the point of being cruel, and subtle as a belch."

1920s GAMES	
1. Sam Rice	1,496
2. Charlie Grimm	1,458
3. Rogers Hornsby	1,430
4. Harry Heilmann	1,417
5. Joe Sewell	1,404
6. Babe Ruth	1,399
7. Frankie Frisch	1,378
8. Joe Judge	1,359
9. George Kelly	1,351
10. George Sisler	1,326
11. C. Jamieson	1,310
12. Bob Meusel	1,294
13. Dave Bancroft	1,264
14. Marty McManus	1,257
15. Bucky Harris	1,251
16. Ken Williams	1,249
17. Jimmy Dykes	1,247
18. Max Carey	1,244
19. Cy Williams	1,239
Wally Gerber	1,239

Right: In 1923, 35-year-old Cy Williams of Philadelphia surprised baseball by smacking 41 home runs when the next nearest competitor in the home run race, Jack Fornier of Brooklyn, was only able to clear the fences 22 times.

Glenn Wright Man for Buc Shortstop Job

Above: *Rogers Hornsby batted over .360 for three teams during three straight years: the '27 Giants, the '28 Braves, and the '29 Cubs.*

1920s RUNS

1.	Babe Ruth	1,365
2.	Rogers Hornsby	1,195
3.	Sam Rice	1,001
4.	Frankie Frisch	992
5.	Harry Heilmann	962
6.	Lu Blue	896
7.	George Sisler	894
8.	Charlie Jamieson	868
9.	Tris Speaker	830
	Ty Cobb	830
11.	Max Carey	818
12.	Joe Sewell	813
13.	Ken Williams	805
14.	Joe Judge	765
15.	Pie Traynor	764
	Bob Meusel	764
17.	Marty McManus	741
18.	Dave Bancroft	740
19.	George Kelly	736
20.	Cy Williams	721
	Bucky Harris	721

In the 20th century, only three shortstops have claimed a National League batting title—Honus Wagner, Arky Vaughan, and Dick Groat—and all three did it while playing for the Pittsburgh Pirates. In the 1920s, the Pirates had another offensive-minded shortstop, Glenn Wright, who was never a batting leader but for many years held the record for the most home runs by a National league shortfielder. In addition, Wright was the first player in senior loop history to compile 100 or more RBI in each of his first two seasons. As a rookie in 1924, Wright registered 111 ribbies, and the following year he hiked his total to 121. Early in his career, Wright was also a fine defensive shortstop, but a shoulder injury suffered while playing handball idled him for almost the entire 1929 season and permanently impaired his throwing. Nonetheless Wright rebounded in 1930 to club 22 home runs.

Fetch

Rogers Hornsby revealed why he preferred baseball to golf: "When I hit a ball I want someone else to go chase it."

Pirate shortstop Glenn Wright missed getting 100 RBI in his third consecutive season, in 1926, when he had 77, but he rebounded in 1927 with 105 RBI.

Williams Shifts Into High Gear

When Cleveland manager Lou Boudreau devised the "Williams Shift" in 1946 to combat Ted Williams's lefty pull-hitting prowess, he was not inventing something new. Boudreau was actually resurrecting a version of the first Williams shift, which had been employed in the early 1920s to thwart Ken Williams. In 1922, the lefty-swinging outfielder nearly spearheaded the St. Louis Browns to their first pennant when he topped the American League with 39 home runs and 155 RBI. Both figures will always stand as Browns' club record now that the team has moved from St. Louis to Baltimore. Like his contemporary namesake, Cy Williams, the National League slugging star, the Browns' bomber played most of his career in the enormous shadow of Babe Ruth. Even in his peak year of 1922, Williams emerged from Ruth's umbra largely because the Babe started the season under suspension for an illegal barnstorming trip the previous fall. Despite not becoming a full-time regular until he was 30 years old, Williams amassed 1,552 hits, eight .300-plus seasons, and a .319 career batting average.

In 1922, Rogers Hornsby sets NL records with 42 homers, 152 RBI, and a .722 slugging average. His .401 batting average made him the first National League player since 1901 to top the .400 mark.

1920s RUNS

1.	Babe Ruth	1,365
2.	Rogers Hornsby	1,195
3.	Sam Rice	1,001
4.	Frankie Frisch	992
5.	Harry Heilmann	962
6.	Lu Blue	896
7.	George Sisler	894
8.	Charlie Jamieson	868
9.	Tris Speaker	830
	Ty Cobb	830
11.	Max Carey	818
12.	Joe Sewell	813
13.	Ken Williams	805
14.	Joe Judge	765
15.	Pie Traynor	764
	Bob Meusel	764
17.	Marty McManus	741
18.	Dave Bancroft	740
19.	George Kelly	736
20.	Cy Williams	721
	Bucky Harris	721

In 1925, Rogers Hornsby set an NL record with a .756 slugging average.

Bill Klem, one of the greatest umpires in history, said to a green pitcher protesting a ball call: "Young man, when you pitch a strike, Mr. Hornsby will let you know."

Philadelphia Foursome Fashions 200 Hits

In 1929, the first of three successive seasons that would constitute the greatest offensive deluge ever, the Philadelphia Phillies led the majors with a .309 batting average. The Phils were paced by left fielder Lefty O'Doul, who topped the National League in batting with a .398 figure and compiled 254 hits to set a new loop record. Three other Phils also had 200 or more hits, making the club the only one in history with four 200-hit men. Right fielder Chuck Klein collected 219 safe blows, third baseman Pinky Whitney had 207, and second sacker Fresco Thompson notched 202. Thompson was the least likely member of the quartet. O'Doul, Klein, and Whitney all had several more fine seasons after 1929, but Thompson amassed just 762 hits in his career and only 183 after 1929. Despite their wealth of offensive punch in 1929, the Phillies finished fifth in the NL, mostly because the Philadelphia pitching staff gave up a National League-high 6.13 team ERA.

Baseball Magazine **reviewed Ken Williams in 1922: "The seeming miracle has happened. Another player rose to the occasion, and did as well as Ruth had ever done in the first weeks of the season. Kenneth Williams was the stalwart figure who picked up the king's idle bludgeon in the true kingly fashion."**

Smokey Joe Wood set a record in 1921 for the most RBI by a player with under 200 at bats when he totaled 60 ribbies in 194 at bats.

In 1929, second baseman George Grantham of the Pirates collected 90 RBI and 93 walks in just 349 at bats.

1920s DOUBLES

1.	Rogers Hornsby	405
2.	Tris Speaker	397
	Harry Heilmann	397
4.	Joe Sewell	358
5.	Sam Rice	346
6.	Bob Meusel	338
7.	George Burns	317
8.	Babe Ruth	314
9.	George Kelly	304
10.	George Sisler	297
11.	Ty Cobb	293
12.	Joe Judge	290
13.	Frankie Frisch	277
14.	Jimmy Dykes	276
15.	Bibb Falk	275
16.	Marty McManus	273
17.	Charlie Jamieson	269
18.	Ken Williams	265
19.	Bing Miller	264
20.	William Jacobson	262

Bengal Bats Blast AL

In Harry Heilmann (.394) and Ty Cobb (.389), the Detroit Tigers had the American League's two top hitters in 1921. The Bengals third outfielder, Bobby Veach, hit .338. Catcher Johnny Bassler finished at .307, first sacker Lu Blue at .308, and third baseman Bob Jones at .303. Second baseman Ralph Young (.299) and shortstop Donie Bush (.281) were the only regulars who fell below .300 as the club hit .316 as a unit to set an all-time AL record. For all the offense the Tigers generated, though, they could finish no better than sixth, 11 games below .500. Indifferent pitching and fielding were the easy culprits to cite, but the St. Louis Browns, who had an even higher staff ERA—4.62 to the Tigers 4.40—and stood only a point higher in fielding average, finished in third place.

Rogers Hornsby as a player and a manager had many detractors, but as Clyde Sukeforth said of Hornsby: "When he had a bat in his hands, he had nothing but admirers."

Paul Strand of Salt Lake City in the Pacific Coast League collected an organized baseball single-season record 325 hits in 1923.

Jim Murray wrote about Babe Ruth's gargantuan appetite: "His stomach used to rumble in the outfield if the other team had a big inning."

In 1926, all three of Detroit's regular outfielders—Heinie Manush, Harry Heilmann, and Bob Fothergill—hit .367 or better.

The Pirates could finish no better than fourth in 1928 despite leading the majors in batting with a .309 average.

1920s TRIPLES

1.	Sam Rice	133
2.	Rogers Hornsby	115
3.	George Sisler	111
	Edd Roush	111
5.	Goose Goslin	110
6.	Pie Traynor	109
7.	Frankie Frisch	107
8.	Curt Walker	106
9.	Jim Bottomley	104
10.	Joe Judge	101
	Harry Heilmann	101
12.	Rabbit Maranville	99
13.	Wally Pipp	87
	Bob Meusel	87
	Charlie Grimm	87
	Lu Blue	87
17.	Ty Cobb	85
18.	Earle Combs	84
19.	Babe Ruth	82
20.	Kiki Cuyler	81

When Tigers rookie Al Wingo hit .370 in 1925, he had the lowest average in the Detroit outfield, trailing Harry Heilmann's .393 and Ty Cobb's .378.

In 1920, Tris Speaker set a major legue record with 11 consecutive base hits.

In 1922, first baseman Ray Grimes of the Cubs set an all-time record when he collected at least one RBI in 17 consecutive games played by him.

Philadelphia's Cy Williams topped the NL in 1920 with 15 homers, 39 fewer than AL leader Babe Ruth.

Harry Heilmann was waived out of the American League after he hit .344 for Detroit in 1929

1920s HOME RUNS	
1. Babe Ruth	467
2. Rogers Hornsby	250
3. Cy Williams	202
4. Ken Williams	190
5. Bob Meusel	146
Lou Gehrig	146
Jim Bottomley	146
8. Harry Heilmann	142
9. Hack Wilson	137
10. George Kelly	134
11. Jack Fournier	121
12. Al Simmons	115
13. Goose Goslin	108
14. Irish Meusel	97
15. Marty McManus	91
George Harper	91
17. Bing Miller	85
Chick Hafey	85
19. Zack Wheat	81
Travis Jackson	81
Gabby Hartnett	81

Wingo, Others Explode On and Off Scene

The 1920s were loaded with odd feats and performers. There was Dick Spalding, a soccer player who didn't turn to professional baseball until he was nearly 34 years old and hit .296 for the Philadelphia Phillies in 1927, his first pro season. A year earlier it had been Cuckoo Christensen, who hit .350 and nearly won the National League batting title as a rookie only to find himself back in the minors before the following season was out. In 1925, Dick Burrus was the story in the NL after he came out of nowhere to hit .340 and notch 200 hits, nearly half of his career total. The oddest note of all was struck by Al Wingo, likewise in 1925, when he batted .370 in his first season as a regular outfielder with the Tigers. It was also to be Wingo's only campaign of regular duty, gaining him the record for the highest batting average by a one-year regular.

Above: *In 1927, Yankees Babe Ruth (right) and Lou Gehrig finished as the top two in the major leagues in home runs, RBI, slugging average, and runs.*

In 1921, Babe Ruth set a major league RBI record with 171, breaking Sam Thompson's mark of 166 set back in 1887. The Bambino also set records that year with 59 homers, 457 total bases, and 177 runs scored.

714×4
"I have only one superstition. I make sure to touch all the bases when I hit a home run."
—Babe Ruth

Lou Gehrig's 175 RBI in 1927 set an American League record.

Reliable Lou Replaces Merkle

Legend would have it that Lou Gehrig's record consecutive games played streak began one day when Wally Pipp, the New York Yankees regular first baseman, had a headache and Larrupin' Lou replaced him. The truth, however, is that the streak began a day earlier when Gehrig pinch hit for Yankees shortstop Pee Wee Wanninger. Pipp's replacement on the afternoon he came down with a headache was not Lou but Fred Merkle, who was in turn replaced by Gehrig after the heat got to Merkle. At one point in Gehrig's streak he played left field, freeing Babe Ruth to pitch.

Bombers Blossom at First

When the 1920s opened, most of the leading sluggers and hit makers, as in the previous three decades, were outfielders. With the exception of George Sisler there remained a notable lack of first basemen who could both hit for average and produce an occasional long ball. During the 1910s, Wally Pipp of the Yankees had been the only first baseman to win an undisputed home run crown in either league, and neither of the two gateway guardians who won hitting crowns, Hal Chase and Jake Daubert, were power hitters. By the end of the 1920s, however, first base was the position with the greatest representation on the batting and slugging charts. The senior loop featured Jim Bottomley and Bill Terry while the junior circuit had Jimmie Foxx and Lou Gehrig; only a cut behind these four were Dale Alexander, who set a new rookie record in 1929 when he amassed 137 RBI; Lew Fonseca, the 1929 AL batting champ; Don Hurst (31 home runs and 125 RBI); and George Kelly, both a home run and an RBI leader.

1920s RUNS BATTED IN		1920s STOLEN BASES	
1. Babe Ruth	1,331	1. Max Carey	346
2. Rogers Hornsby	1,153	2. Frankie Frisch	310
3. Harry Heilmann	1,133	3. Sam Rice	254
4. Bob Meusel	1,005	4. George Sisler	214
5. George Kelly	923	5. Kiki Cuyler	210
6. Jim Bottomley	885	6. Eddie Collins	180
7. Ken Williams	860	7. Johnny Mostil	175
8. George Sisler	827	8. Bucky Harris	166
9. Joe Sewell	821	9. Cliff Heathcote	145
Goose Goslin	821	10. Jack Smith	144
11. Pie Traynor	804	11. Ken Williams	142
12. Charlie Grimm	748	Edd Roush	142
13. Joe Judge	739	13. Bob Meusel	130
14. Marty McManus	738	14. Pie Traynor	129
Frankie Frisch	738	15. Ty Cobb	126
16. Ty Cobb	726	Sparky Adams	126
17. Tris Speaker	724	17. Rabbit Maranville	124
Sam Rice	724	18. Ross Youngs	118
19. Bibb Falk	720	19. Joe Judge	114
20. Cy Williams	715	George Grantham	114

Lee Allen, historian, wrote about Babe Ruth: "For almost two decades he battered fences with such regularity that baseball's basic structure was eventually pounded into a different shape."

The 1929 A's second baseman Max Bishop hit .232 but led in walks with 128.

Bubbles Pops .353 for Crown

Prior to 1926 every position on the diamond, including pitcher, had furnished at least one batting titlist with a single exception. As yet there had never been a catcher who reigned as batting king. The closest to it had been King Kelly, who had won two hitting crowns in the 1880s while shuttling between catcher and several other positions. But 1926 saw the first full-blooded catcher triumph in a batting race when Cincinnati backstopper Bubbles Hargrave hit .353 to edge out rookie teammate Cuckoo Christensen's .350 mark and top the National League. Purists were anguished by the fact that Hargrave had only 326 at bats— for that matter, Christensen had just 329—but the rule at the time required only that a player participate in two-thirds of his team's games to be eligible, and Hargrave qualified since he appeared in 105 of the Reds' 157 contests. A steady .300 hitter throughout his career, Hargrave was the first backstopper to play 10 or more seasons and finish with a .300-plus career average (.310).

George Sisler, wrote Robert Smith, "spent ten years building up the fiction that he could not hit a high inside pitch. He used to strike out on such pitches occasionally, just so he could count on having pitchers throw them to him in tight spots."

The Detroit Tigers set an AL record in 1921 when they posted a .316 team batting average; remarkably the Tigers finished in sixth place that year.

In 1926, Bill Diester of Salina in the Southwestern League hit .444, the highest average this century by a batting title winner.

Tell It Like It Is

When asked by team owner Judge Fuchs whether his club could win the pennant, Braves player-manager Rogers Hornsby responded: "Not with these humpty-dumpties."

1920s BATTING AVERAGE

1. Rogers Hornsby .382
2. Harry Heilmann .364
3. Ty Cobb .357
4. Al Simmons .356
5. Babe Ruth .355
6. Tris Speaker .354
7. George Sisler .347
8. Eddie Collins .346
9. Bob Fothergill .342
10. Riggs Stephenson .340
11. Zack Wheat .339
12. Heinie Manush .338
13. Lou Gehrig .335
14. Edd Roush .332
15. Kiki Cuyler .331
16. Earle Combs .331
17. Goose Goslin .330
18. Jim Bottomley .328
19. Ross Youngs .326
20. Bill Terry .326

Al Simmons amassed 253 base hits in 1925, setting an American League record for outfielders.

Phillie flycatcher Lefty O'Doul's 254 hits in 1929 set a major league record for outfielders.

In 1925, Joe Sewell of Cleveland fanned just four times in 608 at bats, the fewest in a full season by a regular player.

Sunny Jim Bottomley of the St. Louis cards collected a major league record 12 runs batted in against brooklyn on September 16, 1924.

Young Cy Warmoth Rings Up Sewell Twice

In 1923, Cy Warmoth won just seven games for the Washington Senators and collected an unimposing total of 45 strikeouts before disappearing from the majors. But among his strikeout victims was Cleveland shortstop Joe Sewell. Moreover, Warmoth managed to whiff Sewell twice in the same game. It was the first time that Sewell had ever been rung up twice on the same afternoon, and it happened on only one other occasion in his 14-year career. On May 26, 1930, White Sox rookie Pat Caraway, nearly as obscure as Warmoth, zapped the game's greatest contact hitter twice. The second K swelled Sewell's total for the season to three. He then played the rest of the 1930 campaign without fanning again, but his real apex came in 1925 when he went down on strikes a mere four times in 608 at bats. For his career, Sewell in his 7,132 at bats collected 114 whiffs, about the number that the typical free-swinger nowadays posts in a single season.

Cudgel-Wielding Trio Dons Tools of Ignorance

Above: *George Sisler at age 16 signed a contract that would have made him a Pirate, but the National Commission ruled that the pact was nonbinding.*

Outfielder Johnny Frederick of the Brooklyn Dodgers in 1929 set an all-time rookie record with 52 doubles.

By the late 1920s, the majors were stocked for the first time with a wealth of outstanding offensive catchers. Gabby Hartnett was the first to arrive, joining the Chicago Cubs in 1922; 19 years later he would be the first catcher to leave the game with over 200 career homers and more than 1,000 RBI. In 1925, Mickey Cochrane appeared on the scene with the Philadelphia A's and hit .331 as a rookie; when he quit in 1937 he held the record for the highest career batting average (.320) and on-base percentage (.419) by a catcher. The last of the dynamic trio, Bill Dickey, joined the Yankees in 1928 and immediately served notice that he would offer a blend of Hartnett's slugging prowess and Cochrane's bat control. A .313 hitter for his career, Dickey batted .362 in 1936, the highest single-season average in history by a catcher.

In 1920, George Sisler of the St. Louis Browns set an all-time major league record with 257 base hits. He won the 1920 American League batting title with a .407 average.

Not Exactly the Science of Hitting

Babe Ruth said about hitting: "All I can tell you is I pick a good one and sock it. I get back to the dugout and they ask me what it was I hit and I tell 'em I don't know except it looked good."

Pittsburgh's Charlie Grimm set an NL record in 1923 by hitting in 23 consecutive games to begin the season.

Siblings Toxin for NL Hurlers

The 1927 season was the first that a pair of siblings finished one-two on their team in batting. Moreover, the Waner brothers, Paul and Lloyd, ranked first and third among their loop's hitting leaders. What made the feat even more remarkable was that the elder of the two Waners, Paul, was then only in his second major league season and Lloyd, his younger sib, was just a rookie. Playing side by side in the outfield for the Pittsburgh Pirates, the Waners hit a combined .367, Paul topping the National League with a .380 mark and Lloyd hitting .355 and collecting a rookie-record 223 hits and a 20th century frosh-record 133 runs. Between them the fabulous Waners also compiled a single-season brother-record 460 hits. Never again did they scale such heights, individually or collectively, but they nonetheless finished with career records for the most hits, the most runs and the highest combined batting average by a pair of brothers.

On May 11, 1923, right fielder Pete Schneider, a former major league pitcher, clouted five home runs and a double for Vernon of the Pacific Coast League in a 35-11 win over Salt Lake City.

In 1929, Pie Traynor of Pittsburgh hit .356, drove in 108 runs, and fanned just seven times in 540 at bats.

On July 3, 1925, Brooklyn's Milt Stock accumulated four hits for a record fourth day in a row.

George Sisler led the 1922 AL with a .420 batting average, a 20th-century record for first basemen.

Lloyd Waner in 1927 collected a rookie-record 223 hits; he set another record by hitting 198 singles in a season.

Tim-ber!

Zack Wheat, after playing in the 26-inning game between the Braves and the Dodgers in 1920, said: "I carried up enough lumber to the plate to build a house today."

The only NL player in this century to have more than 100 at bats per strikeout in a season is Charlie Hollocher, who fanned just five times in 592 at bats for the 1922 Chicago Cubs.

Pitcher Carl Mays in 1971, just prior to his death, said: "I think I belong in the Hall of Fame. I know I earned it. What's wrong with me?"

Wachtel Moistens Way to 317 Farm Wins

In 1920, as part of the effort to rid the game of its undesirable element, baseball moguls abolished all types of pitches in which a foreign substance was applied to the ball and most especially the unseemly spitball. A total of 17 designated spitball pitchers who were in the majors at the time the spitter was outlawed were permitted to ply their salivary trade until the finish of their careers, but any spitball pitcher then in the minor leagues was barred from throwing a spitter should he happen to reach the majors. Several of the chosen 17 spitballers were marginal hurlers whose major league careers were destined for an early end anyway, while many talented minor league hurlers who had made the spitball the fulcrum of their repertoire were forced either to drop the spitter or remain in the bush leagues. Among the leading victims was Paul Wachtel. Unable to give up the wet one, Wachtel was relegated to a 19-year career in the minors, where he won 317 games.

1920s GAMES PITCHED

1.	Eddie Rommel	423
2.	Eppa Rixey	386
3.	Waite Hoyt	379
4.	Bill Sherdel	378
5.	Burleigh Grimes	373
6.	Jack Quinn	368
7.	Elam Vangilder	364
8.	Sam Jones	363
9.	George Uhle	356
10.	Dolf Luque	353
11.	Herb Pennock	352
12.	Slim Harriss	349
13.	Jesse Haines	346
14.	Tom Zachary	336
15.	Firpo Marberry	333
	Howard Ehmke	333
17.	Urban Shocker	330
18.	Jack Scott	329
19.	Pete Alexander	325
20.	Red Faber	316

Ike Boone of the Mission Reds in the Pacific Coast League collected 553 total bases in 1929.

Grimes Hurls Final Legal Spitball

Stan Coveleski, Burleigh Grimes, and Red Faber all might have suffered the same fate as Paul Wachtel if they had not had the fortune to be established major leaguers by the time the spitball was abolished. Allowed to continue to water his deliveries, each of the trio went on to win over 200 games in the majors and make the Hall of Fame. Coveleski had the most dazzling career stats of any spitballer who remained active in the lively ball era, but Grimes posted the most victories of the 17 designated spitballers—270. Active in the majors from 1916 until 1934, he hurled for seven different teams in both leagues. A starting pitcher throughout most of his career, he was relegated to the bullpen in his last few seasons. In 1934, pitching in relief for the New York Yankees, Grimes posted the final win in major league history by a pitcher legally permitted to employ a spitball.

In 1928, his only year as a regular, Cleveland's Carl Lind topped the American League in at bats with 650 and also led all AL second basemen in assists and double plays.

1920s COMPLETE GAMES	
1. Burleigh Grimes	234
2. Pete Alexander	195
3. Eppa Rixey	185
4. George Uhle	182
5. Red Faber	181
6. Herb Pennock	179
7. Dazzy Vance	171
8. Urban Shocker	168
Dolf Luque	168
Jesse Haines	168
11. Howard Ehmke	162
12. Waite Hoyt	160
13. Wilbur Cooper	151
14. Sam Jones	150
15. Lee Meadows	146
16. Walter Johnson	143
17. Stan Coveleski	138
18. Eddie Rommel	134
19. Dutch Ruether	132
Carl Mays	132

Good Company

"The secret of success as a pitcher lies in getting a job with the Yankees."
—Waite Hoyt

Spitball artist Burleigh Grimes earned his nickname "Ol' Stubblebeard" because he didn't shave on the days he pitched, citing that the slippery elm he chewed to increase saliva irritated his skin.

ChiSox Quartet Win 20, ChiSox Lose Trio

All summer long in 1920, the Chicago White Sox played under a dark cloud as several key members of the club were suspected of having thrown the 1919 World Series. The Sox nevertheless held tough in a heated pennant race. In 1920, the Pale Hose became the first team in history to feature four 20-game winners: Red Faber, Lefty Williams, Dickie Kerr, and Eddie Cicotte. Among them, the four figured in all but 21 of the club's 154 decisions. When the scandal broke late in the campaign and implicated Cicotte and Williams, both were promptly suspended by Sox owner Charlie Comiskey and never pitched another inning. By the commencement of the 1922 season only Faber remained of the foursome that had made the Sox the envy of every club in the game just two short years before.

In 1924, Sloppy Thurston won 20 games for the last-place Chicago White Sox and topped the American League with 28 complete games.

Former major league pitcher Danny Boone, brother of minor-league star Ike Boone, won the Piedmont League Triple Crown in 1928 when he hit .419 with 38 home runs and 131 RBI.

Cardinals third baseman Les Bell, after the seventh game of the 1926 World Series in which Pete Alexander fanned Tony Lazzeri in relief to end a Yankees threat: "Doggone, there wasn't another man in the world I would rather have seen out there at that moment than Grover Cleveland Alexander."

Notching 31 wins, hurler Jim Bagby of the Cleveland Indians was the last AL righty until 1968 to win 30 games in a season.

In 1921, Red Faber had an AL-leading 2.47 ERA; it was the only ERA figure below 3.00 in that circuit.

Chapman's Death Results in Rule Changes

On August 16, 1920, the Cleveland Indians were in first place. Facing Cleveland on that day was Yankees ace Carl Mays. An ethereal fog that hung over the Polo Grounds had been complicated by a drizzle by the time shortstop Ray Chapman led off the fifth inning for Cleveland. Mays's best pitch was delivered with an underhand sweep. Down went his body and out shot his arm from the blur of white shirts and dark suits in the open bleachers in the deep background behind him. The pitch struck Chapman in the temple and killed him—from all indications he never saw it. As a consequence of the only on-the-field fatality, dirty or scuffed balls thereafter were discarded immediately from play and patrons were no longer allowed to sit in the center field bleachers. Mays was quickly exonerated from any wrong doing but the following season fell under suspicion of throwing the 1921 World Series. This, even more than the Chapman incident, would haunt him the rest of his days.

1920s SHUTOUTS

1.	Walter Johnson	24
2.	Dazzy Vance	22
	Urban Shocker	22
4.	Herb Pennock	21
	Dolf Luque	21
	Sam Jones	21
	Jesse Haines	21
	Stan Coveleski	21
9.	Eppa Rixey	20
	Burleigh Grimes	20
	Pete Alexander	20
12.	Jack Quinn	19
13.	Eddie Rommel	17
	Waite Hoyt	17
	Red Faber	17
16.	George Uhle	16
	Pete Donohue	16
	Wilbur Cooper	16
19.	Tom Zachary	15
	Bob Shawkey	15
	Lee Meadows	15
	Hal Carlson	15
	Jesse Barnes	15

Frosh lefty Emil Yde paced the 1924 NL with an .842 win percentage.

Yankee hurler Carl Mays liked pitching against Philadelphia; in August of 1923, he beat the A's for a record 23rd consecutive time.

Trouble In Mind

"The pressure never lets up. Doesn't matter what you did yesterday. That's history. It's tomorrow that counts. So you worry all the time. It never ends. Lord, baseball is a worrying thing."
—Stan Coveleski

Johnny Frederick remarked about Dazzy Vance: "He could throw a cream puff through a battleship."

Dazzy Vance led the NL in strikeouts from 1922 to 1928. His high point was in 1924, when he notched 262 whiffs.

On September 13, 1925, Brooklyn fireballer Dazzy Vance (above) pitched a rare 1920s no-hitter, as he beat Philadelphia 10-1 despite three Dodger errors.

Bagby's Improvement Gives Tribe Flag

Despite the loss of Ray Chapman, Cleveland held on to hoist its first pennant in 1920, thanks in no small part to three pitchers, Jim Bagby, Stan Coveleski, and Ray Caldwell. Caldwell, a reformed alcoholic who had nearly been killed by a lightning bolt while on the mound a few years earlier, won an even 20 games and Coveleski contributed 24 victories. But Bagby was the icing on the cake. A 17-game winner the previous year and scarcely expected to surpass that figure now that he was approaching his 31st birthday, Bagby instead became the last 30-game winner in the American League prior to 1961. The Indians not only won the pennant but added the 1921 World Series trophy to their spoils.

1920s WINS

1.	Burleigh Grimes	190
2.	Eppa Rixey	166
3.	Pete Alexander	165
4.	Herb Pennock	162
5.	Waite Hoyt	161
6.	Urban Shocker	156
7.	Eddie Rommel	154
8.	Jesse Haines	153
9.	George Uhle	152
10.	Red Faber	149
11.	Dazzy Vance	147
12.	Bill Sherdel	139
13.	Dolf Luque	138
14.	Sam Jones	137
15.	Howard Ehmke	136
16.	Stan Coveleski	133
17.	Jack Quinn	131
18.	Tom Zachary	128
	Lee Meadows	128
20.	Carl Mays	126
	Pete Donohue	126

1920s INNINGS

1. B. Grimes — 2,797.2
2. Eppa Rixey — 2,678.1
3. Dolf Luque — 2,479.2
4. Pete Alexander — 2,415.1
5. Red Faber — 2,364.0
6. Waite Hoyt — 2,346.0
7. Jesse Haines — 2,328.1
8. Herb Pennock — 2,313.0
9. George Uhle — 2,309.2
10. H. Ehmke — 2,265.0
11. Eddie Rommel — 2,242.2
12. Sam Jones — 2,230.0
13. U. Shocker — 2,148.2
14. Bill Sherdel — 2,061.1
15. Dazzy Vance — 2,054.0
16. Jack Quinn — 2,042.0
17. Tom Zachary — 2,018.1
18. Pete Donohue — 1,962.0
19. Lee Meadows — 1,946.1
20. Jimmy Ring — 1,941.0

In 1925, Philadelphia A's rookie Lefty Grove led the AL in strikeouts with 116.

Ferrell Rebounds, Tribe Holds Bag

Eighteen years after Vean Gregg burst onto the scene, the Cleveland Indians found themselves blessed with another rookie phenom when Wes Ferrell won 21 games in 1929. Like Gregg, Ferrell proceeded to reach the 20-game circle in each of his first three seasons, then went Gregg one better when he bagged 20 or more for the fourth straight time in 1932. The following year, however, Ferrell seemed to go the way of Gregg and so many other Cleveland rookie stars when he was plagued by arm trouble. Certain he was through, the Tribe dealt him cheap to the Boston Red Sox, only to see him rebound to lead the American League in wins in 1935 and in complete games for three straight years in the mid-1930s. With outfielder Earl Averill, another rookie whiz who joined the club the same year as Ferrell, Cleveland was wiser. The Indians retained Averill until 1939 and saw him set many team career batting marks.

Larry Benton, the National League leader in winning percentage in 1927 and 1928, is the only two-time winning percentage champ to finish with a career winning percentage below .500 (.498).

Excuse Me
Miller Huggins revealed what a player needs when he's in a slump: "A string of alibis."

On April 28, 1921, Cleveland pitcher George Uhle collected six RBI in a game.

Fibber Kremer Wins 143 After 30

Wes Ferrell was not even 20 years old when he played in his first major league game, but many pitchers in Ferrell's era who were equally talented found the path to stardom much more arduous. Hall of Famer Dazzy Vance did not reach the majors to stay until he was past 30. Wilcy Moore had already turned 30 when he led the AL in saves and ERA as a rookie in 1927. In the World Series that year, Moore and the Yankees were opposed by a pitcher for the Pirates who may have faced the hardest climb of all to the majors. Remy Kremer toiled in the minors for 10 seasons before Pittsburgh gave him his first big-league test in 1924. Although really 31, Kremer pretended to be 28. Not until his career was over did he reveal that he had been over 40 when he finally retired in 1933 with 143 wins, all of them achieved after his 31st birthday.

"I think the reason I pitched so long is that I never wasted my arm throwing over to first to keep runners close to the base. There was a time there, for five years, I never once threw to first base." Sam Jones, who spanned the dead-ball era and into the 1930s

In 1921, Eppa Rixey of the Reds gave up only one home run in 301 innings, a National League record since the end of the dead-ball era.

Walter Johnson had 110 shutouts in his career, a total that still is a major league record.

George Sisler in 1922 had an AL record 41-game hitting streak.

Walter Johnson batted .433 in 1925, a single-season record for pitchers with 75-plus at bats.

1920s STRIKEOUTS

1.	Dazzy Vance	1,464
2.	Burleigh Grimes	1,018
3.	Dolf Luque	904
4.	Walter Johnson	895
5.	Lefty Grove	837
6.	Howard Ehmke	824
7.	George Uhle	808
8.	Red Faber	804
9.	Bob Shawkey	788
10.	Urban Shocker	753
11.	Waite Hoyt	748
12.	Jesse Haines	742
13.	Herb Pennock	731
14.	Sam Jones	718
15.	Jimmy Ring	715
16.	Eppa Rixey	686
17.	Bill Sherdel	657
18.	Pete Alexander	653
19.	Slim Harriss	644
20.	Joe Bush	631

Washington's Firpo Marberry Makes Living Out of the Bullpen

Wilcy Moore in 1927 became the first reliever to win a league ERA crown. That year he also led the American League in saves, but the following season he returned the bullpen mantle to the hurler who was the game's reigning relief king throughout the 1920s, Firpo Marberry of the Washington Senators. Marberry was both the first moundsman to compile 100 career saves and the first to make a living exclusively as a bullpen artist. In 1925, he was the first pitcher to lead his league in mound appearances without making a single start. Subsequently the Senators learned that he could also take his turn as a starter without impairing his relief work and began using him in both roles. Marberry continued to do double duty until the end of his career in 1936. He led the loop in appearances in six seasons. He was the only pitcher to retire prior to the expansion era with over 100 saves and 2,000 innings pitched.

Cubs manager Joe McCarthy described Pete Alexander: "I like Alec. Nice fellow. But Alec was Alec. Did he live by the rules? Sure. But they were always Alec's rules."

After the 1927 season, Walter Johnson retired with a major league record 3,506 strikeouts.

Firpo Marberry in 1926 pitched in 64 games, setting a 20th-century major league record.

In 1926, Firpo Marberry compiled 22 saves for Washington, setting a major league record.

On April 30, 1922, White Sox hurler Charlie Robertson threw a perfect game against Detroit; it was the last perfect game that the major leagues would see until 1956.

Herb Pennock topped the AL with 277 innings pitched in 1925, the first time a loop leader worked fewer than 300 innings.

Ehmke One Dribble Away From Back-to-Back No-Hitters

No-hitters were nearly as rare during the hitting-happy 1920s as perfect games are now. The National League had only four no-hitters the entire decade and the American League had none at all between August 21, 1926, and April 29, 1931. When Howard Ehmke tossed a no-hitter against the Philadelphia A's on September 7, 1923, it was therefore a significant event, made all the more impressive by the fact that he was toiling for the last-place Boston Red Sox. Four days later, Ehmke narrowly missed becoming the first hurler in history to throw two successive no-hitters when a ground ball that was misplayed by his third baseman was deemed a hit by official scorer Fred Lieb. Even though the muffed dribbler turned out to be the only hit that day off Ehmke, Lieb refused after the game to buckle to an adamant attempt to get him to reverse his decision.

1920s EARNED RUN AVERAGE	
1. Pete Alexander	3.04
2. Lefty Grove	3.09
3. Dolf Luque	3.09
4. Dazzy Vance	3.10
5. Stan Coveleski	3.20
6. Eppa Rixey	3.24
7. Tommy Thomas	3.24
8. Walter Johnson	3.33
9. Urban Shocker	3.34
10. Red Faber	3.34
11. Wilbur Cooper	3.36
12. Bill Doak	3.38
13. Herb Pennock	3.44
14. Carl Mays	3.44
15. Firpo Marberry	3.44
16. Bob Shawkey	3.45
17. Ray Kremer	3.46
18. Eddie Rommel	3.47
19. Jack Quinn	3.50
20. Waite Hoyt	3.51

"When I couldn't get anybody to catch me, I'd throw against a stone wall or barn door. It wasn't always fun, but I kept plugging away because it meant so much to me."
—Herb Pennock, on how he acquired his marvelous control

In game three of the 1927 World Series, Yankee ace Herb Pennock retired the first 22 batters he faced, on his way to a three-hitter and 8-1 victory, giving the Bronx Bombers a 2-1 Series lead.

> "Wives of
> ballplayers,
> when they teach
> their children
> their prayers,
> should instruct
> them to say:
> 'God bless
> mommy, God
> bless daddy,
> God bless Babe
> Ruth.'"
> —Waite Hoyt

In 1924, the NL
joined the AL in
giving an MVP
award; the first
NL winner was
Brooklyn's
Dazzy Vance.

1920s PITCHER FIELDING AVERAGE

1.	Walter Johnson	.988
2.	Jakie May	.987
3.	Pete Alexander	.986
4.	Urban Shocker	.985
5.	Hooks Dauss	.985

Robertson Routs Tigers

Charlie Robertson had been in the major leagues for only a few weeks when he took the mound on April 30, 1922, for the Chicago White Sox at Detroit's Navin Field. Facing the team that a year earlier had hit .316 to set an American League record, the rookie righthander was expected by Tigers fans to be easy meat. Instead, to their utter dismay, he set the home nine down in order inning after inning. With two out in the bottom of the ninth and Detroit still looking for its first baserunner, Tigers skipper Ty Cobb sent Johnny Bassler up to pinch hit. Among the best-hitting catchers in the game and one of the first to retire with a .300-plus career batting average, Bassler presented a formidable challenge. When Robertson made Bassler his 27th straight victim that afternoon, he tailored the only undisputed perfect game in the majors between 1908 and 1956. It was to be Robertson's lone bright moment in an eight-year career that ended with just 49 wins and a .380 winning percentage.

On May 1, 1920, Joe Oeschger of the Boston Braves and Leon Cadore of the Brooklyn Robins pitched the entire way in a 26-inning 1-1 tie.

Yankee pitcher
Waite Hoyt won
two complete
games in the
1928 World
Series

On August 28, 1926, Dutch Levsen of the Cleveland Indians was the last pitcher to win two complete games in one day.

Cobb, Speaker Accused of Throwing Game

In 1926, it surfaced that former big league pitcher Dutch Leonard had incriminating letters from Smokey Joe Wood regarding bets that Leonard, Wood, Tris Speaker, and Ty Cobb had made on a 1919 game between the Tigers and the Indians. In a quandary, Commissioner Kenesaw Mountain Landis at first induced both Cobb and Speaker to retire quietly. Landis recanted when Cobb and Speaker reconsidered and demanded a hearing with Leonard. When Leonard refused, Landis decided to let the issue die.

Will Rogers said of Judge Kenesaw Mountain Landis's (above) appointment as commissioner: "Somebody said, 'Get that old boy who sits behind first base all the time. He's out there every day anyhow.' So they offered him a season's pass and he jumped at it."

Dramatics

Heywood Broun said of Judge Kenesaw Mountain Landis: "His career typifies the heights to which dramatic talent may carry a man in America if only he has the foresight not to go on the stage."

New York Giant Heinie Groh in 1924 set a record with a .983 fielding average for third basemen.

1920s CATCHER GAMES	
1. Muddy Ruel	1,115
2. Bob O'Farrell	937
3. Cy Perkins	917
4. Wally Schang	895
5. Ray Schalk	822

O'Connell Last to Go

On the closing weekend of the 1924 season, the Giants were facing a stern challenge from the Brooklyn Dodgers in New York's quest for a fourth straight pennant. Giants utility outfielder Jimmy O'Connell approached Phillies shortstop Heinie Sand before a game and told him there was $500 in it for him if he took it easy that day. Sand reported the bribe attempt and both O'Connell and Giants coach Cozy Dolan, who had allegedly given O'Connell his instructions, were called on the carpet by Commissioner Kenesaw Mountain Landis. Despite testimony from O'Connell that several other Giants were involved in the incident, including stars like Frankie Frisch and George Kelly, he and Dolan were the only two made to suffer the consequences. O'Connell's banishment marked the last time a player has been barred for life from the game for baseball-related activities. After leaving the Giants, he played for years in outlaw circuits in the Southwest along with Hal Chase and several members of the 1919 Black Sox.

The 1927 Philadelphia A's had a record seven future Hall of Famers on their active roster in 1927: Ty Cobb, Al Simmons, Mickey Cochrane, Eddie Collins, Zack Wheat, Jimmie Foxx, and Lefty Grove.

Stuffy McInnis of Boston had a .999 fielding average in 1921, a record for first basemen.

1920s FIRST BASE GAMES
1. Charlie Grimm	1,455
2. Joe Judge	1,339
3. George Sisler	1,309
4. Lu Blue	1,199
5. George Kelly	1,159

Playing the outfield in 1928 for the A's with 40-year-old Tris Speaker and 41-year-old Ty Cobb flanking him, Al Simmons said: "If this keeps up, by the end of the season I'll be an old man myself."

Doc Johnston of Cleveland opposed his brother, Jimmy, a hurler for Brooklyn, in the 1920 World Series.

Many accused White Sox owner Charlie Comiskey of being cheap. Before the 1923 season, however, Comiskey bought third baseman Willie Kamm from San Francisco of the Pacific Coast League for $125,000.

1920s SECOND BASE GAMES

1. Rogers Hornsby	1,405
2. Bucky Harris	1,242
3. Eddie Collins	1,010
4. Frankie Frisch	1,006
5. Aaron Ward	805

In 1924, Freddy Lindstrom of the Giants, at age 18, was the youngest player in a World Series.

About the 1929 World Series, Heywood Broun wrote: "When danger beckoned thickest it was always [Lefty] Grove who stood towering on the mound, whipping over strikes against the luckless Chicago batters."

On August 2, 1925, Joe Hauser of the A's set an AL record with 14 total bases in a single game.

Giants outfielder Mel Ott was the youngest player ever to hit 40 homers in a season when, at the age of 20, he smacked 42 in 1929.

Baltimore, Fort Worth in Seventh Heaven

In 1924, even as the New York Giants were about to become the first team in major league history to win four consecutive pennants, the Baltimore Orioles were wrapping up their sixth consecutive International League pennant and the Fort Worth Panthers were claiming their sixth straight Texas League flag. The Giants fell to second place in 1925, but the twin minor league dynasties continued for yet one more season, giving both clubs seven flags in a row. To the Orioles and the Panthers thus belongs the dual honor of the longest pennant skein in professional baseball history. The Orioles were owned and managed by Jack Dunn, a former major league pitcher, while Jake Atz, an erstwhile second baseman with the White Sox, piloted the Panthers. Both clubs fell from their lofty perch in 1926 when age and the forced sale of several of their star players to major league teams caught up to them.

Harry Hooper grumbled about Red Sox owner Harry Frazee: "He sold the whole team down the river to keep his dirty nose above water. What a way to run a ballclub!"

The 1922 New York Giants were the first team to win a pennant without a 20-game winner on their pitching staff.

1920s THIRD BASE GAMES

1. Pie Traynor	1,135
2. Joe Dugan	1,041
3. Willie Kamm	1,035
4. Ossie Bluege	828
5. Milt Stock	750

Farm Star Arlett Buzzes Bigs

Among the stars of the great Baltimore Orioles dynasty were Lefty Grove and George Earnshaw, two pitchers who graduated to fine careers in the majors after they were purchased by the Philadelphia Athletics. For many other minor league stars of their time, graduation to the majors either occurred too late in their careers or in some instances never occurred at all. Frozen for years in the Pacific Coast League when their teams refused to sell their contracts to major league clubs were such great hitters as Lefty O'Doul, Smead Jolley, Ike Boone, and Buzz Arlett. All but Arlett eventually reached the majors before their skills had begun to erode. By the time Arlett joined the Philadelphia Phillies in 1931 he was already 32 years old and on the downside of his career. Nevertheless he amply proved that he could play in exclusive company. In his lone season up top, Arlett hit .313 and ranked fifth in the National League in slugging average and tied for fourth in home runs.

Red Sox owner Harry Frazee was a theatrical producer who often sold his players to raise cash for his shows. In January of 1920, he sold Babe Ruth to the Yankees for $125,000 and a $300,000 loan.

In 1922, Pittsburgh's Max Carey set a stolen base percentage record of .962 when he swiped 51 bases and was caught stealing only two times.

In 1921, the Giants beat the Yanks in the last best-of-nine World Series.

Hornsby-Frisch Swap Biggest Yet

After the St. Louis Cardinals bagged their first pennant in 1926, team owner Sam Breadon judged that player-manager Rogers Hornsby's ego and salary demands would soon be more than he cared to bear. New York Giants manager John McGraw meanwhile began to fear that his star second baseman Frankie Frisch would soon begin having managerial aspirations of his own. Between them Breadon and McGraw thus struck the greatest trade in history to that point, a swap of the game's top two second basemen at the time. Since Hornsby was undeniably the better of the two, the Giants agreed to throw in pitcher Jimmy Ring. When Ring quickly demonstrated he was about washed up—he never won a game for the Cardinals—New York at first seemed to have gotten much the better of the deal as Hornsby belted .361 in 1927 to set a new modern Giants club record. McGraw, however, found Hornsby's ego and personality no more tolerable than Breadon had and sent him to the Boston Braves prior to the 1928 season. Frisch in contrast remained with the Cardinals until the end of his playing career and achieved his managerial ambitions in 1933 when he was named the club's player-pilot. The next year, Frishch's club won the World Series.

The Chicago White Sox were just a game and one-half out of first place in 1920 when news of the 1919 World Series fix broke on September 28 and eight team members were promptly suspended.

1920s SHORTSTOP GAMES

1. Dave Bancroft	1,237
2. Joe Sewell	1,216
3. Wally Gerber	1,201
4. Chick Galloway	976
5. Roger Peckinpaugh	972

George Burns stole home for the 27th time in 1925, setting a National League lifetime record.

No Secrets Here

Dave Bancroft, after being traded from the Phils to the Giants, refused an offer by his new teammates to explain the Giants signs to him, saying, "Unless they've changed, I already know them."

Chewing gum magnate William Wrigley bought the Chicago Cubs in 1921 and soon thereafter changed the name of the team's home park to Wrigley Field.

In 1929, Judge Guchs of the Boston Braves became the last club owner to manage his team for an entire season.

The Boston Red Sox in 1926 lost a club record 107 games.

The Indians and Yankees in 1929 were the first teams to put numbers on their uniforms and keep them on.

Dry

"There is much less drinking now than there was before 1927, because I quit drinking on May 24, 1927."
—Rabbit Maranville

Hub Heroes Stock Bronx Dynasty

During the 1920s, the St. Louis Cardinals became the first major league organization to develop a farm system. Yankees owner Jake Ruppert's fellow American League moguls could be forgiven, however, for feeling that he too had a farm club—the Boston Red Sox. Beginning with the sale of Babe Ruth to the Yankees after the 1919 season, the Red Sox furnished the Yankees with many key members of the cast that made them the game's most formidable team during the 1920s. Among the many stars the Yankees acquired from Boston were Ruth, Everett Scott, Joe Dugan, Carl Mays, Joe Bush, Herb Pennock, Sam Jones, Waite Hoyt, and Red Ruffing.

1920s OUTFIELD GAMES

1.	Sam Rice	1,486
2.	Babe Ruth	1,388
3.	Charlie Jamieson	1,279
4.	Harry Heilmann	1,217
5.	Max Carey	1,204
6.	Bob Meusel	1,192
7.	Curt Walker	1,190
8.	Ken Williams	1,163
9.	Bibb Falk	1,147
10.	Cy Williams	1,122
	Goose Goslin	1,122
12.	Bing Miller	1,108
13.	Edd Roush	1,107
14.	W. Jacobson	1,102
15.	Tris Speaker	1,091

The '27 Yankees beat the Browns 21 times to set the AL season record.

On July 5, 1929, the New York Giants became the first team to employ a public address system in their home park, the Polo Grounds.

In 1924, Goose Goslin (above) posted a .344 batting average, 199 hits, scored 100 runs, and became the first Washington Senator player to lead the AL in RBI, with 129.

1920s MANAGER WINS

1.	Miller Huggins	927
2.	John McGraw	836
3.	Connie Mack	770
4.	Wilbert Robinson	765
5.	Tris Speaker	577
6.	Bill McKechnie	538
7.	Bucky Harris	499
8.	Ty Cobb	479
9.	Jack Hendricks	469
10.	Branch Rickey	404

Us Versus Them

"I never saw a game without taking sides and never want to see one. That is the soul of the game."
—Warren G. Harding

Steady Scott Secures Shortstop with Glove

Lou Gehrig's record of 2,130 consecutive games played is full of ironical twists. Gehrig began the streak when he pinch hit for Pee Wee Wanninger, who in turn had replaced Everett Scott, the consecutive games record holder prior to Gehrig. Before losing his post to Wanninger, Scott had played 1,307 straight games. Even if he had not been so durable, though, Scott would have had a meritorious career. In his 11 seasons as a regular, he played on five American League pennant winners, three in Boston and two in New York, and led all AL shortstops in fielding eight years in a row between 1916 and 1923. When he posted a .976 fielding average in 1918 and then tied his own mark the following year, he set a new fielding average standard for shortstops that would endure until 1942.

The Reading team of the International League in 1926 posted a .194 win percentage, going 31-129.

1920s TEAM WINS

	W	L
1. New York-AL	933	602
2. New York-NL	890	639
3. Pitt.-NL	877	656
4. St.Louis-NL	822	712
5. Chicago-NL	807	728
6. Cincinnati-NL	798	735
7. Wash.-AL	792	735
8. Cleveland-AL	786	749
9. Phila.-AL	770	754
10. Brooklyn-NL	765	768
11. St.Louis-AL	762	769
12. Detroit-AL	760	778
13. Chicago-AL	731	804
14. Boston-NL	603	928
15. Boston-AL	595	938
16. Phila.-NL	566	962

"Funny thing, I played in the big leagues for 13 years—1914 through 1926— and the only thing anybody seems to remember is that once I made an unassisted triple play in a World Series.
—Bill Wambsganss

Taylor Douthit Ranges Into Record Books

Many record-breaking performances seem to come from nowhere. Nothing in the careers of Earl Webb or Chief Wilson could possibly have prepared students of the game for their setting records for doubles and triples, respectively. Taylor Douthit's 1928 season is a similar aberration. Playing center field for the St. Louis Cardinals that year, Douthit made 547 putouts, nine more than any other outfielder in history. He also scored 111 runs with a .295 average that year. In 1930, Douthit again topped NL gardeners in putouts but with just 425, a total much more within reason. His only other flirtation with recognition for his glove work came in 1927, the year before his record feat, when he paced all NL outfielders in errors.

On August 5, 1921, Harold Arlen of radio station KDKA in Pittsburgh announced the first broadcast of a baseball game.

Goose Goslin: "I loved to play against the Yankees, especially in Yankee Stadium. Boy, did I get a kick out of beating those guys. They were so great, you know, it was a thrill to beat them."

Shortstop Specs Toporcer, the first bespectacled infielder in major league history, hit .324 as the Cardinals' shortstop in 1922.

The 1930s

1930s GAMES

Buddy Hassett, commenting on Paul Waner's theory of hitting, wrote: "He said he just laid his bat on his shoulder and when he saw a pitch he liked he threw it off."

Klein Clubless as Cubbie

At the conclusion of the 1933 season, Chuck Klein became the only player ever to be traded after a Triple Crown performance, when he was sent to the Chicago Cubs by the Philadelphia Phillies. The Phillies at the time had the worst pitching staff in the majors, meaning that Klein would now have an opportunity to feast on his former teammates. Too, the Cubs were a much better team, able to surround Klein in the batting order with a corps of strong hitters. Hence it was expected that his slugging would only accelerate in the Windy City. Instead, for reasons that still remain elusive, Klein flopped so egregiously with the Cubs that Chicago returned him gladly to the Phillies early in the 1936 season. Even back in his old haunts, Klein was unable to retrieve his earlier form. He did have one last moment in the sun, though, after his return to the Quaker City club. On July 10, 1936, he slammed four home runs in a 10-inning game at Pittsburgh's Forbes Field, which during the 1930s was the most difficult park in the National League for sluggers to conquer.

In 1933, Chuck Klein of Philadelphia set a 20th century record in the National League when he collected 200 hits for the fifth consecutive year.

Slugger Ott Also Garners Walks

New York Giants star Mel Ott was nicknamed "Master Melvin," largely for his skill at pounding balls over the inviting right field wall in the Polo Grounds, the Giants' home field. But Ott could also have merited the sobriquet for his mastery at working pitchers for walks. Between 1929 and 1944, he led the National League in free passes six times and likewise topped the circuit on four occasions in on-base percentage. During each of those years, he was in the NL's top five in bases on balls. Ott never achieved the monstrous walk totals that Babe Ruth registered, but then no one else did either during Ruth's heyday. Pitchers in the 1930s were quite stingy for the most part with free trips to first base. When Ott paced the NL with 100 walks in 1932, he was the only senior loop performer to garner more than 65 passes. The following year his walk total dropped to 75, but he again led as his closest pursuer could collect only 72. Over his career Ott walked an average of once in every seven trips to the plate.

Durable and consistent, Mel Ott (above) won six National League home run titles in a 22-year career with the New York Giants.

Thirst For Quotes
Joe DiMaggio related how unsophisticated he was as a rookie: "I can remember a reporter asking for a quote, and I didn't know what a quote was. I thought it was some kind of a soft drink."

1930s RUNS
1.	Lou Gehrig	1,257
2.	Jimmie Foxx	1,244
3.	Charlie Gehringer	1,179
4.	Earl Averill	1,102
5.	Mel Ott	1,095
6.	Ben Chapman	1,009
7.	Paul Waner	973
8.	Chuck Klein	955
9.	Al Simmons	930
10.	Joe Cronin	885
11.	Buddy Myer	841
	Doc Cramer	841
13.	Wally Berger	806
14.	Billy Herman	794
15.	Sam West	782
16.	Dick Bartell	781
17.	Joe Vosmik	771
	Joe Medwick	771
19.	Goose Goslin	766
20.	Arky Vaughan	754

Simmons Starts Strong, Stops Swiftly

Few players have managed to collect 100 RBI as rookies. A mere handful have had 100-RBI campaigns in each of their first two seasons, and only one man, Al Simmons, has commenced his career with more than three straight 100-RBI efforts. Simmons assembled no less than 11 consecutive seasons of 102 or more RBI, beginning with his frosh year of 1924 and ending in 1935 when he fell to just 79 ribbies. Between 1929 and 1933, Bucketfoot Al also became the first player in American League history to collect 200 or more hits for five consecutive years. He almost made it six in a row, as he had 192 safeties in 1934. At the finish of the 1939 season, Simmons had 2,864 hits and seemed within easy range of the coveted 3,000 mark. Age caught up to him abruptly, however, the following year, relegating him to spot duty for the remaining four years of his career. Simmons retired in 1944 with 2,927 hits and 1,827 RBI, good for 10th place on the all-time list.

1930s HITS

1. Paul Waner	1,959
2. Charlie Gehringer	1,865
3. Jimmie Foxx	1,845
4. Lou Gehrig	1,802
5. Earl Averill	1,786
6. Al Simmons	1,700
7. Ben Chapman	1,697
8. Chuck Klein	1,676
9. Mel Ott	1,673
10. Joe Cronin	1,650
11. Lloyd Waner	1,585
12. Doc Cramer	1,557
13. Joe Vosmik	1,550
14. Billy Herman	1,540
15. Wally Berger	1,537
16. Dick Bartell	1,504
17. Sam West	1,502
18. Joe Medwick	1,492
19. Gus Suhr	1,442
20. Bill Dickey	1,431

Paul Waner, who was a drinking man, said about hitting: "I see three baseballs, but I only swing at the middle one."

On June 3, 1932, Lou Gehrig knocked four home runs in a game, becoming the first player in the 20th century to do so.

Lou Gehrig of the New York Yankees set an AL record in 1931 when he drove home 184 runs.

Yankee first baseman Lou Gehrig slugged 14 homers against Cleveland in 1936, setting a record against one opponent in a single season

1930s DOUBLES

1. Charlie Gehringer — 400
2. Joe Cronin — 386
3. Paul Waner — 372
4. Earl Averill — 354
5. Joe Medwick — 353
6. Ben Chapman — 346
7. Lou Gehrig — 328
8. Dick Bartell — 325
9. Chuck Klein — 323
10. Billy Herman — 322
11. Joe Vosmik — 319
12. Jimmie Foxx — 316
13. Wally Berger — 297
14. Al Simmons — 292
15. Gus Suhr — 288
16. Mel Ott — 287
17. Sam West — 286
18. Tony Cuccinello — 280
19. Heinie Manush — 275
20. Gee Walker — 269

Joe DiMaggio scored an AL rookie record 132 runs in 1936.

On May 6, 1930, Gene Rye of Waco in the Texas League hit three homers in one inning.

Hafey Wins Photo-Finish '31 Batting Crown

Going into the final day of the 1931 season, Al Simmons had his second consecutive American League batting title locked up, but in the National League the crown was still at issue, so much so that mathematicians began calculating whether it was possible that the race could finish in a flat tie. At the end of the afternoon less than one percentage point separated the top three hitters. When their averages were calculated to the fourth decimal point, St. Louis Cardinals outfielder Chick Hafey stood at .3489; New York Giants first baseman Bill Terry, the defending bat titlist, was at .3486; and Hafey's teammate, first sacker Jim Bottomley, came in at .3482. The three were so tightly packed that if Bottomley had collected just one fewer at bat, he would have won the crown and Hafey would have dropped from the top spot to third place if he had batted one more time without a hit.

2,987 But Who's Counting?

Sam Rice explained why he retired with 2,987 hits: "You must remember, there wasn't much emphasis then on 3,000 hits. And to tell the truth, I didn't know how many hits I had when I quit."

Speak Softly and Carry a Big Stick

Mickey Cochrane on Charlie Gehringer: "He says hello on opening day and goodbye on closing day, and in between he hits .350."

Vosmik Sits, Plays, Loses Both Ways

The American League also had a batting race during the 1930s that resulted in a photo finish. Cleveland outfielder Joe Vosmik entered the last day of the 1935 season with a seemingly safe lead over second sacker Buddy Myer of the Washington Senators. To protect his batting average Vosmik was told to sit out the Tribe's doubleheader that afternoon. Alarmed when word reached the Cleveland press box that Myer was going wild in his finale, the Indians rushed Vosmik into action in the second half of the twin bill. Vosmik went 1-for-4, lowering his average to .348. Myer meanwhile was 4-for-5 in his finale to hike his average to .349, one point above Vosmik's. Vosmik's single enabled him to beat Myer out by one hit for the loop lead in safeties; the irony is that if Vosmik had sat out the second game as well, he and Myer would have finished in a dead heat in both hits and batting average.

In 1930, Cub outfielder Hack Wilson drove in a major league record 190 runs. He also set an NL record with 56 home runs.

Harry Heilmann, with the Reds after years with Detroit, was the first player to homer in every major league park in use during his career.

New York Giants first baseman Bill Terry in 1930 batted .401, the last .400 average in the league.

Josh Gibson said about Cool Papa Bell: "Cool Papa Bell was so fast he could get out of bed, turn out the lights across the room, and be back in bed under the covers before the lights went out."

1930s TRIPLES

1.	Gus Suhr	114
	Earl Averill	114
3.	Paul Waner	112
4.	John Stone	100
	Ben Chapman	100
6.	Arky Vaughan	94
7.	Buddy Myer	92
8.	Lou Gehrig	91
9.	Joe Cronin	90
10.	Al Simmons	89
11.	Heinie Manush	88
12.	Jimmie Foxx	87
13.	Joe Vosmik	86
14.	Sam West	84
	Carl Reynolds	84
16.	Joe Medwick	81
17.	Charlie Gehringer	76
	Kiki Cuyler	76
19.	Lloyd Waner	74
20.	Pepper Martin	71
	Tony Lazzeri	71
	Babe Herman	71

Hurler Lucas Excels in Pinch

The decade of the 1930s saw the emergence of a new phenomenon: the pinch-hitting specialist. For the first time, several teams had at least one player whose main job was to sit patiently in the dugout and await pivotal situations, usually late in the game, when his bat was needed. In 1932 Bill Terry's understudy for the New York Giants' first base job, Sam Leslie, broke Doc Miller's 19-year-old record for the most pinch hits in a season when he garnered 22 pinch blows. Leslie was so much a specialist that he played only two games in the field that season. Four years later, Ed Coleman of the St. Louis Browns was also seldom used in the field when he nabbed 20 pinch hits to set a new American League record. The game's most consistently productive pinch hitter during the 1930s was Red Lucas, a pitcher who in 1929 had led the National League not only in pinch hits but also in complete games. The first player in major league history to accumulate 100 career pinch hits, Lucas retired in 1938 with 114 and still ranks high on the all-time list.

On May 24, 1936, Yankee Tony Lazzeri drove in an AL record 11 runs in a game.

The only player to have two seasons in which he collected 420 or more total bases is Chuck Klein, who did it in 1930 and 1932.

In 1931, Lou Gehrig slammed a record three grand slams in a four-day period.

**"I had most of my trouble with lefthanded hitters. Charlie Gehringer could hit me in a tunnel at midnight with the lights out."
—Lefty Gomez**

1930s HOME RUNS

1. Jimmie Foxx	415
2. Lou Gehrig	347
3. Mel Ott	308
4. Wally Berger	241
5. Chuck Klein	238
6. Earl Averill	218
7. Hank Greenberg	206
8. Babe Ruth	198
9. Al Simmons	190
10. Bob Johnson	186
11. Hal Trosky	180
12. Bill Dickey	168
13. Gabby Hartnett	149
14. Dolph Camilli	148
15. Charlie Gehringer	146
16. Joe Medwick	145
17. Goose Goslin	140
18. Joe DiMaggio	137
19. Ripper Collins	135
20. Harlond Clift	123

Above: *Hall of Fame first baseman Jimmie Foxx played 20 years in the majors. With the Philadelphia A's and Boston Red Sox, "Double X" won three batting championships, and the 1933 Triple Crown.*

1930s RUNS BATTED IN

1.	Jimmie Foxx	1,403
2.	Lou Gehrig	1,358
3.	Mel Ott	1,135
4.	Al Simmons	1,081
5.	Earl Averill	1,046
6.	Joe Cronin	1,036
7.	Charlie Gehringer	1,003
8.	Chuck Klein	979
9.	Bill Dickey	937
10.	Wally Berger	893
11.	Ben Chapman	880
12.	Joe Medwick	873
13.	Hank Greenberg	853
14.	Joe Vosmik	819
15.	Gus Suhr	813
16.	Goose Goslin	788
17.	Tony Lazzeri	787
18.	Gabby Hartnett	777
19.	Hal Trosky	767
20.	Bob Johnson	750

Frederick Is Pinch Fence-Buster

For most of his six-year career with the Brooklyn Dodgers, Johnny Frederick was a regular outfielder who was used only occasionally as a pinch hitter. Indeed, he collected only 62 career pinch at bats and never more than nine pinch blows in a season. Of those nine pinch hits in 1932, nonetheless, six were home runs, giving Frederick a major league record that has endured since. What makes his achievement still more improbable is that he was never regarded as a slugger. His best home run percentage was 4.2 in that 1932 season. Following his record-breaking season, he collected just seven home runs in 1933 in 556 at bats. Released by the Dodgers after the 1934 season, Frederick dropped down to the Pacific Coast League. Even there he rapped a mere 35 home runs in his final six seasons of professional ball.

1930s STOLEN BASES

1.	Ben Chapman	269
2.	Billy Werber	176
3.	Gee Walker	158
	Lyn Lary	158
5.	Pepper Martin	136
6.	Kiki Cuyler	118
7.	Roy Johnson	115
8.	Charlie Gehringer	101
9.	Stan Hack	100
	Pete Fox	100
11.	Frankie Frisch	94
12.	Tony Lazzeri	86
	Luke Appling	86
14.	Joe Kuhel	85
15.	Frankie Crosetti	84
16.	Augie Galan	81
17.	Tony Piet	80
18.	Buddy Myer	78
19.	Carl Reynolds	77
20.	Billy Rogell	76

In 1932, Dale Alexander of the Red Sox became the first AL batting champ from a last place team.

Catcher Lombardi Cruises to Crown

Some purists were still contending that no catcher had ever legitimately won a major league batting title when Ernie Lombardi put an end to the controversy. In 1938, Lombardi hit .342 to cop the NL crown. More important, he had 489 at bats, well above the figure of 400 that many in the game felt should be the true minimum standard. Lombardi was also awarded a second batting crown in 1942 for hitting .330, albeit in only 309 at bats. His latter triumph marked the last time except for the strike-torn 1981 season that a player won recognition as a major league hitting leader with fewer than 400 at bats. It also was the last time to date that a catcher has finished at the top of the heap in a batting race. If the rule had not been changed subsequent to 1942, requiring 400 at bats, backstopper Smokey Burgess, who hit .368 for the Phillies in 105 games, would have been granted the National League batting crown in 1954.

Seventeen years after he hit a record 18 homers in a month, Rudy York in 1954 was earning $150 a month as a fire fighter. In an interview in '54, he said: "I've heard thousands cheer for me, like the time I hit the home run that beat the Cardinals in the first game [of the World Series] in 1946. I've been rich."

Billy Evans explained why he signed Earl Averill: "There was something about the nonchalant Averill that won you over. I guess it was the easy, steady manner in which he did his work, without any great show."

Average NL Hitter Bats .303 in 1930

Hitters had the time of their lives in 1930. Four teams in the American League batted over .300, but pitchers were even more ravaged in the National League where the average hitter in 1930 posted a .303 mark. As a result, Bill Terry's .401 figure—the last .400 season to date in the NL—was only 98 points above the league norm, and he needed to go down to the wire before besting Babe Herman (.393) and Chuck Klein (.386) for the batting crown. Terry's New York Giants were similarly hard-pressed before copping the team batting award. New York's .319 figure, though a 20th century record, was only four points better than the runner-up Philadelphia Phillies', who hit .315 as a unit (although the Phillies had a last-place record). Even Cincinnati, the most punchless club in the loop with 665 runs and a .281 batting average, had marks that would have outhit and outscored every team in the National League in 1917, the last year during the dead-ball era that a full schedule was played.

First baseman Lu Blue hit just one home run in 155 games with the Chicago White Sox in 1931 but nevertheless set a club record when he walked 127 times.

Lou Gehrig set a career record with 23 grand slams.

When he registered a .345 winning percentage in 1938, Larry French of the Cubs set the all-time record for the lowest winning percentage by a full-time starting pitcher on a pennant winner.

The last time Babe Ruth was a league leader in a major offensive department was in 1933 when he paced the AL in bases on balls.

Wait'll Next Year
"Baseball is like this. Have one good year and you can fool them for five more, because for five more years they expect you to have another good one."
—Frankie Frisch

1930s BATTING AVERAGE

1. Bill Terry .352
2. Lou Gehrig .343
3. Joe Medwick .338
4. Paul Waner .336
5. Jimmie Foxx .336
6. Babe Ruth .331
7. Charlie Gehringer .331
8. Arky Vaughan .329
9. Chuck Klein .326
10. Al Simmons .325
11. Heinie Manush .324
12. Mickey Cochrane .323
13. Hank Greenberg .323
14. Cecil Travis .321
15. Babe Herman .321
16. Bill Dickey .320
17. Earl Averill .318
18. Hal Trosky .317
19. Pie Traynor .316
20. Chick Hafey .315

In 1936, Woody Jensen had 696 at bats, the record for a 154-game season.

High Low Card in '30 With .279 Mark

The St. Louis Cardinals' team batting average of .314 made them merely the National League's third-best hitting club in 1930, but the Redbirds used their hits to bag a 20th-century loop record 1,004 runs. Part of the reason the Cards scored so freely was that their batting order was packed from top to bottom with .300 hitters. In 1930, every Cardinals regular hit at least .300, ranging from rookie George Watkins's .373 figure to Taylor Douthit's .303. To add to the Cards' riches, backup outfielder Showboat Fisher rapped .374, and second-string catcher Gus Mancuso finished at .366. The only member of the club's cast to have cause for embarrassment was utility infielder Andy High, a mere .279 hitter. Move the calendar up 38 years to 1968, and High's .279 mark would have tied for second place on the Cardinals' team stats.

Foul

Luke Appling, famed for fouling pitches into stands, was once denied a request for two baseballs to give to admiring fans by a White Sox official because they cost $2.75 apiece. Appling then proceeded to foul 10 straight pitches into the stands. He looked toward the official sitting in the club boxes and yelled: "That's $27.50 and I'm not done yet."

Luke Appling of the Chicago White Sox set a 20th-century record for shortstops when he hit .388 in 1936 to cop the American League batting crown.

Above: Joe "Ducky" Medwick played left field with the Cardinals' hustling "Gashouse Gang." A 10-time .300 batter, he led the NL in doubles and RBI three times each.

Joe "Ducky" Medwick cracked an NL record 64 doubles in 1936.

Medwick Muscles Way to 1937 Triple Crown

Starting in 1933, Cardinals outfielder Ducky Medwick started ringing up impressive statistics, finishing near the top of the league in several offensive categories. After knocking at the door for a few seasons, he finally broke through in 1937 to win the National League batting title. Since Medwick also paced the loop in RBI with 154 and his 31 homers tied Mel Ott for the four-bagger lead, Medwick additionally claimed the Triple Crown. It was to be the last such achievement to date by a National League player. The closest anyone has come in the years since was in 1948 when another Cardinal, Stan Musial, missed the Triple Crown by a margin of one home run. Medwick followed his Triple Crown season by having another good year in 1938, hitting .322, topping the NL in doubles for the third consecutive year, and bagging his second consecutive RBI title. Although just 26 years old that season, he never again was a league leader in a major hitting department.

On April 19, 1938, Dodger Ernie Koy and Phillie Heinie Mueller each homered in their first major league at bat in the same game.

"Baseball must be a great game to survive the fools who run it."
—Bill Terry

"There's no room for sentiment in baseball if you want to win."
—Frankie Frisch

On September 29, 1935, catcher Aubrey Epps of the Pirates went 3-for-4 in his only big league game and had three RBI.

Despite hitting .355 in a late-season trial in 1938 and becoming the first White Sox player to have a three-homer game in Comiskey Park, Merv Connors was dropped by the Sox and never again played in the majors.

Stan Hack said about his hometown: "It's so small we don't even have a town drunk. Everybody has to take a turn."

Johnny Cooney hit his only two home runs on consecutive days.

The St. Louis Cardinals have not had an NL home run king since 1940, when Johnny Mize hit 43.

Twice in 1932, Buzz Arlett socked four homers in a game for Baltimore of the International League.

The last player to lead the NL in both home runs and batting in the same season was Johnny Mize of the St. Louis Cardinals in 1939.

Mize Just Misses Triple Crowns in 1939 and '40

When Stan Musial fell short by one home run in his bid to capture the National League home run crown in 1948, he also missed becoming the Cardinals' first home run leader since 1940 when St. Louis first sacker Johnny Mize snared his second consecutive four-bagger crown. The previous season Mize had topped the senior loop in round trippers with 28 and also copped the batting crown with a .348 mark. RBI, normally Mize's forte, proved to be the lone stumbling block in his quest for a Triple Crown—he finished with 108, 20 behind the leader, Frank McCormick of the Reds. In 1940, Mize easily paced the NL in ribbies with 137 and again took the four-bagger crown with a Cardinals-record 43 round trippers, but this time his quest was thwarted by his .314 batting average, a sizeable 41 points behind Debs Garms's loop-leading figure of .355. If the 400 at bat rule had been in effect in 1940, however, Mize would have missed the Triple Crown by a scant three points. Among NL players with 400 or more at bats, only Stan Hack at .317 ranked ahead of Mize.

Diz Is All-Around Whiz

Dizzy Dean was one of the last great starting pitchers who was also used frequently in relief roles. When he won 30 games in 1934 to become the most recent National League hurler to reach that figure, four of his victories came as a reliever, and he also notched seven saves. Two years later, he became the last pitcher to top his league in both complete games and saves. The colorful Dean was also among the better hitting pitchers during the 1930s and often helped his own cause. In 1931, his last minor league season, he pitched for Houston of the Texas League. One afternoon he hit a solo homer to give his club an early lead. When manager Joe Schultz removed him from the mound after he ran into trouble, Dean stalked out to the scoreboard in center field and took down his marker, arguing that if he wasn't allowed to keep pitching, Houston couldn't have his run.

Dizzy Dean in 1936 was the last major league pitcher to lead his league in complete games (28) and saves (11) in the same year.

"I may not have been the greatest pitcher ever, but I was amongst 'em." —Dizzy Dean

1930s GAMES PITCHED

1.	Larry French	430
2.	Jack Russell	394
3.	Mel Harder	385
4.	Carl Hubbell	383
5.	Charlie Root	377
6.	Paul Derringer	375
7.	Bump Hadley	374
8.	Dick Coffman	366
9.	Lefty Grove	351
10.	Fred Frankhouse	345
11.	Clint Brown	344
12.	Willis Hudlin	338
13.	Red Ruffing	334
14.	Syl Johnson	327
15.	Chief Hogsett	323
	Wes Ferrell	323
17.	Lefty Gomez	322
18.	Lon Warneke	318
19.	Earl Whitehill	317
20.	Guy Bush	316

Dizzy Dean, the famed hurler, commented on his mangled English: "A lot of folks that ain't saying ain't ain't eating."

King Carl

After watching Carl Hubbell in the 1934 All-Star Game fan Babe Ruth, Lou Gehrig, Jimmie Foxx, Al Simmons, and Joe Cronin in a row, Frankie Frisch commented: "I could play second base 15 more years behind this guy. He doesn't need any help."

On August 15, 1932, Tommy Bridges of the Tigers lost a chance at a perfect game when pinch hitter Dave Harris of the Senators hit a bloop single with two out in the ninth inning.

Cardinal rookie Dizzy Dean led the NL with 191 strikeouts in 1932.

Carl Hubbell's 1.66 ERA in 1933 (in 308 frames) was the lowest ever by an NL lefty for over 300 innings.

1930s COMPLETE GAMES

1. Wes Ferrell	207
2. Red Ruffing	201
3. Carl Hubbell	197
Lefty Grove	197
5. Ted Lyons	168
6. Lefty Gomez	163
Paul Derringer	163
8. Larry French	160
9. Tommy Bridges	156
10. Dizzy Dean	151
11. Lon Warneke	146
12. Red Lucas	136
13. Earl Whitehill	134
Mel Harder	134
15. Bobo Newsom	129
16. Danny MacFayden	128
17. Ed Brandt	125
18. Van Mungo	114
19. Bill Lee	110
20. F. Fitzsimmons	109

Pitcher Red Lucas led the National League in pinch hits four times.

Phillies Hurlers Hit Hard

In 1930, when the Philadelphia Phillies hit .315 as a unit under manager Burt Shotton to set a 20th century club record, they averaged over six runs a game. Shotton's men nonetheless finished in last place, winning just 52 of 154 contests, as the team's pitchers surrendered nearly seven runs per nine innings. The leading miscreants were Les Sweetland (7.71 ERA), Claude Willoughby (7.59 ERA), and Hal Elliott (7.67 ERA). This trio was instrumental in dooming the 1930 Phillies to a 6.71 staff ERA, the worst in the 20th century. Philadelphia allowed 16.8 baserunners per nine innings. And although the Phils batted .315 and had a .367 on-base percentage, their opponents were able to bat at a .345 clip and get an on-base average of .405. So ghastly was the club's pitching that only one hurler, Phil Collins (4.78), managed to post an ERA below the NL average mark of 4.97. Amid the chaos, Collins even succeeded in fashioning a winning record of 16-11; the rest of the Phils mound corps meanwhile had an aggregate 36-91 record.

AL Mound City Mound Staff Roundly Unsound

During the 1930s, the St. Louis Browns hill staff never sank to the depths that the Phillies hurlers had in 1930, but in one vital respect the Browns were even more disgraceful. Between 1935 and 1939, the American League Mound City entry posted the junior loop's worst ERA for five straight years. The nadir came in 1936 when the Browns registered a 6.24 ERA and surrendered 1,064 runs; both figures stand as all-time American League negative marks. Poor as St. Louis' pitching was in 1936, the team still managed to dodge the cellar. The following year, however, the Brownies plummeted deep into the AL basement when the pitching improved throughout the junior circuit while their own mound work remained horrendous. In 1937, the Browns' staff ERA of 6.00 was 1.15 runs per game higher than that of the Philadelphia Athletics, the loop's second-worst pitching crew. As a result St. Louis had a dismal .299 winning percentage despite a .285 team batting average that ranked second that year in the AL.

Lefty Grove, asked whether money was important when he played, responded: "Sure, I looked for as much as I could get. But the truth was, I would have played for nothing. Of course I never told Connie (Mack) that."

Detroit's Schoolboy Rowe in 1934 tied Lefty Grove's American League record by notching 16 straight victories.

Cleveland hurler Johnny Allen in 1937 set an American League record with a .938 winning percentage.

When Johnny Vander Meer tossed back-to-back no-hitters in 1938, it marked the only season between 1917 and 1944 that there were two no-nos in the National League.

1930s SHUTOUTS

1.	Larry French	32
2.	Carl Hubbell	31
3.	Red Ruffing	28
4.	Lefty Grove	26
	Lefty Gomez	26
	Dizzy Dean	26
7.	Tommy Bridges	25
8.	Lon Warneke	24
9.	Bill Lee	23
	Paul Derringer	23
11.	Hal Schumacher	20
12.	F. Fitzsimmons	17
	Ed Brandt	17
14.	Van Mungo	16
	Mel Harder	16
	Wes Ferrell	16
17.	Schoolboy Rowe	15
	Tex Carleton	15
19.	Bucky Walters	14
	Bill Walker	14
	Bill Hallahan	14
	Lou Fette	14

In 1933, last-place Cincinnati set an NL record when its pitching staff issued just 257 walks.

Newsom Wins 20 Despite 5.08 ERA

When Dave Stewart of the Oakland Athletics lost his final decision in 1991, he missed becoming the first pitcher since Bobo Newsom in 1938 to post a winning record in 200 or more innings of work despite having an ERA above 5.00. What made Newsom's performance all the more remarkable was that he was pitching for a seventh-place team. In 1938, while his St. Louis Browns mates were finishing with a 55-97 record, Newsom somehow went 20-16 despite notching a 5.08 ERA, the worst in history by a 20-game winner. He also led the loop in complete games and innings pitched that year. Newsom's achievement was by no means without a precedent, though, during the 1930s. In the high-scoring 1930 season, Pittsburgh's Remy Kremer became the first 20-game winner with a 5.00 plus ERA (5.02), and seven years later Roxie Lawson of the Tigers had a dazzling 18-7 record on a 5.26 ERA. Lawson's .720 winning percentage in 1937 stands as the best ever by a pitcher who gave up more than five earned runs a game.

It's Academic

Dizzy Dean revealed his pitching strategy to sportswriter Red Smith: "I never tried to outsmart nobody. It was easier to outdummy them."

Indian hurler Bob Feller's 240 stikeouts in 1938 led the majors; NL strikeout leader Clay Bryant of Chicago totaled just 135.

In 1937, Giants rookie Cliff Melton won 20 games, tied for the National League lead in saves, and was second in the NL in both ERA and winning percentage.

Don't Sweat It

When asked if he ever threw a spitter, Lefty Gomez replied: "Not intentionally, but I sweat easy."

Indian hurler Bob Feller's 240 strikeouts in 1938 led the major leagues.

1930s WINS

1.	Lefty Grove	199
2.	Carl Hubbell	188
3.	Red Ruffing	175
4.	Wes Ferrell	170
5.	Lefty Gomez	165
6.	Mel Harder	158
7.	Larry French	156
8.	Tommy Bridges	150
9.	Paul Derringer	148
10.	Dizzy Dean	147
11.	Lon Warneke	144
12.	Earl Whitehill	131
13.	Bump Hadley	121
14.	F. Fitzsimmons	120
15.	Hal Schumacher	117
	Ted Lyons	117
17.	General Crowder	115
18.	Charlie Root	114
19.	Guy Bush	112
20.	Johnny Allen	108

Red Sox Hurlers Not Durable Goods

By the end of the 1930s, the hitting and scoring onslaught that prevailed throughout the decade had so drained pitchers that in 1939 the New York Yankees nearly became the first team to win a pennant without a single hurler capable of working 200 innings. The previous year, the Boston Red Sox had become the first team to finish as high as second lacking a pitcher good for at least 200 innings of work. In 1939, the Crimson Hose repeated as the American League runner-up without a true staff leader. Jim Bagby Jr. led the 1938 Crimson Hose with 198 2/3 innings, while Lefty Grove topped the '39 club with 191 innings. The BoSox dipped to fourth in 1940, with Bagby (183 innings) the only moundsman who hurled more than 158 frames. When rookie Dick Newsome won 19 games in 214 innings in 1941, he gave the Red Sox their largest hill output since 1937 when Grove, Jack Wilson, and Bobo Newsom all labored over 200 innings.

The 1937 Boston Braves were the only team in this century to have two rookie 20-game winners, Lou Fette and Jim Turner; both were over age 30.

1930s INNINGS

1.	Carl Hubbell	2,596.2
2.	Larry French	2,481.2
3.	Red Ruffing	2,439.0
4.	Lefty Grove	2,399.0
5.	Wes Ferrell	2,345.1
6.	Paul Derringer	2,343.2
7.	Mel Harder	2,326.0
8.	Lefty Gomez	2,234.2
9.	Earl Whitehill	2,129.1
10.	Bump Hadley	2,121.2
11.	T. Bridges	2,083.0
12.	Lon Warneke	2,021.0
13.	D. MacFayden	1,997.0
14.	Ted Lyons	1,972.0
15.	F. Fitzsimmons	1,937.2
16.	Dizzy Dean	1,908.1
17.	Ed Brandt	1,875.1
18.	Charlie Root	1,829.1
19.	H. Schumacher	1,736.2
20.	Willis Hudlin	1,736.1

"I'd rather be lucky than good."
—Lefty Gomez

On June 10, 1938, Bill Lefebvre of the Red Sox became the first pitcher in American League history to homer in his first major league at bat.

In 1931, for the first time in history, no pitcher won 20 games in a major league. Three National League hurlers—Pittsburgh's Heinie Meine, St. Louis' Wild Bill Hallahan, and Philadelphia's Jumbo Jim Elliott—tied for the loop lead with 19 wins.

Murphy Slams Door on Yankee Foes

One important reason that Red Ruffing was the only member of the New York Yankees' hill unit to pitch over 200 innings in 1939 was the mound depth that manager Joe McCarthy enjoyed. McCarthy had seven pitchers who won at least 10 games. Furthermore, the Yankees were equipped with Johnny Murphy, the first hurler to carve an outstanding career while functioning almost exclusively as a relief pitcher. An occasional starter during his early seasons with the Yankees in the mid-1930s (he notched more than 200 innings pitched in 1934, getting 10 complete games), Murphy by 1939 had found a permanent niche in the bullpen. That year he notched a career-high 19 saves, but he had several other seasons nearly as good. Because of the regularity with which he dowsed enemy uprisings, Murphy was nicknamed "Fireman Johnny." He finished in 1947 with 73 career relief wins and 107 career saves; both marks at that juncture were all-time records.

Brown Becomes Relief Ace

The National League had no bullpen operatives of Johnny Murphy's quality during the 1930s. Early in the decade, ancient Jack Quinn of the Brooklyn Dodgers was the loop's top fireman, but by the end of the period Pittsburgh's Mace Brown claimed that honor. Like most of the leading relievers in that era, Brown was also used frequently as a starter. In 1938, however, 49 of his league-leading 51 mound appearances were in relief.

Above: *Paul (left) and Dizzy Dean were teammates and friends. During the 1934 season, Dizzy staged a short strike so Paul could get a raise.*

In 1934, Paul Dean's strikeouts per game ratio of 5.79 was the highest in the majors; Dizzy was second with 5.63.

In 1934, Dizzy Dean's brother Paul hurled the first no-hitter in the National League since 1929 when he beat Brooklyn 3-0 on September 21.

1930s STRIKEOUTS

1.	Lefty Gomez	1,337
2.	Lefty Grove	1,313
3.	Carl Hubbell	1,281
4.	Red Ruffing	1,260
5.	Tommy Bridges	1,207
6.	Dizzy Dean	1,144
7.	Van Mungo	1,022
8.	Paul Derringer	1,018
9.	Bump Hadley	1,006
10.	Bobo Newsom	963
11.	Larry French	901
12.	Lon Warneke	877
13.	Wes Ferrell	867
14.	Johnny Allen	838
15.	Charlie Root	818
16.	Mel Harder	812
17.	Earl Whitehill	783
18.	Bill Hallahan	768
19.	Ed Brandt	743
20.	George Earnshaw	736

Rapid
Bucky Harris, Washington manager, instructed his players before a game in which the Senators were to face Bob Feller: "Go up and hit what you see. And if you don't see it, come on back."

Ferrell Gives Way to Young Feller

In the summer of 1935, the Cleveland brass suffered in silence as Wes Ferrell led the AL in wins after having been traded to the Boston Red Sox the previous year for next to nothing. Much of the abuse heaped on the Tribe's front office turned to praise, however, when the local press got its first look at the 16-year-old pitching phenom Cleveland scout Cy Slapnicka signed. Even at that tender age, Bob Feller's blazing speed was so apparent that it brought instant comparison to Walter Johnson. The problem for Cleveland was that Slapnicka had signed Feller illegally while he was still in high school. When Slapnicka's gaffe came to light, it was expected that Commissioner Kenesaw Mountain Landis would void Feller's contract with Cleveland. Instead Landis elected to accept its validity, thereby averting a potential bidding war for Feller that might have toppled the already shaky financial underpinnings of the game during the last years of the Depression.

On September 23, 1936, 17-year-old Indian Bob Feller set an AL record when he struck out 17 batters in a game. He set the modern major league record in 1938 with 18 Ks in a game.

Lefty Gomez set an All-Star Game record for the longest pitching stint when he went six innings in 1935 in helping the American League to a 4-1 victory.

In 1932, four-year vet Wes Ferrell of Cleveland won 20-plus games for the fourth straight year.

In 1931, Cleveland hurler Wes Ferrell hit a season record nine home runs while serving as a pitcher.

Bob Feller recounted the game on September 13, 1936, when he fanned 17 Philadelphia A's to set a new American League strikeout record at age 17: "I was pretty excited. I knew I was approaching the record. I was counting those whiffs. And the closer I got to the record, the more I wanted to break it. I just kept pouring them in."

1930s EARNED RUN AVERAGE

1.	Carl Hubbell	2.71
2.	Lefty Grove	2.91
3.	Dizzy Dean	2.96
4.	Bill Lee	3.21
5.	Lon Warneke	3.23
6.	Lefty Gomez	3.24
7.	Hal Schumacher	3.38
8.	Larry French	3.42
9.	Van Mungo	3.42
10.	Charlie Root	3.50
11.	Paul Derringer	3.50
12.	Curt Davis	3.50
13.	F. Fitzsimmons	3.54
14.	Bill Swift	3.57
15.	Ed Brandt	3.57
16.	Bill Walker	3.57
17.	Red Ruffing	3.59
18.	Johnny Allen	3.73
19.	Ben Cantwell	3.74
20.	Mel Harder	3.74

Feller Blows 18 Bengals Away

By 1938, though just 19 years old, Bob Feller was already the Cleveland hill ace. That season he captured 17 of 28 decisions despite issuing 208 walks to set a new 20th century record. Feller's penchant for giving up free passes was more than outweighed by his strikeout totals. Massive in any era, his K figures in the late 1930s towered over those of his closest competitors. In 1938, while Clay Bryant was leading the National League in whiffs with 135, Feller bagged 240 Ks to pace the junior circuit. Feller's total was the highest in the majors since 1924. The apex of his season came in his final start when he set down 18 Detroit Tigers on strikes to set a new post-1893 single-game K mark. When Feller again topped the AL with 246 whiffs in 1939, he became the first junior loop hurler since Walter Johnson in 1916 to register back-to-back 200-K campaigns.

Pitcher Russ Van Atta of the Yankees made his major league debut on April 25, 1933, by collecting four hits in the process of shutting out Washington 16-0.

"The secret to my success was clean living and a fast-moving outfield."
—Lefty Gomez

In 1937, Joe Kohlman had a 25-1 record for Salisbury of the Eastern Shore League and then won a late-season start with Washington, giving him an overall 26-1 mark.

Fitzsimmons Wins and Zips Four

In the late 1920s and early 1930s, Freddie Fitzsimmons had been one of the New York Giants' mound mainstays and had won in double figures for nine straight seasons. Perhaps as importantly, he had topped 200 innings from 1926 to 1934. In 1935, however, Fitzsimmons was below par physically, working just 94 innings and notching only six complete games in 15 starts. His record at the season's close was a miserable 4-8 with an earned run average over four. His lousy season contributed heavily to the Giants' disappointing third-place finish. Yet Fitzsimmons contrived to top the National League in a major pitching department. All four of his victories were shutouts, tying him with four other hurlers for the loop lead in whitewashes. The following year Fitzsimmons rebounded to bag 10 wins but failed to hurl a single shutout. In fact, his 1935 total of four tied a personal high in a career that spanned 19 seasons and brought him 217 wins, 29 of them by the shutout route.

In 1937, Johnny Allen won his first 15 starts of the season, then lost on the season's closing day.

Red Hot

Bill Dickey said about Red Ruffing: "If I were asked to choose the best pitcher I ever caught, I would have to say Ruffing."

Ted Lyons, a 260-game winner, hurled 21 seasons in the majors without ever having a 100-strikeout campaign; his high was 74 Ks in 1933.

On July 5, 1935, Al and Tony Cuccinello were the first brothers on opposing teams to homer in the same National League game.

In 1931, Lefty Grove, George Earnshaw, Roy Mahaffey, and Rube Walberg compiled a composite 87-27 record for the Philadelphia A's.

Brooklyn Buys and Then Benches .448 Bopper Boone

In 1930, the action in the minor leagues once again mirrored what fans were seeing on the major league level. All of the top minor circuits were stocked with hitters who produced mammoth stats, but none was more dazzling than Ike Boone's. The property of the Mission Reds in the Pacific Coast League, Boone, a former Boston Red Sox club batting leader, launched the 1930 campaign by hitting at a .448 clip for his first 83 games. Since Boone had hit .407 the previous year with 55 home runs and an all-time professional baseball record 553 total bases, major league magnates began to think that even in an era of superinflated hitting stats Boone might be worth another look in top company. Hence the Brooklyn Dodgers purchased Boone from the Mission club, thereupon depriving him of an opportunity to set a new minor league record for the highest single-season batting average. While it is doubtful that Boone could have maintained his .448 pace over the entire season, in 1930 conditions were such that it was certainly possible. The shame is that the Dodgers didn't really need Boone. After acquiring him, they kept him on the bench for the balance of the season.

1930s CATCHER GAMES

1. Bill Dickey	1,179
2. Al Lopez	1,172
3. Rick Ferrell	1,162
4. Gabby Hartnett	1,123
5. Spud Davis	958

Right: *Bill Dickey caught nearly 1,800 games with the Yankees from 1928 to 1946. In addition to his defensive skills, Dickey hit 102 homers between 1936 and '39, hit over .300 10 times, and batted in more than 1,200 runs.*

Lee, French Maintain Fine Gloves in Minors

Buried under the welter of massive hitting and slugging feats on both the minor and major league level in the early 1930s were the accomplishments of players who made their way in the game with their gloves. Lost in particular were several fine shortstops such as Dud Lee and Ray French, who were relegated to long careers in the minors because the emphasis was so strongly on offense that few major league teams could afford to carry a weak-hitting regular regardless of his defensive talent. In a career that lasted from 1914 to 1941, French played a record 2,736 games in the minors at shortstop. His total major league experience consisted of only 82 games in the early 1920s. Lee played 253 games in the majors during the 1920s, mostly with the Red Sox, but did not really reach his peak until the following decade. In 1930, despite hitting just .275, one of the lowest marks in the Pacific Coast League, Lee was so highly regarded a fielder that he was voted the Most Valuable Player on the loop champion Hollywood Stars.

In 1938, Stan Hack led the NL with 16 steals, an all-time low by an NL leader.

The 1936 New York Yankees won the AL pennant by 19½ games, setting a circuit record.

1930s FIRST BASE GAMES

1.	Gus Suhr	1,399
2.	Lou Gehrig	1,394
3.	Jimmie Foxx	1,377
4.	Joe Kuhel	1,139
5.	Bill Terry	930

In his first 33 seasons as manager of the Philadelphia A's, Connie Mack won nine pennants (the last in 1931); in his last 17 seasons with the club, he finished in the first division just once, bringing the A's home fourth in 1948.

Support Squad

Fresco Thompson, Phillies captain, delivered a lineup card to umpire Bill Klem in 1930 with the following notation in the ninth or pitcher's spot in the batting order: "Willoughby and others."

Browns Shortstops Found Wanting

In the early 1930s, batting averages climbed to their highest level since the mid-1890s, after the pitching distance was increased by 10½ feet. Yet, not all hitters thrived. In 1931, rookie St. Louis Browns shortstop Jim Levey batted just .209. Levey upped his hitting mark the following year to .280, but the bottom fell out on him in 1933. Playing in 141 games, he collected just 103 hits in 529 at bats and clocked a .195 batting average, the lowest of the 1930s decade for a regular. Levey never again appeared in the majors but played for several seasons in the National Football League. In 1934, the Browns gave his shortstop post to rookie Alan Strange, another notoriously weak hitter of the period. After hitting .233 as a frosh, Strange played four more seasons in the majors before departing with a .223 career batting average. He batted .186 in 167 at bats in 1940. Levey's career mark, even including his horrendous 1933 campaign, was seven points higher at .230.

Cleveland is the only team in this century to have two home parks at the same time; between 1932 and 1946 the Indians played in both League Park and Cleveland Municipal Stadium.

Each '35 Tiger received a $6,500 World Series share.

Credits and Debits

"You'd be surprised the amount of guys that were broke after they quit playing. They always thought they were gonna keep making that good money, and as fast as they got the money, they spent it."
—Joe Stripp, third baseman during the 1930s

1930s SECOND BASE GAMES

1. Charlie Gehringer	1,397
2. Billy Herman	1,194
3. Buddy Myer	1,173
4. Tony Cuccinello	1,136
5. Ski Melillo	958

Released by the Yankees in 1935, Babe Ruth signed a three-year contract with the Boston Braves. On May 25, 1935, Ruth hit three homers at Pittsburgh's Forbes Field, then retired a few days later.

*Robert Creamer wrote about the '20s and '30s:
"A man could spend an entire career in the minor
leagues, and major league veterans who had seen
their best days would come back down and play
another half-dozen seasons in the high minors."*

**In 1934, the
Detroit Tigers
won the
franchise's first
flag since 1909.**

*The Detroit Tigers won the
franchise's first world championship
in 1935; Tigers owner Frank Navin
died shortly after seeing his club win
its first fall classic.*

In 1934, Lou Gehrig won the Triple Crown in the AL, batting .363 with 49 homers and 165 RBI. Despite his performance, Detroit player-manager Mickey Cochrane was selected as the AL MVP.

**1930s THIRD BASE
GAMES**

1.	Pinky Whitney	1,055
2.	Pinky Higgins	997
3.	Marv Owen	912
4.	Stan Hack	886
5.	Harlond Clift	873

*The St. Louis Cardinals in 1934 won the World Series
with a rowdy club that went down in history as "The
Gashouse Gang."*

Oliver Twists in Wind Without Homer

In 1922, shortstop Rabbit Maranville, then with the
Pittsburgh Pirates, set the all-time single-season record for
the most at bats without a four-bagger when he went
homerless in 672 turns at the plate. Doc Cramer of the
Boston Red Sox established the corresponding American
League record in 1938 by failing to homer in 658 at bats.
Both Cramer and Maranville hit a fair number of round
trippers during their careers, however. Center fielder Tom
Oliver, on the other hand, played four years with the
Boston Red Sox in the early 1930s without ever connecting
for the distance. Oliver's career homerless skein of 514
games and 1,914 at bats is a 20th century record, made
even more noteworthy by the period in which he was active
and the park in which he performed. A righthanded hitter,
Oliver played his entire career in Fenway Park without ever
being able to clear its inviting left field wall.

A Cincinnati bank took over the bankrupt Reds in 1933, then convinced magnate Powell Crosley to buy the club.

On May 24, 1935, the Reds beat the Philadelphia Phillies 2-1 at Cincinnati's Crosley Field in the first major league night game.

1930s SHORTSTOP GAMES

1.	Joe Cronin	1,360
2.	Dick Bartell	1,348
3.	Leo Durocher	1,316
4.	Billy Rogell	1,148
5.	Arky Vaughan	1,129

Dihigo, Bell, Other Negro Leaguers Play Year-Round

During the Depression years baseball promoters, hoping to appeal to fans of all races and denominations, began to stage more and more games between Negro League all-star teams and white major leaguers. Black stars like Buck Leonard, Josh Gibson, Judy Johnson, Cool Papa Bell, and Martin Dihigo in that way got their only chance to compare their skills to those of the reputedly best players in the land. Because the salaries Negro League players received were far less than their white brethren could earn, many chose to play elsewhere than the United States. Dihigo, for one, spent the bulk of the 1930s playing first in Cuba and then in Mexico. Bell generally stayed stateside during the summer, but the lure of additional money took him south of the border in the winter months. For over two decades he played baseball year-round, not retiring until he was well into his 40s.

Commenting on playing, traveling, and living conditions in the black leagues that drove him to pursue a career in real estate in 1934, Negro League star Dave Malarcher said: "They were conditions which I could not continue to bear."

On April 14, 1936, Cardinal Eddie Morgan became the first player to hit a pinch homer in his first major league at bat.

The Boston Red Sox in 1932 set a club record for losses with 111.

Braves Beaten By the Bushel

In 1934, the Boston Braves finished fourth, rousing hopes in the Hub of their first pennant since 1914. To bolster the club for the 1935 campaign, owner Judge Fuchs made only one significant change; he signed 40-year-old Babe Ruth after the Yankees released the Bambino. Ruth's legs were shot, causing him to retire before the season was barely six weeks old, but by that time the race was over for the Braves anyway. The club went on to lose 115 of 153 decisions and post a .248 winning percentage, the lowest in this century by a senior circuit nine. Boston's opponents scored 277 more runs, an average of 1.8 a game. Center fielder Wally Berger paced the loop with 34 home runs and 130 RBI, but no other Brave was able to collect more than five dingers or 60 ribbies. The pitching staff was equally inept. Frank Frankhouse had a semirespectable 11-15 record, but the rest of the hill corps was an aggregate 27-100. The club finished so far off the pace that it came in 26 games behind the seventh-place Philadelphia Phillies.

The Hall of Fame was established in 1936. In the first vote for enshrinement, the leading vote-getter was Ty Cobb. Other first electees were: Babe Ruth, Honus Wagner, Christy Mathewson, and Walter Johnson.

The New York Yankees in 1934 released two future Hall of Famers, Herb Pennock and Joe Sewell on the same day.

> **"Next to religion, baseball has had a greater impact on the American people than any other institution."**
> **—Herbert Hoover**

1930s OUTFIELD GAMES

1. Paul Waner	1,418
2. Earl Averill	1,412
3. Wally Berger	1,285
4. Chuck Klein	1,275
5. Al Simmons	1,271
6. Ben Chapman	1,270
7. Mel Ott	1,251
8. Joe Vosmik	1,241
9. Sam West	1,238
10. Doc Cramer	1,185
11. Lloyd Waner	1,174
12. Joe Medwick	1,080
13. John Stone	1,068
14. Goose Goslin	1,066
15. Jo-Jo Moore	1,045

Few Practice Art of Base Thievery

After Sam Rice of Washington stole 63 bases in 1920 to pace the American League, thievery totals began a sharp and steady decline that would continue into the late 1950s. Periodically, however, someone would step forward to remind fans of what the game had been like only a generation earlier. In 1930, it was Yankees outfielder Ben Chapman, whose 61 swipes were the most by any major leaguer between 1920 and World War II. Pepper Martin and Augie Galan were the only two National Leaguers who could consistently garner more than 20 steals in a season.

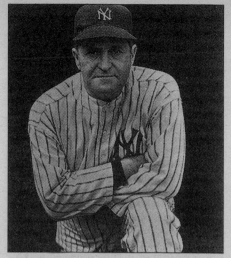

Above: *Joe McCarthy managed the 1929 Chicago Cubs to the National League pennant. When he skippered the 1932 Yankees to the AL flag, he became the first manager in major league history to win pennants in both the NL and the AL.*

The world champion St. Louis Cardinals in 1934 drew only 350,000 fans in home attendance.

"Give a boy a bat and a ball and a place to play and you'll have a good citizen."
—Joe McCarthy

1930s MANAGER WINS

1.	Joe McCarthy	970
2.	Bill McKechnie	739
3.	Bucky Harris	723
4.	Connie Mack	678
5.	Bill Terry	677
6.	Joe Cronin	574
7.	Charlie Grimm	534
8.	Walter Johnson	458
	Frankie Frisch	458
10.	Pie Traynor	457

Warstler Rare '30s Defensive Specialist

Any outfielder during the 1930s who could not keep his batting average above .300 was generally without a job the following year. The same held true of first and third basemen, and even catchers and middle infielders were expected to hit somewhere around .280. It was a rare player who was retained even as a substitute if he fell below .250, which made Rabbit Warstler's performance one of a kind. A middle infielder, Warstler played every year during the 1930s and got into over 1,200 games—even though he never once batted over .250. More typically, Warstler hit in the low .220s. His .229 career batting average and .287 slugging average both are the lowest of any player who was active all 10 seasons of the greatest offensive decade in the game's history. Warstler was occasionally used as a pinch hitter despite his meager offensive output. In 20 pinch at bats, he never once came through with a hit.

In 1938, the Phillies moved to Shibe Park after 51 years in the Baker Bowl.

1930s TEAM WINS

	W	L
1. New York-AL	970	554
2. Chicago-NL	889	646
3. St.Louis-NL	869	665
4. New York-NL	868	657
5. Cleveland-AL	824	708
6. Detroit-AL	818	716
7. Pittsburgh-NL	812	718
8. Wash.-AL	806	722
9. Brooklyn-NL	734	793
10. Phila.-AL	723	795
11. Boston-AL	705	815
12. Boston-NL	700	829
13. Chicago-AL	678	841
14. Cinci.-NL	664	866
15. Phila.-NL	581	943
16. St.Louis-AL	578	951

In 1933, total attendance in the majors fell to 6.3 million, the lowest it had been since the early 1900s.

In 1934, a few members of the Cincinnati Reds flew to a game in Chicago, the first major league teammates to travel together by air.

It Ain't Over
"You can't freeze the ball in this game. You have to play till the last man is out."
—Joe McCarthy

Chapter 7
The 1940s

Dynamic Giants Drive Dingers Downtown

In 1947, Mel Ott, the most prolific home run hitter in New York Giants history, retired as a player and turned his full attention to managing the Polo Grounds tenants. All that summer he watched from the dugout in amazement as his charges, lacking his booming bat for the first time in two decades, nevertheless set off on a home run spree that shattered every then-existing team single-season home run record. When the doors of the Polo Grounds finally closed for the 1947 campaign, the Giants had amassed 221 round-trippers, nearly a quarter of the 886 compiled by the entire National League. Leading the way was first sacker Johnny Mize, whose 51 four-baggers tied Pittsburgh's Ralph Kiner for the National League lead, followed by right fielder Willard Marshall (36), catcher Walker Cooper (35), and center fielder Bobby Thomson (29), who finished third, fourth, and fifth respectively in the NL homer derby. For all the power the Giants packed into their batting order in 1947, they could finish no better than fourth.

New York Giants teammates Johnny Mize and Willard Marshall in 1947 combined for 87 homers, setting an NL teammate tandem record.

1940s GAMES

1.	Bob Elliott	1,455
2.	Lou Boudreau	1,425
3.	Marty Marion	1,396
4.	Bill Nicholson	1,389
5.	Dixie Walker	1,363
6.	Eddie Miller	1,328
7.	Bobby Doerr	1,283
8.	Rudy York	1,259
9.	Frankie Gustine	1,230
10.	Phil Cavarretta	1,217
11.	Wally Moses	1,212
12.	George McQuinn	1,210
13.	Ken Keltner	1,209
14.	F. McCormick	1,191
15.	Luke Appling	1,188
16.	Joe Gordon	1,169
17.	Johnny Hopp	1,159
18.	Tommy Holmes	1,157
19.	Vern Stephens	1,154
20.	Stan Spence	1,112

Pittsburgh's Ralph Kiner in 1946 became the first rookie to lead the NL in homers, socking just 23.

Pirate outfielder Ralph Kiner in 1949 slugged 25 homers on the road, an NL record.

Las Vegas Stakes Prospects on 271 Jackpots

1940s RUNS

1. Ted Williams — 951
2. Stan Musial — 815
3. Bob Elliott — 803
4. Bobby Doerr — 764
5. Lou Boudreau — 758
6. Bill Nicholson — 743
7. Dom DiMaggio — 721
8. Vern Stephens — 708
9. Dixie Walker — 704
10. Joe DiMaggio — 684
11. Joe Gordon — 680
12. Tommy Henrich — 669
13. Phil Cavarretta — 664
14. Johnny Mize — 655
15. Rudy York — 653
16. Tommy Holmes — 651
17. Enos Slaughter — 650
18. Stan Hack — 639
19. Wally Moses — 635
20. George McQuinn — 626

As serious devotees of the game would expect, in 1947 there was a parallel in the minors to the New York Giants' home run binge. The Las Vegas team of the Sunset League clubbed a minor league record 271 four-baggers in 140 games and posted a .338 club batting average. Each of the team's eight regulars hit at least .303. All that firepower enabled Las Vegas to tally 1,261 runs, nine a game, but the team surrendered 1,235 markers and finished with a record of 73-67. The short-lived Sunset League was only one of several Southwestern circuits in the late 1940s that promoted high-scoring contests and provided a haven for hitters whose skills were just a shade below major league standards.

The first National Leaguer to clout 50 or more home runs in a season twice was Ralph Kiner, who accomplished it in 1947 and 1949.

The 1947 New York Giants swatted an NL-record 221 homers.

Lloyd Waner in 1941 played an NL-record 77 straight games without striking out.

Stan Musial, with 429 total bases in 1948, is the only player to top 420 total bases in a season since 1930.

All Business

Robert Smith wrote about Joe DiMaggio: "He never offered the appearance of either gaiety, or anger, or tremendous effort. His smile was self-conscious, his manner withdrawn to the point of a chill."

Crusher Crues Drives 254 Home

Prominent among the minor league loops that became a cradle for sluggers in the years immediately after World War II was the West Texas-New Mexico League. In 1948, Bob Crues, an outfielder with the Amarillo entry, hammered 69 home runs and rang up an all-time professional record 254 RBI. Crues in 1948 was 30 years old and playing his seventh successive season in the circuit, with three years out for military duty during the war. Prior to his service interruption, Crues had been a pitcher and had notched just two home runs and 32 RBI in his first four professional seasons.

During Ted Williams's first spring training with the Red Sox, Bobby Doerr told Ted to wait until he'd seen Jimmie Foxx hit. Ever confident, Williams responded: "Wait'll Foxx sees me hit."

1940s HITS

1. Lou Boudreau	1,578
2. Bob Elliott	1,563
3. Dixie Walker	1,512
4. Stan Musial	1,432
5. Bobby Doerr	1,407
6. Tommy Holmes	1,402
7. Luke Appling	1,376
8. Bill Nicholson	1,328
9. Marty Marion	1,310
10. Phil Cavarretta	1,304
11. Ted Williams	1,303
12. Vern Stephens	1,290
13. Rudy York	1,266
14. F. McCormick	1,261
15. Ken Keltner	1,211
16. Wally Moses	1,205
17. Frankie Gustine	1,198
18. Enos Slaughter	1,190
19. George McQuinn	1,171
20. Joe Gordon	1,165

Above: *Shortstop Lou Boudreau was named player-manager of the Indians at age 25. He paced the AL in fielding percentage eight times and batted as high as .355. In 1948, Boudreau guided Cleveland to the AL crown and won the MVP award.*

Williams, Stephens Set Duo Ribbie Record

In 1949, Ted Williams and Vern Stephens of the Boston Red Sox collected the most RBI of any pair of teammates since World War II, when they tied for the American League ribbie crown with 159 apiece. Stephens in addition set a still-existing record for the most RBI by a shortstop. His 39 home runs also established a mark for shortfielders that was later broken by Ernie Banks. Although always a slugger of the first order, Stephens did not really emerge as an RBI threat until he joined the Red Sox in 1948 after an off-season trade freed him from the lowly St. Louis Browns. With Dom DiMaggio and Johnny Pesky, solid .300 hitters, batting ahead of him, and the specter of Ted Williams following him in the Red Sox batting order, Stephens was usually assured of both coming to the plate with men on base and seeing good pitches to hit. In 1950, with rookie slugger Walt Dropo added to the Red Sox cast, Stephens again tied for the AL RBI lead with 144.

Ink By the Barrel

John Lardner wrote of Ted Williams: "By the time the press of Boston has completed its daily treatment of Theodore S. Williams, there is no room in the papers for anything but two sticks of agate type about Truman and housing, and one column for the last Boston girl to be murdered on a beach."

Hank Greenberg returned from the service on July 1, 1945, and slugged a grand slam on the season's final day to clinch a pennant for Detroit.

First sacker Eddie Robinson was the only member of the Indians infield in 1948 who totaled less than 100 RBI.

1940s DOUBLES

1.	Lou Boudreau	339
2.	Stan Musial	302
3.	Dixie Walker	291
	Bob Elliott	291
5.	Bobby Doerr	272
6.	Ted Williams	270
7.	Tommy Holmes	269
8.	Wally Moses	252
9.	Marty Marion	251
10.	Frank McCormick	246
11.	Bill Nicholson	241
	Phil Cavarretta	241
13.	Eddie Miller	240
	Ken Keltner	240
15.	George McQuinn	233
16.	Rudy York	230
17.	Mickey Vernon	224
	Dom DiMaggio	224
19.	Frankie Gustine	218
20.	Jeff Heath	213

Joe McCarthy said that Joe DiMaggio was "the best baserunner I ever saw. He could have stolen 50, 60 bases a year if I had let him. He wasn't the fastest man alive. He just knew how to run the bases better than anybody. I don't think in all the years [he] played for me he was ever thrown out stretching."

Fritz Ostermueller explained why teammate Ralph Kiner didn't choke up on the bat with two strikes on him: "Cadillacs are down at the end of the bat."

1940s TRIPLES

1.	Stan Musial	108
2.	Enos Slaughter	84
3.	Bob Elliott	80
4.	Jeff Heath	70
	Phil Cavarretta	70
6.	Johnny Hopp	68
	Joe DiMaggio	68
8.	Snuffy Stirnweiss	66
	Bobby Doerr	66
10.	Wally Moses	63
	Charlie Keller	63
12.	Stan Spence	60
13.	Lou Boudreau	59
14.	Dixie Walker	56
	Mickey Vernon	56
16.	Barney McCosky	54
17.	Bill Nicholson	51
18.	Jim Russell	49
	Buddy Lewis	49
	Ken Keltner	49
	Tommy Henrich	49

In 1949, Cincinnati's Virgil Stallcup received just nine walks in 575 at bats.

Joltin' Joe Compiles 56-Game Hitting Streak

Joe DiMaggio was the antithesis of a streaky ballplayer, yet he had an aptitude for batting streaks. Immediately after his major league record 56-game hitting streak in 1941, he started in on a 16-game streak. In 1933, he put together a 61-game hitting streak in the Pacific Coast League. DiMaggio started his infamous major league streak with a scratch single off the White Sox' Eddie Smith on May 15. By the time DiMaggio tied George Sisler's 1922 AL record 41, he was a national sensation. On July 2, DiMaggio homered off Boston's Dick Newsome to move past the major league record of 44 games set by Wee Willie Keeler in 1897. Two weeks later, 67,468 Cleveland fans saw the streak come to an end. Twice, third baseman Ken Keltner made sparkling plays on DiMaggio drives down the line. Joltin' Joe made four hits in a game only four times and 34 times kept the streak alive with a single hit.

Seery's Strikeout Sums Not Endearing

In the 1940s, a hitter who struck out 100 times in a season was still something of a rarity. The emphasis on making contact caused a serious problem for Cleveland outfielder Pat Seerey. After topping the AL in strikeouts for three successive seasons, Seerey was reduced to a part-time role in 1947. When he fanned 66 times in just 216 at bats and hit .171, he was dealt to the White Sox early in '48. Although Seerey got into only 103 games and batted less than 400 times, he still collected 102 Ks to regain his unwanted crown as the game's whiff king. However, on July 18, 1948, some two months after his trade to the White Sox, Seerey became only the second player in AL history to blast four homers in a game (in 11 innings). When his four-bagger binge only resulted in 19 homers for the season to go with his .231 batting average and 102 strikeouts, however, Seerey was released by Chicago early in 1949 and never played in the majors again. One might compare Seerey's 1948 stats, which were judged too skimpy to merit continued major league status, to those produced in 1991 by Rob Deer, who retained his job as a regular Detroit gardener for 1992.

	AB	H	R	HR	RBI	SO	BA	SA	OBP
Seerey	363	84	51	19	70	102	.231	.419	.353
Deer	448	80	64	25	64	175	.179	.386	.314

1940s HOME RUNS

1. Ted Williams 234
2. Johnny Mize 217
3. Bill Nicholson 211
4. Rudy York 189
5. Joe Gordon 181
6. Joe DiMaggio 180
7. Vern Stephens 177
8. Charlie Keller 173
9. Ralph Kiner 168
10. Bobby Doerr 164
11. Jeff Heath 158
12. Stan Musial 146
13. Mel Ott 142
14. Tommy Henrich 138
15. Hank Greenberg 125
16. Ken Keltner 124
17. Sam Chapman 119
18. Bob Elliott 109
    Walker Cooper 109
20. Whitey Kurowski 106

In 1941, Brooklyn's outfield trio of Pete Reiser, Joe Medwick, and Dixie Walker all finished among the top-10 hitters in the National League.

Cleveland's Joe Gordon in 1948 slugged an AL record 32 homers by a second baseman.

Vernon Snatches Two Crowns

In 1946, Washington first sacker Mickey Vernon returned from a two-year military hitch to lead the AL in hitting with a .353 batting average. Prior to World War II, Vernon had done nothing in his five seasons with the Senators to suggest that he was a potential .300 hitter, let alone a future batting titlist, so fans in the nation's Capital were both pleasantly surprised and naturally hopeful that Vernon had somehow matured unexpectedly as a hitter during his service interruption. Instead, he slipped to a .265 average in 1947 and then hit .242 the following year with just 48 RBI in 558 at bats. Approaching his 35th birthday, it seemed certain that his 1946 season had been an inexplicable aberration. Vernon then proceeded to hit .337 in 1953 and snatch his second AL bat crown. He retired in 1960 with a .286 career batting average, the lowest to that point by a two-time bat titlist.

Dale Mitchell's 23 triples for Cleveland in 1949 are the most since 1930.

1940s RUNS BATTED IN

1.	Bob Elliott	903
2.	Ted Williams	893
3.	Bobby Doerr	887
4.	Rudy York	854
5.	Bill Nicholson	835
6.	Vern Stephens	824
7.	Joe DiMaggio	786
8.	Dixie Walker	759
9.	Johnny Mize	744
10.	Joe Gordon	710
11.	Stan Musial	706
12.	Frank McCormick	703
13.	Lou Boudreau	692
14.	Jeff Heath	690
15.	Enos Slaughter	649
16.	Charlie Keller	640
17.	Ken Keltner	639
18.	George McQuinn	605
19.	Phil Cavarretta	598
20.	Eddie Miller	582

Sportswriter Jimmy Powers penned about Jackie Robinson as a rookie: "Robinson will not make the grade in the major leagues. He is a thousand-to-one shot at best. The Negro players simply don't have the brains or the skills."

In 1945, Eddie Stanky set a National League record for walks with 148.

Cleveland outfielder Jeff Heath was the first player in AL history to hit at least 20 homers, 20 triples, and 20 doubles in a season.

In 1947, Roy Cullenbine of Detroit set an all-time record for the most walks by a player in his final season when he amassed 137 free passes.

> "If I had my career to play over, one thing I'd do differently is swing more. Those 1,200 walks I got, nobody remembers them."
> —Pee Wee Reese

The Boston Red Sox in 1949 collected a major league record 835 walks.

Kell Edges Williams's Triple Crown Bid

All during the 1949 campaign, Ted Williams had his sights set on becoming the first player in major league history to bag three Triple Crowns. True, he was being chased hard by teammate Vern Stephens for slugging honors and by Detroit's George Kell for the batting title, but neither Stephens nor Kell was a hitter of Williams's caliber and hence both were expected to fade in the late going. Stephens hung unexpectedly tough, however, finally surrendering the home run crown to Williams 43 to 39, but tying his much more highly regarded Red Sox teammate in RBI with 159. Kell meanwhile proved to be even harder for Williams to shake. When the final batting averages were calculated, both Williams and the Detroit third baseman finished with identical .343 marks, but Kell won out by .00016 of a point. Besides homers and RBI, The Thumper led the AL that year in runs (150), doubles (39), total bases (368), walks (162), on-base percentage (.490), and slugging average (.650).

1940s STOLEN BASES

1.	George Case	285
2.	Snuffy Stirnweiss	130
3.	Wally Moses	126
4.	Johnny Hopp	117
5.	Mickey Vernon	108
	Pee Wee Reese	108
7.	Joe Kuhel	93
8.	Luke Appling	91
9.	Bob Dillinger	90
10.	Jackie Robinson	88
11.	Phil Rizzuto	85
12.	Pete Reiser	81
13.	Thurman Tucker	76
14.	Dom DiMaggio	75
15.	Don Kolloway	73
16.	Johnny Barrett	69
17.	Gee Walker	65
	Stan Hack	65
19.	Joe Gordon	63
20.	Lonny Frey	62

The last batter to lead his loop in strikeouts with fewer than 90 was Hank Sauer, who marked 85 in 1948.

Homer Leader Holmes Has Few Fans

At the beginning of the 1945 season, the Boston Braves had possessed just three National League home run champions since 1900. When the season closed, the Braves for the only time in this century prior to their move to Milwaukee had the top two home run hitters in the senior loop. Outfielder Tommy Holmes slugged 28 round-trippers and third sacker Chuck Workman was the runner-up with 25. Holmes also led the NL in total bases, slugging average, hits, and doubles, but perhaps the most significant offensive department he headed was the fewest strikeouts by a regular player. By fanning just nine times in 636 at bats, Holmes became the only player since the end of the dead-ball era to lead his league in both home runs and fewest Ks. In 1947, he led the league with 191 hits, and he fanned just 16 times in 618 at bats. Holmes currently stands fourth on the list of the hardest batters in this century for pitchers to strike out; he fanned 122 times in 4,992 at bats, and he compiled a .302 batting average.

Tommy Holmes, whose single won the 1948 World Series opener 1-0, whenever he was asked about the famous pickoff play in the game: "Never mind that; let's talk about who got the hit."

In 1945, Tommy Holmes became the only player ever to lead the National League in homers (28) and fewest batter strikeouts (nine).

Boston's Tommy Holmes safely hit in 37 consecutive games in 1945, setting a modern NL record.

The 1943 American League had only three .300 hitters and only five above .290.

1940s BATTING AVERAGE

1. Ted Williams		.356
2. Stan Musial		.346
3. Joe DiMaggio		.325
4. Barney McCosky		.321
5. Johnny Pesky		.316
6. Enos Slaughter		.312
7. Luke Appling		.312
8. Dixie Walker		.311
9. Taffy Wright		.308
10. George Kell		.305
11. Joe Medwick		.305
12. Tommy Holmes		.304
13. Johnny Mize		.304
14. Stan Hack		.303
15. Pete Reiser		.303
16. Harry Walker		.302
17. Phil Cavarretta		.301
18. Lou Boudreau		.300
19. Johnny Hopp		.295
20. Dom DiMaggio		.294

Above: *Ted Williams dominated in the 1940s. Despite missing three years to the war, he captured four homer crowns, six runs scored titles and led the AL in batting four times.*

There's No 'K' in 'Slugger'

With the exception of his magnificent 1945 season, Tommy Holmes was never among the slugging leaders, but several other home run kings of his era were nearly as difficult to fan. Ted Williams and Mel Ott are the only two members of the 500-home run club who finished with fewer than 1,000 career strikeouts. Williams fanned just 709 times in 7,706 at bats and never more than 64 times in a season. In 1941, he had 37 home runs and 27 strikeouts. In 9,456 at bats, Ott went down on strikes 896 times with a high of 69 in 1937. In 1929, Ott had 42 homers and 38 Ks. Both Ott and Williams were free-swingers, however, compared to Joe DiMaggio. When he won his second homer crown in 1948 with 39 round-trippers, he fanned a mere 30 times. DiMaggio is the only slugger who has more than 300 career home runs (361) and fewer than 500 career strikeouts (369).

Boston's Ted Williams was the only player in American League history to win two Triple Crowns; he turned the trick in 1942 and 1947.

Snuffy Stirnweiss, who was a .219 hitter in 1943, led the major leagues in 1944 with 205 hits.

In 1943, Mel Ott of the Giants was runner-up for the National League home run crown with 18 four-baggers, all of which were hit in his home park, the Polo Grounds.

Win One For the Gina

"When you win, you eat better, sleep better, and your beer tastes better. And your wife looks like Gina Lollobrigida."
—Johnny Pesky

Darned Sox Duo Ditched After Title Try

In 1945, circumstances conspired to produce the oddest batting race in American League history. At the top with a .309 average when the season closed was second baseman Snuffy Stirnweiss of the New York Yankees. Behind Stirnweiss were a pair of Chicago White Sox retreads, third baseman Tony Cuccinello and outfielder Johnny Dickshot. The trio were the only three AL batting title qualifiers to hit .300 in 1945, owing to the absence of many of the era's leading stars and the slightly deader brand of ball that was employed during the war years. Stirnweiss was an all-around offensive threat in 1945—he also led the loop in stolen bases, triples, and slugging average—but Cuccinello and Dickshot had little more than their batting averages to recommend them. So little in fact that despite vying all season for the batting title each was released by the White Sox soon after the curtain descended on the last wartime campaign and never played another inning in the majors.

The record for the lowest career batting average by a major league bat crown winner belongs to Snuffy Stirnweiss, who won the AL title in 1945 and retired with a .268 batting average.

Forty-year-old catcher Jimmy Wilson, playing for the injured Enos Slaughter in the 1940 World Series, wound up being the hitting star, as he batted .353.

The 1943 AL had only three .300 hitters and only five above .290.

In 1945, the Washington Senators hit only one four-bagger at home all season, an inside-the-park blow by Joe Kuhel.

Legs Diamond

"I think the game of baseball is just like any other sport, in that you've got to keep your legs in shape. I was able to play for so many years because I took care of my legs."
—Enos Slaughter

Enos Slaughter, when told by a doctor prior to game six of the 1946 World Series that his arm was so badly injured he risked having it amputated if he tried to play that day, responded: "Doc, I guess we'll have to take that gamble."

Detroit rookie Chuck Hostetler, age 41, in 1944 batted .298 in 90 games.

Above: *Cardinals outfielder Enos "Country" Slaughter lost three prime years to World War II but still hit .300 six times during the 1940s. His all-around hustle made him a valuable player.*

War Talent Shortage Launches Stars

Snuffy Stirnweiss was far from the only good player who was shot to greatness during the war years largely by dint of not being summoned for military duty. Nick Etten, a 4-F first baseman for the Yankees with no particular slugging credentials prior to the war, led the AL in home runs in 1944 and RBI the following year. Tigers' bonus baby Dick Wakefield hacked out a .316 batting average and an AL-leading 200 hits as a rookie in 1943 before receiving a service call-up. He then knocked .355 in half a season the following year when he was temporarily released from military duty. Yet many prewar stars, such as Mel Ott, who might have been expected to thrive on pitching staffs that had been diluted by the draft, barely held their own. After leading the NL in home runs in 1942, Ott (then age 34) plummeted to a .234 batting average and just 47 RBI in 1943, the first year that the game was severely impaired by the war effort. He rebounded to 26 and 21 homers in '44 and '45.

1940s GAMES PITCHED

1.	Hal Newhouser	377
2.	Dizzy Trout	374
3.	Kirby Higbe	354
	Harry Gumbert	354
5.	Rip Sewell	316
6.	Clyde Shoun	315
7.	Bobo Newsom	302
	Ace Adams	302
9.	Dutch Leonard	294
10.	Hugh Casey	290
11.	Bob Muncrief	283
12.	Al Benton	280
13.	Joe Haynes	277
14.	Nels Potter	272
15.	Bob Feller	266
16.	Hank Borowy	261
17.	Claude Passeau	258
	Joe Dobson	258
19.	Murry Dickson	248
20.	Ted Wilks	247
	Allie Reynolds	247

Hal Newhouser's 29 wins in 1944 were the most since 1931 by a major league lefty.

Newhouser Top Hurler, Wartime or No

Until 1992, Hal Newhouser was judged unworthy of Hall of Fame selection because he was considered by many panelists to be little more than a wartime fluke who won 29 games in 1944, 25 games in 1945, and then subsequently did little to recommend himself once all the other top-flight pitchers of the era returned from military stints. The fact is, Newhouser led the American League in victories twice after the war and went on to win more games during the decade of the 1940s than any other hurler. In addition, Newhouser was second only to Bob Feller among the game's strikeout artists in the years immediately following the war. When he notched 275 strikeouts in 1946, the first postwar season, it was the highest total by a southpaw since 1905. He was 26-9 that year, and 21-12 in 1948. Everything points to Newhouser being an outstanding pitcher whose peak seasons happened to dovetail with World War II rather than a wartime fluke.

Hal Newhouser in 1946 led the major leagues in ERA (1.94), and was second in AL MVP voting.

In 1946, the New York Giants hit 121 home runs, 40 more than any other National League team, but finished in last place.

Give 'Em the Ball
"You don't save a pitcher for tomorrow. Tomorrow it might rain."
—Leo Durocher

Giant reliever Ace Adams in 1943 appeared in 70 games, a modern mound record.

On May 12, 1941, Lefty Grove of the Red Sox became the only pitcher ever to win 20 consecutive games in his home park.

On September 27, 1940, the last game of the season, Detroit no-name hurler Floyd Giebell beat Cleveland's Bob Feller 2-0 to clinch the flag by a single game for the Tigers over the Tribe.

Reiser Injures Chance at Excellence

No one will ever know how great a player Pete Reiser might have been if he had not had a penchant for bringing his body into bone-shattering contact with pitched balls and outfield walls. The sports pages during the 1940s seemed constantly to be running photos of Reiser either lying in a heap after colliding with a concrete barrier or being hauled off the field on a stretcher after he was decked by an inside fastball. In 1941, though, his only full injury-free season in the majors, Reiser was something extraordinary. At age 22, he became the youngest batting titlist in National League history when he took the loop crown with a .343 average. Reiser also paced the senior circuit that year in doubles (39), triples (17), runs (117), and slugging percentage (.558)—spurring the Brooklyn Dodgers to their first pennant since 1920. Injuries then prevented him from ever again playing more than 125 games in a season.

In 1941, Lefty Grove became the last hurler until 1963 to win 300 career games.

1940s GAMES STARTED

1.	Hal Newhouser	305
2.	Dutch Leonard	274
3.	Bobo Newsom	261
4.	Dizzy Trout	239
5.	Bucky Walters	238
6.	Rip Sewell	231
	Bob Feller	231
8.	J. Vander Meer	219
9.	Mort Cooper	210
10.	Hank Borowy	208
11.	Claude Passeau	207
	Kirby Higbe	207
13.	Tiny Bonham	193
14.	Allie Reynolds	192
15.	Early Wynn	188
16.	Bill Voiselle	183
	Sid Hudson	183
	Denny Galehouse	183
19.	Joe Dobson	182
20.	Bill Lee	178

Two Years Cement Page's Standing

When Joe Page won 14 games and collected 17 saves in 1947 as the Yankees' bullpen ace, he was nicknamed "Fireman" because he brought to mind Johnny Murphy, the stopper whose job he inherited. But Page's postgame escapades were such that he was soon dubbed "The Gay Reliever." His lax approach to conditioning contributed to a poor season in 1948 and probably cost the Yankees the American League pennant. The following year, though, Page recovered his 1947 wizardry and bagged 27 saves to set a record that lasted until 1961 when expansion lengthened the schedule to 162 games. The Gay Reliever then succumbed to his old ways, stumbling so badly in 1950 that he was released by the Yankees at the season's end and left to struggle for the rest of his career in the minors except for a brief and abortive comeback in 1954 with the Pittsburgh Pirates. Page's reputation thus was based almost entirely on his work in two seasons — 1947 and 1949—but no other reliever during the 1940s had even one season nearly as good.

1940s COMPLETE GAMES	
1. Hal Newhouser	181
2. Bob Feller	155
3. Bucky Walters	153
4. Dutch Leonard	139
5. Dizzy Trout	132
Rip Sewell	132
7. Claude Passeau	130
8. Jim Tobin	127
9. Mort Cooper	120
10. Bobo Newsom	115
11. Tiny Bonham	110
12. J. Vander Meer	103
13. Harry Brecheen	101
14. Ed Lopat	99
Tex Hughson	99
16. Early Wynn	97
Thornton Lee	97
18. Hank Borowy	93
19. Johnny Sain	90
20. Spud Chandler	89

Cleveland hurler Bob Feller's 261 strikeouts in 1940 were the most by any pitcher in a major league since 1924.

New York Giant hurler Dave Koslo led the 1949 senior circuit in ERA (2.50)—he became the first loop leader without a shutout.

Young At Heart
"Age is a question of mind over matter. If you don't mind it doesn't matter."
—Satchel Paige

Between the end of the dead-ball era (1920) and expansion (1961), George Uhle (1922, 1923) and Bob Feller (1941, 1946) were the only two pitchers to start 40 or more games in a season twice during their careers.

In '49, Parnell and Kinder had a 48-13 record for Boston. The club's other pitchers were 48-45.

In 1945, Philadelphia Phillie hurler Andy Karl pitched 167 innings in relief to set a National League record that lasted until 1974.

Tribe moundsman Bob Feller pitched the only AL Opening Day no-hitter in history on April 16, 1940, against the Chicago White Sox.

Ace Adams of the Giants was the first hurler in the 20th century to appear in 60 or more games for three consecutive years.

In 1945, Dick Fowler of the A's notched the first no-hitter in more than five years by an AL hurler.

Adams Aces to 65 Games Per Season

Prior to the early 1940s, relief specialists seldom worked more than once every third day or so, but in 1942 Ace Adams of the New York Giants became the first bullpenner to change the notion of how often a stopper could be used and still maintain his effectiveness. In the four seasons between 1942 and 1945, Adams appeared in 261 games, an average of 65 a season. As Adams's career was winding to a close, Andy Karl of the Phillies in 1945 logged 167 relief innings, a record that lasted until Mike Marshall appeared on the scene. After the war, however, the manner in which relievers were used reverted for a time to the previous standard. In 1949, for example, Ted Wilks of the Cardinals and Jim Konstanty of the Phils were the only two National League firemen to work more than 50 games, and they finished one-two in saves with the rather inauspicious totals of nine and seven respectively.

Southworth Stays Sain, Whereas Slogan Spahns Story

The Boston Braves' slogan in 1948 of "Spahn and Sain and pray for rain" made for a good story but took some liberties with the facts. One would think that Braves had only two starting pitchers of any worth that year, Warren Spahn and Johnny Sain. In actuality, rookie righthander Vern Bickford had a fine 11-5 record for the 1948 Braves and Bill Voiselle labored 213 innings and collected 13 wins, only two less than Spahn. And a fifth hurler, Nels Potter, a midseason arrival, was nominated by Braves manager Billy Southworth to start the key fifth game of the World Series against Cleveland when a loss would have knocked Boston out of the postseason picture. Closer to the truth perhaps would have been a slogan that began and ended with Sain, who in 1948 led the National League in wins, innings, and complete games and was third in ERA. Spahn, in contrast, had a 3.71 ERA, the poorest on the club among pitchers in a minimum of 10 decisions or 75 innings.

White Sox Ted Lyons compiled a 14-6 mark in 1942, as he made just 20 mound appearances, all of them complete games.

1940s SHUTOUTS

1.	Hal Newhouser	31
	Mort Cooper	31
3.	Bucky Walters	28
	Bob Feller	28
5.	Dizzy Trout	27
6.	Johnny Vander Meer	26
7.	Dutch Leonard	23
8.	Spud Chandler	22
	Harry Brecheen	22
10.	Claude Passeau	21
	Tiny Bonham	21
12.	Rip Sewell	19
	Bobo Newsom	19
	Tex Hughson	19
15.	Howie Pollet	18
16.	Joe Dobson	17
17.	Allie Reynolds	16
	Max Lanier	16
	Ken Heintzelman	16
	Hank Borowy	16

Bill Dickey, commenting on Hal Newhouser, said: "As far as the Yankees are concerned, we'd rather face anyone else."

Giants rookie Bill Voiselle in 1944 was the last rookie in major league history to pitch 300 or more innngs as he worked 313.

1940s WINS

1.	Hal Newhouser	170
2.	Bob Feller	137
3.	Rip Sewell	133
4.	Dizzy Trout	129
5.	Bucky Walters	122
	Dutch Leonard	122
7.	Mort Cooper	114
8.	Claude Passeau	111
9.	Bobo Newsom	105
	Kirby Higbe	105
	Harry Brecheen	105
12.	Hank Borowy	104
13.	Allie Reynolds	103
	Tiny Bonham	103
15.	Tex Hughson	96
16.	Joe Dobson	94
17.	J. Vander Meer	93
18.	Harry Gumbert	88
19.	Virgil Trucks	87
20.	Spud Chandler	85

The 1944 Detroit Tigers are the last team to date to fail to win a pennant despite having two 25-game winners— Hal Newhouser (29) and Dizzy Trout (27). Their tandem record of 56 wins was a record for teammates after the dead-ball era.

McCarthy Maximizes Parnell, Kinder

In 1949, the Boston Red Sox seemed to borrow a page from their fellow Hub entry as they chased the Yankees all season for the American League pennant before succumbing at the wire. During the final weeks of the season, BoSox manager Joe McCarthy started his twin mound aces Mel Parnell and Ellis Kinder at every opportunity and also had no hesitation about calling on them in relief. As a result, Parnell not only led the American League with 25 wins, 295 innings, and a 2.77 ERA, but he notched two saves and came out of the bullpen on several other occasions late in the campaign. Kinder meanwhile won 23 games and topped the AL with a .793 winning percentage at age 35 but still found the strength to relieve in 13 contests and collect four saves. Between them Parnell and Kinder accounted for exactly half of the BoSox 96 wins. Joe Dobson (14) and Chuck Stobbs (11) were the club's only other hurlers to win more than six.

Howie Krist of the Cardinals set a National League record for the most wins by a pitcher without a loss when he was 10-0 in 1941.

The first pinch home run in World Series history was slugged by Yogi Berra in 1947.

Paige Produces More Than Publicity

When Cleveland owner Bill Veeck inked Satchel Paige to an Indians' contract during the 1948 campaign, his fellow magnates thought it was another of his publicity stunts. The Negro League great was then at least 42 years old, and many believed his true age was closer to 50. In any case, Paige was not expected to provide much more than a couple of relief innings here and there, usually in a lost cause. Veeck, though, had another plan. He saw Paige as still having the wherewithal to serve as a starter, and he was right. Facing the Chicago White Sox in his first major league start, Paige became the first black hurler to throw a shutout. That October, in game five of the World Series, he became the first black to pitch in a fall classic when he gave Cleveland manager Lou Boudreau a perfect relief stint. At the close of the 1948 season, the oldest rookie ever to that point had a 6-1 record and two shutouts to go with his snappy 2.48 ERA in 21 mound appearances.

Legendary Negro League pitcher Satchel Paige (above) didn't reach the majors until into his 40s. Paige, who many consider the greatest hurler ever, collected 12 wins for the seventh-place 1952 St. Louis Browns at age 46.

1940s INNINGS

1.	Hal Newhouser	2,453.1
2.	Dutch Leonard	2,047.1
3.	Dizzy Trout	2,026.1
4.	Bobo Newsom	1,961.1
5.	Bob Feller	1,897.0
6.	Rip Sewell	1,894.0
7.	Bucky Walters	1,868.1
8.	Claude Passeau	1,693.2
9.	Kirby Higbe	1,692.2
10.	Hank Borowy	1,607.1
11.	Mort Cooper	1,606.1
12.	J. Vander Meer	1,589.1
13.	Tiny Bonham	1,551.0
14.	Allie Reynolds	1,484.0
15.	Joe Dobson	1,434.2
16.	Jim Tobin	1,426.1
17.	Early Wynn	1,411.0
18.	Bob Muncrief	1,393.1
19.	Harry Brecheen	1,388.0
20.	Jim Bagby	1,387.2

1940s STRIKEOUTS

1. Hal Newhouser	1,579
2. Bob Feller	1,396
3. Bobo Newsom	1,070
4. J. Vander Meer	972
5. Dizzy Trout	930
6. Kirby Higbe	853
7. Allie Reynolds	791
8. Dutch Leonard	779
9. Mort Cooper	772
10. Virgil Trucks	760
11. Tex Hughson	693
12. Bucky Walters	677
13. Harry Brecheen	666
14. Joe Dobson	665
15. Hank Borowy	650
16. Claude Passeau	646
17. Nels Potter	644
18. Bill Voiselle	620
19. Johnny Niggeling	599
20. Max Lanier	588

The 1944 season was the first since 1915 in which two National League pitchers hurled no-hitters in two different games.

Newcombe Debuts in '49, Wins Rookie Prize

In 1949, for the second time in three seasons, the Brooklyn Dodgers unveiled a black Rookie of the Year Award winner when Don Newcombe debuted with a 17-8 mark and a National League-leading five shutouts. He had 19 complete games in 31 starts, and he also notched a save. Newk began the 1949 campaign with Montreal, the Dodgers' International League affiliate, before being called up to the parent club in May. Soon after his arrival, he became the mainstay of Brooklyn's mound staff, a role he would continue to serve until the team moved to Los Angeles. Newcombe was on the rubber in most of the key games Brooklyn played during his career. It was he who was relieved by Ralph Branca moments before Bobby Thomson hit "The Shot Heard 'Round the World" in 1951. The previous season, Newcombe had been positioned to win his 20th game and bring the Dodgers into a tie for first place with the Phillies on the final day of the campaign before Richie Ashburn of the Phils cut down the pennant-tying run at the plate.

Fireman
Casey Stengel said reliever Joe Page "could get the fire out quick. He just came in and blasted the ball in there."

Cardinals reliever Ted Wilks had a perfect 10-0 record over a two-season span (1946 and 1947).

"In USA Today I was voted one of the 21 all-time hardest throwers. But I would trade it all to have had great control. The thing I'll think about all my life—the frustrating thing—is what that lack of control cost me. Bull on that throwing hard."
—Rex Barney, whose wildness cost him what could have been a remarkable career

Cincinnati pitcher Bucky Walters led the National League in both innings (302) and complete games (27) for three straight years, from 1939 to 1941.

On June 22, 1947, Ewell Blackwell was only two outs away from registering his second consecutive no-hitter when he surrendered a single to Eddie Stanky of the Dodgers.

Harry Brecheen, the winner of three games in the '46 World Series, had a 15-15 record for the Cards during the regular season.

Pale Hose Procure Experienced Pitchers

Ted Lyons was appointed manager of the Chicago White Sox when he returned to the game in 1946 following a three-year military commitment. The Sox career leader in wins, Lyons rallied his 45-year-old arm to make five starts and post a 2.32 ERA before retiring to strictly a dugout role. His performance, however, convinced him that life in the major leagues didn't necessarily end at the age of 40. In 1947, Lyons accordingly designated the 42-year-old Earl Caldwell as his bullpen ace and encouraged the Sox to sign 43-year-old Red Ruffing, who had been released by the Yankees after the 1946 season. Joining Caldwell and Ruffing on Lyons's pitching staff in 1947 was 41-year-old Thornton Lee. The trio made the Pale Hose the first team in major league history with three hurlers who were beyond their 40th birthdays. Lyons himself nearly made a fourth before deciding not to mount a comeback bid in 1947. That season, while Caldwell notched eight saves, Lee was 3-7 and Ruffing was only 3-5.

Bearden Brings Tribe Banner

Going into the final day of the 1948 season, Cleveland needed only to beat Detroit that afternoon to clinch the Tribe's first pennant since 1920. When Tigers ace Hal Newhouser knocked off the Tribe, though, it put Cleveland into a tie with the Boston Red Sox and necessitated the first pennant playoff game in AL history. A coin flip determined that the game would be played in Boston's Fenway Park, the bane of southpaws. When Cleveland player-manager Lou Boudreau named rookie lefty Gene Bearden the Tribe's starter in the do-or-die game, everyone doubted his sanity. Bearden made a genius of Boudreau by taming Boston with his knuckleball and becoming the only pitcher ever to attain his 20th win after the season's regulation closing date. He lost only eight games that year, while giving up 106 walks in 230 innings. A subsequent inability to control his butterfly pitch prevented Bearden from ever again winning more than eight games in a season, but for that one year he was gold.

1940s EARNED RUN AVERAGE

1.	Spud Chandler	2.67
2.	Max Lanier	2.68
3.	Harry Brecheen	2.74
4.	Hal Newhouser	2.84
5.	Bob Feller	2.90
6.	Mort Cooper	2.93
7.	Claude Passeau	2.94
8.	Tex Hughson	2.94
9.	Bucky Walters	2.97
10.	Howie Pollet	2.99
11.	Dizzy Trout	3.01
12.	Hank Wyse	3.03
13.	Whit Wyatt	3.04
14.	Tiny Bonham	3.06
15.	Johnny Niggeling	3.12
16.	Thornton Lee	3.13
17.	Dutch Leonard	3.14
18.	Al Benton	3.16
19.	Ed Lopat	3.28
20.	Johnny Sain	3.28

On August 10, 1944, Red Barrett of the Boston Braves tossed a record low 58 pitches in a complete-game shutout.

The 1949 season was the last time until 1959 that two New York Yankees pitchers lost as many as 10 games.

Orbit

Don Newcombe explained as to the kind of pitch Tommy Henrich hit to beat him 1-0 in the opener of the 1949 World Series, calling it "A change of space."

War Inspires May-December Mound Staffs

Some nine months prior to Joe Nuxhall's major league debut, the Philadelphia A's hired Carl Scheib to finish out the 1943 season in mop-up roles. Scheib, at age 16, was the youngest pitcher ever to appear in an American League game. He lasted 11 seasons in the majors, notching a 45-65 record, before departing in 1954 at age 27. Many other fuzzy-cheeked performers who surfaced during the war years, however, were never seen again. By the end of the war, big league rosters were also dotted with grizzled oldsters such as Detroit's Chuck Hostetler. A career minor leaguer, the 40-year-old Hostetler had been playing semi-pro ball when the Tigers signed him in 1944, making him the oldest rookie in history to that juncture. The pennant-bound St. Louis Browns, meanwhile, solidified their mound staff that same season with Sig Jakucki, out of the majors since 1936. He went 13-9 in '44, helping to secure the Browns flag. The following year, the Yankees activated batting practice pitcher Paul Schrieber, whose last major league appearance had been back in 1923.

In 1946, Bill Kennedy of Rocky Mount in the Coastal Plains League fanned 456 hitters and had a 28-3 record with a 1.03 ERA.

In 1941, Lefty Grove became only the second southpaw in major league history to win 300 games.

Whit Wyatt, a knockdown artist, revealed how to play the game: "You ought to play it mean. They ought to hate you on the field."

Floyd Giebell's final major league win was on September 27, 1940, when he clinched a flag for the Detroit Tigers.

Wes Ferrell retired in 1941 with a career record 38 homers by a pitcher.

In 1941, the New York Yankees amassed 101 victories despite having no hurlers who won more than 15 games.

In 1942, outfielder Danny Litwhiler of the Phils became the first player in major league history to field a perfect 1.000 over a full season.

The 1942 St. Louis Cardinals were the first team since 1923 to beat the New York Yankees in the World Series.

In 1942, shortstop Eddie Miller of the Braves had a .981 fielding average to break Everett Scott's old mark of .976, which had stood since 1919.

New York Yankees second baseman Joe Gordon and Shortstop Phil Rizzuto set an AL keystone record in 1942 when they totaled a combined 234 double plays.

George Ferrell, the elder brother of Wes and Rick Ferrell, concluded a 20-year career in the minors in 1945 with 2,876 hits and a .321 batting average.

The Cincinnati Reds in 1940 won their first untainted world championship.

In 1948, some three years after his 11-year major league career came to an end, Jake Powell shot himself to death in a Washington D.C. police station.

Delinquent Juvenile
Telling William Mead, baseball historian, of his big league debut at age 15, Joe Nuxhall said: "I walked five, gave up two hits and I think a wild pitch. I was just scared to death. Finally, [Bill] McKechnie just walked out and said, 'Well, son, I think you've had enough.'"

In 1946, Buddy Rosar of the A's became the only catcher ever to play more than 100 games behind the plate without making an error.

Gray Bats .218 in Bigs Despite Having One Arm

After Pete Gray was voted Most Valuable Player in the Southern Association in 1944, the St. Louis Browns raised eyebrows by purchasing his contract and announcing that he would compete for an outfield job with the club the following season. Normally a minor leaguer with Gray's credentials would have seemed a fitting addition, but Gray was no ordinary performer. He had only one arm, his left, having lost his right limb in a childhood accident. Gray quickly established that there was a vast difference in the quality of play between the minors and the majors, even in wartime. Because he had little power, swinging with just one arm, outfielders played him so shallow that he was frequently deprived of what would otherwise have been base hits. In the field, Gray needed extra time to remove his glove in order to throw after catching a ball, allowing runners to take liberties. He batted .218 in 77 games, and was returned to the minors during the season.

1940s CATCHER GAMES

1.	Mike Tresh	890
2.	Phil Masi	842
3.	Bob Swift	841
4.	Buddy Rosar	818
5.	Frankie Hayes	816

"Catching a fly ball is a pleasure, but knowing what to do with it after you catch it is a business."
—Tommy Henrich

Above: *Pete Gray in 1944 batted .333 with five homers in the Southern Association. He tied a loop record that year with 68 stolen bases.*

Wheels

"During the war years I ran more match races than anybody who ever put on a uniform. One year I ran five races for purses, and the only guy that ever beat me was Jesse Owens."
—George Case, stolen base king

Bert Shepard Pitches in Majors with Artificial Leg

Pete Gray remains the only one-armed position player in major league history, but there have been two one-armed pitchers—Hugh Daily during the 1880s and Jim Abbott in our own time—as well as numerous other hurlers who have functioned with deformed arms or missing digits. A one-legged player seemed an impossibility, though, at least until 1945. Before then, Monte Stratton, a White Sox pitcher who lost a leg to a hunting accident in the late 1930s, had been the only performer to make a serious attempt to compete in the professional game with an artificial leg. Bert Shepard was a former minor league pitcher turned Army Air Corps pilot who had a leg amputated after his plane was shot down over Germany in World War II; in 1945 he braved the odds to pitch for the Washington Senators in an August 14 game with the Boston Red Sox. In a five-inning relief stint, Shepard gave up only one run. Since the Senators were making one of their rare pennant bids that year, Shepard was not used again, but he later played in the minors.

Bob Considine wrote of Connie Mack in 1948: "When he signals for an obviously wrong move, Al Simmons [A's coach at the time] turns his back on the man . . . and calls for the right move."

1940s FIRST BASE GAMES

1. Rudy York	1,241
2. George McQuinn	1,189
3. Frank McCormick	1,119
4. Mickey Vernon	1,034
5. Johnny Mize	927

Lawrence Berra received the nickname "Yogi" as a youngster in St. Louis. One of his boyhood pals thought that Berra walked like a "yogi," who is someone who practices yoga.

"Leo Durocher is a man with an infinite capacity for immediately making a bad situation worse."
—Branch Rickey

"Nice guys finish last."
—Leo Durocher

Opportunities Expand in Postwar Game

Come the spring of 1946 the Joe Nuxhalls, the Paul Schriebers, and the Chuck Hostetlers were all gone from the major league scene now that the war was over. Missing stars like Joe DiMaggio, Bob Feller, Ted Williams, and Stan Musial had returned from military duty. Major league rosters for the only time in history were expanded from the 25-man limit to 30 so that as many experienced players as possible could be accommodated. The minor leagues too swelled to record proportions, increasing to 43 circuits. Given a sudden wealth of openings, many returning war veterans who might otherwise have either chosen to pass up the game or else been denied an opportunity to find their way in it fashioned long and successful careers in professional baseball.

"Baseball is a game of inches."
—Branch Rickey

Jackie Robinson's 37 stolen bases in '49 were the most since 1930 by an NL performer.

"Prefer the errors of enthusiasm to the complacency of wisdom."
—Branch Rickey

Above: *Shortstop Pee Wee Reese (second from left) and second baseman Jackie Robinson (right) formed a star double-play combo for the powerful Brooklyn Dodgers in the late 1940s and 1950s.*

Dangerous Concoction

Chuck Connors, actor and former Dodgers first baseman, remembered Branch Rickey: "He had both players and money—and just didn't like to see the two mix."

1940s SECOND BASE GAMES	
1. Bobby Doerr	1,279
2. Joe Gordon	1,137
3. Eddie Stanky	833
4. Emil Verban	792
5. Ray Mack	752

Sportswriter Rud Rennie said about Lou Boudreau: "He can't run and his arm's no good, but he's the best shortstop in the game."

If Judy Johnson were white, he could name his price."
—Connie Mack

1940s THIRD BASE GAMES

1. Ken Keltner	1,188
2. Bob Elliott	985
3. Stan Hack	950
4. Whitey Kurowski	868
5. Jim Tabor	821

In 1940, Gabby Hartnett said: "If managers were given permission, there'd be a mad rush to sign up Negroes."

Mexican League Bandit Gardella Sues For Reinstatement

The postwar baseball boom was not without its share of obstacles. In 1946, the two major leagues faced the sternest challenge to their monopoly on the best professional players in the land since the Federal League ceased operation at the finish of the 1915 season. On this occasion the challenge came from south of the border. Mexican League entrepreneur Jorge Pasquel parlayed a chance meeting with New York Giants outfielder Danny Gardella in a Manhattan gym into a raging effort to entice as many major leaguers as possible to play in his loop. Soon not only Gardella but several dozen other performers—such as Mickey Owen, Sal Maglie, and Max Lanier—had been lured to Mexico. To nip the threat, Commissioner Happy Chandler banned all the defectors from the major leagues for five years. The ban was ultimately lifted in 1949 after a series of court battles, led by Gardella, but of all the Mexican League deserters the only one who returned to play in the majors with any great impact was Maglie.

The 1942 to '44 St. Louis Cardinals were the last NL team to win three consecutive pennants and also the last NL team to win 100 or more games three years in a row.

"Problems are the price you pay for progress."
—Branch Rickey

193

> "Baseball is almost the only orderly thing in a very unorderly world. If you get three strikes, even the best lawyer in the world can't get you off."
> —Bill Veeck

1940s SHORTSTOP GAMES

1. Marty Marion	1,383
2. Lou Boudreau	1,372
3. Eddie Miller	1,233
4. Vern Stephens	1,126
5. Luke Appling	1,100

The average player's salary in 1942 was down to $6,400.

> "For the Washington Senators, the worst time of the year is the baseball season."
> —Roger Kahn

Masi Ruled Safe in Controversial Series Play

Not many current baseball fans have been alive long enough to remember when Cleveland last won a pennant. They don't realize what they are missing. When the Indians make a postseason appearance something extraordinary inevitably occurs. In 1920, the Tribe's first World Series experience, there was an unassisted triple play. The Indians' last fall outing in 1954 began with Willie Mays's incredible catch, and Cleveland's only other Series exposure, in 1948, opened with a game that was decided by perhaps the most controversial umpire's decision in fall history. In the lid-lifter at Boston's Braves Field, Cleveland hurler Bob Feller seemingly picked Braves catcher Phil Masi off second base on a carefully timed play with Lou Boudreau, only to have Masi ruled safe by umpire Bill Stewart. Moments later the Boston backstopper scored the game's only run on a single by Tommy Holmes. Photographs from every angle later demonstrated that Masi had been out, but by then it was too late for Feller. That 1-0 defeat in the 1948 opener was the closest he ever came to gaining a Series victory.

"A baseball fan has the digestive apparatus of a billy goat. He can—and does—devour any set of statistics with insatiable appetite and then muzzle hungrily for more."
—Arthur Daley, sportswriter

1940s OUTFIELD GAMES

1. Bill Nicholson	1,325
2. Dixie Walker	1,268
3. Tommy Holmes	1,134
4. Wally Moses	1,083
5. Jeff Heath	1,043
6. Ted Williams	1,021
7. Stan Spence	990
8. Enos Slaughter	985
9. Dom DiMaggio	964
10. Doc Cramer	956
11. George Case	941
12. Joe DiMaggio	921
13. Charlie Keller	899
14. Jim Russell	883
15. Danny Litwhiler	879

Above: *Duke Snider was known affectionately as "Lord of Flatbush." He hit a career .295 with 407 home runs. He led the NL in runs scored from 1953 to 1955.*

Dillinger's Stone Hands Rob Him of Career

Bob Dillinger is the only third baseman since World War II who could not hold a major league job despite being a steady .300 hitter. Probably the best good-hit, no-field third sacker ever, Dillinger is also the only hot corner man in this century to sweep three consecutive stolen base crowns. After struggling at second base in the first few seasons of his professional career, Dillinger was stationed at third in 1942 by the Toledo Mud Hens of the American Association. Returning from a three-year service interruption, Dillinger joined Toledo's parent club, the St. Louis Browns, in 1946 and hit .280 as a rookie. It was to be his lowest batting average in his brief but eventful major league sojourn that saw him finish in 1951 with a .306 career mark.

"A king may be king because his father was, but a ballplayer is a major leaguer only so long as his averages show he is."
—Jim Murray

"I believe in God, but I'm not too clear on the other details."
—Bill Veeck

Here Today, Gone Today
Bill Veeck, when asked what his first act would be if named baseball commissioner, answered: "Resign."

Gordon-Reynolds Swap Helps Both Teams

The number of trades that have made both teams who were party to them into a pennant-winner can be counted on the fingers of one hand. Some analysts even contend the count begins and ends with the deal made prior to the 1947 season that sent Joe Gordon from New York to Cleveland and Allie Reynolds from the Tribe to the Yankees. Gordon immediately shored up a gaping second base hole, brought punch to the middle of the Indians' batting order, and perhaps most importantly, lent his experience with the Yankees to help Cleveland learn how to win. In 1948, his second season with the Tribe, the Forest City club hoisted its first flag since 1920. Reynolds meanwhile spurred New York to a pennant in his very first season with the Bronx Bombers. Before he finished in 1954 he participated in five more World Series, bagged 182 victories, and also logged 49 saves. Gordon retired in 1950 with 253 career home runs, still the most by an American League second baseman. Many observers consider the pair the best two players from the 1940s not yet in the Hall of Fame.

"I find now at this stage of the game that if I had my life to live over again, I'm inclined to think that I'd have to try and do something that's more fundamental for humanity than a professional athletic career."
—Dick Wakefield, some years after his playing days were over

1940s MANAGER WINS

1.	Billy Southworth	890
2.	Joe McCarthy	768
	Leo Durocher	768
4.	Joe Cronin	662
5.	Connie Mack	638
6.	Lou Boudreau	636
7.	Frankie Frisch	581
8.	Bill McKechnie	565
9.	Steve O'Neill	509
10.	Mel Ott	464

How 'Bout That Game?

Bruce Catton, historical novelist, remarked: "Say this much for baseball—it is beyond any question the greatest conversation piece ever invented in America."

"Looking back, it seemed like it was all good times. Some people don't like to look back, but I don't find the view all that bad."
—Kirby Higbe on his career

Veeck Early Promotion Developer

In 1948, a Cleveland night watchman named Joe Early wrote a letter to Indians owner Bill Veeck lamenting the numerous special days the Tribe was constantly giving to heap rewards on such players as Bob Feller and Lou Boudreau, who scarcely needed the booty, let alone the recognition. Why not honor an average fan for a change, Early inquired. Why not indeed, responded Veeck, and then promptly scheduled a night for Early at Cleveland Stadium which brought the Tribe rooter an outhouse, a backfiring Model T, some weird animals, a Ford convertible, and plenty more. Joe Early Night was just one of the multitude of promotional gimmicks that Veeck dreamed up to make his product as entertaining as possible. Between them and some good old-fashioned solid baseball from Veeck's players in 1948, the Tribe drew 2,620,627 spectators.

Browns manager Luke Sewell said to William Mead, war-time game historian, that Pete Gray "didn't belong in the majors, and he knew he was being exploited."

Above: *Leo Durocher's first big league managerial job came with the Dodgers, and from 1939 to 1946 his charges fell lower than third place only once.*

1940s TEAM WINS

	W	L
1. St.Louis-NL	960	580
2. New York-AL	929	609
3. Brooklyn-NL	894	646
4. Boston-AL	854	683
5. Detroit-AL	834	705
6. Cleveland-AL	800	731
7. Cincinnati-NL	767	769
8. Pittsburgh-NL	756	776
9. Chicago-NL	736	802
10. New York-NL	724	808
11. Boston-NL	719	808
12. Chicago-AL	707	820
13. St.Louis-AL	698	833
14. Wash.-AL	677	858
15. Phila.-AL	638	898
16. Phila.-NL	584	951

Chapter 8

The 1950s

Rocky Creams Quartet, Gets Traded

On June 10, 1959, Cleveland outfielder Rocky Colavito became only the third player in American League history to belt four home runs in a single game. Colavito's feat occurred in Baltimore's Memorial Stadium, at the time one of the toughest parks in the majors for sluggers to conquer. In 1959, it housed the team with the second-fewest homers in the majors, as the resident Orioles reached the seats just 109 times. Colavito began swinging for the fences after the four-homer game, causing his batting average to drop to .257 from his .303 mark the previous year. Although he finished tied with Harmon Killebrew for the American League home run crown in 1959, Colavito's thirst for the long ball helped frustrate the Indians in their bid for the AL flag that year and made them receptive to trade offers. When the Tribe was offered batting titlist Harvey Kuenn by Detroit even up for the Rock, they jumped at the bait.

1950s GAMES

1.	Richie Ashburn	1,523
2.	Nellie Fox	1,512
3.	Gil Hodges	1,477
4.	Stan Musial	1,456
5.	Alvin Dark	1,441
6.	Eddie Yost	1,439
7.	Willie Jones	1,419
8.	Duke Snider	1,418
9.	Yogi Berra	1,396
10.	Gus Bell	1,380
11.	Minnie Minoso	1,337
12.	Chico Carrasquel	1,325
13.	Del Ennis	1,317
14.	Whitey Lockman	1,314
15.	Carl Furillo	1,307
16.	Jackie Jensen	1,301
17.	Bobby Thomson	1,286
18.	Hank Bauer	1,284
19.	Mickey Vernon	1,280
20.	R. Schoendienst	1,272
	Ted Kluszewski	1,272

From '46 to '52, Ralph Kiner won or tied each year for the NL lead in home runs.

Brooklyn first baseman Gil Hodges socked four homers in one game, on August 31, 1950.

No Problem

"All I want out of life is that when I walk down the street people will say, 'There goes the greatest hitter who ever lived.'"
—Ted Williams

1950s RUNS

1. Mickey Mantle	994
2. Duke Snider	970
3. Richie Ashburn	952
4. Stan Musial	948
5. Nellie Fox	902
6. Eddie Yost	898
Minnie Minoso	898
8. Gil Hodges	890
9. Alvin Dark	860
10. Yogi Berra	848
11. Eddie Mathews	821
12. Willie Mays	777
13. Larry Doby	768
14. Jackie Jensen	746
15. Gus Bell	737
16. Red Schoendienst	732
17. Hank Bauer	730
18. Pee Wee Reese	729
19. Bobby Avila	722
20. Jim Gilliam	705

On August 1, 1954, Milwaukee's Joe Adcock hit four homers and a double, collecting 18 total bases.

Fain Gains Two Batting Claims

Ferris Fain—a fine-fielding, singles-hitting first baseman—won back-to-back batting titles in 1951 and 1952. To find a repeat batting champion as unlikely as Fain, one must go back to 1913 and '14, when Brooklyn first baseman Jake Daubert copped consecutive National League hitting crowns. But in his own way Fain was one of a kind. A first baseman with little power and not much run production, Fain nevertheless accumulated an inordinate number of bases on balls. As a result, his on-base percentage was almost always higher than his slugging average, an extreme rarity for a first baseman. Indeed, Fain retired in 1955 with a .425 career on-base percentage, the highest in history by a player with a sub-.300 career batting average. Fain's first batting championship in 1951 was somewhat tainted because an injury idled him for the last part of the season, freezing his average at .344 after 117 games. In 1952, however, he played in 145 games while posting a .327 mark.

"If somebody came up and hit .450, stole 100 bases, and performed a miracle in the field every day I'd still look you in the eye and say Willie [Mays] was better."
—Leo Durocher

About teammates Whitey Ford and Billy Martin, Mickey Mantle commented: "If I hadn't met those two guys at the start of my career, I would have lasted another five years."

Westrum, Others Amass Free Passes

Ferris Fain was not the only player during the 1950s who was neither a slugger nor a high-average hitter but was nonetheless deft at collecting walks. In 1951, Giants second baseman Eddie Stanky, who had collected a National League record 148 walks in 1945, garnered exactly the same number of free passes as hits (127) to go with a .247 batting average. Washington third baseman Eddie Yost meanwhile lived up to his nickname of "The Walking Man," as he retired as the only member of the top-10 list in free passes who registered fewer than 2,000 hits. Probably the most striking stats in this genre, nevertheless, belong to Giants catcher Wes Westrum. Notwithstanding his .217 career batting average, Westrum posted a .357 on-base percentage, largely aided by his performance in 1951 when he achieved 104 walks but only 79 hits, the fewest ever by a player who topped 100 free passes.

1950s HITS

1.	Richie Ashburn	1,875
2.	Nellie Fox	1,837
3.	Stan Musial	1,771
4.	Alvin Dark	1,675
5.	Duke Snider	1,605
6.	Gus Bell	1,551
7.	Minnie Minoso	1,526
8.	R. Schoendienst	1,517
9.	Yogi Berra	1,499
10.	Gil Hodges	1,491
11.	Carl Furillo	1,399
12.	Mickey Mantle	1,392
13.	Del Ennis	1,390
14.	Ted Kluszewski	1,380
15.	Harvey Kuenn	1,372
16.	Billy Goodman	1,347
17.	Jackie Jensen	1,332
18.	Eddie Yost	1,312
19.	Willie Jones	1,298
20.	Bobby Avila	1,293

On May 2, 1954, Cardinal Stan Musial slugged a record five homers in a doubleheader.

In 1956, Yankees center fielder Mickey Mantle won the only Triple Crown of the decade, batting .353 with 52 homers and 130 RBI.

Mickey Mantle in 1956 was the first switch-hitter to lead a major league in batting since 1889.

Lay One Down

Robin Roberts offered this as his greatest All-Star game thrill: "When Mickey Mantle bunted with the wind blowing out in Crosley Field."

BoSox Bat .300, Score 1,000

In 1950, the Boston Red Sox became the last team to date to compile a .300 batting average when they hit .302 as a unit and tallied 1,027 runs, only 40 less than the American League record of 1,067, set by the 1931 New York Yankees. The BoSox that year featured Billy Goodman, whose .354 average copped the American League batting crown, and three other regulars—Walt Dropo, Al Zarilla, and Dom DiMaggio—who hit better than .320. So deep was the club in offense that Goodman could not win a regular job and nearly did not acquire enough at bats to qualify for the bat title. Manager Steve O'Neill instead used Goodman to spell tired regulars until Ted Williams was shelved by an All-Star Game injury. At that point, Goodman went to left field, where he continued to hit well but never with the power of Williams. In fact, it was the loss of Williams for over two months that for the third straight season prevented the top-scoring team in the majors from claiming a pennant.

The only player since 1939 to hit .360 or better and fail to win a batting title is Mickey Mantle, who was runner-up to Ted Williams for the American League crown in 1957 with a .365 average.

On April 17, 1953, in Washington, Mickey Mantle swatted a 565-foot home run, the longest measured round-tripper in history.

"There have been only two geniuses in the world—Willie Mays and Willie Shakespeare."
—Tallulah Bankhead, actress and personality

In 1955, the National League had four catchers—Roy Campanella, Del Crandall, Stan Lopata, and Smoky Burgess—who had 20 or more home runs.

Stan Musial in 1957 was the first player since Paul Waner to collect 3,000 hits.

Take the Santa Fe Railway

Jimmy Dykes commented about Ernie Banks: "Without him the Cubs would finish in Albuquerque."

"Trying to sneak a pitch past Hank Aaron is like trying to sneak the sunrise past a rooster."
—Joe Adcock

Al Rosen of Cleveland in 1953 just missed winning the Triple Crown when he lost the batting title by failing to beat out a ground ball in his final at bat of the season.

1950s DOUBLES

1.	Stan Musial	356
2.	Red Schoendienst	284
3.	Alvin Dark	282
4.	Duke Snider	274
5.	Gus Bell	269
6.	Minnie Minoso	259
7.	Nellie Fox	254
8.	Richie Ashburn	252
9.	Mickey Vernon	251
10.	Harvey Kuenn	244
11.	Jackie Jensen	238
	Gil Hodges	238
13.	Billy Goodman	237
14.	Carl Furillo	235
15.	Eddie Yost	232
16.	George Kell	224
	Del Ennis	224
18.	Yogi Berra	222
19.	Ted Kluszewski	220
20.	Granny Hamner	216

Dale Long of the '56 Pirates slugged homers in a record eight consecutive games.

Rosen Smashes Hot-Corner Records

When he stepped to the plate for his final at bat of the 1953 season, Al Rosen stood to win the Triple Crown if he hit safely. A single would lift his batting average to .33722 and squeeze him in ahead of Washington's Mickey Vernon by .00005 of a point for the American League hitting crown. Rosen already had slugging honors sewed up with 43 home runs and 145 RBI. But, alas, the Cleveland third sacker hit a grounder and then missed beating the throw to first by half a step. Rosen could only be proud of his overall accomplishments in 1953. He set all-time single-season records for the most total bases (367) and the most RBI (145) by a third baseman. His 43 round-trippers also still stand as the American League mark for the most by a hot-corner man. Seemingly just reaching his prime, Rosen was shelved by a broken finger in '54 that severely hampered him for the remainder of his career.

Mathews Joins Hot-Corner Hit Parade

In 1953, even as Al Rosen was enjoying what is arguably the best season ever by a third baseman, Eddie Mathews helped the Braves celebrate their first campaign in Milwaukee by putting up some of the best numbers of any National League third baseman in history. Mathews swatted 47 home runs (the most ever by a third sacker until 1980 when Mike Schmidt rapped 48) and piled up 135 RBI, still the NL record for a hot-corner performer. The Milwaukee slugger also amassed 363 total bases. Mathews also had a slugging percentage of .627, which was even better than Rosen's astounding .613 mark. Rosen was second in the AL with a .422 on-base percentage, while Mathews was fifth in the National League with his .406 on-base mark. Never before and never again would two performers at the same position conjoin in the same campaign to establish so many loop and all-time marks.

Above: *Eddie Mathews is the only player to perform regularly on the same team in three different cities. After breaking in with the Boston Braves in 1952, he moved with the club to Milwaukee the following year and then to Atlanta in 1966.*

1950s TRIPLES

1.	Nellie Fox	82
	Richie Ashburn	82
3.	Willie Mays	79
4.	Minnie Minoso	74
5.	Bill Bruton	66
6.	Stan Musial	61
7.	Mickey Vernon	60
8.	Alvin Dark	58
9.	Duke Snider	57
	Gus Bell	57
11.	Bobby Thomson	56
	Jim Rivera	56
13.	Mickey Mantle	54
	Jim Gilliam	54
15.	Pete Runnels	53
16.	Granny Hamner	52
17.	Red Schoendienst	51
18.	Enos Slaughter	49
	Hank Bauer	49
20.	Ernie Banks	48

McDougald, Minoso Surpass Two Other 'M' Rooks

In the spring of 1951, the New York Yankees were laboring to convert an enormously talented but erratic-fielding shortstop named Mickey Mantle to the outfield and the New York Giants were trying to decide whether to install rookie Willie Mays in center field and move incumbent center gardener Bobby Thomson to third base. Mantle eventually opened the campaign in right field for the Yankees while Mays started the season at Minneapolis, the Giants' top farm club. Before the summer was out both would show flashes of the brilliance that would soon establish them as the two best center fielders of their era; Mays would even do enough to gain selection as the National League Rookie of the Year. While Mantle hit .267 and collected 13 home runs as a yearling, his rookie teammate Gil McDougald batted .306 and swatted 14 home runs to bag the AL Rookie of the Year honor. Chicago White Sox frosh Minnie Minoso meanwhile rapped .326 to out-hit all rookies that year; in addition, he paced the majors with 14 triples.

Boston Red Sox utility player Billy Goodman was the 1950 American League batting leader with a .354 average; he was the only player ever to win a hit title without having a regular position.

In 1950, George Kell became the only 20th-century third baseman prior to Wade Boggs to hit .340 or better two years in a row.

> "You've got to be a man to play baseball, but you've got to have a lot of little boy in you too."
> —Roy Campanella

1950s HOME RUNS

1.	Duke Snider	326
2.	Gil Hodges	310
3.	Eddie Mathews	299
4.	Mickey Mantle	280
5.	Stan Musial	266
6.	Yogi Berra	256
7.	Willie Mays	250
8.	Ted Kluszewski	239
9.	Gus Zernial	232
10.	Ernie Banks	228
11.	Ted Williams	227
12.	Hank Sauer	215
	Larry Doby	215
14.	R. Campanella	211
15.	Del Ennis	204
16.	Ralph Kiner	201
17.	Roy Sievers	199
18.	Vic Wertz	195
19.	Al Rosen	192
20.	Jackie Jensen	186

1950s RUNS BATTED IN

1. Duke Snider — 1,031
2. Gil Hodges — 1,001
3. Yogi Berra — 997
4. Stan Musial — 972
5. Del Ennis — 925
6. Jackie Jensen — 863
7. Mickey Mantle — 841
8. Ted Kluszewski — 823
9. Larry Doby — 817
   Gus Bell — 817
11. Minnie Minoso — 790
12. Carl Furillo — 784
13. Eddie Mathews — 777
14. Vic Wertz — 745
15. Bobby Thomson — 740
16. Gus Zernial — 738
17. Mickey Vernon — 730
18. Ted Williams — 729
    Roy Campanella — 729
20. Al Rosen — 712

Yogi Berra, when joshed for his homely appearance, replied: "I hit with a bat, not with my face."

Robinson Reaches Rookie Round-Tripper Record

Even though he hit just .263 and clouted a mere 12 home runs for Columbia of the Sally League in an injury-marred 1955 season, Frank Robinson demonstrated enough talent to induce several National League clubs to try to pry him away from the Cincinnati Reds. The Reds, though, elected not to listen to trade offers for Robinson, and events could not have proved them more right. As a 21-year-old rookie in 1956, Robinson tied Wally Berger's then-existing frosh record for home runs, when he slammed 38 round-trippers. Equally impressive to many observers was the fact that he tallied 122 runs to set a new 20th-century club record. In addition, Robinson served notice of the give-no-quarter type of batter he would be throughout his career when he was hit by pitches 20 times to pace the National League and also establish a second new Cincinnati record. He batted .290 and had 83 RBI. To no one's surprise, Robinson was named Rookie of the Year.

Ted Williams in 1957 led the American League with a .388 batting average, the highest in the major leagues since Williams himself batted .406 in 1941. Williams was age 39 when he won the batting crown. In 1958, Williams again won the AL bat crown (with a .328 average), this time at age 40.

Ted Williams of the Boston Red Sox reached base a record 16 times in 16 consecutive plate appearances in 1957.

1950s STOLEN BASES

1.	Willie Mays	179
2.	Minnie Minoso	167
3.	Richie Ashburn	158
4.	Jim Rivera	150
5.	Jackie Jensen	134
	Luis Aparicio	134
7.	Jim Gilliam	132
8.	Pee Wee Reese	124
9.	Bill Bruton	121
10.	Jackie Robinson	109
11.	Johnny Temple	105
12.	Sam Jethroe	98
	Earl Torgeson	98
	Mickey Mantle	98
15.	Jim Busby	93
16.	Dee Fondy	84
17.	Bobby Avila	78
18.	Duke Snider	77
19.	Nellie Fox	68
20.	Ken Boyer	65
	Don Blasingame	65

Above: Ernie Banks clubbed more home runs than he did doubles and triples combined. Mr. Cub accounted for 512 career round-trippers but just 90 triples and 407 two-baggers.

Banks Bags Tribute Despite Bad Ballclub

It is a rare player who can overcome voter prejudice to win an MVP Award while playing for a second-division team. Until Hank Sauer of the Cubs broke through in 1952, no member of a noncontender had bagged the award since the Baseball Writers Association of America had established the honor in 1931. Six years after Sauer collected his trophy with the fifth-place Cubs, Bruins shortstop Ernie Banks became only the second MVP winner in history from a second-division club. When Banks was accorded the honor again in 1959, it marked the only time a player from an also-ran has been so feted twice during his career. In 1959 the Cubs finished fifth with Banks but probably would have finished last without him. His 143 RBI were 91 more than the Cubs' second-most productive run producer collected in 1959. He batted .304 with 45 homers.

Zernial Slugs For Lowly Clubs

When the names of all the great sluggers during the 1950s who won home run and RBI crowns are bandied about, Gus Zernial's is the one most often forgotten. Much of the reason is that Zernial played most of his career with the Philadelphia-Kansas City Athletics, generally the game's worst team all during the decade. After hammering 29 home runs in 1950 to set a new Chicago White Sox club record, Zernial was dealt to the A's in a gigantic three-club deal at the beginning of the following season. He then promptly became the first player ever to win both a home run and an RBI crown in a campaign divided between two different teams when he pounded 33 taters in 1951 and knocked home 129 runs. Zernial never repeated as a loop home run or RBI leader, although on three occasions he paced the American League in home-run percentage. His nickname of "Ozark Ike," after the comic strip character of the postwar era, was pinned on him in 1948 while a member of the Hollywood Stars by Fred Haney, later a major league manager but then a broadcaster for the Stars.

Giants outfielder Monte Irvin described the clubhouse scene after Bobby Thomson's "Shot Heard 'Round the World": "When we fell behind in the late innings, the clubhouse people must have lost heart, because they didn't ice the champagne. So when we finally got around to toasting our pennant, we had to do it with warm champagne. Can you imagine that?"

In 1958, Richie Ashburn of the Phillies became only the second batting titlist in National League history from a last-place team.

White Sox second baseman Nellie Fox, with 192 hits, was the only American League player in 1952 to collect more than 179 safe blows.

Ernie Banks of the Cubs in 1955 set a major league record by whacking six grand slams.

Campy, Yogi Load Up on MVPs

For the first two decades the baseball writers' Most Valuable Player awards were given, catchers had been very infrequent recipients. In the 1950s, however, Yogi Berra and Roy Campanella combined to bring an abrupt end to the backstoppers' drought, as both players emerged as perhaps the two best all-around catchers in the game's history. In 1951, each was named his respective league's MVP, marking the first time that receivers had swept the honor. Both Berra and Campanella then proceeded to win two more MVP plaques during the decade, enabling them to become the only receivers to be so often feted. Campanella's other victories came in 1953 and 1955 while Berra's additional triumphs occurred in 1954 and 1955, making him the lone backstopper ever to sweep consecutive honors. Berra furthermore was among the top four finishers for the AL MVP Award in every year between 1950 and 1956, an achievement unmatched by any other player during the era. Campy's 41 home runs and 142 RBI in 1953 set records for backstoppers.

In 1959, Cleveland's Tito Francona set a 20th-century record for the most hits by a player in under 400 at bats when he bagged 145 safeties and hit .363.

Brooklyn's Roy Campanella in 1953 pounded 41 homers to set a major league record for catchers.

In 1956, Ron Northey of the White Sox notched 23 RBI in 48 at bats and was 15-for-39 as a pinch hitter.

Yankees second baseman Billy Martin in 1953 tied a World Series record with 12 hits.

"The game's not over till it's over."
—Yogi Berra

Peanuts Lowrey of the Cardinals collected 22 pinch hits in 1953 to tie a major league record.

1950s BATTING AVERAGE

1. Ted Williams — .336
2. Stan Musial — .330
3. Hank Aaron — .323
4. Willie Mays — .317
5. Harvey Kuenn — .314
6. Richie Ashburn — .313
7. Jackie Robinson — .311
8. Al Kaline — .311
9. Mickey Mantle — .311
10. George Kell — .308
11. Duke Snider — .308
12. Minnie Minoso — .306
13. Ted Kluszewski — .302
14. Billy Goodman — .302
15. Dale Mitchell — .301
16. Nellie Fox — .300
17. Carl Furillo — .299
18. Smoky Burgess — .298
19. Ferris Fain — .297
20. R. Schoendienst — .297

After debuting as an out-fielder in 1945, Red Schoendienst (above) took the Cardinals second base job from Emil Verban the following year and held it for 10 seasons.

Solid Backstoppers Develop in 1950s

Although Yogi Berra and Roy Campanella were the only two catchers to bag MVP honors during the 1950s, several other backstoppers put together seasons that caused quite a stir. In 1956, Stan Lopata of the Philadelphia Phillies rocked 32 home runs and notched 95 RBI, figures that were matched by only two other National League receivers, Campanella and Walker Cooper, between the end of World War II and expansion. Two years earlier, another Phils catcher, Smoky Burgess, stroked .368, the highest batting average in this century by a receiver in 100 or more games. Lopata and Burgess were a successful lefty-righty combo the three years that they were teammates. From 1952 to '54, Burgess had five homers and 46 RBI a year, while Lopata had eight homers and 33 RBI a year. Berra had no such rivals in the American League until the late 1950s when Gus Triandos emerged. In 1958, Triandos became only the second catcher in AL history to total 30 home runs when he posted exactly 30 with Baltimore.

Better Late . . .

Yogi Berra explained the tough late-inning shadows in left field in Yankee Stadium: "It gets late early out there."

The first major league player to achieve 40 home runs and less than 100 RBI was Duke Snider of the Brooklyn Dodgers in 1957 with 40 four-baggers and 92 ribbies.

The only player to collect 400 total bases in a season during the 1950s was Hank Aaron, who had exactly 400 in 1959.

Stan Musial in 1957 won his final NL batting title with a .351 mark at age 36.

Deep Depth

"In 1950, I led the American League in batting with a .354 average, and when I came to spring training the next year, I was considered a utility man. You see, you have to remember what kind of ballclub the Red Sox had in those years—an All-Star at just about every position."
—Billy Goodman

In 1953, Tommy Byrne's only hit in 18 pinch at bats was a game-winning grand-slam homer for the White Sox.

Also-Ran Reds Benefit from Power Boost

Entering the 1956 season, the Cincinnati Reds had finished in the second division for eleven straight seasons, and few saw much hope for improvement in the near future. Regardless, the arrival of rookie star Frank Robinson and the sudden emergence of catcher Ed Bailey as a bona fide slugger helped the Reds vault all the way up to first place early in the season and remain in contention until the last week of the campaign. The Reds slipped to third, just two games back of the pennant-winning Dodgers. Not even the vaunted Dodgers, though, could match the Reds at smacking balls into the seats. Led by Robinson's 38 home runs, Wally Post's 36, and Ted Kluszewski's 35, Cincinnati tied the 1947 New York Giants' then-existing major league record of 221 round-trippers. One more four-base blow by Gus Bell (29) and two more by Bailey (28) were all that kept the Reds from being the only team in history with five 30-homer men.

Klu Last of Low K Sluggers

Ted Kluszewski during the 1950s continued the tradition of such sluggers from the 1940s as Ted Williams, Mel Ott, and Joe DiMaggio by compiling huge home run totals while seldom striking out. In 1954, Big Klu fanned just 35 times when he paced the National League with 49 homers. Other fence-busters, though, such as Mickey Mantle and Duke Snider, regularly led their respective leagues in whiffs, usually with figures well over 100. Kluszewski proved to be the last slugger of his kind as by the end of the decade even lesser hitters thought little of fanning with a frequency that had earned Pat Seerey a ticket to the minors 10 years earlier. When he topped the American League in strikeouts in 1957 with 94, Jim Lemon became the last AL player to lead with under 100. The following year Harry Anderson of the Phils became the last leader in either loop with under 100 after his 95 Ks paced the National League.

Ted Kluszewski of the Cincinnati Reds in 1954 broke Johnny Mize's National League record by scoring at least one run in 17 consecutive games.

The Eyes Have It

Dan Parker, sportswriter, penned this poem about Johnny Mize, aging Yankees first baseman: "Your arm is gone; your legs likewise/ But not your eyes, Mize, not your eyes."

First sacker Rocky Nelson won the Triple Crown in the International League in both 1955 and 1958.

The 1953 Dodgers slugged home runs in a record 24 straight games. They went on to blast 208 on the season.

St. Louis Cardinals rookie Eldon John "Rip" Repulski collected two or more hits in a major league record 10 consecutive games during the 1954 season. For the year, he batted .283, a career high.

Herb Scores Sizable Strikeout Sums

In the fall of 1954, American League hitters everywhere but in Cleveland cringed when they read Indians farmhand Herb Score's stats that season with Indianapolis of the American Association. All Score had done was top the AA in wins (22), winning percentage (.815), and ERA (2.62) while notching 330 strikeouts in just 251 innings. Since the Indians already had the deepest pitching staff in the game, if Score was anywhere near as formidable as his minor league numbers made him seem, the rest of the AL was in trouble. In 1955, his rookie campaign, he set a new modern frosh record when he fanned 245 hitters and in addition became the first hurler in history to average more than a strikeout per inning. His average of 9.7 Ks in 1955 for every nine innings he worked is still a rookie record. Score went 16-10 with a 2.45 ERA, and he held opposing batters to a .194 batting average.

The Brooklyn Dodgers in 1953 tied a major league record with six players scoring 100 runs or more.

1950s GAMES PITCHED

1.	Hoyt Wilhelm	432
2.	Gerry Staley	430
3.	Clem Labine	412
4.	Robin Roberts	405
5.	Johnny Klippstein	400
6.	Warren Spahn	389
7.	Murry Dickson	376
8.	Early Wynn	374
9.	Chuck Stobbs	359
10.	Turk Lown	358
11.	Mike Garcia	355
12.	Billy Pierce	353
13.	Ellis Kinder	346
14.	Jim Konstanty	344
15.	Bob Friend	342
16.	Lew Burdette	333
17.	Bob Rush	327
18.	Marv Grissom	325
19.	Roy Face	324
20.	Bob Lemon	311

Bob Lennon won the Triple Crown in the Southern Association in 1954 when he hit .345 for Nashville with 64 home runs and 161 RBI.

Billy Goodman assessed the pitching staff of the 1959 White Sox: "What a staff! I'll tell you, if we would have had those guys in Boston during those big years [in the early 1950s], we would have had some fun. We could have closed shop in August and gone fishing."

Endowed With Deprivation

Dizzy Dean said at his induction into the Hall of Fame: "The Good Lord was good to me. He gave me a strong body, a good right arm, and a weak mind."

Dodger hurler Preacher Roe in 1951 notched an .880 winning percentage; it was the highest in history by a 20-game winner in the NL.

1950s GAMES STARTED

1.	Robin Roberts	370
2.	Warren Spahn	350
3.	Early Wynn	339
4.	Billy Pierce	306
5.	Bob Rush	278
6.	Bob Friend	262
7.	Mike Garcia	261
8.	Bob Lemon	260
9.	Ned Garver	257
10.	Don Newcombe	246
11.	Johnny Antonelli	241
12.	Murry Dickson	230
	Lew Burdette	230
14.	Curt Simmons	223
15.	Sal Maglie	222
	Alex Kellner	222
17.	Harvey Haddix	214
18.	Whitey Ford	208
19.	Carl Erskine	204
20.	Chuck Stobbs	202

In his only taste of big league action, Jim Baxes, a 31-year-old rookie, hammered 17 homers for Cleveland in 1959 in just 280 at bats.

Score Hit in Face with Line Drive

After winning 16 games as a rookie in 1955 and 20 the following season while leading the majors in strikeouts both years, Herb Score earned regard as one of the premier pitchers in the game. In his third campaign, he had a 2-1 record after four starts and once again was on a record-setting strikeout pace. His fifth start came in a night game against the New York Yankees. Score's pitching delivery had long been a source of concern to the Indians because he put so much effort behind his fastball that he was often left off balance and unable to field his position after he released it. Facing Gil McDougald on that fateful night in the spring of 1957, Score paid the full price for his awkward delivery. McDougald's line drive back through the box shattered Score's cheekbone, endangered the vision in his eye, and came within a hair of killing him. Like Gene Bearden, the great Cleveland rookie southpaw of a few years earlier, albeit for a very different reason, Score was prevented by the fates from delivering on his enormous promise.

1950s COMPLETE GAMES

1.	Robin Roberts	237
2.	Warren Spahn	215
3.	Early Wynn	162
	Billy Pierce	162
5.	Bob Lemon	139
6.	Ned Garver	125
7.	Don Newcombe	116
8.	Bob Rush	105
9.	Lew Burdette	104
10.	Mike Garcia	103
11.	Murry Dickson	100
12.	Curt Simmons	99
13.	Johnny Antonelli	98
14.	Whitey Ford	94
15.	Bob Friend	89
16.	Bob Porterfield	87
17.	Sal Maglie	86
	Harvey Haddix	86
19.	Alex Kellner	80
20.	Frank Lary	78

In 1954, their first season in Baltimore, the Orioles were led in both homers and RBI by third sacker Vern Stephens with eight four-baggers and 46 ribbies.

Don Newcombe Wins First Cy Young Award

At a special meeting on July 9, 1956, the Baseball Writers' Association of America, by a narrow 14-12 vote, approved Commissioner Ford Frick's recommendation to establish an annual Cy Young Award honoring the game's best pitcher. Frick had campaigned hard for the award because he was bothered by pitchers' lack of representation in MVP balloting. It was a problem that had hit particularly hard in 1952, when Robin Roberts won 28 games for the fourth-place Phillies but lost the MVP to Hank Sauer, a .270 hitter with the fifth-place Cubs. Ironically, the first Cy Young Award winner, Don Newcombe of Brooklyn, had a season so overwhelmingly dominant that he also won the MVP Award. Newcombe fashioned a 27-7 mark for the pennant-winning Dodgers, with a 3.06 ERA and 18 complete games. Newk received 10 of the 16 ballots cast; four of the remaining six went to Sal Maglie, who also finished the season with the Dodgers after being released by Cleveland when Tribe manager Al Lopez felt he was washed up.

Dodger pitcher Don Newcombe in 1955 knocked 42 hits.

Scooper?
"My best pitch is anything the batter grounds, lines, or pops in the direction of [Phil] Rizzuto."
—Vic Raschi

In 1952, when Robin Roberts was 28-7 for the Philadelphia Phillies, the club's other moundsmen combined for a composite record of 59-60.

Yankee hurler Vic Raschi in 1950 set a major league record when he retired 32 batters in a row.

Bobby Shantz, Yankees pitcher and witness to Herb Score's accident, advised: "Baseball can be a lot of fun, but, boy, you never know what can happen. Look what happened to Herb Score. I was there when he got hit in the eye with that line drive. Man, did he get belted. You heard the crack of the bat and he was down, just like that. Never had a chance to protect himself."

Baltimore's Dave Philley in 1959 compiled a major league record nine consecutive pinch hits.

In 1956, Robin Roberts of the Phillies was tagged for a National League-record 46 home runs.

1950s SHUTOUTS

1. Early Wynn	33
Warren Spahn	33
Billy Pierce	33
4. Robin Roberts	30
5. Whitey Ford	24
6. Johnny Antonelli	23
7. Bob Porterfield	22
Sal Maglie	22
Mike Garcia	22
10. Bob Turley	21
Lew Burdette	21
12. Allie Reynolds	20
13. Virgil Trucks	19
Don Newcombe	19
15. Curt Simmons	18
Bob Lemon	18
Harvey Haddix	18
Murry Dickson	18
19. Jim Wilson	17
20. Vic Raschi	16
Ken Raffensberger	16
Billy Hoeft	16
Bob Friend	16

In the 1957 World Series, Milwaukee Brave hurler Lew Burdette had three complete-game World Series wins, including two shutouts, against the New York Yankees.

Cardinals first baseman Steve Bilko registered the top strikeout total in the National League in the 1950s when he fanned 125 times in 1953.

'51 Yanks Discover Ford in Their Future

In the spring of 1951, Whitey Ford insisted that he was ready to make the leap from Class-A Binghampton of the Eastern League to the majors. The Yankees instead farmed him out to Kansas City of the American Association. Short a starting pitcher, Casey Stengel persuaded the team's brass to summon Ford to the Bronx. Despite not making his big league debut until July 1, Ford was voted the top rookie pitcher in 1950. Used both as a starter and in relief roles, he won his first nine decisions before dropping his final verdict to finish with a glittering 9-1 record.

> **"Hitting is timing. Pitching is upsetting timing."**
> **—Warren Spahn**

In 1951, Chet Nichols of the Boston Braves became the first rookie to top the National League in ERA since Jim Turner of the Braves did it in 1937.

1950s WINS

1.	Warren Spahn	202
2.	Robin Roberts	199
3.	Early Wynn	188
4.	Billy Pierce	155
5.	Bob Lemon	150
6.	Mike Garcia	128
7.	Don Newcombe	126
	Lew Burdette	126
9.	Whitey Ford	121
10.	Johnny Antonelli	116
11.	Sal Maglie	114
12.	Bob Rush	110
13.	Carl Erskine	108
14.	Ned Garver	106
	Murry Dickson	106
16.	Gerry Staley	104
17.	Curt Simmons	103
	Bob Friend	103
19.	Harvey Haddix	95
20.	Virgil Trucks	90

Above: Whitey Ford's 9-1 rookie mark with a .900 winning percentage remained an American League frosh record until it was broken by Kansas City's Jim Nash in 1966.

Braves Bilk Bronx Bombers Out of Burdette

During the 1950s, rival general managers were loath to talk turkey with Yankees general manager George Weiss because of the Yankees reputation for bilking other teams in the trade mart. One of Weiss's specialties was working out complicated interleague waiver deals with National League clubs that would put aging senior loop stars, like Johnny Mize, in pinstripes just in the nick of time to aid the Yankees in another of their patented stretch drives. Usually these transactions cost the Bombers little in player talent, so no one in the Yankees camp thought much of it when Weiss in late August of 1951 sweetened a cash deal with the Boston Braves for pitcher Johnny Sain by adding minor league hurler Lew Burdette to the $50,000 package. But for once it was the Yankees who were robbed. Sain was a helpful pitcher for several more years, but Burdette was destined to win 203 games after he left the Yankees chain and three more in the 1957 World Series when he faced his original teammates.

In the '58 Series against the Yankees, Brave Lew Burdette went 1-2 with a 5.64 ERA.

1950s INNINGS

1. Robin Roberts	3,011.2
2. Warren Spahn	2,822.2
3. Early Wynn	2,562.0
4. Billy Pierce	2,383.0
5. Bob Rush	2,047.0
6. Bob Lemon	2,015.1
7. Bob Friend	1,976.0
8. Mike Garcia	1,960.1
9. Murry Dickson	1,918.0
10. Ned Garver	1,904.1
11. Lew Burdette	1,863.2
12. Don Newcombe	1,773.2
13. J. Antonelli	1,721.1
14. Sal Maglie	1,638.2
15. Curt Simmons	1,625.1
16. Chuck Stobbs	1,588.1
17. Alex Kellner	1,581.1
18. Carl Erskine	1,575.0
19. Harvey Haddix	1,572.0
20. Whitey Ford	1,561.2

On May 6, 1953, St. Louis Browns hurler Bobo Holloman became the only pitcher this century to toss a no-hitter in his first major league start.

Jittery

Lew Burdette fidgeted so much on the mound that his Milwaukee manager Fred Haney said: "Lew would make coffee nervous."

Cleveland Indians pitchers led the American League in complete games for five straight seasons between 1951 and 1955.

Cleveland Hoards Heroic Hurlers

Students of the game are still puzzled that the Indians could manage to win only one pennant in the early 1950s. In 1952, Cleveland became the only team in history to come up empty despite having the loop home run and RBI kings as well as three 20-game winners; poor fielding was cited as the culprit. A year earlier, however, the Tribe had paced the American League in fielding, featured their usual three 20-game winners and fallen short because . . . well, just because. No one really knew why Cleveland didn't win, but pitching was certainly not the reason. When the Indians finally ended the Yankees' five-year monopoly on the AL flag in 1954, their pitching staff had one future 300-game winner (Early Wynn), three 200-game winners (Bob Lemon, Bob Feller, and Hal Newhouser), and in Mike Garcia a fifth hurler who at times was better than any of the other four. In 1954, Garcia had the top ERA in the AL, Lemon and Wynn tied for the loop lead in wins, and Newhouser and Feller contributed stats that gave the quintet an aggregate 85-33 record and a .720 winning percentage.

The 1952 Indians are the only team ever to have three 20-game winners, plus the league home run and RBI leaders, yet fail to win the pennant.

Cleveland hurler Early Wynn topped the 1950 American League with a 3.20 ERA, the highest ERA in major league history by a loop leader.

Antonelli Eventually Returns Investment

A few days after he graduated from high school in 1948, mound prospect Johnny Antonelli was given a $65,000 bonus to sign with the Boston Braves. Since the rules at that time forbade major league teams from farming out bonus babies to the minors for seasoning, the Braves were forced to keep Antonelli on their roster while he learned his pitching craft. In 1948, the high-priced southpaw got into just four games. The following two seasons he collected only five wins against 10 losses. Antonelli then spent all of the 1951 and 1952 campaigns in the military service, where he apparently matured. Returning to the Braves in 1953, their first season in Milwaukee, he won 12 games and exhibited enough artistry to tempt the New York Giants to trade Bobby Thomson for him. In 1954, Antonelli became the first bonus-baby hurler to make the heavy investment in him seem worth it, when he won 21 games for the Giants and paced the National League with a .750 winning percentage and a 2.29 ERA.

Robin Roberts discussed why he had such pinpoint control: "I can neither understand it nor explain it. I can't comprehend why other pitchers are wild."

When he bagged 20 victories for the last-place Browns in 1951, Ned Garver also topped the American League with 24 complete games.

Bob Turley collected two wins and a save in the last three games of the 1957 World Series as the Yankees became the first American League team to rebound from a 3-1 deficit.

When at the helm of the '52 Browns, Rogers Hornsby contended that rookie Jim Rivera was the only major leaguer he would pay to see.

In 1950, Yankee Vic Raschi established a major league record when he retired 32 batters in a row.

1950s EARNED RUN AVERAGE

1. Whitey Ford	2.66
2. Hoyt Wilhelm	2.79
3. Warren Spahn	2.92
4. Billy Pierce	3.06
5. Allie Reynolds	3.07
6. Ed Lopat	3.12
7. Bob Buhl	3.14
8. Johnny Antonelli	3.18
9. Sal Maglie	3.19
10. Early Wynn	3.28
11. Frank Sullivan	3.29
12. Frank Lary	3.32
13. Robin Roberts	3.32
14. Mike Garcia	3.32
15. Bob Lemon	3.34
16. Lew Burdette	3.39
17. Curt Simmons	3.44
18. Bob Turley	3.47
19. Virgil Trucks	3.47
20. Jack Harshman	3.48

Toothpick Sam Jones in 1955 set a National League record by issuing 185 walks.

Bonus Babies Go Boom-Boom

In the period between World War II and expansion, bonus babies posed the same problem for major league magnates that multiyear player contracts do now. Much as owners knew that the financial risk far exceeded the probable dividend, they were compelled to take the plunge because so many of their fellow moguls were doing it. The bonus baby era officially ended when the present amateur free-agent draft began in 1965; its actual end came some years earlier after too many teams had been stung too often by expensive prospects who never materialized. For every Johnny Antonelli who grew into a bona fide major leaguer, there were a dozen Paul Pettits and Billy Joe Davidsons. After taking the Pirates for $100,000, Pettit won just one game in the majors. At that, he was made to seem like a bargain by Davidson, who never even pitched a single inning in the bigs after looting the Indians of some $125,000.

Harvey Haddix described the prelude to his famous perfect game: "I didn't feel good. But about the middle of the afternoon I had a hamburger and a milkshake. I went out to the ballpark, still not feeling good. Yet I intended to pitch, no matter what."

In game five of the 1956 World Series, Yankees hurler Don Larsen pitched the only perfect game in fall classic history.

"The space between the white lines—that's my office. That's where I conduct my business."— Early Wynn

Reynolds Wraps Up No-Hitter Pair

With the departure of Joe Page after his miserable 1950 season, the Yankees lacked a bullpen ace. In the spring of 1951, manager Casey Stengel toyed with the notion of converting starter Allie Reynolds into a fireman. Reynolds rebelled, though, and he convinced Stengel that his arm was still strong enough to serve both functions. The results certainly bore Reynolds out. In 1951, not only did he lead the Yankees in saves but he topped the American League in shutouts and became the first junior loop hurler to toss two no-hitters in the same season. The first was a 1-0 masterpiece against Cleveland. Reynolds's second gem came against the Boston Red Sox in his final start of the season. With the Yankees ahead 8-0 the verdict was scarcely in doubt when the Red Sox batted in the ninth inning, but Reynolds was nonetheless nervous. The screws tightened in him when Ted Williams stepped to the plate with two out, especially after Yankees catcher Yogi Berra muffed Williams's pop foul. Moments later Reynolds induced Williams to loft another foul fly, and when Berra squeezed it the Yankees double-duty ace had his second no-no.

Despite leading the National League in both ERA and winning percentage as a yearling in 1952, Hoyt Wilhelm (above) lost the Rookie of the Year Award to Joe Black of the Dodgers.

**"Never win 20 games, because then they'll expect you to do it every year."
—Billy Loes**

In 1954, Bob Grim of the Yankees became the first and, to date, only pitcher in history to win 20 games in a season while hurling less than 200 innings.

Trucks Picks Up Two No-Nos

Just one year after Allie Reynolds's double no-hit feat, the first of its kind in the American League, Tigers righthander Virgil "Fire" Trucks matched it. But while Reynolds had won 17 games in 1951, Trucks could post only a 5-19 record for the season. Much of the reason for his poor mark was because he was pitching for the first team in Tigers' franchise history to finish in the cellar, going 50-104. He had a 3.97 ERA that year, while the loop average was a 3.67. In 1952, Detroit had so little bite on offense that Trucks was given just one run to work with on both occasions when he no-hit the opposition. Trucks also tossed a 1-0 one-hit victory that year over Washington that was marred only by leadoff batter Eddie Yost's single on the first pitch of the game. Traded the following year to the Chicago White Sox, Trucks blossomed immediately into a 20-game winner.

The 1957 Kansas City A's were the first club in major league history that did not have a single pitcher who worked enough innings to qualify as an ERA leader.

"I had my bad days on the field, but I didn't take them home with me. I left them in a bar along the way."
—Bob Lemon

In 1954, Karl Spooner of the Dodgers hurled shutouts in his first two major league starts—they were his only two major league games that year.

The only American League hurler to work 300 innings in a season during the 1950s was Cleveland's Bob Lemon, who toiled 309⅔ frames in 1952.

Carl Erskine of the Brooklyn Dodgers in 1953 struck out a World Series record 14 hitters in game three.

In 1950, after being sent to the Giants by the Cardinals early in the season, Jim Hearn became the first hurler to win an ERA crown while dividing the campaign between two teams.

In 1952 Larry Jackson had a 28-4 record for Fresno of the California League.

When he notched 11 saves in 1953, his last full season in the majors, Satchel Paige came within one save of tying the St. Louis Browns' club record of 12, set by George Caster.

On May 25, 1953, Max Surkont of the Milwaukee Braves became the first player in the 20th century to fan eight batters in a row during a game.

When Sam Jones of the St. Louis Cardinals racked up 225 strikeouts in 1958, he became the first NL hurler since 1941 to collect 200 or more whiffs in a season.

On August 31, 1959, Dodger Sandy Koufax became the first National League hurler in this century to fan 18 batters in a game.

Sam Jones in 1955 tossed a no-hitter against the Pirates after walking the bases full in the ninth and then fanning the side.

Cleveland pitchers Mike Garcia, Bob Lemon, and Early Wynn in 1954 were the top three AL pitchers in ERA, with Garcia leading at 2.64.

On July 1, 1951, Cleveland pitcher Bob Feller became the first hurler in the 20th century to toss three career no-hitters.

When Bob Turley suffered 13 losses in 1955, he became the only New York Yankees pitcher to lose as many as 10 games in a season between 1952 and 1956.

Asked if he ever tired of talking about his World Series perfect game, Don Larsen answered, "No. Why should I?"

In 1952, Detroit's Fred Hutchinson served the team as both a pitcher and a manager.

Braves Success in Milwaukee Triggers Franchise Shifts

In 1948, just two years after a new ownership group headed by contractor Lou Perini took over the club and hired Billy Southworth as manager, the Boston Braves won their first pennant since 1914. Since the Red Sox were also contenders at the time, the city of Boston had no difficulty supporting two teams. Four years later, however, the Braves plunged to seventh, and home attendance was less than a fifth of what it had been in 1948. The following spring, Perini moved the club to Milwaukee for the 1953 season, marking the National League's first realignment since the close of the 1899 season, when four teams were dropped from the senior loop. It was the first realignment in either major circuit since the Baltimore Orioles moved to New York prior to the 1903 campaign. The move was such a spectacular success—the Braves rebounded to finish second in 1953 and attendance in Milwaukee jumped 649 percent over the last figure in Boston—that it quickly triggered the departure of the weak-sister entry in every city but Chicago that had at least two major league teams.

1950s CATCHER GAMES

1. Yogi Berra   1,316
2. Sherm Lollar   1,116
3. Jim Hegan   1,011
4. Roy Campanella   978
5. Sammy White   967

In 1954, Willie Mays made the most famous catch in World Series history in game one, snaring a long line drive by Vic Wertz on a dead run in center field of the Polo Grounds.

Connie Mack said upon his retirement in 1950: "I'm not quitting because I'm too old. I'm quitting because I think people want me to."

Eddie Mathews described the diving stop he made to end the 1957 World Series: "I'd made better plays, but that big one in the spotlight stamped me the way I wanted to be remembered."

The first bespectacled catcher in a major league game was Clint Courtney of the Yankees in 1951.

Bums, Jints Flee to California

In 1946, Paul Fagan, part-owner of the San Francisco Seals, spearheaded an attempt to have the Pacific Coast League certified as a third major league. Although the bid ultimately failed, wiser moguls like Brooklyn's Walter O'Malley recognized that it was only a matter of time before big-league ball came to the West Coast. When attendance began slipping at antiquated Ebbets Field in the mid-1950s, and the borough of Brooklyn seemed disinclined to build the Dodgers a new stadium, O'Malley opted to cast his oar westward to Los Angeles at the finish of the 1957 season. To make the venture economically feasible, a second team had to be planted on the West Coast. O'Malley thus persuaded Giants owner Horace Stoneham to abandon the Polo Grounds, which also was in a state of decay, and flee to San Francisco. When the Giants and the Dodgers opened the 1958 season at San Francisco's Seals Stadium, it was the first major league game ever to be played in the Pacific Time Zone.

In 1950, the Chicago White Sox stole just 19 bases, the fewest in the majors; the following year, under manager Paul Richards, they became the "Go-Go White Sox" and topped the majors with 93 thefts.

1950s FIRST BASE GAMES

1. Gil Hodges	1,407
2. Ted Kluszewski	1,142
3. Mickey Vernon	1,128
4. Earl Torgeson	1,126
5. Walt Dropo	1,084

On May 18, 1950, Cardinal third sacker Tommy Glaviano made errors on three straight plays, blowing the game against the Dodgers.

"Show me a good loser and I'll show you an idiot. Show me a sportsman, and I'll show you a guy I'm looking to trade."
—Leo Durocher

Modern Management
"The secret of managing a ballclub is to keep the five guys who hate you away from the five guys who are undecided."
—Casey Stengel

> "Most
> ballgames are
> lost, not won."
> —Casey Stengel

1950s SECOND BASE GAMES

1. Nellie Fox   1,502
2. Red Schoendienst 1,214
3. Bobby Avila   1,163
4. Johnny Temple   948
5. Jim Gilliam   681

In 1955, Billy Bruton of the Milwaukee Braves became the first National Leaguer in history to pace the loop in steals in each of his first three major league seasons.

Bauman Blasts 72

By 1954, the number of minor leagues had diminished to 36 from a high of 59 five years earlier, but among the circuits that continued to flourish was the Longhorn League, a bastion in the Southwest for players who lived more than anything else to hit. Making his home in the Longhorn League for the third successive season in 1954 was first sacker Joe Bauman of the Roswell Rockets. The previous two years, Bauman had been with Artesia and had topped the circuit on both occasions in homers with totals of 50 and 53, respectively. In 1954, he racked Longhorn loop hurlers for an all-time organized baseball record 72 home runs. Bauman also netted 224 RBI and tallied 188 runs, all in only 498 at bats. In addition to setting the record for the most four-baggers in a season, he also set the all-time mark for the best home run percentage as he tagged 14.46 round-trippers per every 100 at bats.

The last NL contest that ended with a forfeit occurred on July 18, 1954, when the Phils were declared 9-0 victors over the Cardinals after St. Louis was guilty of stalling for darkness at Busch Stadium.

Tough Crowd

"All literary men are Red Sox fans. To be a Yankee fan in literary society is to endanger your life."
—John Cheever, novelist and short story writer

"Rooting for the New York Yankees is like rooting for U.S. Steel."
—Red Smith, sportswriter

Three Thump 60 in '56

Beginning in 1925, when Tony Lazzeri clubbed 60 home runs for Salt Lake City of the Pacific Coast League, hitters in the minor leagues began reaching the 60-homer plateau with fair regularity. The spate ended abruptly, however, just two years after Joe Bauman's record-setting achievement. But it ended with an unprecedented bang as no fewer than three minor league sluggers cracked the 60-homer barrier in 1956. The pacesetter was Dick Stuart, an outfielder with Lincoln of the Western League who slammed 66 taters. Most followers of the game better remember Stuart for his later escapades as a first baseman in the majors. Ironically, neither of the other two 60-homer men in 1956 ever again played regularly on the professional level. After hammering 62 dingers and 143 RBI for Shreveport of the Texas League in 1956, Ken Guettler performed for three more seasons as a part-time outfielder and pinch hitter before retiring in 1959. First sacker Frosty Kennedy played just 53 more games professionally following his monster 1956 season of 60 homers and 184 RBI for Plainview of the Southwestern League.

> **"I don't like them fellas who drive in two runs and let in three."**
> **—Casey Stengel**

> *In 1959, Walter Alston of the Dodgers became the only pilot to lead the same franchise to world championships in two different cities.*

Money's Worth

"One thing you learn as a Cubs fan: When you bought your ticket, you could bank on seeing the bottom of the ninth."
—Joe Garagiola

1950s THIRD BASE GAMES

1. Willie Jones	1,388
2. Eddie Yost	1,380
3. Eddie Mathews	1,157
4. Al Rosen	918
5. George Kell	896

After the 1954 season, the New York Yankees and the Baltimore Orioles fashioned a record 18-player swap. The principles included Don Larsen and Bob Turley going to the Yankees, while Gene Woodling and Gus Triandos went to Baltimore.

The 1950 Phils clinched their pennant on the last day of the season, as Dick Sisler's 10th-inning homer beat the second-place Dodgers.

1950s SHORTSTOP GAMES

1. Chico Carrasquel	1,241
2. Johnny Logan	1,192
3. Roy McMillan	1,186
4. Alvin Dark	1,134
5. Pee Wee Reese	1,031

Above: *White Sox receiver Sherm Lollar awaits the throw as Dodgers outfielder Wally Moon slides home in this piece of action from the 1959 World Series, won by Los Angeles.*

"Being traded is like celebrating your 100th birthday. It might not be the happiest occasion in the world, but consider the alternatives."
—Joe Garagiola

Coliseum Suitable for Moon Shots

After moving to Los Angeles in 1958, the Dodgers played their first four seasons on the West Coast in Memorial Coliseum. The Dodgers set an all-time single-game attendance record on May 7, 1959, when they drew 93,103 for an exhibition game against the Yankees honoring Roy Campanella. The Coliseum was built for football, however, and the Dodgers were forced to be inventive in order to make its contours work for a baseball game. Among the innovations was a towering 42-foot high screen in left field, reminiscent of Philadelphia's Baker Bowl in the 1930s, designed to prevent cheap home runs. The distance of 251 feet to the stands in left, nevertheless, remained so tempting that lefthanded hitters began tailoring their swings to loft fly balls off the screen. Wally Moon, a Dodgers outfielder in the late 1950s, gained the most notoriety for his screen shots.

Two Blue Slew Taboo

1950s OUTFIELD GAMES	
1. Richie Ashburn	1,515
2. Duke Snider	1,372
3. Gus Bell	1,352
4. Del Ennis	1,262
5. Jackie Jensen	1,260
6. Carl Furillo	1,258
7. Minnie Minoso	1,251
8. Hank Bauer	1,238
9. Mickey Mantle	1,213
10. Larry Doby	1,179
11. Jim Busby	1,127
12. Gene Woodling	1,112
13. Bobby Thomson	1,069
14. Willie Mays	1,058
15. Don Mueller	1,056

For many years, umpires concealed their faulty or failing eyesight either by wearing contact lenses or relying on their fellow arbiters to see what they no longer could. By the mid-1950s, however, the taboo against an umpire wearing glasses to officiate had been broken. Former major league pitcher Ed Rommel became the first arbiter to take the field in specs on April 26, 1956, at Washington in a game between the Senators and the Yankees. Larry Goetz shortly thereafter was the first NL umpire to follow suit. Both could afford to risk criticism because they were well-established in their profession.

Richie Ashburn explained why the 1950 Phillies "Whiz Kids" never won another pennant: "We were all white."

Warren Brown, after Minnie Minoso joined the White Sox, said the team "was off and running, but now, for the first time since 1920, they had a general idea of why and where."

Unable to displace Pete Suder at second base, Nellie Fox (above) was traded by the A's to the White Sox in 1950 for sub catcher Joe Tipton. Fox debuted in 1947 at age 19.

1950s TEAM WINS

	W	L
1. NY-AL	955	582
2. Brooklyn-		
L. A.-NL	913	630
Brooklyn-NL	754	479
L. A.-NL	159	151
3. Cleveland-AL	904	634
4. Boston-		
Milwaukee-NL	854	687
Boston-NL	223	238
Milwaukee-NL	631	449
5. Chicago-AL	847	693
6. New York-		
San Fran.-NL	822	721
New York-NL	659	576
San Fran.-NL	163	145
7. Boston-AL	814	725
8. St.Louis-NL	776	763
9. Phila.-NL	767	773
10. Cincinnati-NL	741	798
11. Detroit-AL	738	802
12. Chicago-NL	672	866
13. Wash.-AL	640	898
14. St.Louis-		
Baltimore-AL	632	905
Baltimore-AL	404	517
St.Louis-AL	228	388
15. Pittsb.-NL	616	923
16. Philadelphia-		
KC-AL	624	915
Phila.-AL	311	459
KC A's-AL	313	456

> "They had room at the Los Angeles Coliseum for 93,000 people and two outfielders."
> —Lindsay Nelson

Courtney First Backstopper to Wear Specs

Long before the 1950s, there had been bespectacled players at every position but one—catcher. While umpires eschewed wearing glasses on the field of play mostly for psychological and cosmetic reasons, the assumption was that it would be both too cumbersome and too dangerous for a player in spectacles to don a mask and go behind the plate. The first receiver to end the stigma against catchers wearing cheaters was Clint Courtney, when he caught a few innings for the Yankees on September 29, 1951. Courtney's scholarly looking spectacles belied his true demeanor, which was captured by his nickname of "Scrap Iron." He caught nearly 1,000 games in the majors before retiring in 1961. It was nearly three years after Courtney's debut before the National League unveiled a receiver wearing glasses—Brooklyn's Tim Thompson.

1950s MANAGER WINS

1. Casey Stengel	955
2. Al Lopez	836
3. Paul Richards	692
4. Walter Alston	526
5. Leo Durocher	523
6. Bucky Harris	510
7. Fred Haney	504
8. Lou Boudreau	472
9. Fred Hutchinson	426
10. Chuck Dressen	414

Pee Wee Reese said about making the transition from a player to a coach: "I felt like a mosquito in a nudist colony. I didn't know where to begin."

Rules Make Game Safer

In 1957, the American League became the first major circuit to make batting helmets mandatory equipment, and the National League quickly followed suit. Prior to then, many players had already begun wearing either helmets or protective liners inside their caps. Also during the 1950s, as another measure to guard against disabling injuries, warning tracks were required for the first time in the outfields of all major league parks. Padded fences, however, would not become mandatory until the 1970s. The rules requiring helmets and warning tracks met with instant approval from the game's fraternity. Another rule that came into effect in 1954, albeit, resulted in the passing from the scene of a tradition whose departure is still lamented by many fans with memories that reach back into the early 1950s. The 1954 season was the first in which players were no longer allowed to leave their gloves on the field of play while their team was at bat.

In 1957, Richie Ashburn of the Phillies hit a fan with a foul ball. While the fan was being taken out of the stadium, Ashburn again fouled the pitch off, and again struck the patron.

Wes Westrum, catcher and manager, said about baseball: "It's like church. Many attend, but few understand."

The major league attendance record for a single game was set by 93,103 Los Angeles Dodgers fans on May 7, 1959, when they attended an exhibition game to pay tribute to Roy Campanella.

America's Pastime
"Whoever wants to know the heart and mind of America had better learn baseball, the rules and realities of the game."
—Jacques Barzun, American historian

**"Ballplayers who are first into the dining room are usually last in the averages."
—Jimmy Cannon, sportswriter**

Chapter 9

The 1960s

'60s Start Stresses Safeties Scarcity

When the New York Yankees broke open a close three-team race in the American League in 1960 by ending the season with 15 straight wins, attention focused on who would be the loop's MVP winner. The baseball writers suddenly realized that there were no especially compelling candidates. None of the loop's pitchers had won more than 18 games, and it was certainly not because hitters had worn out hurlers. In fact, for the first time since the war-abbreviated 1918 season no AL batsman managed to accumulate as many as 190 hits. The pacesetter, Minnie Minoso of the White Sox, notched just 184 base hits, and at that he topped the AL by the fairly wide margin of nine safeties. In the National League, there were also strong indications that the game was about to descend to its lowest offensive ebb since the end of the dead-ball era. Willie Mays of the Giants led both the senior loop and the majors with just 190 safeties.

Willie Mays collected 1,903 ribbies in his career, including a high of 141 in 1962, but never was a league leader in RBI.

1960s GAMES

1.	Brooks Robinson	1,578
2.	Hank Aaron	1,540
3.	Ron Santo	1,536
4.	Vada Pinson	1,516
5.	Maury Wills	1,507
6.	Willie Mays	1,498
7.	Curt Flood	1,496
8.	Ernie Banks	1,495
9.	Luis Aparicio	1,494
10.	Frank Robinson	1,468
11.	Roberto Clemente	1,464
12.	Billy Williams	1,454
13.	Norm Cash	1,442
14.	Johnny Callison	1,432
15.	Bill Mazeroski	1,431
16.	Harmon Killebrew	1,429
17.	Orlando Cepeda	1,400
18.	Clete Boyer	1,390
	Felipe Alou	1,390
20.	Carl Yastrzemski	1,383

"It isn't hard to be good from time to time in sports. What's tough is being good every day."
—Willie Mays

Willie Mays in 1965 hammered an NL record 17 homers in one month.

Runnels Wins Bat Crown, Makes 169 Hits

Minnie Minoso milked his league-leading 184 hits in 1960 for a .311 batting average, third best in the AL, and also finished second in the loop in RBI and tied for third in total bases. Had the White Sox won the pennant, he probably would have copped the MVP Award, but the prize went instead to Roger Maris, the loop pacesetter in RBI and slugging average. The AL batting leader in 1960 was Pete Runnels of the Red Sox with a .320 average, the lowest to top either major circuit since 1945. Runnels also set a record for the fewest total bases in history (208) by a hitting titlist with 500 or more at bats. He had 169 base hits, and he finished 17th in MVP balloting.

The 45-year-old John F. Kennedy remarked to 42-year-old Stan Musial at the 1962 All-Star Game: "A couple of years ago they told me I was too young to be President and you were too old to be playing baseball, but we both fooled them."

Even though he bagged Rookie of the Year honors in 1959, Willie McCovey (above) did not win a regular job until 1963.

1960s RUNS

1.	Hank Aaron	1,091
2.	Willie Mays	1,050
3.	Frank Robinson	1,013
4.	Roberto Clemente	916
5.	Vada Pinson	885
6.	Maury Wills	874
7.	Harmon Killebrew	864
8.	Billy Williams	861
9.	Ron Santo	816
10.	Al Kaline	811
11.	Carl Yastrzemski	795
12.	Brooks Robinson	787
13.	Norm Cash	779
14.	Johnny Callison	774
15.	Orlando Cepeda	773
16.	Curt Flood	771
17.	Lou Brock	767
18.	Luis Aparicio	765
19.	Felipe Alou	742
20.	Willie McCovey	728

Cash Profits from Expanded Pitching Staffs

By adding two new teams in 1961, the American League also brought some 20 pitchers into the majors who otherwise would have spent the campaign in the minors. Hitters who had suffered in 1960 feasted on the diluted pitching staffs in the junior loop. Mickey Mantle vaulted from a .275 average to .317 and Al Kaline from .278 to .324. No batsman, however, profited more than Norm Cash of the Tigers. After hitting .286 in 1960 while sharing the Tigers' first base job with Steve Bilko, Cash ripped .361 in the first expansion season, adding 41 home runs and 132 RBI. All those figures turned out to be Cash's personal highs by a whopping margin. In 1962, with pitchers once again gaining the upper hand in the junior loop, he sagged to a .243 average. Cash's 118-point drop was the largest in history by a defending batting titlist. Moreover, his .361 mark was 75 points higher than he ever hit before or after 1961.

"When I was 17 years old I realized I was in a form of show business. It's like being an actor on the Broadway stage. He doesn't phrase his part exactly the same way every day. He thinks up new things. So I played for the fans, and I wanted to make sure each fan that came out would see something different I did each day."
—Willie Mays

Roger Maris broke Babe Ruth's major league single-season home run record in 1961 by swatting 61 homers.

The '61 Yankees had a record six players who hit 20 or more homers.

In 1966, Mickey Mantle became the first player in history to fan 1,500 times.

Giant Willie Mays in 1966 played in 150 or more games for a major league record 13th consecutive year.

Mickey Mantle holds the record for most home runs in a season by a switch-hitter, with 54 in 1961.

1960s HITS

1. Roberto Clemente 1,877
2. Hank Aaron 1,819
3. Vada Pinson 1,776
4. Maury Wills 1,744
5. Brooks Robinson 1,692
6. Curt Flood 1,690
7. Billy Williams 1,651
8. Willie Mays 1,635
9. Frank Robinson 1,603
10. Ron Santo 1,592
11. Luis Aparicio 1,548
12. Felipe Alou 1,530
13. Orlando Cepeda 1,522
14. Carl Yastrzemski 1,517
15. Ernie Banks 1,460
16. Johnny Callison 1,438
17. Bill White 1,413
18. Lou Brock 1,406
19. Al Kaline 1,399
20. Bill Mazeroski 1,385

Bronx Bombers Blast Benchmark

Even with Roger Maris and Mickey Mantle hammering a teammate-record 115 home runs between them in 1961, the Yankees were not the top offensive team that year in the junior circuit. That honor fell to the Tigers, which hit .266 and tallied 841 runs. No team out-homered the Bombers, however, either in 1961 or in any other campaign. Their 240 circuit clouts shattered the old major league team record of 221. Maris and Mantle contributed nearly half the total, but four other sluggers joined with them to make the Yankees the only team ever to showcase six players with 20 or more home runs. The other bammers were first sacker Bill Skowron (28), left fielder Yogi Berra (22), catcher Ellie Howard (21), and backup catcher and pinch hitter deluxe Johnny Blanchard (21). Blanchard's home-run percentage of 8.6 was nearly as high as that of the two M&M boys, as Johnny found the seats 21 times in just 243 at bats.

Mickey Mantle holds the record for the highest career slugging average—.557— by a player who failed to post a .300 career batting average.

During the 1960s, Willie Mays and Hank Aaron became the only two players to win home run crowns while playing for the same franchise in two different cities.

Stan Musial retired in 1963 with the NL record for hits (3,630).

1960s DOUBLES

1.	Carl Yastrzemski	318
2.	Vada Pinson	310
3.	Frank Robinson	309
	Hank Aaron	309
5.	Brooks Robinson	297
6.	Orlando Cepeda	268
7.	Johnny Callison	265
8.	Billy Williams	263
9.	Felipe Alou	260
10.	Willie Mays	259
	Roberto Clemente	259
12.	Ron Santo	247
	Al Kaline	247
	Curt Flood	247
15.	Lou Brock	243
	Ernie Banks	243
17.	Bill White	221
18.	Luis Aparicio	220
19.	Zoilo Versalles	219
20.	Pete Rose	218

In 1965, Boston's Tony Conigliaro led the AL with 32 homers, and at age 20, he was youngest player to ever win a league homer crown.

RBI Totals Expand Everywhere

Expansion created temporarily inflated offensive statistics in both major leagues during the early 1960s and led to several performances that proved to be nearly as anomalous as Norm Cash's .361 batting average in 1961. When the National League swelled to 10 teams the season following Cash's stunner, Tommy Davis of the Dodgers logged 153 RBI while topping the National League with 230 hits and a .346 batting average. Davis's ribbie total remains the highest in the senior loop since 1937—when Ducky Medwick of the Cardinals drove home 154 mates— and the highest in either major league since 1949. RBI figures were also up in 1961, the year the American League expanded, as both loop leaders, Roger Maris and Orlando Cepeda, posted an identical total of 142. Cepeda's numbers were accomplished on a 154-game schedule, however, and in several respects is a more impressive achievement than Davis's the following year. Baltimore first baseman Jim Gentile in '61 had 141 RBI, the only season that he had more than 100 runs batted in.

Roger Maris confided to sportswriter Joe Reichler: "It would have been a hell of a lot more fun if I had never hit those 61 home runs. All it brought me was headaches."

Stan Musial is the only player who ranks among the top 20 in career singles, doubles, triples, and home runs.

1960s TRIPLES

1.	Roberto Clemente	99
2.	Vada Pinson	93
3.	Lou Brock	85
4.	Johnny Callison	84
5.	Billy Williams	69
6.	Willie Davis	68
7.	Jim Fregosi	64
8.	Zoilo Versalles	63
9.	Maury Wills	62
10.	Dick Allen	60
11.	Dick McAuliffe	59
	Luis Aparicio	59
13.	Tony Taylor	55
14.	Ron Santo	54
	Donn Clendenon	54
16.	Willie Mays	53
	Tony Gonzalez	53
18.	Pete Rose	52
19.	Brooks Robinson	50
20.	Bill White	49

In his 23 seasons with the Red Sox, Carl Yastrzemski (above) logged 3,419 hits but batted .300 just six times.

Billy Herman, one of Carl Yastrzemski's first managers with the Red Sox, said of Yaz: "How did I get along with Yastrzemski? Like everybody else. By that I mean nobody ever got along with Yastrzemski."

'68 AL Batting Averages Hit Bottom

At the beginning of the final week of the 1968 season, it seemed a very real possibility that for the first time in history a major league batting titlist would hit below .300. Only a closing rush by Boston's Carl Yastrzemski that lifted his average to .301 spared the American League its most ignominious moment. Yaz's figure topped runner-up Oakland's Danny Cater by 11 points. Rounding out the top five hitters in the AL in 1968 were Tony Oliva of the Twins (.289), Willie Horton of the Tigers (.285), and Minnesota's Ted Uhlaender (.283). In 1968, Yaz was not only the AL's sole bat title qualifier to hit .300, he was also the lone player in the loop with over 100 at bats to top the .300 figure.

ChiSox Scoring Severely Suffers

As might be expected, with batting averages in the AL so low all across the board in '68, hit totals were equally meager. The A's Bert Campaneris topped the circuit in safe blows with just 177, 10 ahead of runner-up Cesar Tovar. With Campaneris, Danny Cater, and Rick Monday all placing among the top 10 in hitting, the A's paced the AL with a .240 batting average, the lowest ever by a loop leader. Second to the A's with a .237 mark were the Twins, who also had three hitters in the top 10—Tony Oliva, Ted Uhlaender, and Tovar. The Yankees brought up the rear in batting at .214, the lowest team average since the dead-ball era. The Chicago White Sox, though, got the least mileage from their hits. Despite finishing at .228, some 14 points above the Yankees, the White Sox saw the Bombers outscore them by 73 runs and finished last in the majors with 463 tallies, less than three a game.

Above: *Zoilo Versalles broke in with the Washington Senators in 1959. Four years after he won the 1965 American League MVP Award, he was released by the expansion Senators at age 29.*

1960s HOME RUNS

1.	Harmon Killebrew	393
2.	Hank Aaron	375
3.	Willie Mays	350
4.	Frank Robinson	316
5.	Willie McCovey	300
6.	Frank Howard	288
7.	Norm Cash	278
8.	Ernie Banks	269
9.	Mickey Mantle	256
10.	Orlando Cepeda	254
11.	Ron Santo	253
12.	Billy Williams	249
13.	Rocky Colavito	245
14.	Bob Allison	225
15.	Roger Maris	217
16.	Eddie Mathews	213
17.	Al Kaline	210
18.	Carl Yastrzemski	202
	Boog Powell	202
20.	Leon Wagner	193

1960s RUNS BATTED IN

1. Hank Aaron	1,107
2. Harmon Killebrew	1,013
3. Frank Robinson	1,011
4. Willie Mays	1,003
5. Ron Santo	937
6. Ernie Banks	925
7. Orlando Cepeda	896
8. Roberto Clemente	862
9. Billy Williams	853
10. Brooks Robinson	836
11. Frank Howard	835
12. Norm Cash	830
13. Willie McCovey	821
14. Vada Pinson	792
15. Rocky Colavito	786
16. Al Kaline	773
17. Carl Yastrzemski	767
18. Bill White	735
Ken Boyer	735
20. Bob Allison	704

The only player during the 1960s to total more than 15 triples in a season was Johnny Callison with 16 in 1965.

Switch-Hitting Pete Rose to NL Top

When Pete Rose hit .335 in 1968 to capture the first of his three National League batting titles, it also represented the first hitting crown in senior loop history won by a switch-hitter. Just 12 years earlier, Mickey Mantle had broken the ice in the American League, becoming the first two-way batsman to be a league leader since Tommy Tucker of Baltimore paced the American Association in 1889. Rose bagged his second consecutive bat crown in 1969 with a .348 mark that tied the then-existing post-1900 National League record for the highest batting average by a switch-hitter, first set in 1923 by Frankie Frisch of the New York Giants. Maury Wills in 1962 had broken the National League record for most at bats by a switch-hitter when he accumulated 695 at bats. The all-time senior loop switch-stickers mark belongs to George Davis, also of the Giants, who slapped .362 in 1893. Mickey Mantle holds the post-1893 major league record with his .365 average in 1956.

Mr. Clutch of 1962

Discussing Tommy Davis in 1962, Sandy Koufax said: "Every time there was man on base he'd knock him in, and every time there were two men on base, he'd hit a double and knock them both in."

Willie Davis of the Dodgers compiled the longest hitting streak during the 1960s when he hit safely in 31 straight games in 1969.

Matty Alou Bats Over .330
Four Straight Years

After annexing the National League batting title in 1966 with a .342 average, Matty Alou of the Pirates embarked on a run that would make him the last senior looper to date to hit .330 or better for four consecutive years. Alou followed his hit crown by rapping .338 in 1967, .332 in 1968, and .331 in 1969. His four-season skein marked the only time in his 15-year career that he topped .330. Nevertheless, he ended his career in 1974 with a .307 career average, among the highest of the postexpansion, prefree-agency era that encompassed the years from 1961 through 1975. He had 231 base hits and 41 doubles to lead the NL in '69. Prior to Alou, the last NL player to enjoy a comparable stretch of hitting success was Stan Musial. Between 1948 and 1954 Musial belted .330 or better for seven consecutive seasons. Roberto Clemente (1969 to '71) is the only other NL hitter since Musial to reach the .330 figure as many as three years in a row.

In 1968, George Scott of the Red Sox became the only first sacker in American League history to collect fewer than 100 total bases in 350 or more at bats when he hit .171 and had just 83 total bases.

Pinnacle
When asked what was his career high point, Bob Uecker replied: "In 1967 with St. Louis, I walked with the bases loaded to drive in the winning run in an intersquad game in spring training."

Chuck Hinton holds the expansion Washington Senators' record for the highest batting average with a .310 mark in 1962.

The 1966 American League had only two hitters with batting averages above .288—Frank Robinson (.317) and Tony Oliva (.307).

In 1968, Dick McAuliffe of Detroit became the first player in AL history to participate in 150 or more games without grounding into a double play.

Cleveland was the first AL team to hit four consecutive homers, on July 31, 1963.

1960s STOLEN BASES

1.	Maury Wills	535
2.	Lou Brock	387
3.	Luis Aparicio	342
4.	Bert Campaneris	292
5.	Willie Davis	240
6.	Tommy Harper	208
7.	Hank Aaron	204
8.	Vada Pinson	202
9.	Don Buford	161
10.	Tony Taylor	157
11.	Jose Cardenal	149
12.	Frank Robinson	145
13.	Chuck Hinton	130
14.	Willie Mays	126
15.	Julian Javier	123
16.	Cesar Tovar	117
17.	Jim Wynn	115
18.	Joe Morgan	113
19.	Tommy McCraw	107
20.	Dick Howser	105

"During my 18 years I came to bat almost 10,000 times. I struck out about 1,700 times and walked maybe 1,800 times. You figure a ballplayer will average about 500 at bats a season. That means I played seven years in the major leagues without ever hitting the ball."
—Mickey Mantle

Alous Dominate '66 NL Batting Race

When Matty Alou won the National League bat title in 1966, the runner-up to him with a .327 average was his brother Felipe of the Atlanta Braves. It marked the only time in big league history that a pair of brothers finished one-two in a loop batting race. Also playing in the senior circuit in 1966 was a third Alou brother, Jesus of the San Francisco Giants. The youngest of the three Alou siblings, Jesus was also the least prominent, but each member of the trio played at least 15 years in the majors and compiled well over 1,000 hits. Felipe was the only one with power, once slugging 33 homers in a season, more than either Jesus or Matty accumulated in their career. Their aggregate career stats helped the Alous to lay claim to being the best threesome of brothers in major league history with the sole exception of the DiMaggios. All three broke in with the San Francisco Giants and in 1963 were teammates for one season before Felipe was traded to the Braves.

Howard Hammers for Hapless Senators

Had he played in the 1930s, Frank Howard might be nearly as well remembered now as Jimmie Foxx and Hank Greenberg. Because his prime years came in the late 1960s and roughly paralleled the most difficult span of time for hitters since the depths of the dead-ball era, Howard's career totals are dwarfed by Foxx's and seem significantly lesser than Greenberg's. Further hampering Howard's case is the fact that his peak stats were produced for a lackluster Washington Senators team. In 1968, while Howard was blasting an American League-leading 44 homers and knocking home 106 runs for the last place Senators, only one other club member, Ken McMullen with 62, produced more than 40 RBI. A year earlier, Howard's 36 home runs represented nearly a third of Washington's total of 115. In 1970, Howard's last monster season, he became one of a very few sluggers to lead his loop in both homers and RBI while playing for a tail-ender as the Senators finished last in the AL East.

Gates Brown of Detroit was the first black player to homer in his first at bat in an American League game, on June 19, 1963.

On May 9, 1961, Jim Gentile hit grand slams in two consecutive innings for Baltimore.

Double Dip
Ernie Banks, upon arriving at the ballpark each day, would exclaim: "Let's play two!"

Dave Philley set a record when he collected 24 pinch singles in 1961.

Mack Jones of the Milwaukee Braves collected four hits in his first major league game on July 13, 1961.

In 1965, when he topped the National League with 130 ribbies, Deron Johnson notched 100 RBI for the only time in his 16-year career.

The White Sox finished 16 games over .500 (89-73) in 1967 despite hitting a meager .225 and tallying only 531 runs.

Class
"Most of what I know about style I learned from Roberto Clemente."
—John Sayles

The Milwaukee Braves hit four consecutive homers on June 8, 1961.

Williams Works Magic for New Nats

The expansion Washington Senators customarily brought up the rear of either the American League or the AL East in each year of their existence from 1961 until the franchise was moved to Texas. Only once in the club's 11-year sojourn in the nation's capital did it break .500. The watershed season came in 1969, the Senators' first under rookie skipper Ted Williams. After replacing Jim Lemon at the helm following a last-place finish in 1968, Williams seemed at first to be that rare great hitter who could convey his batting genius to his charges. In 1969, the Senators rocketed to an 86-76 finish, aided in large part by the team's .251 batting average, tied for the third-best in the AL. Even slugger Frank Howard seemed to benefit from Williams's tutelage, cutting his strikeout total below 100 while still managing to hammer 48 home runs. Williams's magic quickly deserted him, however. In 1970, his second season at the Senators' helm, the club fell into the AL East basement and tied for last in hitting.

In 1968, the New York Yankees posted the lowest team batting average since the dead-ball era when they hit just .214.

1960s BATTING AVERAGE

1.	Roberto Clemente	.328
2.	Matty Alou	.312
3.	Pete Rose	.309
4.	Tony Oliva	.308
5.	Hank Aaron	.308
6.	Frank Robinson	.304
7.	Dick Allen	.300
8.	Willie Mays	.300
9.	Manny Mota	.297
10.	Curt Flood	.297
11.	Tommy Davis	.296
12.	Al Kaline	.296
13.	Orlando Cepeda	.295
14.	Felipe Alou	.294
15.	Carl Yastrzemski	.293
16.	Joe Torre	.293
17.	Vada Pinson	.292
18.	Billy Williams	.292
19.	Tony Gonzalez	.290
20.	Smoky Burgess	.290

Oliva, Allen Top Class of '64

In 1964, Tony Oliva of the Twins became the only rookie since Pete Browning in 1882 to win a major league batting title. Oliva accomplished something nearly as rare when he also paced the American League in total bases. The first frosh total base leader in the AL since George Stone in 1905, Oliva could have expected to have the pedestal all to himself in a normal season. But 1964 was a very unusual year. The National League, for the first time since 1918, also had a yearling player, Dick Allen of the Phillies, garner the total base crown. Oliva in addition tied Hal Trosky's 1934 mark for the most total bases by a frosh (374) and Allen set an all-time NL frosh record with 352. Rather surprisingly, however, neither of the pair was a unanimous Rookie of the Year selection in his loop. Oliva fell one vote short of perfection while Allen missed obtaining two of the 20 ballots cast by NL writers. Rico Carty and Jim Ray Hart received ballots for the NL honor, while Wally Bunker received an AL vote.

"I don't think those people at Wrigley Field ever saw but two players they liked—Billy Williams and Ernie Banks. Billy never said anything, and Ernie always said the right thing."
—Fergie Jenkins

Bobby Richardson in 1962 and Tony Oliva in 1964 were the only American Leaguers to enjoy 200-hit seasons during the 1960s.

Tony Oliva led the American League in hits in each of his first three seasons in the majors, 1964 to '66.

In 1968, the only Yankees player in 400 or more at bats to hit higher than .240 was Roy White at .267.

Boston's 19-year-old Tony Conigliaro in 1964 knocked 24 homers and notched a .530 slugging average—both records for a teenage player.

In 1963, Houston's Ernie Fazio fanned 70 times in just 228 at bats.

When he went down on strikes 103 times as a rookie with Houston in 1963, John Bateman became the first catcher to compile 100 whiffs in a season.

In 1963 and '64, Dave Nicholson of the White Sox fanned 301 times in 743 at bats, including a then-record 175 Ks in 1963 alone.

Bobby Bonds of the '69 Giants set a major league record by striking out 187 times.

Cleveland shortstop Dick Howser had a mere six RBI in 107 games and 307 at bats in 1965.

In 1967, Luis Aparicio of Baltimore became the first player to be a league leader in fewest strikeouts despite fanning over 40 times (44).

Tresh, Other Rookies Swing and Miss

Tony Oliva and Dick Allen both followed their outstanding rookie campaigns in 1964 by fashioning long and noteworthy careers, but numerous other performers in the 1960s, after starring at the plate as rookies, soon fell prey to the home-run-or-bust syndrome that permeated the game all during the decade. Among the leading victims were Pete Ward of the White Sox, Curt Blefary of the Orioles, Tom Tresh of the Yankees, and Jimmie Hall of the Twins. All followed their exceptional freshmen seasons with sophomore campaigns that were in some instances even better before beginning to succumb to the lure of the long ball. Hall hit .260 his rookie year, .254 for his career; Ward hit .295 his first year, .254 for his career; and Blefary hit .260 his rookie season, .237 for his career. Tresh was probably the most talented of the four and also the most disheartening to watch disintegrate at the plate. After hitting .286, .269, .246, and .279 in his first four seasons, he slipped to .233, .219, .195, and .211 in his last four campaigns.

Gibson's Stats Shave Mound, Strike Zone

In 1968, Bob Gibson of the Cardinals notched 13 shutouts, the most by any hurler since 1916. He also registered a 1.12 ERA, which set a new low for the game after the dead-ball era. He led the league in fewest hits per game, strikeouts, opponents batting average, and opponents on-base percentage. Gibson's overwhelming stats earned him both the Cy Young and the MVP awards. Alarmed by how far the balance scale had so obviously tilted in the favor of pitchers, baseball officials shaved the regulation height of pitchers' mounds and also squeezed the size of the strike zone prior to the 1969 season. Gibson's ERA swelled correspondingly to 2.18 in 1969 and his shutout total dipped to four, but he continued to be perhaps the most dominant pitcher in the game. In 1970, toiling for a Cardinals team that had a 76-86 record, Gibson went 23-7 and topped the majors with a .767 winning percentage.

1960s GAMES PITCHED

1.	Ron Perranoski	589
2.	Lindy McDaniel	558
3.	Hoyt Wilhelm	557
4.	Don McMahon	547
5.	Roy Face	524
6.	Ron Kline	519
7.	Stu Miller	468
	Eddie Fisher	468
9.	Bob Miller	450
10.	Turk Farrell	445
	Jack Baldschun	445
12.	Ted Abernathy	444
13.	Gary Bell	442
14.	John Wyatt	435
15.	Phil Regan	434
16.	Al McBean	401
17.	Al Worthington	393
18.	Dick Hall	392
19.	Larry Sherry	388
20.	Ron Taylor	385

A fine all-around athlete, Bob Gibson (above) would probably have found a home in baseball even if he had failed as a pitcher. Playing in the toughest era ever for hitters, he batted .206 and notched 24 home runs during his 17 years with St. Louis.

Drysdale Pitches Zips for 58 Frames

Don Drysdale began the 1968 season as if he were invincible. He pitched four consecutive shutouts for the Dodgers in May and was on the brink of breaking the record for the most consecutive shutout innings pitched on the final day of the month when he took a 3-0 lead into the ninth inning against the Giants. He proceeded to load the bases with none out, though, then hit Giants catcher Dick Dietz with a pitch to seemingly force home a run. Plate umpire Harry Wendelstadt ruled instead that Dietz hadn't tried to avoid the pitch. Dietz subsequently popped out, and Drysdale retired the next two hitters to preserve his streak and run his record to 58 consecutive scoreless innings before he was stopped. His shutout skein notwithstanding, the 1968 season was not an unqualified success for Drysdale. After his five straight whitewashes, his arm seemed to run out of gas, and he finished with a so-so 14-12 record.

**"Regrets about not winning 300? No, not really. A lot of people thought I was striving for 300 wins. But what I was really striving for was to pitch until I was 44 or 45 years old. I knew if I could do that the wins would take care of themselves."
—Robin Roberts**

When the Dodgers moved to L.A. in 1957, Don Drysdale (above) remained the franchise's most durable hurler for 11 more years

1960s GAMES STARTED

1. Jim Bunning 360
2. Don Drysdale 359
3. Larry Jackson 321
4. Juan Marichal 320
5. Jim Kaat 316
6. Dick Ellsworth 308
7. Milt Pappas 302
   Bob Gibson 302
9. Claude Osteen 287
10. Earl Wilson 281
11. Camilo Pascual 273
12. Steve Barber 263
13. Ray Sadecki 261
    Dean Chance 261
15. Jack Fisher 258
16. Jim Maloney 255
17. Mike McCormick 251
18. Mudcat Grant 246
19. Don Cardwell 243
20. Joe Horlen 240

1960s Witness to Three Perfect Games

After Harvey Haddix of the Pirates hurled 12 perfect innings on May 29, 1959, before losing to the Braves in the 13th frame, a door swung ajar that had been sealed shut for nearly 40 years. His effort marked the first time since 1922 that a pitcher had achieved perfection for the first nine innings of a regular-season game. On Father's Day in 1964, the Phillies' Jim Bunning, himself the sire of a multitude of offspring, became the first hurler in 42 years to win a perfect game during the regular season and the first National Leaguer to toss a perfect contest since 1880, when he blanked the Mets 6-0. The following year, Sandy Koufax of the Dodgers was letter-perfect against the Cubs 1-0. That game nearly marked the second double no-hitter in big league history, as Chicago's Bob Hendley surrendered just one hit on the day. In 1968, Catfish Hunter of the A's made the 1960s the first decade in history to feature three perfect games, when he bested Minnesota 4-0 on May 8.

1960s COMPLETE GAMES	
1. Juan Marichal	197
2. Bob Gibson	164
3. Don Drysdale	135
4. Sandy Koufax	122
5. Larry Jackson	116
6. Jim Bunning	108
7. Jim Kaat	102
8. Warren Spahn	95
9. Camilo Pascual	93
Denny McLain	93
11. Gaylord Perry	88
12. Dick Ellsworth	87
13. Mel Stottlemyre	85
14. Dean Chance	82
15. Claude Osteen	80
16. Milt Pappas	79
17. Chris Short	76
18. Mike McCormick	74
Jim Maloney	74
Bob Friend	74

"They called us 'The Miracle Mets.' Miracle, my eye. What happened was that a lot of good young players suddenly jelled and matured all at once."
—Tom Seaver

Early Wynn won his 300th game on July 13, 1963.

Whatta Break

"Bob Gibson is the luckiest pitcher I ever saw. He always pitches when the other team doesn't score any runs."—Tim McCarver

Granger Toes Rubber 90 Times

In 1964, John Wyatt of the Kansas City Athletics became the first pitcher to appear in 80 or more games in a season, when he took the mound in 81 of the A's 163 contests. The following year Ted Abernathy of the Cubs upped the record to 84 appearances, a mark that held until 1968, when Wilbur Wood of the White Sox worked in 88 games. Wood's record, which seemed to push the limit beyond the endurance of the human arm, lasted only one year. In 1969, Wayne Granger, then in his second season, came on in relief for the Reds 90 times. Granger was used so often by Cincinnati manager Dave Bristol out of necessity. The Reds in 1969 had one of the most uninspiring crews of starting pitchers in the majors. Largely owing to Granger and Clay Carroll, however, who posted 34 saves and 21 wins between them, Cincinnati topped the majors with 44 saves and finished at 89-73. The following year, with Granger and Carroll again forming a sterling relief tandem, the Reds won the National League pennant.

When Phillie hurler Jim Bunning pitched a perfect game against the Mets on June 21, 1964, it was the first perfect game in the NL in this century.

Dave McNally of the Orioles tied an American League record when he won 17 consecutive games in 1968 and '69.

Cleveland's Sam McDowell in 1965 set an AL southpaw record for Ks with 325.

Bob Gibson of the St. Louis Cardinals posted a 1.12 ERA in 1968, the lowest in the major leagues since 1914. Opponents managed just 198 hits off Gibson in 304⅔ innings for a .184 batting average.

In 1968, Card hurler Bob Gibson notched 13 shutouts, the most in the major leagues since 1916.

1960s SHUTOUTS

1.	Juan Marichal	45
2.	Bob Gibson	41
3.	Don Drysdale	40
4.	Sandy Koufax	37
5.	Jim Bunning	35
6.	Dean Chance	32
7.	Jim Maloney	30
	Larry Jackson	30
9.	Milt Pappas	28
10.	Camilo Pascual	26
	Denny McLain	26
12.	Claude Osteen	23
13.	Mel Stottlemyre	22
14.	Luis Tiant	21
	Mickey Lolich	21
	Whitey Ford	21
	Steve Barber	21
18.	Chris Short	20
	Bob Friend	20
20.	Bob Veale	19
	Jim Perry	19
	Sam McDowell	19
	Vern Law	19

Righthander Jack Sanford of the San Francisco Giants won 16 straight games in 1962.

Relieving Develops into Laudable Livelihood

A career as a relief pitcher first became a worthy profession during the 1960s. For every failed starter—such as Phil Regan or Ted Abernathy, or Dave Giusti or Stu Miller—who found a second life in the majors as a fireman, there was a Ron Perranoski or a Dick Radatz or a Wayne Granger who began and ended his major league career in the bullpen. Perranoski was the first hurler in history to work in more than 700 contests without ever pitching a complete game. The first pitcher to average more than a strikeout an inning throughout his career, Radatz appeared in 381 games during his seven seasons in the majors without ever making a start. Granger also never received a starting assignment during his nine-year career. Fred Gladding—the National League save leader in 1969—made just one start in his 13 seasons and surprised everyone, most of all himself, by going five innings. Gladding made such a specialty of short relief stints that he labored just 601 career innings in 450 games.

Mickey Lolich said after his Series MVP performance in the 1968 World Series: "All my life somebody else has been the big star and Lolich was No. 2. I figured my day would come."

Minnesota pitcher Jim Kaat in 1962 and '63 won a record 14 consecutive complete games.

Gibson, Lolich Take Series Trio

Since pitchers reigned supreme during the regular season in the late 1960s, it was only to be expected that they would also dominate the action in World Series play. The 1966 fall classic saw Baltimore hurlers cede the Los Angeles Dodgers two runs in the early innings of the opening game and then shut them out for the remaining 33 frames. In the 1967 Series, Bob Gibson of the Cardinals and Jim Lonborg of the Red Sox paired off in the crucial seventh game with two fall victories apiece and identical 0.50 ERAs. Gibson, working on one more day of rest than Lonborg, prevailed 7-2 to become the last National League hurler to date to post three victories in a World Series. The 1968 fall affair again came down to a game seven that featured two hurlers in search of their third Series wins—Gibson and Mickey Lolich of the Tigers. Like Lonborg, Lolich had one less day of rest than Gibson, but on this occasion it was the Cards ace who faltered, bowing 4-1. Lolich's triumph marked the only time in Series history that a hurler bagged three wins two years in a row.

1960s WINS

1.	Juan Marichal	191
2.	Bob Gibson	164
3.	Don Drysdale	158
4.	Jim Bunning	150
5.	Jim Kaat	142
6.	Larry Jackson	141
7.	Sandy Koufax	137
8.	Jim Maloney	134
9.	Milt Pappas	131
10.	Camilo Pascual	127
11.	Earl Wilson	115
	Chris Short	115
	Whitey Ford	115
	Dean Chance	115
15.	Jim Perry	114
	Claude Osteen	114
	Denny McLain	114
18.	Dick Ellsworth	112
19.	Mudcat Grant	111
	Steve Barber	111

Prior to the 1966 season, Sandy Koufax and Don Drysdale staged the first dual holdout by teammates in major league history.

White Sox pitchers Joe Horlen, Gary Peters, and Tommy John finished 1-2-4 in 1967 in ERA.

"Baseball is such a great life that anyone who complains about it, I think, is a little clouded. I could never find the time to complain."
— Jim Lonborg

'Stros Stockpile Strikeouts

Strikeout totals zoomed in the 1960s, culminating in the 1969 expansion season when seven pitching staffs registered 1,000 or more Ks. The previous year, five teams had whiff totals in four figures, led by Cleveland, which topped the majors for the second year in a row and the fourth time in five seasons. In 1967, Tribe hurlers established a new record by setting 1,189 enemy hitters down on strikes, then threatened their own mark in 1968 before finishing with 1,157. Sam McDowell and Luis Tiant both pitched more than 200 innings in 1967 and '68, and they contributed a strikeout an inning to the Tribe's mark. Cleveland's record, however, was toppled by Houston in the last year of the decade. The Astros hill staff logged 1,221 Ks in 1969, led by Don Wilson (235), Larry Dierker (232), and Tom Griffin (200). Wilson and Griffin both averaged at least one strikeout per inning, as did Jim Ray, a starter-reliever.

In 1966, former Tigers starter Phil Regan led the National League with 21 saves and compiled a 14-1 record with a 1.62 ERA for the Dodgers.

Sandy Koufax explained why he quit so young with an arthritic elbow: "When I'm 40 years old, I'd still like to be able to comb my hair."

**"Pitching is the art of instilling fear by making a man flinch."
—Sandy Koufax**

1960s INNINGS

1.	Don Drysdale	2,629.2
2.	Jim Bunning	2,590.1
3.	Juan Marichal	2,550.0
4.	Bob Gibson	2,447.0
5.	Larry Jackson	2,335.2
6.	Jim Kaat	2,223.2
7.	Dick Ellsworth	2,079.1
8.	Claude Osteen	2,077.0
9.	Milt Pappas	2,033.2
10.	Dean Chance	1,900.2
11.	Jack Fisher	1,887.0
12.	Earl Wilson	1,867.0
13.	Camilo Pascual	1,864.2
14.	Chris Short	1,843.2
15.	Mudcat Grant	1,834.2
16.	Sandy Koufax	1,807.2
17.	Jim Perry	1,806.0
18.	Jim Maloney	1,802.0
19.	M. McCormick	1,786.1
20.	Ray Sadecki	1,778.0

Pirate Elroy Face in '62 set the NL save record with 28.

In 1963, Boston's Dick Radatz went 15-6 with 25 saves for a seventh-place team.

On September 12, 1962, Washington's Tom Cheney struck out 21 Orioles in a 16-inning game, winning 2-1.

In 1961, Warren Spahn became the first NL southpaw to win 300 games.

Los Angeles Dodgers hurler Sandy Koufax in 1963 was the first unanimous choice for the Cy Young Award.

In 1960, Detroit's Frank Lary led the American League with 15 complete games, setting a record for the lowest total to lead a major league.

1960s STRIKEOUTS

1.	Bob Gibson	2,071
2.	Jim Bunning	2,019
3.	Sandy Koufax	1,910
	Don Drysdale	1,910
5.	Juan Marichal	1,840
6.	Sam McDowell	1,663
7.	Jim Maloney	1,585
8.	Jim Kaat	1,435
9.	Bob Veale	1,428
10.	Camilo Pascual	1,391
11.	Dean Chance	1,361
12.	Mickey Lolich	1,336
13.	Earl Wilson	1,332
14.	Chris Short	1,329
15.	Gaylord Perry	1,234
16.	Larry Jackson	1,206
17.	Milt Pappas	1,201
18.	Ray Sadecki	1,174
19.	Denny Lemaster	1,161
20.	Steve Barber	1,144

Koufax Strikes Out 382 in 1965

After Van Lingle Mungo led the National League with 238 strikeouts in 1936, 21 seasons would pass before another senior loop hurler would collect as many as 225 strikeouts. Once Sam Jones broke the dry spell in 1958, not until the strike-abbreviated 1981 season would an NL whiff leader again bag fewer than 225 Ks. A similar phenomenon occurred in the American League, where only Bob Feller, Herb Score, and Hal Newhouser had prevented an equally long string of seasons with lackluster strikeout totals. In the free-swinging expansion-packed 1960s, however, whiff totals went through the roof. In 1963, Sandy Koufax of the Dodgers became the first NL pitcher since 1892 to score 300 or more Ks in a season. Two years later, Koufax set a new modern record with 382 whiffs, averaging 10.24 Ks per nine innings. Sam McDowell of Cleveland became only the third hurler in American League history to enjoy a 300-K season in '65, when he amassed 325 strikeouts. Koufax in 1966 enjoyed his third 300-strikeout season by notching 317.

Hurlers on Pale Hose Lack Support

Picture a team that had a 2.75 staff ERA, only .09 runs higher than the best mark that year in its league. Add the fact that the club allowed just 527 runs, a fraction more than three a game. Note that the team had the best relief corps in its loop and led the majors with 40 saves. Finally, take a guess where this pitcher-rich crew finished. The answer is next to last in a 10-team circuit—and at 67-95, only one and one-half games out of the cellar. Those who well remember the 1960s will have already recognized that the team being described here is the 1968 Chicago White Sox. That year the Sox had so little punch that any Pale Hose hurler who allowed more than two earned runs a game was virtually guaranteed a losing record. Among pitchers who figured in at least 10 decisions, only Tommy John (1.98 ERA and 10-5) and Wilbur Wood (1.87 ERA and 13-12) won more often than they lost as the Sox finished 36 games out of first. Joe Horlan (12-14, 2.37 ERA), Jack Fisher (8-13, 2.98) and Gary Peters (4-13, 3.75 ERA) were other pitchers of note on that club.

Jim Maloney of Cincinnati no-hit Houston on April 30, 1969; the next day, Houston's Don Wilson no-hit Cincinnati.

Whitey Ford in 1967 retired with a .690 career winning percentage, the best in history among 200-game winners.

Stout Reasoning

Mickey Lolich defended his portly physique: "All the fat guys watch me and say to their wives, 'See? There's a fat guy doing okay. Bring me another beer.'"

Roger Craig of the New York Mets in 1963 tied the major league single-season record when he lost 18 consecutive games.

From 1968 to 1969, runs per game rose by 20 percent in the American League.

Ken Holtzman was 9-0 for the Cubs in 1967 when his season was brought to an end by a military call-up.

Above: *Before Tom Seaver, few Mets pitchers had ever had a winning season. Seaver called Shea Stadium home for 12 campaigns and never had a losing season in Mets livery until his finale in 1983.*

1960s EARNED RUN AVERAGE

1.	Hoyt Wilhelm	2.16
2.	Sandy Koufax	2.36
3.	Juan Marichal	2.57
4.	Bob Gibson	2.74
5.	Mike Cuellar	2.76
6.	Dean Chance	2.77
7.	Tommy John	2.81
8.	Joe Horlen	2.83
9.	Bob Veale	2.83
10.	Don Drysdale	2.83
11.	Whitey Ford	2.83
12.	Luis Tiant	2.84
13.	Mel Stottlemyre	2.86
14.	Sonny Siebert	2.91
15.	Gary Peters	2.92
16.	Gaylord Perry	2.95
17.	Fergie Jenkins	2.95
18.	Sam McDowell	2.95
19.	Jim Bunning	3.01
20.	Denny McLain	3.04

'68 Mets Finish Ninth Despite 2.72 ERA

Any who guessed the 1968 New York Mets were the team that fared so poorly despite having a wealth of pitching can easily be forgiven. In 1968, the Mets also finished next to last, a mere one game away from the basement, with an even better staff ERA than the White Sox (2.72) and also surrendered fewer runs than the Hose (499). The Mets had a 73-89 record and two young pitchers, Jerry Koosman and Tom Seaver, who fashioned winning records of 19-12 and 16-12, respectively, with ERAs above 2.00. Also on that club was a young hurler named Nolan Ryan, who was 6-9 with a 3.09 ERA in 134 innings pitched. Unlike the White Sox, who suffered a mound collapse the following year and again finished near the bottom, the Mets maintained their stellar hill work in 1969 and added just enough offensive zip to improve to a 100-62 mark, good enough for their first National League pennant.

In 1962, Ralph Terry of the Yankees became the first hurler to win the seventh and deciding game of a World Series 1-0.

Jim Nash set an AL rookie record in 1966 when he compiled a .923 winning percentage by going 12-1.

"There are only two places in this league: first place and no place."
—Tom Seaver

Chance Ensures Cy Young

Juan Marichal, arguably the most consistently outstanding pitcher during the 1960s, never won a Cy Young Award, the honor often going instead to a hurler like Mike McCormick or Vern Law who had only one truly exceptional season. Dean Chance was another hurler in the McCormick and Law mold, a good pitcher throughout his career but never brilliant except in the one season when he copped his lone Cy Young Award. Chance's year of destiny was 1964. Toiling for a mediocre Los Angeles Angels team that barely broke .500, Chance tailored a magnificent 20-9 record and a 1.65 ERA, tops in the majors. He led the league with 287⅓ innings pitched, and had 207 strikeouts opposed to 86 bases on balls. The frosting on the cake, however, was his 11 shutouts, the most since 1913 by an AL pitcher. At the finish of the 1964 season, Chance, although just 23, already had 47 career victories and seemed headed for Cooperstown. He won only 81 more games, however, before departing in 1971.

When he posted a 1.65 ERA in 1964, Dean Chance recorded the lowest ERA in the American League since World War II.

In 1968, Wilbur Wood of the White Sox set a major league record by pitching in 88 games.

In 1969, Hoyt Wilhelm, then with the Angels, became the first pitcher in major league history to log 200 saves.

In 1969, Houston hurlers struck out a major league record 1,221 hitters.

"First thing I do when I wake up in the morning is breathe on a mirror and hope it fogs."
—Early Wynn

In 1964, Bill Wakefield set a record for the most mound appearances by a pitcher in his only big league season when he toed the rubber in 62 contests for the Mets.

Jackson Misses Chance for Cy Young

The National League's top hurler in 1964 was the antithesis of Cy Young winner Dean Chance. Larry Jackson was in his 10th major league season that year and had never been more than a steady workmanlike performer, good for around 14 or 15 wins a season. But in 1964, then in his second campaign with the Cubs after coming to them from St. Louis in a trade the previous year, Jackson snared 24 wins to lead the majors. He pitched almost 300 innings that year, and completed 19 of his 38 starts. Since only one Cy Young Award was given in 1964 and Chance was the popular choice by virtue of his dazzling ERA and shutout total, Jackson was doomed to disappointment in his lone brush with stardom. For the remaining four years of his career, Larry reverted to his earlier form, winning in double figures but losing as often as he won. Minus his snazzy 24-11 season in 1964, Jackson's career record was two games below .500 (170-172).

In 1964, Johnny Wyatt of Kansas City was the first pitcher in major league history to appear in at least half of his team's games (81 of 162).

Pack a Lunch
Early Wynn, asked about his retirement plans when he was still pitching in his 40s, responded: "Somebody will have to come out and take the uniform off me, and the guy who comes after it better bring help."

In 1965, Arnold Earley appeared in 57 games in relief for the Boston Red Sox without earning a single save and figuring in just one decision, a loss.

In 1961, Luis Arroyo of the New York Yankees set a major league record when he notched 29 saves.

In 1968, Luis Tiant of the Cleveland Indians struck out 19 batters in a 10-inning game.

Jay Leads Cincy to Pennant

Eight years after the Braves had signed him to a mammoth bonus contract, Joey Jay had yet to mature as a pitcher. His 9-8 record in 1960 at age 25 convinced Milwaukee to package him with Juan Pizzaro, another young hurler of perennial promise but meager output, and ship the pair to Cincinnati on December 15, 1960, for shortstop Roy McMillan. That same day, the Reds sent Pizarro to the White Sox as part of a deal for third baseman Gene Freese, but they kept Jay and threw him into their starting rotation the following spring. Given his first chance to work on a regular basis, Jay in 1961 blossomed into the National League's leading winner with 21 victories. He lost only 10 games, although his ERA actually increased from his 1960 earned run average. He spearheaded the '61 Reds to their first pennant in 21 years. Jay won 21 games again the following year but then stumbled to a 7-18 mark in 1963 and never again was more than a second-line hurler.

Houston's Ken Johnson in 1964 was the first major league hurler to lose a complete-game no-hitter in nine innings.

Dennis Ribant, with an 11-9 mark in 1966, was the first Mets pitcher to achieve a winning record.

Denny McLain explained his philosophy on conditioning: "All that running and exercise can do for you is make you healthy."

In 1960, Art Ditmar led the Yankees in wins with 15 and innings pitched with just 200.

At age 65, Satchel Paige was the oldest player ever in a major league game when he hurled three scoreless innings for the Kansas City A's against Boston on September 25, 1965.

On April 30, 1967, Steve Barber and Stu Miller of the Orioles tossed the first combined no-hitter in major league history.

In 1963, the Mets had six pitchers who lost 14 or more games, led by Roger Craig with 22 defeats.

Jim Brosnan, relief pitcher and author, when asked if it bothered him that bullpen seats afford a poor view of the game, responded: "That's the best part of it."

After tying for the American League lead in wins as a soph in 1960, Jim Perry (above) was little more than a mediocre hurler for the next eight seasons. He revived in 1969 to post the first of back-to-back 20-win seasons with the Twins.

Cincy Pitchers Breathe Cy of Despair

Even though he paced the National League in wins in 1961, the Reds' Joey Jay failed to garner a single first-place vote for the Cy Young Award. His disappointment was shared by every pitcher on his team during the 1960s. Throughout the decade, Cincinnati had a wealth of pitchers who had fine seasons but were always judged to be just a cut below Cy Young status. In fact, the only Reds hurler to receive so much as a single vote for the top pitching honor was Bob Purkey, when he put together a 23-5 season in 1962 and topped the majors with an .821 winning percentage. Other Reds hurlers who were blanked in the Cy Young balloting during the 1960s despite enjoying fine seasons were Sammy Ellis (1965: 22-10, 3.79 ERA), Jim O'Toole (1961: 19-9, 3.10 ERA), and Jim Maloney. In 1963, Maloney's 23-7 record with 265 strikeouts got him nowhere with voters as Sandy Koufax chose that year to go 25-5 with a 1.88 ERA.

Expansion Alters Schedule

When expansion swelled the American League from eight teams to 10 in 1961, and the composition of the National League was likewise altered a year later, the major league schedule was revised for the first time since 1904. After playing a 154-game slate for over half a century, both leagues adopted a 162-game season. Under the old schedule, every team played 22 contests against each of the other seven clubs in its loop. With two new franchises added, the number of contests teams played against their rivals was pared to 18. Expansion thereby made for a longer schedule but shorter series. Instead of customarily playing one another four contests each time they met, teams now usually played only three per meeting. One casualty was the traditional weekend series, which began with a night game on Friday, followed by a Ladies' Day game on Saturday and then a doubleheader on Sunday.

Don Kessinger on Bill Mazeroski: "He was as good as I've ever seen at turning the double play. They called him 'No Hands' because he threw so quickly he never seemed to touch the ball."

1960s CATCHER GAMES

1. Johnny Roseboro	1,206
2. Tom Haller	990
3. Clay Dalrymple	974
4. Earl Battey	967
5. Elston Howard	961

Mickey Stanley of the Detroit Tigers was awarded an American League Gold Glove as outfielder in 1968; in the 1968 World Series, however, he played all seven games of the affair at shortstop.

Luis Aparicio led the American League in steals a record nine consecutive years, from 1956 to 1964.

"To a pitcher, a base hit is a perfect example of negative feedback."
—Steve Hovley, outfielder and flake

National (Not Quite) Geographic

Rod Carew tied Pete Reiser's major league record when he stole home successfully seven times in 1969.

In the 1963 fall classic, the Los Angeles Dodgers swept the New York Yankees. It was the first time New York was swept since 1922.

1960s FIRST BASE GAMES
1. Norm Cash	1,375
2. Bill White	1,265
3. Orlando Cepeda	1,181
4. Ernie Banks	1,177
5. Donn Clendenon	992

In 1969, a second wave of expansion, which created two new teams in both major leagues, resulted in each circuit splitting into two six-team divisions rather than balloon to an unwieldy 12-team loop. The schedule remained at 162 games, with clubs playing 18 contests against each of their five division rivals and 12 against each of the six clubs in the other division. It was decided that the two division champions would play a best three-of-five League Championship Series at the conclusion of the regular season. Only the World Series format was left unchanged by schedule-makers in 1969. The restructuring that was done to divide the two leagues into separate divisions resulted in several quixotic geographical arrangements that lasted until the NL again expanded in 1993. Atlanta was placed in the National League West as was Cincinnati, while St. Louis and Chicago got spots in the East.

Gus Triandos retired in 1965 with the record for the most consecutive games without being caught stealing; in his 1,206-game career Triandos was successful in his one and only stolen base attempt.

I'm the Wanderer
Joe Pepitone, complaining about his move from first base to the outfield, said: "In center field you've got too much time to think about everything but baseball."

"A great catch is like watching girls go by. The last one you see is always the prettiest."
—Bob Gibson

Hodges Transforms Mets

In 1961, Gil Hodges retired after a long career as one of the game's top sluggers to take a dugout post with the Washington Senators. Although Hodges was unable to lift the Senators out of the second division in any of his five seasons at their helm, the New York Mets thought highly enough of his managerial skills to offer Washington pitching prospect Bill Denehy if the Senators would agree to release Hodges from his contract so that he could take over the Mets' reins. It turned out to be the Mets' greatest deal. Denehy never won a game in Washington. Hodges, however, turned around a franchise that had previously been close to a travesty, and brought a pennant to Shea Stadium after only two seasons. After the Miracle Mets' triumph in 1969, Hodges kept the club in contention during the next two years. Near the end of spring training in 1972, after playing a round of golf, Hodges suffered a fatal heart attack.

In 1964, the New York Yankees tied their own record by winning their fifth consecutive flag in the AL.

1960s SECOND BASE GAMES

1. Bill Mazeroski	1,421
2. Julian Javier	1,330
3. Bobby Richardson	1,075
4. Jerry Lumpe	1,038
5. Tony Taylor	940

Casey Stengel, after he was fired by the Yankees following the club's 1960 World Series loss, said: "I'll never make the mistake again of being 70 years old."

The New York Yankees had winning seasons in 39 consecutive years, from 1926 to 1964. The second-longest streak was 18 straight seasons, owned by the Baltimore Orioles from 1968 to 1985.

The last time the Cleveland Indians finished above .500 two years in a row was in 1965 and '66.

Willie Had Better Hands
Jimmy Breslin wrote about the early Mets: "Having Marv Throneberry play for your team is like having Willie Sutton play for your bank."

262

Cubs Collapse

As the 1960s drew to a close, the Chicago Cubs seemed about to mark their second consecutive decade without a pennant. Then in 1969, in their fourth season under manager Leo Durocher, the Bruins roared out of the starting gate at such a furious pace that it seemed certain they would make their first postseason appearance since 1945. In early August, the Cubs led the second-place Mets by 9 1/2 games. The Bruins then went into a tailspin that left them only 2 1/2 games in front when they faced New York on September 8 in the first of a two-game set. Three days later the Mets were in first place by percentage points, a margin that swelled to eight full games when the season closed. What triggered the Cubs' late-season collapse was the lack of an adequate center fielder, plus some sniping by Durocher that helped to undermine the team's morale.

Ed Kranepool said about his manager on the Mets, Gil Hodges: "You played his way or you didn't play. He molded young players. He was the turning point."

1960s THIRD BASE GAMES	
1. Brooks Robinson	1,576
2. Ron Santo	1,526
3. Clete Boyer	1,253
4. Ken Boyer	1,169
5. Eddie Mathews	1,024

Amazin'

Richie Ashburn, on playing with the 1962 Mets, said: "I don't know what's going on, but I know I've never seen it before."

Dodger manager Walter Alston in 1965 won an NL record fourth world championship.

Before the 1968 season, the Athletics moved from Kansas City to Oakland.

In 1960, the Cincinnati Reds set a 20th-century record for the lowest winning percentage (.435) by a team destined to win the pennant the following year. That record was broken by the 1990 Atlanta Braves, who fashioned a .401 winning percentage.

Ashford Breaks Blue Color Bar

In 1966, Emmett Ashford broke a color barrier that had been even more difficult to surmount than the one faced by Jackie Robinson, when Ashford became the first black umpire in major league history. Hired by the American League, Ashford served as a junior loop official for five seasons. Two years after his departure, Art Williams joined the National League arbiters staff as the senior loop's first black umpire and remained on its rolls until 1977. Neither Ashford nor Williams was a particularly outstanding official, lending support to historians who have since written that they were both hired simply because the timing was right. With all the documentation there is about the many great Negro League stars who were denied access to the majors because of their color, astonishingly little has been written about early day black umpires.

Ty Cobb in 1960, on why he would only hit .300 against modern pitching, said: "You've got to remember I'm now 73 years old."

1960s OUTFIELD GAMES

1. Hank Aaron	1,513
2. Vada Pinson	1,494
3. Willie Mays	1,464
4. Curt Flood	1,461
5. Roberto Clemente	1,443
6. Billy Williams	1,438
7. Johnny Callison	1,379
8. Carl Yastrzemski	1,353
9. Frank Robinson	1,340
10. Willie Davis	1,314
11. Rocky Colavito	1,261
12. Al Kaline	1,235
13. Tony Gonzalez	1,216
14. Lou Brock	1,180
15. Frank Howard	1,179

Manager Casey Stengel was fired after the 1960 World Series loss, despite winning nine world championships in 12 seasons at the helm of the New York Yankees.

1960s SHORTSTOP GAMES

1. Luis Aparicio	1,482
2. Leo Cardenas	1,298
3. Zoilo Versalles	1,212
4. Maury Wills	1,172
5. Jim Fregosi	1,143

Elderly?

Bill DeWitt, Cincinnati president, revealed why he traded Frank Robinson prior to the 1966 season although Robinson was just 30 years old and seemingly in his prime: "Because he's an old 30."

In 1963, Harmon Killebrew (above) led the AL in slugging despite batting .258 with 18 doubles and no triples.

"Old-timers weekends and airplane landings are alike. If you can walk away from them, they're successful."
—Casey Stengel

The New York Mets in 1963 lost a big league record 22 straight games on the road.

"The only good thing about playing in Cleveland is you don't have to make road trips there."
—Richie Scheinblum

Bigs Hire Schools of Umps

In its 1959 edition, the *Baseball Register* discontinued its annual custom of listing the playing records of umpires along with those of active players, coaches, and managers. The change was made in part because not many umpires by the late 1950s had had careers of any substance as players. Among the few who had, only Ken Burkhart, Ed Sudol, and Frank Secory would still be in blue by the end of the following decade. Others, such as Vinny Smith, Jocko Conlan, and Dusty Boggess all retired during the 1960s. To replace them, the two major leagues drew new recruits from the graduates of the many umpiring schools that sprang up after World War II rather than, as before, from the ranks of former players who had turned to officiating after their retirement. The trend has only increased in recent years. For every former major league player like Bill Kunkel, there are a dozen umpires who never played so much as a single inning professionally.

In 1960, the Tigers and Indians engineered the only managerial trade in history when Skipper Jimmy Dykes came to Cleveland in return for Tribe pilot Joe Gordon.

In 1968, the Player Relation Committee and the Player Association hammered out their first "Basic Agreement."

In 1967, Detroit outfielder Al Kaline won his last of 10 Gold Gloves.

"Once I get on first I become a pitcher and catcher as well as a baserunner. I am trying to think with them."
—Maury Wills

One Small Step
"I'm anxious to see one of the moon-rock samples the astronauts brought back. I'm sure there are a few of my home run balls in that crowd."
—Wilmer Mizell, former congressman and 1950s NL hurler

NL Clubs Recruit Blacks, Latinos

In All-Star play, considered by many to be the best measure of talent in the two rival major leagues, the National League won all but two of the games played between 1961 and 1978. Much of the reason was the greater zeal with which senior loop teams scouted, signed, and developed black and Latino players in the late 1950s and early 1960s. Between 1961 and 1978, only four NL bat titles, one slugging championship, and five home run crowns were won by white players. The huge disparity between the two leagues in their recruitment of black and Latino players was apparent as early as 1961. The AL's top five hitters and sluggers in the first expansion season were all white, but the three top sluggers and three of the five leading hitters in the NL were either black or Latino. No team was more guilty of shortsightedness or suffered harder for it than the New York Yankees. The club's stubborn refusal to stock its farm system with young black and Latino talent, more than anything else, caused the end of its long dominance of the game.

Brosnan, Bouton Bull-Pen Baseball Books

Few of Jim Bouton's teammates in 1969 on the Seattle Pilots and the Houston Astros were aware that he was occupying himself in the bullpen by keeping a journal that would soon appear under the title of *Ball Four*. Bouton's sense of the absurd in the game and his irreverent expose of the adolescent male egos that were both playing it and running it in 1969 was a joy to read for everyone but his former teammates. *Ball Four* followed in the footsteps of *The Long Season* and *Pennant Race*, two books by Jim Brosnan, a relief pitcher who broke the ground for Bouton nearly a decade earlier. When the first of Brosnan's books appeared, there was general amazement that a baseball player could write both wittily and coherently, to say nothing of the shock that one would actually tell the truth about the game and the men who played it.

"The charm of baseball is that, dull as it may be on the field, it is endlessly fascinating as a rehash."
—Jim Murray, sportswriter

Above: *Brooks Robinson (left) and Clete Boyer vied all during the 1960s for recognition as the game's best fielding third baseman. Boyer's older brother Ken was also in the running.*

1960s MANAGER WINS

1.	Walter Alston	878
2.	Gene Mauch	698
3.	Bill Rigney	658
4.	Alvin Dark	640
5.	Ralph Houk	610
6.	Hank Bauer	594
7.	Al López	574
8.	Sam Mele	524
9.	Gil Hodges	494
10.	Danny Murtaugh	456

Shortstop Maury Wills of the Dodgers in 1962 swiped a major league record 104 bases.

Robinson Swap Leaves Cincy Red-Faced

On November 30, 1959, shortly after restrictions on interleague trading were lifted, at least during the off-season, the Baltimore Orioles sent pitchers Billy O'Dell and Billy Loes to the San Francisco Giants for outfielder Jackie Brandt and two other players. Among the more significant transactions between the two leagues in the early 1960s was one that took former bat titlist Harvey Kuenn from Cleveland to San Francisco for Johnny Antonelli and Willie Kirkland prior to the 1961 season. But probably no interleague deal will ever surpass in impact the December 1965 exchange between Baltimore and Cincinnati that gave the Orioles Frank Robinson for pitcher Milt Pappas and two lesser players. In his initial year with Baltimore, Robinson won the Triple Crown and sparked the Birds to their first AL pennant.

"Open up a ballplayer's head and you know what you'd find? A lot of broads and a jazz band."
—Mayo Smith, manager and former player

Ball Four
"You spend a good part of your life gripping a baseball, and in the end it turns out it was the other way around all the time."
—Jim Bouton

1960s TEAM WINS

	W	L
1. Baltimore-AL	911	698
2. San Fran.-NL	902	704
3. New York-AL	887	720
4. St.Louis-NL	884	718
5. Detroit-AL	882	729
6. L.A.-NL	878	729
7. Washington-Minnesota-AL	862	747
Wash. 1960-AL	73	81
Minnesota-AL	789	666
8. Cincinnati-NL	860	742
9. Chicago-AL	852	760
10. Milwaukee-Atlanta-NL	851	753
Milw.-NL	515	441
Atlanta-NL	336	312
11. Pittsburgh-NL	848	755
12. Cleveland-AL	783	826
13. Boston-AL	764	845
14. Phila.-NL	759	843
15. Chicago-NL	735	868
16. Kansas City-Oakland-AL	686	922
K.C. A's-AL	516	768
Oakland-AL	170	154
17. Los Angeles-California-AL	685	770
L.A.-AL	308	338
California-AL	377	432
18. Wash. 1961-69-AL	607	844
19. Houston-NL	555	739
20. N.Y.-NL	494	799
21. K.C.-AL	69	93
22. Sea. Pilots-AL	64	98
23. San Diego-NL	52	110
24. Montreal-NL	52	110

Players Flourish in Both Leagues

Previous to the cessation of the ban on interleague trading, it was a rare player who accomplished something of significance in both major leagues during his career. Generally a player was waived from one circuit to the other only when, like Babe Ruth, he seemed near the end of the line, or, like Lew Burdette, before he had established himself. By the mid-1960s, though, many players had been swapped from one circuit to the other while at their peak. In 1963, after joining the Boston Red Sox, former Pirates first baseman Dick Stuart became the first player in history to hit 35 or more homers in a season in each major league. Frank Howard marked the beginning of the 1960s by being named the National League Rookie of the Year and the beginning of the 1970s by pacing the American League in homers and RBI. And in 1970, Jim Bunning became the first hurler in this century to win 100 or more games in each league.

Prior to his death in 1969, John Hollison was the last surviving major league pitcher who threw from inside a rectangular box only 50 feet from home plate.

It's the Thought That Counts

"I was a bonus baby. I got two autographed baseballs and a scorecard from the 1935 All-Star Game."
—Bob Feller

"You can't get rich sitting on the bench—but I'm giving it a try."
—Phil Linz, highly paid utility infielder

In 1960, Jim Brosnan wrote *The Long Season*, regarded as the best baseball book written by a player.

White Sox owner Bill Veeck in 1960 was the first owner to put player names on backs of his team's uniforms. He also unveiled the first exploding scoreboard that year.

Chapter 10
The 1970s

Carew Cruises to Crown

Ted Williams hit .406 in 1941 and George Brett hovered around the .400 mark for much of the 1980 season before finishing at .390. But Williams, who received tons of walks, had only 456 at bats and Brett came to bat officially just 449 times. Since 1930, only once has a player made a serious bid to hit .400 while collecting far more than the minimum number of plate appearances. In 1977, Rod Carew of the Twins sizzled to a .388 mark with 239 hits in 616 at bats. Carew's performance was tarnished somewhat by the fact that 1977 was an expansion year in the American League, with the addition of two new teams in Toronto and Seattle. His .388 figure exceeded the league average of .266 by 122 points, a staggering amount in the current era when few batting titlists outhit the average player in their loop by even a 100 point margin.

In 1977, the Dodgers became the first team in history with four 30-homer men—Ron Cey, Steve Garvey, Dusty Baker, and Reggie Smith.

1970s GAMES

1.	Pete Rose	1,604
2.	Graig Nettles	1,557
3.	Sal Bando	1,527
4.	Bobby Murcer	1,500
5.	Larry Bowa	1,489
6.	Carl Yastrzemski	1,479
	Bobby Bonds	1,479
8.	Tony Perez	1,471
9.	Lee May	1,464
10.	Amos Otis	1,462
11.	Joe Morgan	1,458
12.	Reggie Jackson	1,440
13.	Al Oliver	1,438
14.	George Scott	1,437
15.	Johnny Bench	1,435
16.	Rusty Staub	1,433
17.	Ted Simmons	1,412
18.	Ken Singleton	1,405
19.	Mark Belanger	1,402
20.	A. Rodriguez	1,400
	Lou Brock	1,400

In 1972, Rod Carew of the Twins was the first batting crown winner to go homerless since Zach Wheat in 1918.

"Babe Ruth will always be No. 1. Before I broke his home run record it was the greatest of all. Then I broke it and suddenly the greatest record is Joe DiMaggio's hitting streak."
—*Hank Aaron*

1970s RUNS

1.	Pete Rose	1,068
2.	Bobby Bonds	1,020
3.	Joe Morgan	1,005
4.	Amos Otis	861
5.	Carl Yastrzemski	845
6.	Lou Brock	843
7.	Rod Carew	837
8.	Reggie Jackson	833
9.	Bobby Murcer	816
10.	Johnny Bench	792
11.	Cesar Cedeno	777
12.	Reggie Smith	776
13.	Graig Nettles	773
14.	Al Oliver	767
15.	Sal Bando	759
16.	Roy White	752
17.	Tony Perez	740
18.	Rusty Staub	732
19.	Larry Bowa	725
20.	George Scott	724

Above: *George Foster was not an instant star after coming to Cincinnati in a 1971 deal with the Giants; his maturation did not really begin until 1975.*

Giants Taken in Trades

The player who posted the highest single-season home run and RBI totals during the 1970s and the first pitcher to win a Cy Young Award in each league began the 1970s as teammates with the San Francisco Giants. Unfortunately for the Giants, both had moved on to other teams by the time they accomplished their feats, and in return for them the Bay Area club received next to nothing. In 1977, at Cincinnati, George Foster amassed 52 dingers and 149 ribbies. In May of 1971, the future home run and RBI king was shipped to the Reds for pitcher Vern Geishert and shortstop Frank Duffy. Geishert never threw a single pitch in Giants livery; Duffy had time to appear in only 21 games with San Francisco before he was packaged with Gaylord Perry at the end of the 1971 season and tossed Cleveland's way for sore-armed Sam McDowell. Sudden Sam had only nine wins left in him, a mere 170 less than Perry would accumulate in the years ahead along with his two Cy Young trophies.

Bull Market
"I came to the Braves on business, and I intended to see that business was good as long as I could."
—Hank Aaron

George Foster had only 79 career home runs in nearly 2,000 at bats before he blasted 52 dingers for the Reds in 1977.

Johnson Fails to Utilize Talent

Fans in every city where Alex Johnson played came out in droves just to watch him take batting practice. In pregame drills, he always looked as if he was ready to go 4-for-4, and some days he actually did. He hit over .300 two years in a row, with the 1968 and '69 Reds. In 1970, Johnson became the only member of the California Angels franchise ever to win an American League batting title, when he hit .329. At the time he was spending his first season in Anaheim after having played for three National League teams. The surly and self-centered Johnson would remain with the Angels for one more year before beginning an odyssey that would take him to four other AL teams in the next five seasons. With each move the quality of his play grew more lackadaisical and his stats declined. After winning the AL bat crown, Johnson never again hit anywhere near .300. He played for seven ballclubs and had a career .288 batting average. But he continued to look great in batting practice.

1970s HITS

1. Pete Rose	2,045
2. Rod Carew	1,787
3. Al Oliver	1,686
4. Lou Brock	1,617
5. Bobby Bonds	1,565
6. Tony Perez	1,560
7. Larry Bowa	1,552
8. Ted Simmons	1,550
9. Amos Otis	1,549
10. Bobby Murcer	1,548
11. Ralph Garr	1,546
12. T. Munson	1,536
13. Bob Watson	1,507
14. Carl Yastrzemski	1,492
15. Rusty Staub	1,487
16. George Scott	1,475
17. Steve Garvey	1,469
18. Dave Cash	1,464
19. Lee May	1,461
20. Joe Morgan	1,451

Fore!

"It took me 17 years to get 3,000 hits in baseball. I did it in one afternoon at the golf course."
—Hank Aaron

Stan Musial was the only living member of the 3,000-hit club when Hank Aaron hit his 3,000th. Musial said: "It was getting awfully lonely. Congratulations, Henry."

In 1973, the Atlanta Braves had three players with at least 40 homers.

In 1973, Hank Aaron set a record for the most home runs (40) by a player who collected fewer than 400 at bats.

Carty Battles Knee and TB to DH

The National League batting titlist in 1970, Rico Carty of the Atlanta Braves, also never again approached the hitting form he displayed that season. In Carty's case, though, the reason was physical rather than psychological. Tuberculosis compounded by a severe knee injury caused Carty to miss the entire 1971 season and held him to just 82 games the following year. Lacking the mobility to play the outfield any longer, he was then traded by the Braves to Texas in the American League, which had just adopted the designated hitter rule. But Carty's knee was still so shaky that he could not handle even a DH role. Not until late in the 1974 campaign, after being picked up by Cleveland, did he start to regain the form that had made him a .322 career hitter prior to his illness and injury. Carty served as a regular DH for five seasons before retiring in 1979 with a .299 average.

Giant Bobby Bonds in 1973 just missed becoming the first "40-40" player in major league history, when he hit 39 homers and swiped 43 bases.

After signed by the Phils as a free agent, Pete Rose said: "With all the money I'm making, I should be playing two positions."

Hank Aaron slugged a major league record 715th career homer on April 8, 1974, off Al Downing of the Dodgers.

In 1974, Hank Aaron defeated Japanese slugger Sadaharu Oh 10-9 in a specially arranged home run contest in Tokyo.

Giants outfielder Bobby Bonds fanned 189 times to set a major league record that still stands.

In 1974, the Chicago White Sox led the American Legue in home runs for the first time.

After winning the NL batting crown in 1970, Rico Carty was idled all of the following season and was never again able to play regularly except as a DH.

As a rookie in 1977, Mitchell Page led the Oakland A's in batting (.301) and RBI (75) and was second on the club in homers with 21.

In 1979, Garry Templeton of the Cardinals became the first switch-hitter to collect 100 hits in a season from each side of the plate.

In 1978, Bobby Bonds had 30 homers and 30 steals for a record fifth time.

"The only way I can't hit .300 is if there is something physically wrong with me."
—Pete Rose

1970s DOUBLES

1. Pete Rose	394
2. Al Oliver	320
3. Tony Perez	303
4. Ted Simmons	299
5. Cesar Cedeno	292
6. Amos Otis	286
7. Hal McRae	285
8. Joe Morgan	275
9. Reggie Jackson	270
10. Willie Montanez	266
11. Johnny Bench	264
12. Rusty Staub	263
13. Bobby Bonds	255
14. Willie Stargell	253
15. Chris Chambliss	252
16. Joe Rudi	251
17. Bob Watson	250
18. Steve Garvey	248
19. Carl Yastrzemski	247
Reggie Smith	247

Sanguillen, Simmons Strive for Stick Summit

No catcher has won a batting crown since 1942, but during the 1970s, the National League had two receivers who made a serious bid to end the long drought. In 1970, Manny Sanguillen of the Pirates hit .325 to tie for the second-best average in the loop. Five years later, Sanguillen finished third in the NL bat race with a .328 mark. Four points ahead of him at .332 was Ted Simmons, the Cardinals' switch-hitting backstopper. He also was in the top five with 193 base hits. Simmons made a second run at the NL hitting title in 1977 before finishing at .318, some 20 points behind champion Dave Parker. Although he never again hit .300 after 1975, Sanguillen retired in 1980 with a .296 career average, the sixth highest mark in history by a receiver. He batted over .300 in four seasons. A string of poor seasons near the end of his career dropped Simmons's average to .285, but he nonetheless remains the top switch-hitting catcher in history. He batted over .300 in seven seasons.

'70s AL Receivers Swing Sweet Sticks

Eighth on the list for the highest career batting average by a catcher is Thurman Munson at .292. The Yankees backstopper finished among the top five hitters in the American League just once, in 1975, but prior to his death in 1979 he bettered .300 on five occasions, the most by any AL catcher since World War II. Carlton Fisk, while never the hitter for average that Munson was, ranked as the AL's equivalent to Johnny Bench as a slugging receiver during the 1970s. In 1977, his finest all-around season, Fisk stood seventh in the AL when he hit .315 to go with his 26 homers and 102 RBI. The receiver who might have been the AL's best-hitting backstopper of all during the 1970s if not for an injury was Ray Fosse. In 1970, his first full season with Cleveland, Fosse was batting well over .300 before being sent to the disabled list after a bone-crunching All-Star game home-plate collision with Pete Rose. Even though he managed to hold his average at .307 in 1970, Fosse was never again able to generate the same pop at the plate.

1970s TRIPLES	
1. Rod Carew	80
2. Larry Bowa	74
3. George Brett	73
4. Roger Metzger	71
5. Willie Davis	70
6. Pete Rose	64
Ralph Garr	64
8. Al Oliver	63
9. Mickey Rivers	61
10. Lou Brock	56
11. Don Kessinger	55
12. Amos Otis	53
Garry Maddox	53
Dave Cash	53
15. Garry Templeton	52
16. Manny Sanguillen	51
Dave Parker	51
Bobby Bonds	51
19. Jim Rice	49
20. Joe Morgan	47
Jose Cruz	47
Cesar Cedeno	47

Ted Simmons of the Cardinals set an all-time season record for catchers when he logged 193 hits in 1975.

In 1979, catcher Brian Downing of the Angels finished third in the American League in batting with a .326 mark.

Terrifying

Willie McCovey, when asked how he'd recommend pitchers pitch to him, responded: "I'd walk me."

Torre! Torre! Torre!

Few players have performed as regulars at three different positions during their careers. Fewer still have posted 100-RBI seasons as regulars at three different positions. Only one, Joe Torre, has achieved it with catcher among his three positions. After two 100-RBI campaigns as a backstopper with the Braves, Torre was swapped to the Cardinals in 1969 and converted to a first baseman. He promptly rang up 101 ribbies. In 1971, the Cards moved Torre to third base and saw him have the finest all-around season of any National League player during the decade when he stroked .363 and added 230 hits and 137 RBI. He also had 24 homers, a .424 on-base average, and a .555 slugging percentage. Torre's monster year earned him the MVP Award by a comfortable margin over slugger Willie Stargell, whose 48 homers led the majors. In his first year at the hot corner, Torre also led all NL third sackers in putouts.

1970s HOME RUNS

1.	Willie Stargell	296
2.	Reggie Jackson	292
3.	Johnny Bench	290
4.	Bobby Bonds	280
5.	Lee May	270
6.	Graig Nettles	252
	Dave Kingman	252
8.	Mike Schmidt	235
9.	Tony Perez	226
10.	Reggie Smith	225
11.	Willie McCovey	207
12.	George Scott	206
13.	Greg Luzinski	204
14.	Carl Yastrzemski	202
15.	George Foster	201
	Hank Aaron	201
17.	Bobby Murcer	198
	John Mayberry	198
19.	Sal Bando	195
20.	Rusty Staub	184
	Darrell Evans	184

Catfish Hunter, a teammate of Reggie Jackson's on both the A's and the Yankees, said that Jackson would "give you the shirt off his back. Of course, he'd call a press conference to announce it."

Count Your Lucky Stars
"I don't want to be a hero. I don't want to be a star. It just works out that way."
—Reggie Jackson

The last NL player to top the major leagues in both batting average and slugging percentage in the same season was Billy Williams of the Cubs in 1972.

Yearling Lynn Wins MVP

Frosh players generally fare poorly in MVP balloting regardless of how sensational their yearling campaigns are. In 1964, when he led the American League in batting and total bases as a rookie, Tony Oliva finished a distant fourth on the MVP list. All leading the majors with 49 homers as a frosh in 1987 brought Mark McGwire was the sixth spot at MVP time. In 1975, however, Fred Lynn of the Red Sox had an inaugural season so sensational that he forced AL writers to break with tradition and vote him the MVP prize. Lynn's credentials included a .331 average (second in the AL), the loop's top slugging average of .566, and 105 RBI (only four behind leader George Scott). In addition, Lynn manned center field, a trouble spot for the Red Sox in 1974, and was instrumental in bringing the AL pennant to Boston. He finished with 326 points in the MVP voting, more than twice the total of runner-up John Mayberry.

In 1975, Dave Cash set a single-season record with 699 at bats.

1970s RUNS BATTED IN

1.	Johnny Bench	1,013
2.	Tony Perez	954
3.	Lee May	936
4.	Reggie Jackson	922
5.	Willie Stargell	906
6.	Rusty Staub	860
7.	Bobby Bonds	856
8.	Carl Yastrzemski	846
9.	Bobby Murcer	840
10.	Graig Nettles	831
11.	Ted Simmons	828
12.	Bob Watson	822
13.	Al Oliver	812
	Sal Bando	812
15.	George Scott	802
16.	Greg Luzinski	755
17.	Amos Otis	753
18.	Reggie Smith	750
19.	Steve Garvey	736
20.	Willie Montanez	730

In 1972, San Diego Padre Nate Colbert drove home 13 teammates during a doubleheader to break a big league record; he had five homers during the twin bill to tie a major league record.

In 1979, Dave Winfield and Gene Tenace combined to hit 54 of the Padres' 93 home runs

> "I'd rather hit than have sex."
> —Reggie Jackson

In 1970, Chicago Cubs outfielder Billy Williams set an NL record when he played in his 1,117th consecutive game.

"If I'm hitting, I can hit anyone. If not, my 12-year-old son can get me out."
—Willie Stargell

Manny Mota, an NL outfielder from 1962 to 1982, not only holds the record for the most career pinch hits with 150 but also the mark for the highest batting average (.297) among players with at least 100 career pinch hits.

The last player to collect 400 or more total bases in a season was Boston's Jim Rice, who netted 406 in 1978.

Lynn Wins, but Rice Also Nice

Third in the American League MVP balloting in 1975 was a second rookie. Even more remarkable, he too played for the Red Sox—and right beside center fielder Fred Lynn. In left field for Boston in 1975, replacing incumbent Juan Beniquez, was Jim Rice, a Triple Crown winner the previous year with Pawtucket of the Triple-A International League (.337 average, 25 homers, 97 RBI). Rice was the minor loop's Most Valuable Player. Ironically Lynn also played with Pawtucket in 1974 but did not particularly distinguish himself (.282 average, 21 homers, 68 RBI). It was Rice who was regarded by the Red Sox in the spring of 1975 as their rookie prize, and he in no way disappointed Hub followers. His frosh season was, in fact, the second best of the decade, with a .309 average, 22 home runs, and 102 RBI. Rice's misfortune was that his teammate chose that same year to have one of the best yearling campaigns ever.

1970s STOLEN BASES

1.	Lou Brock	551
2.	Joe Morgan	488
3.	Cesar Cedeno	427
4.	Bobby Bonds	380
5.	Davey Lopes	375
6.	Freddie Patek	344
7.	Bert Campaneris	336
8.	Billy North	324
9.	Amos Otis	294
	Ron LeFlore	294
11.	Rod Carew	253
12.	Larry Bowa	251
13.	Frank Taveras	248
14.	Don Baylor	240
15.	Mickey Rivers	226
16.	Dave Concepcion	220
17.	Omar Moreno	217
18.	Tommy Harper	200
19.	Garry Maddox	193
20.	Pat Kelly	192

In 1974, Pittsburgh's Richie Zisk notched 21 RBI in a 10-game span.

The first player to collect 100 career pinch hits in the AL was Gates Brown, who played with Detroit from 1963 to 1975 and retired with 108 pinch safeties.

The longest hitting streak in the American League during the 1970s was Ron LeFlore's 30-game skein in 1976.

In 1970, seven players in the majors collected 200 or more hits, led by Billy Williams and Pete Rose with 205 each.

America's *Pastime*

"Nobody ever said, 'Work ball!' They say, 'Play ball!' To me, that means having fun."
—Willie Stargell

Jose Morales of the Expos set a major league record that still stands. He rapped 25 pinch hits in 1975.

In 1974, Ed Kranepool of the Mets hit a major league record .486 as a pinch hitter with 17 hits in 35 pinch at bats.

Brett Shaves McRae with Gift Hit

In 1910, Nap Lajoie won the American League batting title when rookie St. Louis Browns third baseman Red Corriden was instructed to play deep on the last day of the season and allow Lajoie to bunt at will for hits. Joe DiMaggio nearly won the Pacific Coast League hitting crown in 1935 on a similar gift. No batting chase, nonetheless, in either major league or minor league history was ever decided in a more disputed fashion than the American League race in 1976. George Brett of the Kansas City Royals won out by a single point—.333 to .332—over teammate Hal McRae. Twins outfielder Steve Brye allowed to fall safely a routine fly ball that Brett hit on his final at bat of the season. Brye made only a token disclaimer that he'd deliberately thrown the bat title to Brett. Brye justified his maneuver by maintaining that Brett, a third baseman, was more deserving of the crown than McRae, a designated hitter who played only 31 games in the field in 1976.

Madlock Wins Second Crown at Third

Like the AL race, the National League batting chase also went right down to the wire in 1976 before Bill Madlock of the Cubs emerged triumphant on the final day of the season. Madlock, Chicago's third baseman, won by three points over Cincinnati's Ken Griffey. Madlock's .339 mark was down 15 points from his .354 figure the previous year, which brought him the first of what would be four hitting crowns before he finished. His 1976 batting title also made him the first third baseman in major league history to win more than one. Madlock has since been joined in this select company by George Brett and Wade Boggs. When both Madlock and Brett won in 1976, it marked the first season that the batting crown in each major league had been captured by a third sacker. Madlock enjoys yet another distinction. He and Roberto Clemente are the only two righthanded hitters since Rogers Hornsby to win four batting titles.

Willie Stargell, when told Dave Parker had called him his idol, said: "That's pretty good, considering that Dave's previous idol was himself."

Johnny Bench revealed his hitting success, calling it: "Inner conceit. It's knowing within yourself you can meet any situation."

The Giants hoped Bill Madlock (above) would end the hex that plagued hitters in Candlestick Park when they acquired him in 1977. Madlock's best year at the Stick was 1978 when he batted .309. Later he won two more hitting titles with Pittsburgh.

Gloveless

In 1973, the 12 American League clubs then in existence, after voting unanimously in favor of the designated-hitter rule, used designated hitters for pitchers for the first time in major league history. The National League disdained the rule and refused to go along with it. Interestingly, however, the notion of a designated hitter was first proposed in 1928 by National League president John Heydler; NL owners were all for it, but the proposal died a quick death when American League moguls roundly vetoed it. The introduction of the DH rule in 1973 immediately gave new life to such players as Tony Oliva, Orlando Cepeda, Frank Robinson, Carlos May, and Tommy Davis, all of whom were too crippled to play regularly anymore in the field. The new position also provided a home for others like Hal McRae, whose fielding was so suspect it made them a liability anywhere but with a bat in their hands.

1970s BATTING AVERAGE

1.	Rod Carew	.343
2.	Bill Madlock	.320
3.	Dave Parker	.317
4.	Pete Rose	.314
5.	Manny Mota	.313
6.	Jim Rice	.310
7.	George Brett	.310
8.	Ken Griffey	.310
9.	Fred Lynn	.309
10.	Ralph Garr	.307
11.	Steve Garvey	.304
12.	Joe Torre	.303
13.	Al Oliver	.303
14.	Bob Watson	.301
15.	Tony Oliva	.299
16.	Bake McBride	.298
17.	Greg Gross	.298
18.	Lou Brock	.298
19.	Ted Simmons	.297
20.	Ron LeFlore	.297

In 1971, the San Diego Padres became the last team to date to score fewer than 500 runs (486) in a season when a full schedule of games was played.

Forest For the Trees
John Candelaria, when told by Pirates teammate Dave Parker that he was a vegetarian, asked: "What do you eat, redwoods?"

Prior to 1985, the New York Mets had just one player in their 23-year history who collected as many as 100 RBI in a season—Rusty Staub with 105 in 1975.

Kaline Designates 3,000th

In 1973, the Detroit Tigers made Gates Brown their first regular designated hitter. Brown, so indifferent an outfielder that he had previously been employed mostly as a pinch hitter, flopped in his new role, hitting just .236 in 125 games. His failure enabled the Tigers to turn the job over to Al Kaline in 1974 without any qualms. Nearing 3,000 hits, Kaline opted to play one more year in an effort to reach the coveted figure when he was given the DH assignment. By collecting 146 hits in 1974 to put him over the top and allow him to retire with 3,007 lifetime base hits, Kaline became the first player the DH rule permitted to reach a significant career milestone stat that otherwise might have eluded him. There have been numerous others in the years since, including George Brett, whose conquest of the 3,000-hit mark was made possible by the DH rule. Whether career attainments like Kaline's and Brett's should be viewed with a certain amount of cynicism is still a subject of debate.

In 1971, Enzo Hernandez of the Padres set a record for the fewest RBI by a player with 500 or more at bats when he knocked home just 12 runs in 549 at bats.

Curt Gowdy announced about Brooks Robinson: "Brooks is not a fast man, but his arms and legs move very quickly."

In 1978, Pete Rose became the first switch-hitter to earn his 3,000th career base hit.

Pete Rose in 1978 set a modern National League record by hitting in 44 consecutive games.

The last player to top the NL in both batting average and slugging average in the same season was Dave Parker of the Pittsburgh Pirates in 1978.

Cincy's Scoring Apparatus a Hit

When the Cincinnati Reds outscored every other team in the National League by at least 105 runs in 1975, rival NL clubs were hopeful it was just a momentary show of offensive force. But the Reds proceeded to tally 857 runs in 1976, 232 more than any of the other five teams in their division and at least a run a game more than every other team in the NL but the Phillies. The offensive deluge earned Sparky Anderson's Cincinnati club the nickname of "The Big Red Machine." Anderson had under his command in the mid-1970s three almost certain Hall of Famers in Joe Morgan, Pete Rose, and Johnny Bench, plus four other players—Tony Perez, Dave Concepcion, George Foster, and Ken Griffey—who would also put up numbers before they retired that merited Cooperstown consideration. The Reds' only regular in 1975 and '76 who was something less than an All-Star was center fielder Cesar Geronimo, but even he was hardly a weak link. In 1975, Geronimo led all NL gardeners in putouts and double plays.

Four of the six key members of the "Big Red Machine" in the mid-1970s were, from left; Tony Perez, Johnny Bench, Joe Morgan, and Pete Rose. Missing are George Foster and Ken Griffey.

Dick Allen said about artificial turf: "If a horse can't eat it, then I don't like it."

In 1974, Cincinnnati's Pete Rose made a major league-record 771 plate appearances.

In 1979, the Houston Astros hit just 49 home runs and were led by Jose Cruz with nine four-baggers.

In 1971, Bill Melton became the first member of the Chicago White Sox to lead the AL in home runs; the following year Dick Allen became the second Sox player to do it.

Bobby Knoop retired in 1972 with a .236 career batting average, the lowest in history by a second baseman with 3,000 or more at bats.

Cardinal outfielder Vic Davalillo in 1970 tied a record with 24 pinch hits.

Melton Dissolves ChiSox Pale Homer History

The Chicago White Sox began the 1971 campaign as the only major league franchise in existence since 1901 that had never had a home run champion. By the end of that season, third baseman Bill Melton had removed that stigma from the Pale Hose. Melton's 33 dingers gave him the American League crown by a margin of one over Detroit's Norm Cash and Reggie Jackson of the A's. Prior to 1971, no White Sox player had ever finished higher than third in the AL home run derby, and only three had ranked that high. The trio were Eddie Robinson in 1951, Jack Fournier in 1914, and Ping Bodie in 1913. In 1951, Gus Zernial had given the Sox a minuscule claim on a home run crown when he won the honor with the A's after beginning the season in Chicago. But Zernial had played only four games before exiting from the Windy City and departed with no home runs. Braggo Roth, on the other hand, hit three of his AL-leading seven homers in 1915 for the Sox before being swapped.

Roger Angell said Joe Morgan "has the conviction that he should affect the outcome of every game he plays in every time he comes up to bat and every time he gets on base."

Reggie Jackson in the 1977 World Series earned the nickname "Mr. October." He had four home runs in four straight official times at bat.

In 1977, Duane Kuiper hit his only home run in 3,379 at bats in the majors.

Allen Spurs White Sox to First Homer Title

Bill Melton's homer crown in 1971 was considerably facilitated by changes made in the design of Comiskey Park in the late 1960s, shortening the distance to and the height of the outfield walls. The alterations brought a second home run leader to Comiskey immediately on the heels of Melton in the person of Dick Allen. The 1972 American League four-bagger king, Allen hit 37 homers in his first year with the Sox after being acquired over the winter in a deal with the Dodgers. Injured much of the following season, Allen rebounded in 1974 to again pace the AL with 32 round-trippers. Help from Melton and outfielder Ken Henderson, who contributed 21 and 20 homers respectively, enabled the Sox to claim their first-ever team home run crown that season. In 1975, after Allen was traded to the Phillies, the Pale Hose reverted to form and hit just 94 homers, the second-fewest in the AL.

"When I was a little boy I wanted to be a baseball player and join the circus. With the Yankees I've accomplished both."
—Graig Nettles

The 1972 season was the only one during the 1970s in which no players in either league managed to compile 200 hits.

On April 6, 1973, Yankee Ron Blomberg became the first designated hitter in a big league game.

In 1970, Dal Maxvill of the Cardinals set a major league record for the fewest hits by a player in 150 or more games when he compiled just 80 singles in 152 contests.

The Conigliaro brothers, Tony and Billy, hit a sibling record 54 homers for the 1970 Boston Red Sox.

Tidy Bowl
John Lowenstein revealed how he stays ready when he's a designated hitter: "I flush the john between innings to keep my wrists strong."

Baltimore Four Take 20

In 1971, manager Earl Weaver of the Orioles had the good fortune to establish his pitching rotation on Opening Day and never have to veer from it. Of the Orioles' 158 games (four were postponed and not made up), Weaver's regular rotation of Mike Cuellar, Pat Dobson, Dave McNally, and Jim Palmer started 142. The quartet furthermore made Baltimore the only team other than the 1920 White Sox to exhibit four 20-game winners. McNally led the Orioles with 21 victories and the other three members of the club's Big Four all kicked in an even 20 wins apiece. Oddly, McNally, the top winner, was idled for part of the season by a sore arm. The Orioles' rotation helped Baltimore take the AL team ERA crown by posting a 2.99 earned run average. The 16 games that were not started by the 20-game winning foursome were distributed by Weaver among Grant Jackson (nine), Dave Leonard (six), and Dave Boswell (one).

Above: *Jim Palmer won 20 games eight times during the '70s. Injuries held him below 20 in the other campaigns.*

1970s GAMES STARTED

1.	Phil Niekro	376
2.	Gaylord Perry	368
3.	Steve Carlton	366
4.	Fergie Jenkins	354
5.	Jim Palmer	352
6.	Bert Blyleven	350
7.	Don Sutton	349
8.	Tom Seaver	345
9.	Nolan Ryan	333
10.	Catfish Hunter	327
	Vida Blue	327
12.	Mike Torrez	313
	Jerry Koosman	313
14.	Rick Wise	303
15.	Jack Billingham	296
16.	Ken Holtzman	294
17.	Jim Kaat	290
18.	Jerry Reuss	287
19.	Paul Splittorff	286
20.	Luis Tiant	285

Ouch
After being hit by a record 50 pitches in 1970, Ron Hunt explained: "Some people give their bodies to science. I give mine to baseball."

Tom Seaver became the first pitcher to claim his third Cy Young Award when he triumphed in 1975, after previously winning in 1969 and 1973.

Who'd Start Doubleheader? Wilbur Wood

Wilbur Wood's knuckleball delivery was so effortless that his arm seemed almost indefatigable. A reliever early in his career, he was converted to a starter when it grew apparent to the White Sox that they were not getting full value out of his rubber wing in just a bullpen role. In 1973, Wood was used so extensively by Sox manager Chuck Tanner that Wilbur became the last American League pitcher to date who was both a 20-game winner and a 20-game loser. Wood's 24-20 record was achieved in 48 starts and 359 innings. Two of his starts came on the same day. When Wood took the hill in each game of a doubleheader against the Yankees on July 20, 1973, he gained the distinction of being the last pitcher to start both ends of a twin bill. The Yankees treated Wood rudely on the occasion, though, knocking him out early in each contest and pinning two losses on him for the day.

1970s GAMES PITCHED

1.	Rollie Fingers	640
2.	Sparky Lyle	600
3.	Pedro Borbon	561
4.	Dave LaRoche	543
	Darold Knowles	543
6.	Tug McGraw	542
7.	Mike Marshall	528
8.	Dave Giusti	470
9.	Paul Lindblad	460
10.	Tom Burgmeier	458
11.	Clay Carroll	447
12.	Al Hrabosky	445
13.	Gene Garber	444
14.	Grant Jackson	443
15.	Randy Moffitt	436
16.	John Hiller	426
17.	Elias Sosa	423
18.	Ron Reed	412
19.	Phil Niekro	406
20.	Dick Drago	396
	Stan Bahnsen	396

In 1973, Nolan Ryan broke Sandy Koufax's old mark of 382 strikeouts in a season when he notched his 383rd strikeout by fanning Rich Reese of the Twins on his last pitch of the campaign.

When asked whether he'd rather face Jim Palmer or Tom Seaver, Merv Rettenmund replied: "That's like asking if I'd rather be hung or go to the electric chair."

In a game on April 22, 1970, Tom Seaver of the Mets fanned a major league record 10 San Diego Padres in a row. He went on to tie a major league record by fanning 19 batters during the game.

Wood, Lolich, Others Prove that Life Starts at 40

Wilbur Wood's 48 starts in 1973 were one less than he made the previous year, when he drew more starting assignments than any hurler since Ed Walsh in 1908. Wood started 42 or more games for five successive seasons between 1971 and 1975 to set a 20th century record for the most starts (223) over a five-year period. Right behind Wood was Mickey Lolich of the Tigers. Between 1970 and 1974, Lolich logged 208 starts, with a high of 45 in 1971. Phil Niekro, who also started more than 40 games on several occasions during the 1970s, like Wood was a knuckleballer who found the delivery so untaxing he seemed apt to pitch forever. Some of the other hurlers who were able to start 40 games at least a couple of years during this time included: Gaylord Perry, Catfish Hunter, Stan Bahnsen, Steve Carlton, Joe Coleman, Bill Singer, Fergie Jenkins, Dave McNally, and Don Sutton. Lolich, unlike Wood, threw hard, as well as often. In 1971, while making 45 starts to set a Detroit club record, he also set a Tigers mark for the most strikeouts, with 308.

After the 1979 season, the Houston Astros signed free-agent pitcher Nolan Ryan for $1 million.

In both the 1973 and '74 seasons, Minnesota's Bert Blyleven fanned 507 hitters and averaged more than seven and one-half strikeouts for every nine innings he pitched.

1970s COMPLETE GAMES

1.	Gaylord Perry	197
2.	Fergie Jenkins	184
3.	Jim Palmer	175
4.	Steve Carlton	165
5.	Nolan Ryan	164
6.	Phil Niekro	160
7.	Tom Seaver	147
8.	Bert Blyleven	145
9.	Catfish Hunter	140
10.	Mickey Lolich	133
11.	Vida Blue	124
12.	Luis Tiant	120
13.	Don Sutton	117
14.	Mike Cuellar	115
15.	Wilbur Wood	113
16.	Rick Wise	107
17.	Mike Torrez	100
18.	Ken Holtzman	97
19.	Bob Gibson	89
20.	Andy Messersmith	86

In 1972, Milt Pappas of the Cubs became the first pitcher in history to bag 200 career victories without ever winning 20 games in a season.

Tim McCarver said about Steve Carlton: "Carlton does not pitch to the hitter, he pitches through him. The batter hardly exists for Steve. He's playing an elevated game of catch."

On September 2, 1972, Milt Pappas of the Chicago Cubs lost a perfect game by walking the 27th man on a 3-2 pitch. He went on to get the no-hitter.

In 1979, Phil Niekro of Atlanta and his brother, Joe Niekro of Houston, tied for the National League lead in wins (21).

Reggie Jackson said about Tom Seaver: "Blind people come to the park just to listen to him pitch."

The record for the highest ERA by an NL Cy Young winner is held by Bob Gibson, with a 3.12 ERA in 1970.

Phil Niekro Wins 287 After 30, 121 After 40

Phil Niekro is the only 300-game winner who began as a relief pitcher. He also is the only 300-game winner who did not reach the majors to stay until he was 26 years old. As a result of his belated arrival and starting out as a relief pitcher, Niekro had only 31 wins in the majors when he turned 30. No one could possibly have predicted then that he was less than a 10th of the way to his career total of 318. Niekro made at least 32 starts in every season during the 1970s. Twice, he led the National League in wins, and on four occasions, he paced the senior loop in losses. In 1979, when he finished at 21-20, Niekro became the only hurler since Jim Whitney in 1881 to top his league in both wins and losses. Interestingly, Whitney labored for the Boston Red Stockings, later to become the Boston Braves, then the Milwaukee Braves, and finally the Atlanta Braves, the team with which Niekro was affiliated in 1979 and for most of his career.

In 1972, Jim Barr of the San Francisco Giants retired a major league-record 41 batters in a row over a two-game period.

Niekro Induces Batters to Knuckle Under

What saved Phil Niekro from a lifetime in the minor leagues was learning to throw a knuckleball. His mastery of the butterfly pitch was also much of the reason that his early managers in both the minors and the majors could not envision him as a starting pitcher. Most of the knuckleballers who preceded Niekro settled into careers as firemen, such as Hoyt Wilhelm and Eddie Fisher. Some, such as Gene Bearden and Roger Wolff, bloomed for a season or two as starters only to flounder after batters, catching on that they had no more idea than anyone else where their dipsy-doodles were going, simply waited for them to fall behind in the count and then sat on their fastballs. Niekro was the first pitcher to make his name as a starter on little more than a knuckler. The pitch was so effective for him, however, that his other deliveries often caught batters with their bats on their shoulders in surprise. In 1977, Niekro even snuck past such flamethrowers as J.R. Richard, Steve Carlton, and Tom Seaver to lead the National League in strikeouts.

The last pitcher to win 25 or more games and not win a Cy Young Award was Mickey Lolich in 1971.

1970s SHUTOUTS

1.	Jim Palmer	44
2.	Nolan Ryan	42
3.	Tom Seaver	40
4.	Don Sutton	39
	Bert Blyleven	39
6.	Gaylord Perry	36
7.	Fergie Jenkins	33
8.	Steve Carlton	32
	Vida Blue	32
10.	Catfish Hunter	30
11.	Luis Tiant	28
	Jon Matlack	28
13.	Jack Billingham	27
14.	Phil Niekro	25
	Mike Cuellar	25
16.	Wilbur Wood	24
	Frank Tanana	24
	Andy Messersmith	24
19.	Rick Wise	22
	Jerry Reuss	22
	Rudy May	22
	Ken Holtzman	22

Cincinnati's Wayne Granger in 1970 set a major league record with 35 saves.

Sprinkles?

Reggie Jackson said about Nolan Ryan: "Every hitter likes fastballs just like everybody likes ice cream. But you don't like it when somebody's stuffing it into you by the gallon."

Perrys' Cy Young Awards Fill Family Mantle

Jim Perry retired at the finish of the 1975 season with the satisfaction of knowing that he and his younger brother Gaylord held the record for the most career wins by pitching siblings. Jim had 215 wins, and at that point Gaylord had 216 Ws, beating John, Dad, and Walter Clarkson, who had 385. The younger Perry later extended the record to 529 wins before retiring himself in 1983. The mark was shortlived, however, lasting only until 1987 when it was broken by the Niekro brothers, who finished with 539 wins between them. But to the Perrys belongs a distinction they need not share with any other siblings. In 1970, Jim snagged the American League Cy Young Award. When Gaylord took the same honor two years later, it was the first and to date the only time that a pair of brothers has each received so high a tribute. Later in the decade Gaylord garnered a second Cy Young after he returned to the National League, giving the Perrys another first.

Above: Gaylord Perry won 314 games in the majors but never appeared in a World Series game; Phil Niekro is the only other 300-game winner in this century to suffer the same fate.

1970s WINS

1.	Jim Palmer	186
2.	Gaylord Perry	184
3.	Tom Seaver	178
	Fergie Jenkins	178
	Steve Carlton	178
6.	Catfish Hunter	169
7.	Don Sutton	166
8.	Phil Niekro	164
9.	Nolan Ryan	155
	Vida Blue	155
11.	Bert Blyleven	148
12.	Luis Tiant	142
13.	Wilbur Wood	136
14.	Jack Billingham	135
15.	Mike Torrez	134
16.	Rick Wise	133
	Tommy John	133
18.	Ken Holtzman	126
19.	Jerry Koosman	124
20.	Paul Splittorff	123

Perry Pitch Packs Petroleum Jelly

Jim Perry was a fairly straightforward hurler during his career, but brother Gaylord was another kettle of fish. Enemy batters were certain the younger Perry cheated by throwing a spitter or some kind of spitball and Vaseline™ ball combination, and he did little to disabuse them of their suspicions. Perry seemed actually to relish the accusations, perhaps because he knew that as long as the flames were fanned it could only give hitters something more to think about. In any case, Gaylord Perry hung up his spikes in 1983 with the issue still unresolved. Did he throw the wet one or didn't he? Had he ever been caught in the act, the rules would have demanded Perry's ejection. But not since 1944, when Nels Potter of the St. Louis Browns was asked to leave the mound in a game against the Yankees, has a hurler been ousted expressly for violating the spitball prohibition.

> "Why pitch nine innings when you can get just as famous pitching two?"
> —Sparky Lyle

1970s INNINGS

1.	Gaylord Perry	2,905.0
2.	Phil Niekro	2,881.0
3.	Steve Carlton	2,747.0
4.	Jim Palmer	2,745.0
5.	Fergie Jenkins	2,706.2
6.	Tom Seaver	2,652.1
7.	Bert Blyleven	2,624.2
8.	Don Sutton	2,557.1
9.	Nolan Ryan	2,465.0
10.	Catfish Hunter	2,399.0
11.	Vida Blue	2,398.2
12.	Jerry Koosman	2,281.1
13.	Wilbur Wood	2,150.1
14.	Mike Torrez	2,138.2
15.	Rick Wise	2,121.0
16.	Mickey Lolich	2,110.0
17.	Ken Holtzman	2,073.2
18.	Luis Tiant	2,063.0
19.	Jack Billingham	2,045.2
20.	Jim Kaat	2,004.1

In 1972, Steve Carlton of the Phillies tied Sandy Koufax's record, set just six years earlier, for the most wins since 1900 by an NL southpaw when Carlton logged 27 wins.

On June 23, 1971, Rick Wise of the Philadelphia Phillies no-hit Cincinnati and clobbered two homers.

> "When you're a winner you're always happy, but if you're happy as a loser you'll always be a loser."
> —Mark Fidrych

See Ya

Graig Nettles remarked when Yankees teammate Sparky Lyle was traded to Texas after the 1978 season: "He went from Cy Young to sayonara in a year."

Hoyt Wilhelm was the last pitcher to win at least 100 games in the majors and minors.

1970s STRIKEOUTS

1.	Nolan Ryan	2,678
2.	Tom Seaver	2,304
3.	Steve Carlton	2,097
4.	Bert Blyleven	2,082
5.	Gaylord Perry	1,907
6.	Phil Niekro	1,866
7.	Fergie Jenkins	1,841
8.	Don Sutton	1,767
9.	Vida Blue	1,600
10.	Jerry Koosman	1,587
11.	Jim Palmer	1,559
12.	Mickey Lolich	1,496
13.	J.R. Richard	1,374
14.	A. Messersmith	1,340
15.	Joe Coleman	1,319
16.	Catfish Hunter	1,309
17.	Rudy May	1,238
18.	Luis Tiant	1,229
19.	Jon Matlack	1,215
20.	Fred Norman	1,208

Fergie Jenkins, with 25 victories in 1974, was the last 20-game winner to date for the Texas Rangers.

John's Surgery Regreases Elbow

In the winter of 1965, Cleveland, desperate since 1960 to get Rocky Colavito back into a Tribe uniform, engineered a three-team deal involving Kansas City and the Chicago White Sox that transferred a young Tribe lefty named Tommy John to the Windy City club. In some respects, the trade to reobtain Colavito proved even more devastating to Cleveland than the one in which he'd been lost, for John proceeded to win more games than any postexpansion southpaw except Steve Carlton. John's career did not really begin to accelerate, though, until he was swapped to the Dodgers in 1972. Even then, he first had to overcome a seemingly impossible obstacle. An elbow injury in 1974 forced him to submit to an experimental surgical procedure that offered only guarded hope he would ever pitch again. After sitting out all of the 1975 campaign while his elbow mended, John returned in 1976 with his wing as good as new. The following year, at age 34, he nailed the first of what would be three 20-win seasons before he retired in 1989 with 288 victories.

Vida Blue After Big 1971 Campaign

Who is the only 200-game winner in this century whose best season came when he was 22 years old? Who was the first black switch-hitter to win an MVP Award? Who is the only hurler to fan 300 batters in a season but never before or never again in his career fan as many as 200? The answer to all three questions is Vida Blue, and his glorious year came in 1971 when he notched 24 wins, 301 Ks, and a 1.82 ERA while spurring the Philadelphia-Kansas City-Oakland A's franchise to its first postseason appearance in 40 years. Blue actually did not turn 22 until the 1971 campaign was deep into its fourth month. By then he had become the youngest winning pitcher in All-Star game history and brought the American League its first midsummer victory since 1962. When Blue faded somewhat in the second half of the season and the A's failed to beat Baltimore in the League Championship Series, Oakland owner Charlie Finley rejected his young pitcher's salary demands. After a long and bitter holdout, Blue was ineffective in 1972 and never again matched his early brilliance.

In 1971, Vida Blue of the A's became the first hurler in major league history to strike out at least 300 batters (301) and not lead the league, as Mickey Lolich of the Tigers notched 308 Ks that year.

In 1978, Ron Guidry tied Babe Ruth's American League record for most shutouts in a season by a lefty with nine.

Tug McGraw said about relief pitching: "Some days you tame the tiger. And some days the tiger has you for lunch."

In 1974, the Baltimore Orioles set an AL record when they won five straight games by shutouts.

California's Nolan Ryan set a major league record in 1972 by allowing only 5.26 hits per game.

1970s EARNED RUN AVERAGE

1.	Jim Palmer	2.58
2.	Tom Seaver	2.61
3.	Bert Blyleven	2.88
4.	Rollie Fingers	2.89
5.	Gaylord Perry	2.92
6.	Frank Tanana	2.93
7.	Andy Messersmith	2.93
8.	Jon Matlack	2.97
9.	Mike Marshall	2.98
10.	Don Wilson	3.01
11.	Don Sutton	3.07
12.	Vida Blue	3.07
13.	Tommy John	3.09
14.	Mel Stottlemyre	3.11
15.	Don Gullett	3.11
16.	Dennis Eckersley	3.12
17.	Steve Rogers	3.13
18.	Nolan Ryan	3.14
19.	Catfish Hunter	3.17
20.	Ken Forsch	3.18

In 1972, Steve Carlton had a 27-10 record for the Phillies while the rest of the Phils pitchers had a combined 32-87 record.

Guidry Gains Grand Campaign

In the fall of 1976, southpaw Ron Guidry had shown so little evidence of becoming a major league pitcher that he was nearly left unprotected by the Yankees in the expansion draft to stock the new Seattle and Toronto franchises. The following spring, Yankees skipper Billy Martin became so exasperated with Guidry that he said, "Show me somebody you can get out and I'll let you pitch to him." Finally given his chance in relief against the Kansas City Royals, Guidry struggled but managed to post his first major league victory. By the fall of 1978, he was the toast of New York after collecting 25 triumphs, a 1.74 ERA, and an .893 winning percentage, the best ever by a 25-game winner. He led the American League by hurling nine shutouts, yielding 8.6 baserunners per nine innings, and holding batters to a .193 batting average. Like Vida Blue, the southpaw sensation in 1971, Guidry never had another season as good as 1978, although he remained a fine pitcher for another decade.

I Agree

"In baseball you're supposed to sit on your ass, spit tobacco, and nod at stupid things."
—Bill Lee, zany pitcher

Ron Guidry of the Yankees set an AL record for lefties in 1978 when he notched 18 strikeouts in a game.

In 1974, Detroit's John Hiller went 17-14—as a relief pitcher.

Hurlers Not Good Buys

The advent of free agency opened the flood gates for disgruntled players to sell their services to the highest bidder. With the advent of the era, pitchers who were looking to make a change often went where the money was, no matter the quality of the team offering it, and the results were sometimes catastrophic. Andy Messersmith, after bagging 19 wins while pitching without a contract for the Dodgers in 1975, signed with the lowly Braves for 1976 and collected just 18 more victories in his career. In 1977, Cleveland, hungering for a staff bulwark, wooed Wayne Garland away from Baltimore where he had been a 20-game winner the previous year. Determined to get their money's worth from their expensive free-agent acquisition, the Indians overworked Garland in 1977 and saw him go down with a torn rotator cuff. Surgery enabled Garland to fulfill his multiyear contract, but in five seasons with Cleveland he won a mere 28 games against 48 losses.

The 1975 World Series was the first to feature two teams that lacked a 20-game winner, as Rick Wise led the Red Sox with 19 victories and the Reds had three hurlers with 15 wins apiece.

In 1973, John Hiller of the Tigers was 10-5 with a 1.44 ERA, and he set a major league record for saves with 38.

Range
Ralph Kiner, Mets announcer, described Phillies outfielder Garry Maddox: "Two-thirds of the earth is covered by water; the other one-third is covered by Garry Maddox."

"Almost every batter guesses a few times a game. This is an advantage for me. Hell, most of the time I don't know what I'm going to throw."—Sam McDowell, wild and woolly lefty.

Al Hrabosky explained why he refused to shave: "How can I intimidate batters if I look like a !*@ $%? golf pro?"

Jones Loses Dominance After Cy Young Season

In the 1975 ALCS, won by the Red Sox over Oakland three games to none, Ken Holtzman was the starting pitcher in two of the A's three losses and became the only starter to register two decisions in a three-game LCS.

Owing to the inclement weather that caused a five-day gap between games five and six of the 1975 World Series, Luis Tiant of the Red Sox was able to start three of the first six games of the seven-game set.

Arm and elbow miseries have plagued pitchers since the invention of the curveball in the late 1860s, but never have more hurlers fallen prey to the pitfalls of their profession than in recent times. Steve Stone, the American League Cy Young winner in 1980 on the basis of his 25 victories with the Orioles, threw his last pitch before the following season was out. Another Cy Young recipient whose arm went soon after his triumph was Randy Jones. The sinkerballer went 20-12 with 18 complete games in 1975 for a Padres team that climbed out of the NL West basement for the first time in franchise history. Jones finished second in Cy Young voting. Logging 22 wins for the Padres in 1976 and pacing the National League with 25 complete games earned Jones the NL's top pitching honor the next year, but the price was high. An ailing flipper hounded him for much of the following season, sending him crashing to a 6-12 record with just one complete game in 25 starts. Jones rebounded somewhat in 1978 but was never again able to win as often as he lost or to complete more than seven games in a season.

When Gaylord Perry's agent approached the makers of Vaseline™ for a possible endorsement contract, a company representative replied: "We soothe babies' asses, not baseballs."

Vida Blue in 1971 struck out 301 batters in his first full major league season.

Bryant Denied '73 Cy Young

By all the laws of probability, Ron Bryant ought to have been another pitcher during the 1970s who fizzled after winning a Cy Young Award. In 1973, Bryant won 24 games for the Giants, five more than any other National League hurler. However, Mike Marshall chose that year to shatter the major league record for both the most mound appearances and the most relief innings (he broke both of his own marks in 1974). The other NL East teams also decided that year to let the Mets cop the pennant with a .509 winning percentage. As a result, Bryant finished in the show position in the Cy Young chase, behind Marshall, the place hurler, and Tom Seaver of the Mets, the winner. The writers who voted for Seaver defended their choice by pointing out that although Seaver had just 19 wins, he led the NL in ERA, complete games, and strikeouts, but Bryant's supporters nonetheless felt cheated. After reporting in less than top condition the following spring, Bryant slipped to just three victories in 1974 and never won another game.

Charley Lau, the hitting guru of the Royals and others, said after a particularly rough outing against Phil Niekro: "There are two theories on hitting the knuckleball. Unfortunately neither of them works."

Let It Roll
"The way to catch a knuckleball is to wait until the ball stops rolling and then pick it up."
—Bob Uecker

The last pitcher to hurl as many as 30 complete games in a season was Catfish Hunter of the New York Yankees in 1975.

Above: *Catfish Hunter led all hurlers in World Series starts during the 1970s with nine but completed only one.*

Red Sox Regret Letting Lyle Leave

Yankee Sparky Lyle in 1977 was the first reliever to win the AL Cy Young Award.

The Montreal Expos have only had one 20-game winner in their history—Ross Grimsley, who won 20 on the nose in 1978.

On May 31, 1979, Detroit's Pat Underwood made his major league debut against brother Tom of Toronto; Pat beat Tom 1-0.

Which team got the better of the deal that sent Tom Seaver to the Reds in 1977 is still an open question, but there is little dispute over who took a reaming in the trade between the Yankees and the Red Sox during spring training in 1972. Ticketed for New York was reliever Sparky Lyle while Boston made ready to welcome first baseman Danny Cater. It seemed a fairly even swap on the surface, but it turned out to be the steal of the decade. After joining the Red Sox, Cater was never again more than a part-time player, whereas Lyle immediately established himself as the American League's premier fireman. Lyle led the loop in saves his first season in the Bronx and repeated his conquest three years later. The following season Lyle became the first AL reliever to win a Cy Young Award. Cater by then had been out of the majors for two years.

On August 27, 1977, pitching against the Texas Rangers, Ken Clay of the New York Yankees allowed two inside-the-park home runs on successive pitches, to Toby Harrah and Bump Wills.

In 1973, with the new designated hitter rule in place, the American League posted 167 more complete games than the National League.

"Trying to hit Phil Niekro is like trying to eat Jell-O with chopsticks."
—Bobby Murcer

You Say Goodbye, and I Say Hello

Billy Martin was a perfect 3-for-3 in the summer of 1975. Three times he had been hired to manage floundering American League teams, and three times he had almost instantly led them either to a division title or else their best showing in years only to be fired before the following season was out when his volatile personality shot away his welcome. Yankees owner George Steinbrenner was convinced that Martin had the right chemistry to restore the Bombers to their pre-1965 supremacy, nonetheless. Hence, Steinbrenner dumped Bill Virdon late in the 1975 season and gave the Yankees dugout post to Martin, thereupon beginning a love-hate relationship between the two that would last until Martin's death in December 1989. As had happened in Minnesota, Detroit, and Texas, Martin quickly hoisted the Yankees into contention and then was fired just as quickly. Steinbrenner, however, proved to be as mercurial as Martin. Between 1975 and 1988, George hired and fired Martin no fewer than five times.

After Brooks Robinson made three errors in the Orioles' first eight games in 1974, Dave McNally said to the third baseman: "You've gone from being a human vacuum cleaner to a litterbug."

Billy Martin won his only world championship as manager with the New York Yankees in 1977.

Hoover
After being robbed of a hit by Brooks Robinson in the 1970 World Series, Johnny Bench said: "I walked back to the dugout appreciating his play for what it was—a thing of beauty."

1970s CATCHER GAMES

1. Ted Simmons	1,305
2. Johnny Bench	1,299
3. Thurman Munson	1,253
4. Manny Sanguillen	973
5. Darrell Porter	893

After his reconstructive elbow surgery, Tommy John said: "When they operated, I told them to put in a Koufax fastball. They did—but it was Mrs. Koufax's fastball."

It Takes a Thief

Mickey Stanley on his sore arm: "I knew how different my arm was. Maybe others didn't know. I didn't advertise it. Every day when infield was practicing and outfielders were taking their positions, I would not line up in my normal position but about 30 feet in. I did everything I could to keep people from noticing."

1970s FIRST BASE GAMES

1. George Scott	1,297
2. Chris Chambliss	1,252
3. John Mayberry	1,193
4. Tony Perez	1,186
5. Lee May	1,079

Baseball has had its share of unsavory characters, but the game's magnates have always been loath to take on players they know to have a criminal record. In the 1930s, the Washington Senators sent a shudder through the major league community when they scouted and signed a convict named Alabama Pitts, but to the relief of most Pitts proved unable to hit top-caliber pitching. Ron LeFlore recalled memories of Pitts when he joined the Detroit Tigers in 1974. A product of the Motor City ghetto, LeFlore came to the Bengals only after serving a prison stint for armed robbery that made him a persona non grata to most of the other teams in the majors. Tigers skipper Ralph Houk, though, swiftly recognized that the fleet LeFlore was the answer to the club's center field hole. In 1976, LeFlore's second full season, he led the club in hitting with a .316 batting average. Two years later he paced the American League in runs and stolen bases. Convicted of thievery, LeFlore spent nine years in the majors being paid for being a thief, swiping an average of 50 bases a season.

Lou Brock commented on stealing: "It's almost like choosing weapons. The runner chooses, the pitcher chooses, you step off three paces, and come out firing."

In 1978, Joe Morgan's record streak of 91 consecutive errorless games at second base ended.

1970s SECOND BASE GAMES

1.	Joe Morgan	1,415
2.	Dave Cash	1,190
3.	Ted Sizemore	1,162
4.	Tito Fuentes	1,078
5.	Felix Millan	1,077

Lou Brock retired after the 1979 season with a major league record for career stolen bases (938).

The last major league player to post a season fielding average below .900 was third baseman Butch Hobson of Boston in 1978, with an .899 fielding average.

Dodger Quartet Consistent

In 1973, the Dodgers moved Steve Garvey from third base to first base to free a spot for rookie hot corner prospect Ron Cey. The following year Garvey, Cey, second baseman Davey Lopes, and shortstop Bill Russell formed an infield unit for Los Angeles that would remain intact a record eight seasons until Steve Sax replaced Lopes in 1982. During that span, the Dodgers won four pennants and two world championships and just once, in 1979, finished lower than second place in their division. Four different All-Star Games saw three of the four on the NL team, but never did all four make it in the same year. Each of the quartet except Russell eventually took advantage of free agency to move on and play elsewhere. Lopes left in 1982 to join the Oakland A's. A year later Garvey signed with the Padres and Cey with the Cubs. Russell remained in Los Angeles, retiring in 1986 after 18 seasons in Dodger blue.

Heaven on Earth

"Ninety feet between bases is the nearest to perfection that man has yet achieved."
—Red Smith, sportswriter

In 1979, Philadelphia Phillie outfielder Del Unser slugged home runs in three consecutive pinch-hit plate appearances.

"The rhythms of the game are so similar to the patterns of American life. Periods of leisure, interrupted by bursts of frantic activity."
—Roger Kahn

Dodger Skippers Stay the Course

From its inception in 1884, the Dodgers franchise has displayed extraordinary continuity. Nowhere is it more prominent than in the way the club has treated its managers. Since 1900, the Dodgers have had only 13 different skippers. By contrast, the Giants have had 21, the Pirates 23, the Cards 33, the Phillies 38, the Braves 39, the Cubs 40 and the Reds 41. All but one of the Dodgers' 13 different managers since 1900—Harry Lumley, who sat at the reins in 1909—has manned the wheel for at least two full seasons. The three who have enjoyed the greatest longevity are Wilbert Robinson, Walter Alston, and Tommy Lasorda. Alston piloted the club for nearly 23 years, breaking Robinson's record of 18 seasons in 1972. When Alston stepped down voluntarily on September 28, 1976, turning the job over to Lasorda, it forged a chain that reaches back 40 years. Not since Chuck Dressen was relieved of command at the end of the 1953 season have the Dodgers had to resort to firing a manager.

Jeff Torborg exposed the art of catching: "There must be some reason we're the only ones facing the other way."

St. Louis Cardinal outfielder Lou Brock in 1974 broke the major league swipe record by stealing 118 bases.

In 1975, Bob Watson of the Astros scored the millionth run in major league history.

1970S THIRD BASE GAMES

1. Graig Nettles	1,547
2. Sal Bando	1,449
3. Aurelio Rodriguez	1,389
4. Doug Rader	1,102
5. Ken Reitz	1,086

**"If there is such a thing as a good loser, then the game is crooked."
—Billy Martin**

Above: *Don Baylor became primarily a designated hitter after winning the MVP Award in 1979 but was so effective in the role that he played nearly 10 more seasons.*

Cheap Suds Brew Trouble

For the past 30 years, the Cleveland Indians management has tried everything short of summoning Bill Veeck's ghost in a vain effort to boost attendance and revive the fan interest that made the Forest City the envy of the majors in the late 1940s. Most of the promotional stunts have failed miserably and some have even resulted in near disaster. The closest brush with catastrophe came on June 4, 1974, when the club staged a special "10-cent Beer Night" for a game with the Texas Rangers. At a dime a throw, the suds flowed so freely that the crowd raged out of control before the verdict was settled. With the score tied 5-5, fans began pouring out of the stands while the game was in progress and invading the field. Unable to restore order, the umpires forfeited the contest to Texas. On two other occasions during the decade, at Chicago's Comiskey Park in 1979 and at RFK Stadium in 1972 near the end of the Senators' last game in Washington, unruly crowds similarly gave arbiters no choice but to declare a forfeit.

Jim Bouton described how he prepared to make a comeback at age 38: "This winter I'm working out every day, throwing at a wall. I'm 11 and 0 against the wall."

"Mike Ivie is a $40,000,000 airport with a $30 control tower."
—Rick Monday

1970s SHORTSTOP GAMES

1. Larry Bowa	1,481
2. Mark Belanger	1,385
3. Bert Campaneris	1,320
4. Freddie Patek	1,306
5. Dave Concepcion	1,303

The first general strike in major league history was a 13-day strike by the players in 1972 that delayed the opening of the season for 10 days.

In '76, the Yanks won their first flag since 1964.

The Milwaukee Brewers are the only major league team to be a member of both divisions in its league while based in the same city; now in the AL East, the Brewers were stationed in the AL West in 1970 and '71, their first two seasons in Milwaukee.

Luis Aparicio retired in 1973 with almost every major career fielding record for a shortstop, including the most chances accepted and the most games played at the position.

Fame and Fortune

Jim Bouton explained why he wrote *Ball Four* while he was still an active player: "I thought if I ever got to be famous or great I'd write a book about it. Unfortunately, I couldn't wait any longer."

Punch Line

"Lots of people look up to Billy Martin. That's because he just knocked them down."
—Jim Bouton

1970s OUTFIELD GAMES

1.	Bobby Murcer	1,467
2.	Amos Otis	1,422
3.	Bobby Bonds	1,386
4.	Lou Brock	1,327
5.	Reggie Jackson	1,318
6.	Ken Singleton	1,310
7.	Roy White	1,190
8.	Paul Blair	1,189
9.	Cesar Cedeno	1,181
10.	Al Oliver	1,174
11.	Ralph Garr	1,167
12.	Cesar Geronimo	1,145
	Dusty Baker	1,145
14.	Reggie Smith	1,140
15.	Greg Luzinski	1,116

In 1975, the Pittsburgh Pirates beat the Cubs 22-0; it was the most one-sided shutout in the major leagues since 1901.

Cleveland Bottoms Out

Anyone who has followed the plight of the Cleveland Indians since the Tribe won its last pennant in 1954 knows why the club for years has had the most execrable attendance figures in the majors. The last time the Indians played a game after the month of July in which they had anything significant at stake was in 1959. The last time Cleveland finished more than 10 games above .500 was in 1968. After enjoying more than its share of batting leaders and home run champs in the first half of the century, the Tribe has not had a batting king since Bobby Avila in 1954 and the club's last home run leader was Rocky Colavito, who tied for the top spot in 1959. The last MVP winner? Al Rosen in 1953. The one and only Cy Young celebrant? Gaylord Perry in 1972. Two years after his triumph Perry posted 21 victories, the Tribe's last 20-game winner.

Bicentennial Freshmen Flop

The record for the fewest career wins by a pitcher who received a Rookie of the Year Award (18) belongs to Butch Metzger, one of the National League's co-honorees in 1976. Metzger, a reliever with the Padres, shared the prize with Pat Zachry of the Reds. After going 11-4 with 16 saves as a yearling, Metzger collapsed almost at once, collecting only seven more saves and five more wins before departing from the majors a mere two years after his rookie triumph. Zachry likewise never lived up to his frosh billing, finishing in 1985 with a 69-67 career mark. Most of the rest of the rookie crop in 1976 fared little better. Hector Cruz, rated the National League's top frosh regular after he led the Cardinals in home runs and RBI, never again appeared in enough games to be a batting title qualifier. Of the 1976 yearling stars, only receiver Butch Wynegar of the Twins went on to have a productive career.

Dick Williams in 1973 said of A's owner Charlie Finley: "He has been wonderful to me. I have nothing but the highest regard for him." A year later the deposed manager said: "A man can take just so much of Finley."

The first American League MVP Award winner to wear glasses was Dick Allen of the White Sox in 1972.

1970s MANAGER WINS

1. Earl Weaver	944
2. Sparky Anderson	919
3. Gene Mauch	771
4. Chuck Tanner	770
5. Billy Martin	719
6. Ralph Houk	697
7. Dick Williams	681
8. Bill Virdon	646
9. Walter Alston	636
10. Danny Ozark	594

In 1975, Frank Robinson became the first black manager in major league history, as he was named the manager of Cleveland.

In 1975, Fred Lynn of the Red Sox became the only rookie in major league history to win an MVP Award.

**"Baseball was made for kids, and grownups only screw it up."
—Bob Lemon**

Staub Gets 500 Hits with Four Teams

Free agency and the corresponding frequency with which players nowadays are traded have made for so much mobility that fans seldom have an opportunity to form the sort of allegiance that a Ted Williams or a Mickey Mantle or a Bob Feller once commanded. At one point during the 1970s, Mike Torrez won 14 or more games five years in a row with five different teams. Rusty Staub meanwhile achieved a distinction that would have seemed impossible prior to expansion. When he made his 500th hit as a member of the Detroit Tigers in 1978, Staub became the first player in history to collect 500 or more hits with four different teams. The clubs that benefited from Staub's bat were the Astros, the Expos, the Mets and, finally, the Tigers. In addition, Staub notched 102 hits with the Texas Rangers in 1980. He completed his 23-year career in 1985 with 2,712 base hits.

Pennies From Heaven
Vida Blue once paid a fine of $250 to Charlie Finley all in coins, saying: "I wanted to make it all in pennies, but they're hard to come by."

Willie Stargell of the Pittsburgh Pirates in '79 became the oldest MVP in history at age 39.

Gates Brown, an ex-convict who preceded Ron LeFlore on the Tigers, said of high school "I took a little English, a little math, some science, a few hubcaps, and some wheel covers."

On September 12, 1976, Minnie Minoso (age 54) of the White Sox became the oldest player to get a hit in a major league game.

Their Biggest Fan
Cesar Geronimo commented on being the 3,000th strikeout victim of both Nolan Ryan and Bob Gibson: "I was just in the right place at the right time."

High Averages
"It isn't really the stars that are expensive. It's the high cost of mediocrity."
—Bill Veeck

In 1973, it was made public that Yankee pitchers Mike Kekich and Fritz Peterson swapped wives.

1970s TEAM WINS

	W	L
1. Cincinnati-NL	953	657
2. Baltimore-AL	944	656
3. Pittsburgh-NL	916	695
4. Los Angeles-NL	910	701
5. Boston-AL	895	714
6. New York-AL	892	715
7. Kansas City-AL	851	760
8. Oakland-AL	838	772
9. Philadelphia-NL	812	801
10. Minnesota-AL	812	794
11. St.Louis-NL	800	813
12. San Fran.-NL	794	818
13. Houston-NL	793	817
14. Detroit-AL	789	820
15. Chicago-NL	785	827
16. California-AL	781	831
17. NY Mets-NL	763	850
18. Chicago-AL	752	853
19. Montreal-NL	748	862
20. Washington-		
Texas-AL	747	860
Wash.-AL	133	188
Texas-AL	614	672
21. Milwaukee-AL	738	873
22. Cleveland-AL	737	866
23. Atlanta-NL	725	883
24. San Diego-NL	667	942
25. Seattle-AL	187	297
26. Toronto-AL	166	318

Weaver Winds Up Winning

In 1948, his first year in organized baseball, Earl Weaver led all second basemen in the Class-D Illinois State League in putouts and fielding average and also topped the loop in games played. Promoted to St. Joseph in the Class C Western Association the following year, Weaver hit .282 and was fourth in the circuit in RBI with 102. Year by year Weaver continued to advance up the ladder in the minors, until he got to the Class-AA Texas League. There he found himself in over his head and was forced to drop back a notch to the Class-A Western League. Realizing that the major leagues were out of reach, Weaver did what another scrappy minor league second baseman named Joe McCarthy had done 40 years earlier. He turned to managing. In his 17 seasons at the Baltimore helm, he bagged four pennants ('69 to '71, 1979) and six division titles ('69 to '71, '73 and '74, 1979). He won the Series in 1970.

"We will scheme, connive, steal, and do everything possible to win the pennant—except pay big salaries."
—Bill Veeck, White Sox owner, in the 1970s

No, Thanks
"I'm not sure which is more insulting, being offered in a trade or having it turned down."
—Claude Osteen

Above: Mike Torrez won at least 11 games for eight different major league teams.

The only "rainout" in Astrodome history occurred on June 15, 1976, when heavy rains prevented fans and the umpires from getting to the dome.

"Isn't it amazing that we're worth so much on the trading block and worth so little when we talk salary with the general manager?"
—Jim Kern, Texas reliever

Murtaugh Murder on Pirate Foes

Danny Murtaugh was in many ways a near mirror image of Earl Weaver. Murtaugh's 15 seasons as a big league pilot all came with one club, Pittsburgh. And, like Weaver, Murtaugh was a scrappy second baseman during his playing days who had more brains than talent. The difference was that Murtaugh got to play in the majors for nearly a full decade. Perhaps the best indication of how he succeeded in finessing his way to the top came in his rookie season of 1941. Even though he played in just 85 games, Murtaugh paced the National League in stolen bases— albeit with a .219 batting average. Time and again, a heart condition forced Murtaugh to surrender his managerial responsibilities, but his dugout expertise was so sorely missed that on each occasion he was begged by the Pirates to return, until at last he succumbed to his ailing heart at the finish of the 1976 season.

Perfection Plus

"They expect an umpire to be perfect on opening day and to improve as the season goes on."
—Nestor Chylak, umpire

The Los Angeles Dodgers in 1978 were the first team to draw more than 3 million fans in a single season.

Chapter 11
1980-1993

Brett Flirts With .400 Batting Average

In 1979, George Brett became only the second player in American League history to compile 20 or more doubles, triples, and home runs in the same season. The following year, a lengthy stay on the disabled list with a foot injury held him to just 117 games and prevented him from repeating his 1979 achievement. In 1980, however, Brett accomplished something even more remarkable—he hit .390 to post the highest batting average since 1941. In addition, the Kansas City third baseman achieved another rarity by collecting 118 RBI to give him an average of more than one ribbie for every game he played. He also had a .461 on-base percentage and a .664 slugging average. Brett's performance in 1980 earned him both the AL MVP Award and selection as the *Sporting News* Man of the Year. More importantly, it sparked Kansas City to its first pennant and a date with the Phillies in the World Series. Even though Philadelphia prevailed in six games, it was no fault of Brett's. He batted .375 in the fall classic.

In 1987, the Toronto Blue Jays set a major league record by belting 10 homers in one game.

1980-1993 GAMES

1.	Eddie Murray	2,118
2.	Ozzie Smith	2,034
3.	Robin Yount	2,011
4.	Cal Ripken	1,962
	Harold Baines	1,962
6.	Andre Dawson	1,956
7.	Lou Whitaker	1,937
8.	R. Henderson	1,904
9.	Tim Wallach	1,900
10.	Dave Winfield	1,895
11.	Dale Murphy	1,888
12.	Brett Butler	1,834
13.	Willie Wilson	1,831
14.	Ryne Sandberg	1,822
	George Brett	1,822
16.	Tim Raines	1,813
17.	Alfredo Griffin	1,778
18.	Alan Trammell	1,777
19.	Wade Boggs	1,768
20.	Steve Sax	1,762

The last player to top the majors in both batting and slugging in the same season was George Brett of the Kansas City Royals in 1980.

Pill
"George Brett could get good wood on an aspirin."
—Jim Frey

Above: At the end of 1988, Wade Boggs had a .356 career batting average.

1980-1993 RUNS

1.	R. Henderson	1,537
2.	Robin Yount	1,254
3.	Paul Molitor	1,235
4.	Tim Raines	1,210
5.	Eddie Murray	1,164
6.	Wade Boggs	1,150
7.	R. Sandberg	1,143
8.	Lou Whitaker	1,132
9.	Cal Ripken	1,130
10.	Brett Butler	1,128
11.	Dave Winfield	1,113
12.	Dale Murphy	1,070
13.	Dwight Evans	1,057
14.	A. Dawson	1,056
15.	George Brett	1,051
16.	A. Trammell	1,026
17.	Ozzie Smith	1,008
18.	Willie Wilson	999
19.	Harold Baines	929
20.	Tony Gwynn	912

Kansas City manager Jim Frey revealed the advice he gave to George Brett about hitting: "I tell him, 'Attaway to hit, George.'"

Boggs Establishes Batting Mastery

Even after Wade Boggs hit .349 in 108 games as a rookie in 1982, the Boston Red Sox were still not convinced he was for real. With considerable trepidation, they traded incumbent third baseman Carney Lansford to Oakland and installed Boggs at the hot corner in 1983. The Sox' anxiety quickly evaporated after Boggs hit .361 as a sophomore and claimed the American League batting title. At the conclusion of the 1988 season, Boggs had four more batting crowns to his credit and a .356 career average, the highest of any player at a comparable point in his career since Al Simmons in 1931. He batted .361 in 1983, .325 in 1984, .368 in '85, .357 in '86, .363 in '87, and .366 in 1988. That same season, Boggs collected his sixth successive 200-hit season to break Simmons's old AL mark of five. In 1989, Boggs added a 20th-century record seventh straight 200-hit season despite being hounded by a palimony suit that for a time eclipsed all of his on-the-field feats.

Only three third basemen in major league history—Bill Madlock, Wade Boggs, and George Brett—have won more than one batting title and all were active during the 1980s.

Gwynn Gives San Diego Batting Champ

As the 1991 season entered its final lap, Tony Gwynn seemed poised to snag his fifth National League batting title. But a knee injury froze his average at .317, two points behind the eventual winner Terry Pendleton. Few doubted, however, that Gwynn would rebound from off-season surgery to challenge for more hitting crowns, since he had always been in the running for a decade. His .328 career average at the finish of the 1991 season stood as the highest by any NL performer since Stan Musial retired in 1963. Gwynn appeared on the major league scene in 1982, and he won his first batting crown in 1984, getting a .351 average on 213 base hits. His high-water mark came in 1987, when he hit .370, and the next year he led the loop with a .313 mark. In 1989, Gwynn became the first senior loop performer since Musial in 1952 to nab three consecutive batting crowns.

1980-1993 HITS

1.	Eddie Murray	2,294
2.	Robin Yount	2,271
3.	Wade Boggs	2,267
4.	Paul Molitor	2,162
5.	Andre Dawson	2,132
6.	Cal Ripken	2,087
7.	Ryne Sandberg	2,080
8.	George Brett	2,072
9.	Harold Baines	2,060
10.	Tim Raines	2,050
11.	R. Henderson	2,043
12.	Tony Gwynn	2,039
13.	Dave Winfield	2,034
14.	Kirby Puckett	1,996
15.	Ozzie Smith	1,989
16.	Willie Wilson	1,962
17.	Brett Butler	1,958
18.	Steve Sax	1,943
19.	Lou Whitaker	1,932
20.	Alan Trammell	1,927

Tony Gwynn described his hitting success: "See the ball, hit the ball, run like hell."

Willie McGee in 1990 became the first major league player to win a batting title without being in the league at the time he won it, because he was traded from St. Louis to Oakland in August.

San Diego's Tony Gwynn established a record in 1988 when he batted .313, the lowest mark ever by a league leader.

In 1987, Eric Davis of the Reds set a record for the most combined home runs and steals by a 30-30 Club member when he had 37 homers and 50 thefts for a total of 87.

Pittsburgh's Barry Bonds in 1990 became the first player in major league history to hit .300 with 30 homers, 100 RBI, and 50 stolen bases.

In 1987, Mark McGwire of the A's pounded a rookie record 49 homers.

A Brewers official said about Robin Yount: "When Robin was 20, the fear was that he had none [no fear]. It still is."

In 1988, Jose Canseco of the Oakland A's became the first player to steal 40 bases and hit 40 homers in the same season.

In 1981, Joe Lefebvre led San Diego in home runs with eight.

On August 17, 1990, Carlton Fisk hit his 329th homer as a catcher—a major league record.

On July 6, 1986, Bob Horner of the Atlanta Braves became the first player in the 20th century to hit four home runs in a game lost by his team.

McGee Atypical Two-Time Titlist

Willie McGee ranks as the strangest two-time batting titlist since Mickey Vernon. McGee's first crown came in 1985, when he emerged from nowhere in his fourth season with the Cardinals to stroke .353 and establish a new post-1900 record for a National League switch-hitter. McGee followed his glittering 1985 campaign by sagging to .256 in 1986, a drop of 97 points, the largest in history by a defending senior loop hitting champ. Three years later, he reached a career nadir, hitting just .236 in an injury-plagued season. Then in 1990, he came out of nowhere again to hit .335 and win his second batting crown, albeit the first one ever claimed in absentia. Late in the campaign, McGee was shipped to the American League Oakland A's by the Cardinals, meaning that he was no longer even in the NL at the season's close. He returned to the senior loop prior to the 1991 campaign, however, signing with San Francisco as a free agent.

In 1986, when Bert Blyleven of the Twins set a record by allowing his 47th homer of the season, the blow was struck by Cleveland's Jay Bell in his first major league at bat.

On September 20, 1981, Twins Gary Gaetti, Kent Hrbek, and Tim Laudner homered in their first major league game.

Parker Finds New Life as Designated Hitter

During the 1980s, the American League continued to be a haven for aging or disabled veterans who could no longer cut it in the field but still had enough offensive pop to serve as a designated hitter. Several, such as Dave Parker, even made the transition a highly profitable one for them. After a mediocre year with the Reds in 1987, Parker was traded to Oakland for Jose Rijo. In 1989, Parker had 22 homers and 97 RBI as the A's designated hitter. He signed that winter as a free agent with the Brewers. Parker's luck ran out in 1991, however, when his .239 average and huge salary made the Blue Jays, his fourth AL team in three seasons, loath to offer him a new contract. Parker's departure left Brian Downing of the Texas Rangers as the oldest reigning DH both in terms of age and longevity in the role. The 1992 season marked the 41-year-old Downing's fifth straight year as a designated hitter.

A *Los Angeles Times* columnist instructed how to conduct a paternity test to determine whether a baby was Steve Garvey's: "If the baby's hair is mussed, it's not Garvey's."

Rafael Palmeiro, Julio Franco, and Ruben Sierra of the Rangers all notched more than 200 hits in 1991 to tie an AL team record.

Winfield Still Chasing Flies

In remarkable contrast to Dave Parker and Brian Downing, Dave Winfield celebrated his 18th major league season in 1991 by turning 40 and still taking his regular turn in the outfield. Idled all of the 1989 season by a back ailment, Winfield upon his return in 1990 collected just 475 at bats, the fewest since his rookie year. In 1991, however, he performed in 150 games with the Angels and slammed 28 home runs, his highest total in eight seasons. Winfield then joined the Blue Jays prior to the 1992 campaign as a free agent and continued to defy his age. Although finally relegated to the DH role, he batted .290 with 26 homers and 108 RBI. On September 14, 1991, he became the first 40-year-old ever to drive in 100 runs in a season. Winfield helped the Jays to the '91 world title by driving in the winning run in the sixth game of the World Series. Winfield joined the Twins in 1993 and hit a solid .271 with 21 dingers and 76 RBI.

1980-1993 TRIPLES

1.	Willie Wilson	130
2.	Brett Butler	109
3.	Tim Raines	100
4.	Robin Yount	98
5.	Juan Samuel	89
6.	Andy Van Slyke	86
7.	Willie McGee	84
8.	Tony Fernandez	81
9.	Tony Gwynn	78
10.	Mookie Wilson	71
	Paul Molitor	71
12.	Vince Coleman	70
13.	Alfredo Griffin	68
14.	Ryne Sandberg	67
15.	Lloyd Moseby	66
16.	Andre Dawson	65
17.	George Brett	64
18.	Lonnie Smith	58
	Omar Moreno	58
20.	Larry Herndon	56

Mike Hargrove set a Cleveland Indians club record in 1980 when he walked 111 times.

In 1986, Willie Aikens set a 20th-century record for the highest batting average to lead a professional league when he hit .454 for Puebla of the Mexican League.

Monthly

In 1981, George Steinbrenner reviewed expensive free-agent Dave Winfield after Steinbrenner let Reggie Jackson go as free agent to Angels: "I let Mr. October get away and I got Mr. May."

The Kansas City Royals hit .286 in 1980—the highest team batting average of the decade.

Mattingly Mashes Myriad Marks

In 1986, Don Mattingly shattered two all-time New York Yankee franchise marks when he logged 238 hits and rapped 53 doubles. He batted .352 and slugged .573 that year. The following year, his hit totals and slugging figures dropped across the board, but he continued to set records. In 1987, he tied Dale Long's 31-year-old record by homering in eight consecutive games. Next, Mattingly broke Ernie Banks's 32-year-old mark of five grand slams in a season by clubbing six four-ribbie round-trippers. Finally, on July 20, Mattingly tied a major league record for first basemen when he handled 22 chances in a game. For the season, Mattingly compiled 30 home runs and 115 RBI, good totals but hardly awesome. He nevertheless packed two remarkable all-time slugging records into his stats, plus a fielding mark as a bonus. Although just age 26 at the time, Mattingly has not matched any of his 1987 slugging totals since.

Toronto outfielder George Bell was the first player in major league history to hit three home runs on Opening Day in 1988.

Brotherly Love
"Philadelphia is the only city where you can experience the thrill of victory and the agony of reading about it the next day."
—Mike Schmidt

1980-1993 HOME RUNS

1.	Eddie Murray	362
2.	Dale Murphy	352
3.	Andre Dawson	343
4.	Dave Winfield	319
5.	Mike Schmidt	313
6.	Cal Ripken	297
7.	Darryl Strawberry	290
8.	Kent Hrbek	283
9.	Lance Parrish	281
10.	Dwight Evans	275
	Joe Carter	275
12.	Jack Clark	274
13.	George Bell	265
14.	Tom Brunansky	261
	Harold Baines	261
16.	Gary Gaetti	245
	Jose Canseco	245
18.	George Brett	243
19.	Jesse Barfield	241
20.	Ryne Sandberg	240

A premier hitter early in his career, Don Mattingly (above) fell prey to an ailing back and a poor supporting cast. He is the only Yankee to play 10 straight years without reaching the postseason.

1980-1993 RUNS BATTED IN

1. Eddie Murray   1,380
2. Andre Dawson   1,256
3. Dave Winfield   1,247
4. Harold Baines   1,144
5. George Brett   1,135
6. Dale Murphy   1,107
7. Cal Ripken   1,104
8. Robin Yount   1,103
9. Kent Hrbek   1,033
10. George Bell   1,002
11. Dwight Evans   1,001
12. Don Mattingly   999
13. Joe Carter   994
14. Tim Wallach   967
15. Dave Parker   960
16. Jack Clark   933
17. Chili Davis   930
18. Mike Schmidt   929
19. Gary Gaetti   922
20. Lance Parrish   919

The first member of an expansion team to lead the NL in slugging was Darryl Strawberry of the Mets in 1988.

Pendleton Arrives to Advance Atlanta

Few in the Mound City mourned when Terry Pendleton left the Cardinals at the end of the 1990 season to sign with the Braves. After a peak of .286 with 96 RBI in 1987, Pendleton had declined steadily thereafter, reaching bottom in 1990 when he hit just .230 with a .280 on-base percentage and a .324 slugging average. In his first season with the Braves, Pendleton posted a batting average that nearly matched his 1990 slugging average as he hit .319 to win the National League batting crown. Moreover, he hoisted his on-base percentage to .363 and his slugging average to .517. Voted both the NL's MVP and Comeback Player of the Year, Pendleton culminated his stunning 1991 season by spurring the Braves from a cellar finish in 1990 to their first pennant since moving to Atlanta. The third sacker in addition became only the third switch-hitter in NL history to seize a batting crown. He backed up his strong 1991 stats with an equally good season in '92 to prove that his stirring comeback was not a fluke.

In 1986, Mike Schmidt set a major league record by leading his league in homers for the eighth time, as he clubbed 37.

Mike Schmidt during his career frequently led the National League in homers, RBI, and assists, but was not always a favorite of sportswriters. One scribe said Schmidt also "led the league each year in false humility."

Lansford Joins List of High-Average Hot Corner Men

Prior to 1975, only two third basemen—Heinie Zimmerman in 1912 and George Kell in 1949—won major league batting titles. When Bill Madlock of the Chicago Cubs triumphed in 1975, it seemed to set off a chain reaction among third sackers in both leagues. Indeed, since 1975 no fewer than five different hot corner men have grabbed hitting crowns. A sixth, Mike Schmidt, gave it a run in 1981 before finishing at .316, good for fourth in the National League. In the American League that year, third sacker Carney Lansford of Boston joined with Seattle's Tom Paciorek to mark the first season in the junior loop since 1959 that a pair of righthanded hitters finished one-two in the batting race. Lansford's .336 average established a career high that he matched in 1989 when he nearly copped a second hitting crown before finishing three points behind winner Kirby Puckett of the Twins.

In 1993, the White Sox concluded their all-time record 50th consecutive season without having a batting crown winner; Luke Appling in 1943 was the team's last champ.

Cal Ripken in 1991 became the first shortstop in AL history to hit .300 with 30 or more homers and 100 or more RBI.

Blame It On Rio
Toby Harrah, Cleveland third baseman, compared baseball statistics to a girl in a bikini: "They both show a lot, but not everything."

1980-1993 STOLEN BASES

1.	Rickey Henderson	1,062
2.	Tim Raines	749
3.	Vince Coleman	648
4.	Willie Wilson	530
5.	Ozzie Smith	495
6.	Brett Butler	476
7.	Steve Sax	444
8.	Paul Molitor	371
9.	Lonnie Smith	363
10.	Juan Samuel	358
11.	Gary Pettis	354
12.	Otis Nixon	352
13.	Mookie Wilson	327
14.	Ryne Sandberg	323
15.	Gary Redus	322
16.	Willie McGee	317
17.	Eric Davis	301
18.	Dave Collins	291
19.	Lloyd Moseby	280
	Barry Bonds	280

Armas: Free Swings, Not Free Passes

In 1984, Tony Armas of the Red Sox set a record for the fewest walks by a player with more than 40 home runs when he collected just 32 free passes en route to claiming the American League four-bagger crown with 43 dingers. He retired in 1989 with 251 career homers and 260 career bases on balls. Armas was so impatient at the plate that one must wonder why pitchers ever gave him a decent pitch to hit. In 1983, the slugger set an even more dubious record in his first season with the Hub team after coming to Boston from Oakland. Despite amassing 36 homers and 107 RBI, Armas registered a meager .258 on-base percentage, the lowest ever by an outfielder who had 500 or more at bats. The comparable post-1900 record for an outfielder with more than 400 at bats is held by another contemporary free-swinger, Cory Snyder. Playing for the Indians in 1989, Snyder compiled a .253 on-base percentage when he collected just 23 walks to go with a .215 batting average.

Willie Wilson explained why he refuses to sign autographs: "When I was a little kid, teachers used to punish me by making me sign my name 100 times."

In 1982, Kansas City Royal Hal McRae led the majors with 133 RBI, setting a record for the most RBI by a designated hitter.

In 1982, Robin Yount became the first shortstop in American League history to top the circuit in total bases (367) and slugging percentage (.578).

The American League record for the most RBI in a season since expansion is held by Don Mattingly with 145 in 1985.

When Rod Carew collected his 3,000th hit in 1985, he was the first infielder since Eddie Collins to attain the 3,000-hit circle.

On September 11, 1985, Pete Rose tallied his 4,192 career hit, breaking Ty Cobb's major league record.

Dave Kingman set records for the most home runs and the most RBI by a player in his final season when he put up 35 and 94 in 1986.

Darrell Evans in 1985 became the first hitter to smack 40 or more homers in a season in each league, as he pummeled a league-high 40 for Detroit.

Both Evans Are Even

Darrell and Dwight Evans were not kin, but there are so many parallels between them they might have been brothers. Both were born in the Los Angeles area, both played 20 or more seasons in the majors, and both were effective up to the end of their careers. Both collected more than 1,300 runs, more than 1,300 RBI, and more than 2,200 hits. In addition, each seldom hit much for average but nevertheless compiled outstanding on-base percentages, owing to high walk totals. Darrell led the National League in free passes twice while Dwight topped the American League in walks on three occasions. Last but not least, both were sluggers of the first order. Dwight tied for the AL four-bagger lead in 1981. Four years later, at age 38, Darrell cracked 40 homers to snare the AL crown. The two amassed 799 circuit clouts between them, almost evenly divided—414 for Darrell and 385 for Dwight.

Babe Ruth and Dave Kingman are the only two players who were active 10 or more seasons and posted career slugging averages that were more than double their career batting averages.

Saddle Up

Johnny Bench explained why he waited so long before he converted to third base: "A catcher and his body are like an outlaw and his horse. He's got to ride that nag until it drops."

When the Mets' Dave Kingman hit a league-high 37 homers in 1982, he batted just .204, the lowest ever for a home run leader.

Rose's Renown Reduced

Pete Rose retired as a player in 1986 with the career records for the most hits (4,256), the most at bats (14,053), and the most games (3,562). He continued at his post as manager of the Cincinnati Reds for two more seasons and part of a third before a probe into his gambling activities grew so intense in 1989 that he was forced to accept banishment from the game. Compounding Rose's problems was a conviction for income tax evasion that brought a prison sentence. A Hall of Fame committee then rendered a decision in 1991 that no player or official who had been expelled from baseball could have his name put on the Hall of Fame ballot unless he was first reinstated. Since Rose is still under suspension and there are no indications from the commissioner's office that his ouster is likely to be lifted anytime soon, the possibility looms that the holder of the most major career longevity marks may never have a plaque in Cooperstown.

"There's no such thing as bragging. You're either lying or telling the truth."
—Al Oliver

1980-1993 BATTING AVG.

1.	Wade Boggs	.335
2.	Tony Gwynn	.329
3.	Kirby Puckett	.318
4.	Rod Carew	.314
5.	Don Mattingly	.309
6.	Mike Greenwell	.307
7.	Al Oliver	.307
8.	Paul Molitor	.307
9.	Mark Grace	.304
10.	Ken Griffey	.303
11.	George Brett	.302
12.	Pedro Guerrero	.300
13.	Julio Franco	.300
14.	Cecil Cooper	.300
15.	John Kruk	.300
16.	Will Clark	.299
17.	Willie McGee	.298
18.	Barry Larkin	.298
19.	Tim Raines	.298
20.	Lee Lacy	.298

In 1985, the Cardinals took the World Series to seven games and nearly won it in six games, even though they tallied just 13 runs in the fray on a .185 batting average.

Pete Rose in 1983 was the first first baseman for a pennant winner to not hit a home run since Red Sox first baseman Stuffy McInnis in 1918.

In the 1983 fall classic, Pete Rose, the oldest World Series regular in history at age 42, batted .313 in the Series.

Kuenn's Crushers Tear Down the Walls

Harvey Kuenn took over the reins of the staggering Milwaukee Brewers a third of the way into the 1982 season. Kuenn then molded the team into the top slugging and scoring outfit in the majors, so much so that it fairly begged that his crew be dubbed "Harvey's Wallbangers." Leading the Brewers and the American League with 39 homers was Gorman Thomas, followed by Ben Oglivie (34), Cecil Cooper (32), Robin Yount (29), and Ted Simmons (23). Third baseman Paul Molitor nearly gave Milwaukee a record-tying sixth 20-homer man before finishing with 19, and part-time DH Don Money added 16 taters in just 275 at bats. The Brewers parlayed their 216 home runs into 891 tallies, 77 more than any other club in the majors. The Brew Crew's .455 slugging percentage was 22 points better than California's, the second-place club. A mere two years later, with all of the main 1982 Wallbangers except Thomas still on the club, Milwaukee finished last in the AL and compiled both the fewest runs and the fewest homers in the loop.

The Milwaukee Brewers set an American League record for most base hits in a nine-inning game with 31 on August 28, 1992. The Brew Crew tied a modern major league record set by the New York Giants, who had 31 hits on June 9, 1901, against the Cincinnati Reds.

In 1987, Brewer Paul Molitor got hits in 39 consecutive games, the most in the American League since Joe DiMaggio's 56 in 1941.

Reggie Jackson in 1987 retired with a major league record 2,597 Ks.

Brewer Paul Molitor in 1982 notched a World Series record five hits in one game.

Among players with 500 or more career home runs, Reggie Jackson posted the lowest career slugging average (.490).

In 1983, Expo Tim Raines set an NL record when he scored 19.6 percent of his team's runs, as he led the major leagues with 133 runs while his team tallied just 643.

Above: Tim Raines ranks as the most savvy base thief in history. His success rate and number of steals have declined in recent years, but he continues to excel at scoring runs.

Goofball

"Yeah, I was a little nutty. If there'd be some guy on a pogo stick with three girls around him, it would be me."
—pitching flake Dave Rozema

On September 14, 1987, the Toronto Blue Jays hit 10 home runs against the Baltimore Orioles. The Orioles hit one homer to tie the major league record of 11 home runs by both teams in one game.

Fielder Returns From Far East, Fires 51

In his first four seasons with the Toronto Blue Jays, first sacker Cecil Fielder displayed good power, but his propensity for striking out kept his average below .250. Few in the Canadian city grieved when he opted to play in Japan for the 1989 campaign. A year in the Far East was evidently all that Fielder needed. He returned from Japan to hammer 51 home runs and silence critics who jeered the Tigers for giving him a two-year $3 million contract. Fielder's four-bagger total was the highest in the American League since the two M&M boys, Roger Maris and Mickey Mantle, both topped the 50 mark in 1961. Big Cecil also led the loop with 132 RBI, thus becoming the first Bengal to top the circuit in both homers and RBI since Hank Greenberg did so in 1946. The first player to use the game in Japan as a launching pad to major league stardom, Fielder claimed his second homer crown in 1991 when he tied Jose Canseco for the AL lead with 44 dingers.

Tigers Swing For Fences

Despite his advancement as a slugger, Cecil Fielder did little in Japan to learn how to cut down his strikeout totals. In 1981, he fanned 151 times to help boost the Tigers to 1,184 Ks, a new American League record. Other heavy contributors to the whiff total were outfielder Rob Deer (175), second-year infielder Travis Fryman (149), and catcher Mickey Tettleton (131). The staggering number of Ks helped result in a .247 team batting average, the lowest in the AL. Nevertheless Detroit scored 817 runs, second in the loop only to Texas, which tallied 829. A circuit-leading 209 home runs and an AL-best 699 walks nearly made the free-swinging Tigers the first team in history to lead its league in runs despite finishing last in batting. Fielder (44 homers), Tettleton (31), Deer (25), Lou Whitaker (24), and Fryman (21) all notched over 20 round-trippers. As it was, the club's offensive production overrode woeful pitching to allow Detroit to finish with an 84-78 record.

In the 1989 NLCS the two opposing first basemen, Will Clark of the Giants and Mark Grace of the Cubs, collected 24 hits and 16 RBI and hit a combined .649 in the five-game set.

**"The key to this game is to do the things it takes to stay, day in and day out."
—Andre Dawson**

Andre Dawson in 1990 became the second player in major league history to compile 2,000 hits, 300 homers, and 300 steals (Willie Mays was the first).

"Baseball has been very good to me since I quit trying to play it."
—Whitey Herzog

The Cubs batted a rousing .303 in the 1989 NLCS, led by Mark Grace at .647, but nevertheless continued to lose the series to the Giants four games to one, Chicago's ERA was 5.57.

Cincinnati's Billy Hatcher in 1990 hit an all-time Series record .750 (9-for-12), as he collected seven hits in his first seven at bats.

Dave Henderson's two-out, two-strike, two-run homer in the ninth inning of game five saved the 1986 Boston Red Sox from ALCS elimination, helping Boston to its first AL flag since 1975.

Long Time Comin'

San Francisco first baseman Will Clark was drafted in 1985 and spent his first season in the major leagues in 1986. When the Giants clinched their division in 1987, Will roared: "I've waited so long for this."

Hobbled Dodger Kirk Gibson won game one of the 1988 World Series with a pinch-hit homer in the bottom of the ninth.

Joel Youngblood in 1982 got hits for two different teams in two different cities in the same day when he was traded from the Mets to the Expos.

In 1988, there were only 3,180 homers hit in the major leagues—1,278 fewer than in 1987.

In 1986, DH Johnny Grubb of Detroit slugged 13 homers and had 51 RBI in just 210 at bats.

Will the Thrill Fills the Bill

In an era studded with wildly fluctuating team and individual performances, there has been no more consistently excellent player at all phases of the game than Will Clark of the Giants. Others have posted higher batting averages and slugging totals and outperformed Clark in the field and as a baserunner, but none has exceeded his dedication to becoming the best player his skills will allow him to be. In his first major league at bat in 1986, Clark homered against Nolan Ryan at the Astrodome, giving San Francisco fans the first of many moments that quickly led to him being nicknamed "Will the Thrill." He is a tough, hard-working, and gutsy player. Through the 1991 season, Clark's career was a model of consistency. His batting averages ranged between .282 and .333, and he consistently drove in about 100 runs a year. He did drop off in 1990 and '93, however.

Welch Wins 27

At the onset of the 1990 campaign, Bob Welch of the Oakland A's was 33 years old and had been in the majors for 12 years without ever winning more than 17 games in a season. He had accomplished both 17-win years with the A's in 1989 and '90. Welch proceeded to notch 27 wins in 1990, the most of any AL hurler since 1968 and the most in the majors since Steve Carlton of the Phillies also won 27 in 1972. Welch lost only six for a winning percentage of .818, notching a 2.95 ERA. His career year earned Welch the Cy Young Award and left him only 24 victories short of 200. In 1991, Welch returned to earth, winning just 12 of 25 decisions and posting a 4.56 ERA.

"I'm sick of hearing about J.R. Richard. We all know what he can do with his stuff. He's tremendous. But what I'd like to see is what he could do with my stuff."
—Don Sutton

Baltimore's Gregg Olson set an AL rookie saves record in 1989 with 27.

1980-1993 GAMES STARTED

1.	Jack Morris	464
2.	Bob Welch	429
	Frank Tanana	429
4.	Nolan Ryan	411
5.	Frank Viola	405
6.	Charlie Hough	404
7.	Dave Stieb	391
8.	Mike Moore	390
9.	Dennis Martinez	384
10.	Bill Gullickson	371
11.	F. Valenzuela	353
12.	Bruce Hurst	351
13.	Scott Sanderson	349
14.	Rick Sutcliffe	347
15.	Charlie Leibrandt	346
16.	Bert Blyleven	335
17.	Mark Langston	331
18.	Jim Clancy	327
19.	Ron Darling	318
20.	Bob Knepper	313

Above: *Bob Welch in 1994 stands to perform what was once a rare achievement: winning at least 100 games in each major league.*

White Sox Bobby Thigpen in 1990 shattered the major league save record by 11, as he slammed the door 57 times.

Polished Stone Becomes Jewel With 25 Gems

As Bob Welch began the 1990s by unexpectedly producing a Cy Young season, so Steve Stone of the Orioles opened the 1980s with an upset win in the Cy Young derby. Like Welch, Stone had never before had a 20-win season when he registered 25 victories in 1980; and also like Welch, Stone was age 33 at the time, just two years short of Burleigh Grimes's record for the oldest 25-game winner since 1920. Stone's best season had been a 15-12 record with the 1977 White Sox. He had been in the bigs since 1971. Stone stood alone in history, however, after arm trouble decked him permanently midway through the 1981 season. He set a new American League mark for the fewest career triumphs subsequent to a 25-win season when he logged just four more victories before he was forced to retire. Stone also became the only hurler other than Sandy Koufax to cop a Cy Young Award in his last full season. Upon leaving the playing field, Stone simply moved upstairs, launching a new career in the broadcast booth.

Gipper

Ronald Reagan told Gaylord Perry before Perry won his 300th game at age 43: "I just know it's an ugly rumor that you and I are the only two people alive who saw Abner Doubleday throw the first pitch out."

Rollie Fingers in 1981 became the first relief pitcher to win both the MVP Award and the Cy Young Award in the same season.

In 1983, Dan Quisenberry of the Kansas City Royals set a major league record with 45 saves.

1980-1993 COMPLETE GAMES

1.	Jack Morris	164
2.	F. Valenzuela	112
3.	Charlie Hough	106
4.	Bert Blyleven	97
5.	Dave Stieb	96
6.	Roger Clemens	91
7.	Bruce Hurst	83
8.	Mark Langston	75
9.	Frank Viola	74
	Mike Moore	74
11.	Mike Witt	72
12.	Dennis Martinez	71
13.	Mario Soto	70
14.	Bret Saberhagen	69
15.	Rick Sutcliffe	67
	Dwight Gooden	67
17.	Orel Hershiser	64
18.	Mike Boddicker	63
19.	Scott McGregor	62
20.	Rick Langford	61
	Jim Clancy	61

"Natural grass is a wonderful thing for little bugs and sinkerball pitchers."
—Dan Quisenberry

Underhanded Quiz Passes Test

From day one of his professional career, Dan Quisenberry was bred for a career as a relief pitcher. He nevertheless needed a four and one-half year apprenticeship in the minors before he reached the show. He surfaced with the Kansas City Royals in 1979 at age 26, a rather ripe age for a rookie. Quiz swiftly made up for lost time, however, topping the American League in saves in five of his first six full seasons. In 1983, his unorthodox sidearm-to-underhanded slants gained him a new major league record when he racked up 45 saves in just 69 appearances. Quiz retired in 1990 after hurling in 674 games without ever making a start, but he was still a long way from the record for startless mound appearances in the majors. The previous year, Kent Tekulve had departed after seeing action in 1,050 games, all in relief. Tekulve was furthermore only the second hurler in history to work 1,000 games in the majors.

When Doug Drabek won 22 games for Pittsburgh in 1990, he was the first Pirates pitcher to be a 20-game winner since John Candelaria in 1977.

The only A's player to reach double figures in triples since 1976 is Luis Polonia with 10 in 1987.

Stroke Halts Richard's Career

The Houston Astros at first thought J.R. Richard was malingering when he claimed halfway into the 1980 season that he felt too weak and disoriented to take his regular turn on the mound. A thorough physical examination, however, revealed that Richard had a blocked artery. He again started pitching when he suffered a stroke. The Astros top pitcher at the time with a 10-4 mark, Richard was expected to join with expensive free-agent acquisition Nolan Ryan to give the club the most potent strikeout tandem in history. In 1979, Richard had set a franchise record when he bagged 303 strikeouts and then broke his own mark a year later by whiffing 313 enemy hitters. Since he was only 30 in 1980, the Astros were prepared to give him every chance to recover from the effects of his stroke. But Richard's comeback attempt stalled before he could ever again throw a single pitch in the majors. He departed with a .601 career winning percentage and 1,493 strikeouts in 1,606 innings.

Mike Scott of the Astros no-hit the San Francisco Giants on September 25, 1986; it was the only no-hitter in NL history to clinch a pennant or division crown.

Dan Quisenberry appraised his unorthodox pitching style: "I found a delivery in my flaw."

Are We Having Fun Yet?

"People say baseball players should go out and have fun. No way. To me, baseball is pressure. I always feel it. This is work. The fun is afterwards, when you shake hands."
—Dennis Eckersley

The Seattle Mariners will begin their 18th season of operation in the majors in 1994 still in search of their first 20-game winner.

Cardinal Bruce Sutter in 1984 tied the major league record with 45 saves.

1980-1993 SHUTOUTS

1.	Roger Clemens	35
2.	Fernando Valenzuela	31
3.	Dave Stieb	29
4.	Jack Morris	27
5.	Bob Welch	25
6.	Orel Hershiser	24
7.	Bruce Hurst	23
	Dwight Gooden	23
9.	Mike Scott	22
10.	Bert Blyleven	21
11.	Bob Knepper	20
12.	Nolan Ryan	19
13.	Geoff Zahn	18
	Dennis Martinez	18
	Charlie Leibrandt	18
	Doug Drabek	18
17.	Rick Sutcliffe	17
	Jerry Reuss	17
	Scott McGregor	17
20.	Frank Viola	16
	John Tudor	16
	Bret Saberhagen	16
	Steve Rogers	16
	Bob Ojeda	16
	Mike Moore	16
	Mark Langston	16
	David Cone	16
	Mike Boddicker	16
	Tim Belcher	16

Astros Lose Promising Young Hurlers

The Astros overcame the loss of J.R. Richard in 1980 to win their division but then faltered in the League Championship Series with Philadelphia. The 'Stros are still in search of their first pennant. Much of the reason for Houston's lengthy fruitless quest can be traced to the fate that has befallen not only Richard but many of its talented young pitchers. Larry Dierker won his first big league game when he was 18 years old and had a 20-win season in 1969 at age 23. Dierker had several more productive seasons, but he saw his arm run out of steam before he was 30. In 1969, 21-year-old rookie Tom Griffin fanned 200 hitters in just 188 innings but never again collected more than 110 Ks in a season. And Don Wilson, a staff bulwark for several seasons in the early 1970s, committed suicide in January 1975.

When both Phil Niekro and Tom Seaver won their 300th games in 1985, it marked the first time since 1890 that two hurlers had notched 300 career wins in the same season.

WIN

Famed reliever Mike Marshall had a bad season in 1980 while with the Twins. After some Minnesota fans booed him, he said: "If they worked as hard at their jobs as I do at mine, this country wouldn't have the inflation problem it now has."

Don Sutton in 1985 became the first pitcher in major league history to fan 100 or more hitters in 20 consecutive seasons.

Among the all-time top nine hurlers in career strikeouts, Walter Johnson is the only one who was not active in 1983.

I♥NY

"I never could play in New York. The first time I ever came into a game there, I got in the bullpen car and they told me to lock the doors."
—Mike Flanagan

Above: *Lee Smith seems only to grow stronger as he ages. At age 33 in 1991, he saved a National League record 47 games. He followed that up with consecutive 43-save seasons.*

Starter Stieb Stars North of Border

In June 1978, the Toronto Blue Jays selected Dave Stieb in the fifth round of the free-agent draft. Barely a year later, Stieb was a regular member of the Canadian team's starting rotation. By 1980, in only his first full season, he was already the staff leader, a role that he held for 10 years. Shoulder and back trouble idled Stieb for most of the 1991 season after he had become the first pitcher in club history to author a no-hitter the previous year. Stieb nevertheless entered the 1992 season with 170 career wins, all for Toronto, and without the distinction of ever having a 20-win season. He is also known as a fine fielder and perhaps the best-hitting pitcher of the current era, although he has had little chance to show it. Because of the designated hitter rule, Stieb has collected just one at bat in his 14 major league seasons.

1980-1993 WINS

1.	Jack Morris	223
2.	Bob Welch	198
3.	Frank Viola	174
4.	Dave Stieb	167
5.	Charlie Hough	165
6.	Roger Clemens	163
7.	Dennis Martinez	162
8.	Dave Stewart	158
	Bill Gullickson	158
10.	Nolan Ryan	157
11.	Dwight Gooden	154
12.	F. Valenzuela	149
	Frank Tanana	149
14.	Rick Sutcliffe	148
15.	Mike Moore	145
16.	Mark Langston	144
17.	Bruce Hurst	143
18.	Scott Sanderson	141
19.	Charlie Leibrandt	140
20.	Bert Blyleven	139

Mariners Lose Moore, Langston

Toronto's sister American League expansion club, Seattle, has been unable to satisfy the salary and competitive demands of their youthful mound stars. The M's selected Mark Langston in the third round of the June '81 draft. Rather than lose him to free agency, Seattle dealt him to Montreal in 1989 after he had led the American League in strikeouts three times as a Mariner. Prior to the 1989 season, Mike Moore, the first player chosen in the same 1981 draft as Langston, availed himself of the free-agency escape hatch to slip away to Oakland. The Langston swap at least brought Seattle two young quality hurlers, Brian Holman and Randy Johnson, in exchange, but Moore's loss left the Mariners with only an extra draft choice in compensation.

1980-1993 INNINGS

1.	Jack Morris	3,333.1
2.	Charlie Hough	2,920.1
3.	Bob Welch	2,830.2
4.	Frank Tanana	2,777.0
5.	Frank Viola	2,760.2
6.	Dave Stieb	2,715.2
7.	Nolan Ryan	2,694.2
8.	Dennis Martinez	2,621.0
9.	Mike Moore	2,544.2
10.	F. Valenzuela	2,534.0
11.	Bill Gullickson	2,443.2
12.	Dave Stewart	2,413.1
13.	Rick Sutcliffe	2,381.1
14.	Bruce Hurst	2,379.1
15.	Bert Blyleven	2,345.1
16.	Mark Langston	2,329.0
17.	C. Leibrandt	2,303.2
18.	Danny Darwin	2,284.2
19.	Roger Clemens	2,222.2
20.	S. Sanderson	2,183.1
	Jim Clancy	2,183.1

In 1981, with the season shortened by a strike to just 109 games, A's pitchers turned in 60 complete games, the most in the past 10 years.

Doctors In the House

Don Sutton after a meeting with Gaylord Perry remarked: "He handed me a tube of Vaseline™. I thanked him and gave him a sheet of sandpaper."

"Let me put it this way: There's a lot of luck in getting to the majors."
—Mark Funderburk, who spent most of his career in the minors

Steve Bedrosian of the Braves established a major league record in 1985 when he started 37 games and completed none of them.

1980-1993 STRIKEOUTS

1.	Nolan Ryan	2,805
2.	Jack Morris	2,189
3.	Roger Clemens	2,033
4.	Mark Langston	2,001
5.	F. Valenzuela	1,842
6.	Dwight Gooden	1,835
7.	Frank Viola	1,813
8.	Bob Welch	1,795
9.	Charlie Hough	1,786
10.	Bruce Hurst	1,665
11.	Frank Tanana	1,653
12.	Bert Blyleven	1,619
13.	Dave Stieb	1,590
14.	Dave Stewart	1,571
15.	Mike Moore	1,541
16.	Rick Sutcliffe	1,533
17.	Danny Darwin	1,495
18.	Jose DeLeon	1,462
19.	Sid Fernandez	1,458
20.	Steve Carlton	1,453

"Luck is the by-product of busting your fanny."
—Don Sutton

Rickey Henderson is the first player to swipe 100 bases in three different seasons.

Gooden Great, Career Has Promise

In 1984, when he was still just 19 years old, Dwight Gooden broke Herb Score's modern rookie strikeout record by fanning 276 National League hitters in only 218 innings. The following year, at age 20, the Mets young fireballer led the NL with 24 wins, a 1.53 ERA, and 268 strikeouts. After Gooden dipped to 17 wins and a mere 200 Ks in 1986, Mets fans speculated on what could be wrong with him and talked as if he were a has-been at 21. Gooden's problem turned out to be cocaine usage, which he has since conquered, but in recent years shoulder woes have prevented him from matching his early achievements. Nevertheless, Gooden began the 1993 season still short of his 29th birthday but with 142 career wins and a stellar .683 winning percentage. At the time, it was the fifth-best mark in major league history.

Rick Langford of the 1980 A's was the last pitcher to hurl at least 25 complete games when he tossed 28.

Mike Torrez was the first pitcher in history to win 10 or more games in a season for seven different teams.

ChiSox hurler LaMarr Hoyt in 1983 issued 1.07 walks per game, the loop's fewest per game since Tiny Bonham's 0.96 in 1942.

In 1981, Rollie Fingers won or saved 55 percent of Milwaukee's victories.

Mets Mound Masters Crumble

In 1986, Dwight Gooden, though he dipped to just 17 wins, remained the crown jewel in the Mets' pitching staff, regarded by the end of the season as the best and the deepest in recent history. Joining Gooden in the starting rotation were Ron Darling (15-6), Bob Ojeda (18-5), Sid Fernandez (16-6), and Rick Aguilera (10-7). Roger McDowell (14-9, 22 saves) and Jesse Orosco (8-6, 21 saves) anchored the bullpen. Should any of these seven falter manager Davey Johnson had only to pick up the phone and call for help to the club's well-stocked farm operation, where such trainee hurlers as David Cone and Randy Myers waited in the wings. The following season, though, the Mets' vaunted pitching corps staggered as only Aguilera matched his 1986 win total, and after rallying in 1988, thanks to a 20-3 season from Cone, it began to unravel completely in 1989. The club that seemed poised in 1986 to build a dynasty around its pitching staff has yet to win another pennant.

On September 26, 1981, Nolan Ryan tossed his fifth career no-hitter, breaking Sandy Koufax's record of four. Ryan pitched his sixth no-hitter on June 11, 1990. He got his seventh no-hitter on May 1, 1991.

Five of the top nine pitchers in career innings pitched were active during the 1980s: Phil Niekro, Nolan Ryan, Gaylord Perry, Don Sutton, and Steve Carlton.

Floyd Bannister in 1982 became the first Mariner to lead the AL in Ks, with 209.

"When I'm on the road, my greatest ambition is to get a standing boo."
—Al Hrabosky, relief pitcher

After making his first pitching appearance in several weeks for the Orioles, Doyle Alexander divulged: "When I got to the mound, catcher Johnny Oates reminded me that the lower mask was his and the upper one was the umpire's."

Kingman Tosses Twenty Setbacks

In 1979, Phil Niekro of Atlanta became the last National League pitcher to date to lose 20 games in a season. A year later, Brian Kingman became the majors' last 20-game loser when he clocked an 8-20 mark for Oakland, made more remarkable by the fact that the A's finished second in their division with an 83-79 record. Kingman pitched in 211 innings, and he notched a 3.83 ERA (the AL had a 4.03 ERA). Since 1980, no hurler has lost more than 19 games in a season. The last to do it was Tim Leary with the Yankees in 1990, when he finished at 9-19. Once he was perched on the threshold of his 20th loss, Leary was spared the ignominy by being held out of the starting rotation, as had happened to several other 19-game losers earlier in the decade. One of them, Jose DeLeon of Pittsburgh, set a National League record for the lowest winning percentage by a pitcher in 20 or more decisions (.095) when he finished at 2-19 in 1985.

1980-1993 EARNED RUN AVERAGE

1. Dan Quisenberry — 2.74
2. Lee Smith — 2.91
3. Roger Clemens — 2.94
4. Orel Hershiser — 2.95
5. Dwight Gooden — 3.04
6. John Tudor — 3.07
7. Jose Rijo — 3.13
8. Dave Dravecky — 3.13
9. Jeff Reardon — 3.14
10. David Cone — 3.14
11. Sid Fernandez — 3.15
12. Greg Maddux — 3.19
13. Doug Drabek — 3.21
14. Nolan Ryan — 3.22
15. Bret Saberhagen — 3.24
16. Steve Rogers — 3.24
17. Steve Bedrosian — 3.31
18. Rick Reuschel — 3.31
19. Dave Righetti — 3.33
20. Mario Soto — 3.37

In the mid-1980s, Nolan Ryan (above) looked to be fading. Nearly a decade later his heater was still mowing batters down.

Jose DeLeon of the Pirates set the 20th-century National League record for the lowest winning percentage by a pitcher in a minimum of 20 decisions when he went 2-19 in 1985, for an .095 winning percentage.

Vin Scully on the quiet Burt Hooton: "The night the Dodgers won the World Series [in 1981] he went out and painted the town beige."

When John Tudor of the Cardinals racked up 10 shutouts in 1985, he fell only one short of the modern southpaw record of 11, set in 1963 by Sandy Koufax.

Minnesota's Bert Blyleven in 1986 allowed a major league record 50 home runs.

The Cincinnati Reds are the only one of the eight NL franchises that have been in existence since 1892 that has never had a 30-game winner.

Martin's Starters Amass Complete Games

Despite logging 20 losses in 1980, Brian Kingman turned in 10 complete games. At that he was by far the low man in the A's rotation, as Oakland starters compiled 94 complete games, the most in either major league since 1946 (when Detroit also had 94). Whereas every other American League team fashioned at least 61 complete games in 1946, only the Milwaukee Brewers in 1980, with 48 complete games, registered even half of Oakland's total. The credit was assigned to A's skipper Billy Martin, who believed his young hurlers—Rick Langford, Mike Norris, Matt Keough, Steve McCatty, and Kingman—could only profit from the work. Langford pitched a league-top 290 innings and 28 complete games. Norris had 284 innings pitched and 24 complete games, Keough 250 innings and 20 complete games, and McCatty 222 and 11 complete games. The following year, Martin's strategy paid off in a division title, but the credit given him turned to blame when all of the A's young starters in 1980 were either gone from the majors or reduced to mop-up roles by 1984.

In 1982, Rollie Fingers became the first pitcher in major league history to collect 300 saves.

LA's Fernando Valenzuela in 1981 became the first player in major league history to win Rookie of the Year and Cy Young honors in the same year.

Steve Carlton became the first lefthander to collect 3,000 career strikeouts, in 1981, and the first to collect 4,000, in 1986.

Fernando Accepts Frequent, Extensive Outings

A contemporary hurler whose career probably was shortened by overwork was Fernando Valenzuela. In 1986, the Dodgers southpaw became what may well be the last pitcher to author 20 complete games in a season. The following year he again led the NL in complete games for the third time in the 1980s. Fernando then tumbled to five wins in 1988 and collected his 141st major league victory in 1990 before his 30th birthday. Valenzuela was out of the bigs until he staged a comeback with Baltimore, winning eight games in 1993. From 1982 to '87, he pitched at least 250 innings a year. Valenzuela was a workhorse from the inception of his career. As a rookie in 1981, he paced the NL in innings, starts, complete games, and strikeouts. The last frosh hurler to approach Valenzuela's performance was the Giants' Bill Voiselle, who in 1944 topped the NL in all of the same departments except complete games.

Tom Lasorda said about his young star pitcher from Mexico, Fernando Valenzuela: "All last year we tried to teach him English, and the only word he learned was 'million.'"

Tom Seaver extended his own major league record when he started his 16th consecutive Opening Day game for the White Sox in 1986.

Sparky Lyle was the first pitcher to play 15 or more full seasons in the majors without ever receiving a starting assignment.

Despite a history of great pitching, the Orioles completed their 39th season in 1993 without having had a loop strikout leader. The Birds' Bob Turley led the AL in Ks in 1954.

Tom Browning of the Cincinnati Reds was the last rookie 20-game winner, with a 21-9 mark in 1985.

Len Barker of Cleveland pitched a perfect game against Toronto on May 15, 1981.

Completion Games On Endangered List

When Jack McDowell of the White Sox churned out 15 complete games in 1991, he was the first pitcher in three years to compile that many. Even as McDowell was topping the American League, Tom Glavine of Atlanta and Bruce Hurst of San Diego shared the National League complete-game crown in 1991 with just nine, the first time a loop leader posted fewer than 10. The previous record low of 10 had belonged to Hurst and Tim Belcher of Los Angeles, who tied for the NL lead in 1989. That year, Bret Saberhagen led the AL with 12, despite having the DH rule that protects pitchers from being lifted for pinch-hitters. In 1987, the Cincinnati Reds finished second in their division despite collecting just seven complete games, one short of the loop record low set by the 1977 Padres. The Toronto Blue Jays also finished second in their division in 1990 when they established a new AL negative mark with a mere six complete games.

Toronto's Dave Stieb was denied no-hitters in each of two consecutive games by a two-out base hit in the ninth inning in 1988.

After failing to win the Cy Young after his second straight 20-win season, Joaquin Andujar complained: "If there was nobody else pitching, they still wouldn't give it to me."

Tom Browning of Cincinnati hurled a perfect game against the Dodgers on September 16, 1988.

On August 11, 1991, Wilson Alvarez of the Chicago White Sox threw a no-hitter in his second major league game after failing to survive the first inning in his first outing.

Good ERA

Jose Rijo, after he filed for a divorce from his wife, said: "My wife, she takes half of everything I make. I give up six runs and three are charged to her."

Rich Gale in 1980 set a Royals record with 11 straight wins.

On April 23, 1983, Tiger Milt Wilcox missed a perfect game when he gave up a single with two out in the ninth inning.

The American League record for the most starts in a season without registering a complete game is held by Milt Wilcox of the Tigers with 33 in 1983.

The 1982 season was the first campaign since 1949 that failed to see a no-hit game in either major league.

Tanana Tallies 220 Without 20-Win Season

Frank Tanana finished the 1991 campaign with 220 career victories, the most of any pitcher in history who never had a 20-win season. The previous year, he had become the first hurler to log 200 wins without ever coming to bat or scoring a run in a major league game. A power pitcher early in his career, Tanana led the American League in strikeouts in 1975 with 269. Four years later, an arm ailment forced him to begin winning with guile rather than speed. He came within one victory of winning 20 in 1976, when he had a 19-10 record for the Angels. His career high point came in 1987, when he blanked Toronto on the last day of the season to clinch the division title for Detroit. In his lone League Championship Series start in 1987, he was bombed by the Twins, however, to further frustrate his bid to pitch in a World Series. Although twice on a division champion, Tanana marked his 21st season in 1993 without ever being a member of a pennant winner.

Stewart Takes Trio of 20-Win Seasons

In the 1980s, only two National League pitchers were able to win 40 or more games during a two-year period. Dwight Gooden collected 17 victories as a rookie in 1984 and 24 as a sophomore. Meanwhile, Joaquin Andujar was the only NL hurler to have consecutive 20-win seasons (1984 and '85). By contrast, the AL had several hurlers who did the 40-in-two thing. In fact, from 1987 through 1989, Dave Stewart tallied three consecutive 20-win seasons. And in 1986 and '87, Roger Clemens racked up 44 victories.

Since joining the Red Sox regular rotation in 1986, Roger Clemens (above) has been a model of consistency, winning in double figures every season.

On September 29, 1986, Greg Maddux of the Cubs and brother Mike of the Phils became the only rookie siblings in major league history to face each other as starting pitchers.

Roger Clemens jokingly complained about Nolan Ryan: "If Ryan would act his age, there might be a few records left for me."

Roger Clemens of the Boston Red Sox fanned a major league record 20 batters on April 30, 1986.

Saberhagen's Career on Royal Roller Coaster

Bret Saberhagen was, if nothing else, amazingly consistent in his inconsistency from his rookie year in 1984 through the 1991 campaign, his eighth in the majors. As a frosh hurler with Kansas City, he had an undistinguished 10-11 mark that offered no suggestion he would go 20-6 the next year at age 21 to become the youngest Cy Young Award winner ever. He had a 2.87 ERA and allowed only 9.6 baserunners a game. Saberhagen followed his eye-popping soph season with a 7-12 junior year. He then rebounded to 18-10 in 1987. But again the even-year jinx caught up with him as he finished the 1988 season at 14-16. In 1989, Saberhagen won his second Cy Young prize on the coattails of a 23-6 season. He led the league with 12 complete games, 262⅓ innings, and a 2.16 ERA. Hopes were riding high that he would finally stop the every-other-year jinx, only to crash once more in an even year, tumbling to 5-9 in 1990. After Saberhagen went 13-8 in 1991, the Royals unloaded him to the Mets prior to the 1992 season where injuries limited him to 3-5.

Willie Wilson said about Roger Clemens: "He struts around out there like 'Hey, man, I'm God. I'm Roger God Clemens, and nobody's going to hit me.'"

In 1991, Dennis Eckersley became the first pitcher in major league history to collect both 150 career wins and 150 career saves.

On July 1, 1990, Yankee hurler Andy Hawkins no-hit Chicago in a regulation nine-inning game, but lost 4-0.

In 1984, Tigers reliever Willie Hernandez earned a record 32 saves in his first 32 save opportunities; he won the AL's Cy Young and MVP honors that year.

Steve Carlton in 1982 set a major league record by winning his fourth Cy Young Award.

Oakland Loses Series, Dynasty Claim

By ending the 1980s with their second straight flag, the Oakland A's became the only team during the decade to cop two consecutive pennants. A third flag in a row followed in 1990, making the club the first since the 1976 to 1978 Yankees to sweep to three straight World Series appearances. Bidding to match the Yankees' two successive world titles in 1977 and '78, the A's instead dropped four straight contests to the Cincinnati Reds in one of the hugest upsets in professional sports history. A similar unexpected and egregious loss to the Dodgers in the 1988 fall classic doomed Oakland's chance to rank among the top dynasties since expansion. Indeed, by winning three straight pennants but emerging with just one World Championship for the effort, the A's invited comparison to the 1969 to 1971 Baltimore Orioles, unquestionably the game's strongest team at the time but ignored in most discussions of dynasties because they too came away from their skein of dominance with but one world title in three tries.

The 1984 Tigers won 26 of their first 30 games, and 35 of their first 40—which were the best starts for any major league team this century.

The 1984 Tigers won an AL record 17 straight games on the road.

Peter Gammons wrote of the 1986 Series: "When the ball went through Bill Buckner's legs, 41 years of Red Sox history flashed before my eyes."

In 1982, Phillie outfielder Garry Maddox won his eighth straight Gold Glove.

In 1982, the Atlanta Braves opened the season with 13 consecutive wins, a National League record.

33⅓
"No matter how good you are, you're going to lose a third of your games. No matter how bad you are, you're going to win a third of your games. It's the other third that makes the difference."
—Tom Lasorda

LaRussa Oversees Oakland's Ascent

Many observers felt the Oakland A's had the best talent in the American League West during the mid-1980s but lacked the leadership to go over the top. In 1986, with the season more than half over and the A's lagging in the rear 21 games under .500, the club's brain trust speedily hired Tony LaRussa to bring order to the dugout after he was dumped by the Chicago White Sox. LaRussa—the first successful manager with a law degree since Hughie Jennings—boosted the A's from 21 games below .500 to 10 under by the close of the 1986 season. After bringing the A's home third in 1987, just four games back of division-winning Minnesota, LaRussa then guided the club to three easy division triumphs followed in each case by a mercilessly one-sided League Championship Series win. LaRussa's commanding presence in the dugout along with his devotion to detail and skill at choosing coaches to whom he can comfortably delegate responsibility combine to make him one of the most respected American League managers.

"There are three types of baseball players—those who make it happen, those who watch it happen, and those who wonder what happens."
—Tom Lasorda

1980-1993 FIRST BASE GAMES

1. Eddie Murray	2,012
2. Kent Hrbek	1,537
3. Don Mattingly	1,412
4. Pete O'Brien	1,377
5. Keith Hernandez	1,363

1980-1993 CATCHER GAMES

1. Tony Pena	1,714
2. Gary Carter	1,488
3. Lance Parrish	1,480
4. Mike Scioscia	1,395
5. Carlton Fisk	1,354

Off and Running
Doc Medich said about Rickey Henderson: "He's like a little kid in a train station. You turn your back on him and he's gone."

In 1984, the Philadelphia Phillies set a franchise record when they finished with a .500 or better record for the 10th straight season.

Steve Garvey's record streak of 1,207 consecutive games ended in 1983.

Above: *Ozzie Smith celebrated his 15th season as the major leagues' top all-around shortstop in 1992 by collecting his 2,000th hit. A weak hitter early in his career, Smith has steadily hiked his career batting average since the mid-1980s.*

Smith Snares a Dozen Glove Awards

In 1992, Ozzie Smith of the Cardinals claimed his record 13th straight Gold Glove Award at shortstop. The skein began in 1980 while Smith was still a member of the San Diego Padres. What launched him that year in the voters' eyes were his 621 assists, establishing a new single-season record for shortstops. Smith has since topped the NL in assists seven more times for a total of eight, another major league mark. Smith's glove alone would demand that a place be found for him in the lineup, but the fact is that he is among the better-hitting shortstops of the current era. At the conclusion of the 1991 season he had a .285 career batting average. Early in the 1992 campaign, he collected both his 2,000th hit and 500th stolen base. At the season's finish, Smith stood second only to Luis Aparicio in games played at shortstop.

In 1987, Lou Whitaker and Alan Trammell of the Tigers became the first major league keystone combo to play regularly for the same team for 10 consecutive years.

Not to Mention Their Curlers

Bob Lemon, while managing the Yankees in 1981, remarked: "Today's players like to play their stereos early because after the game their hair dryers cause static."

1980-1993 SECOND BASE GAMES

1. Lou Whitaker	1,891
2. Steve Sax	1,673
3. Ryne Sandberg	1,666
4. Willie Randolph	1,580
5. Frank White	1,475

Super Joe Jinxed, Job Junked

For a Cleveland frosh, being named Rookie of the Year can be more of a curse than a blessing. Only Chris Chambliss, the choice in 1971, has escaped the jinx, largely perhaps because he was traded soon thereafter to the Yankees. Gene Bearden, the American League's top rookie in 1948, and Herb Score, everyone's favorite in 1955, both were unable to capitalize on their early promise. Likewise Sandy Alomar, the AL's top yearling in 1990, was decked the following year by rotator cuff problems and has still not regained his frosh form. No Cleveland rookie toppled more precipitously after bagging freshman honors than Super Joe Charboneau. Two consecutive minor league batting titles earned him a shot at a Tribe outfield post in 1980, and he seized the opportunity to hit .289 with 23 homers and 87 RBI, making him a runaway choice for loop rookie honors. Charboneau played only 70 more games in the majors after 1980. Injuries and a lack of motivation stymied his comeback bids and relegated him to softball.

Manager Dave Bristol addressed his Giants team after a loss: "There'll be two buses leaving the hotel for the park tomorrow. The 2 o'clock bus will be for those of you who need a little extra work. The empty bus will leave at 5 o'clock."

In 1984, Steve Garvey of the Padres became the only regular first baseman ever to go errorless for an entire season.

Cornered

Brewers manager Harvey Kuenn, after the Angels led the ALCS two games to none in 1982, explained: "They had us with the walls to our back."

Joe DiMaggio, upon being named greatest living player at age 66, said: "At my age I'm just glad to be named the greatest living anything."

Billy Martin was fired as Yankee manager a record fifth time, in 1988.

Atlanta Ascends From Ashes

In 1890, the Louisville Colonels, spared by Players' League raiders because they had few performers coveted by the rebel loop, won the American Association pennant after finishing dead last the previous year. Almost exactly a century later, the Atlanta Braves became the first major league team to match Louisville's feat. The Braves copped the National League pennant in 1991 after spending the season before in the loop's basement. In 1990, the Braves were 65-97, with a .401 winning percentage. The next season, Atlanta went 94-68 for a .580 win average. Prior to 1991, the two closest parallels in this century to the 1889 and '90 Louisville Colonels were the 1967 Boston Red Sox, who won the AL pennant after finishing only half a game out of the cellar in 1966, and the 1914 and '15 St. Louis Terriers. After finishing last in the first Federal League season, the Terriers in 1915 missed winning the FL flag by a single percentage point, losing out to the Chicago Whales .566 to .565.

1980-1993 THIRD BASE GAMES

1. Tim Wallach	1,754
2. Wade Boggs	1,654
3. Gary Gaetti	1,609
4. Carney Lansford	1,446
5. Terry Pendleton	1,375

Stan Musial assessed the new domed stadiums: "I got started too early in baseball. In air conditioning I could have lasted another 20 years."

The 1983 White Sox won their division by 20 games, and Chicago was the only team in the American League West to break .500.

Blink of an Eye

"It's a mere moment in a man's life between an All-Star Game and an old-timer's game."
—Vin Scully, Dodgers broadcaster

In 1981, Buddy Bell of the Rangers set a modern record for third basemen when he totaled 2.93 assists per game.

"All I ever wanted to be president of was the American League.
—A. Bartlett Giamatti

Home Dome Advantage

The Minnesota Twins in a sense matched the Braves' feat in 1991 by rising to the American League pennant following a last-place finish in their division. The Twins did not perform a true worst-to-first leapfrog because their record in 1990 of 74-88 was better than the Yankees (67-95) and the same as the Brewers, meaning that the Twins finished in a tie with Milwaukee as the 12th-best team in the 14-club circuit. To the Twins, however, belongs a distinction that is as remarkable in its own right as the Braves' achievement. When Minnesota beat Atlanta in the World Series, it marked only the second time a team had claimed a fall classic without winning a single game in its opponent's park. The first victorious team to win all four of its Series triumphs on its home ground was none other than the 1987 Twins. Minnesota thus has won two world titles even though it has yet to win a Series game on the road.

1980-1993 OUTFIELD GAMES

1. Dale Murphy	1,853
2. Brett Butler	1,795
3. Rickey Henderson	1,792
Andre Dawson	1,792
5. Willie Wilson	1,742
6. Tim Raines	1,692
7. Tom Brunansky	1,631
8. Tony Gwynn	1,570
9. Willie McGee	1,532
10. Lloyd Moseby	1,529
11. Dave Winfield	1,505
12. Kirby Puckett	1,492
13. K. McReynolds	1,422
14. Chet Lemon	1,402
15. Jesse Barfield	1,387

The New York Yankees' .414 winning percentage during the 1990 season was the team's worst since 1912.

"All baseball fans can be divided into two groups: those who come to batting practice and the others. Only those in the first category have much chance of amounting to anything."
—Thomas Boswell, sportswriter

1980-1993 SHORTSTOP GAMES

1. Ozzie Smith	2,008
2. Cal Ripken	1,885
3. Alfredo Griffin	1,687
4. Alan Trammell	1,673
5. Garry Templeton	1,455

In 1987, the Twins set a record for the lowest winning percentage by a world championship team when they went 85-77 to finish with a .525 mark.

Mauch Thwarted From Championship Bid

In 1964, Gene Mauch piloted the Philadelphia Phillies to a 6½-game lead in the National League with just 12 contests to play, only to see his club go into a monumental skid that handed the pennant to the St. Louis Cardinals. Eighteen years later, Mauch, still without a flag in 23 seasons as a helmsman, had the 1982 California Angels needing only one win in three games at Milwaukee to claim their first American League pennant. The Angels then dropped all three contests to the Brewers to become the only AL team ever to lose a five-game League Championship Series after leading 2-0 in games. Disappointed again, Mauch felt he finally had a lock on his first pennant when the Angels led the Red Sox 3-1 in games in the 1986 ALCS. The Angels were ahead 5-2 in the ninth inning of game five. California, though, lost that contest 7-6 and then dropped the next two games in Boston to leave Mauch high and dry once again. He managed just one more season before departing after a record 26 years as a skipper without winning a pennant.

In their last seven World Series appearances — 1946, 1964, 1967, 1968, 1982, 1985, and 1987—the St. Louis Cardinals have been forced to go the full seven games on each occasion.

"Fenway Park in Boston is a lyric little bandbox of a ballpark. Everything is painted green and seems in curiously sharp focus, like the inside of an old-fashioned peeping-type Easter egg."

Boo!
"Philly fans are so mean that on Easter Sunday, when the players staged an Easter-egg hunt for their kids, the fans booed the kids who didn't find any eggs."
—Bob Uecker

Since the start of the free-agent draft in 1965, 16 players have made pro debuts in the major leagues.

Glovemen Gather at Gateway Bag

First base has traditionally been the province of slew-footed sluggers and murderously inept fielders, such as Dick Stuart ("Doctor Strangeglove") and Zeke Bonura. In recent years, though, first base has become a bastion for some of the slickest glovemen in the game. In 1988, Keith Hernandez of the Mets set a new mark for gateway guardians when he acquired his 11th consecutive Gold Glove. Three years earlier, Bill Buckner, although never a Gold Glove winner, shattered his own all-time record of 161 assists, set in 1983, when he tossed out 184 runners from his first base post. Buckner at one point held both the American League and the National League record for the most assists in a season, but his NL mark fell in 1986 to Sid Bream of the Pirates, who notched 166 assists. Bream's record stood only until 1990 when the Cubs' Mark Grace racked up 180 assists, only four shy of Buckner's all-time mark.

Hot Stove

"There is no off-season in Chicago. It is only when the teams start playing that the fans lose interest."
—Steve Daley, writer

1980-1993 MANAGER WINS

1.	Tony LaRussa	1,175
2.	Sparky Anderson	1,162
3.	Tom Lasorda	1,148
4.	Whitey Herzog	822
	Bobby Cox	822
6.	Bob Rodgers	768
7.	John McNamara	739
8.	Jim Leyland	667
9.	Davey Johnson	648
10.	Joe Torre	643

"One of my goals in life was to be surrounded by unpretentious, rich young men. Then I bought the Braves and I was surrounded by 25 of them."
—Ted Turner

Cardinal Vince Coleman swiped a major league record 50 straight bases over two seasons (1988 and '89) without being caught.

The five players who were drafted who did not have seasoning in the minors include Dave Winfield of San Diego (drafted in June 1973), Bob Horner of Atlanta (June 1978), Pete Incaviglia of Texas (June 1985), Jim Abbott of California (June 1988), and John Olerud of Toronto (June 1989).

Skipper Howser Leads KC to Crown

In his senior year at Palm Beach High School in Florida, Dick Howser hit below .200 and was moved to second base because his arm was judged too weak for shortstop. Seven years later, as an AL rookie, he hit .280 and swiped 37 bases while serving at shortstop for the Kansas City A's. Owing to injuries, Howser enjoyed only one other season as a full-time player before retiring to the coaching lines in 1969. After 10 years as a Yankees coach, Howser was given a chance to manage the club in 1980. He responded by taking the Bombers to the AL East title but was fired when New York fell to Kansas City in the League Championship Series. If Howser was underappreciated in New York, though, Kansas City knew his true worth. Hired to replace Whitey Herzog at the Royals' helm in 1981, Howser led Kansas City to the second-half division title. Two more postseason appearances followed in the next four years, including the Royals' first world championship in 1985. But in 1986, during the All-Star break, Howser learned he had an inoperable brain tumor. The Royals have not appeared in postseason play since his death in 1987.

In 1992, Robin Yount (above) became the youngest righthanded hitter to amass 3,000 hits. Just 37, he seems good for many more.

After hearing umpire Ron Luciano signed to become a sportscaster, Earl Weaver stated: "I hope he takes this job more seriously than he did his last one."

Hostile
"The old fan used to yell, 'Kill the umpire.' The new fan tries to do it."
—Psychiatrist Arnold Beisser

Sandberg Second to None as Slugger

Observers of the game cannot be blamed for looking askance at the many record errorless skeins and high fielding averages in recent years. Not only are official scorers nowadays loath to charge fielders with miscues on anything less than an egregious error, but players themselves join in the conspiracy to make a mockery of fielding records. Ryne Sandberg, for one, helped protect his record 123-game errorless streak at second base in 1989 and '90 by removing himself from several contests in the late innings. Although historically his fielding mark was sullied, he is still a fine fielder. Also, his offensive output in 1990 left nothing to dispute. By rapping 40 circuit blows, he became the only second baseman since the end of the dead-ball era other than Rogers Hornsby to win a loop home run crown in a season when a full schedule was played. Sandberg also became the first second sacker since Hornsby to be a league leader in total bases by collecting 344 total sacks, the most in the majors.

1980-1993 TEAM WINS

	W	L
1. Toronto-AL	1,185	1,026
2. Detroit-AL	1,162	1,052
3. NY-AL	1,156	1,054
4. Oakland-AL	1,154	1,061
5. St.Louis-NL	1,149	1,058
6. Mont.-NL	1,148	1,062
LA-NL	1,148	1,066
8. Boston-AL	1,146	1,065
9. KC-AL	1,139	1,068
10. Hous.-NL	1,125	1,092
11. Milw.-AL	1,122	1,090
12. Chi.-AL	1,119	1,089
13. Balt.-AL	1,117	1,091
14. NY-NL	1,115	1,091
15. Cinc.-NL	1,109	1,103
16. San F.-NL	1,108	1,108
17. Phila.-NL	1,105	1,106
18. Pitt.-NL	1,096	1,109
19. Calif.-AL	1,087	1,127
20. Atlanta-NL	1,073	1,132
21. San D.-NL	1,064	1,151
22. Minne.-AL	1,063	1,151
23. Chicago-NL	1,051	1,151
Texas-AL	1,051	1,156
25. Clev.-AL	996	1,211
26. Seattle-AL	979	1,235
27. Color.-NL	67	95
28. Florida-NL	64	98

"When I am right, no one remembers. When I am wrong, no one forgets."
—Doug Harvey, umpire

The Oakland A's swept the San Francisco Giants in the 1989 fall classic, in the most one-sided World Series ever. A massive earthquake in the San Francisco Bay area prior to game three forced a 10-day delay of the World Series.

All-Time Leaders

GAMES

1. Pete Rose — 3,562
2. Carl Yastrzemski — 3,308
3. Hank Aaron — 3,298
4. Ty Cobb — 3,035
5. Stan Musial — 3,026
6. Willie Mays — 2,992
7. Rusty Staub — 2,951
8. Brooks Robinson — 2,896
9. Robin Yount — 2,856
10. Dave Winfield — 2,850
11. Al Kaline — 2,834
12. Eddie Collins — 2,826
13. Reggie Jackson — 2,820
14. Frank Robinson — 2,808
15. Honus Wagner — 2,792
16. Tris Speaker — 2,789
17. Tony Perez — 2,777
18. Mel Ott — 2,730
19. George Brett — 2,707
20. Graig Nettles — 2,700
21. Darrell Evans — 2,687
22. R. Maranville — 2,670
23. Joe Morgan — 2,649
24. Lou Brock — 2,616
25. Dwight Evans — 2,606
26. Luis Aparicio — 2,599
27. Eddie Murray — 2,598
28. Willie McCovey — 2,588
29. Paul Waner — 2,549
30. Ernie Banks — 2,528
31. Cap Anson — 2,523
32. Sam Crawford — 2,517
   Bill Buckner — 2,517
34. Babe Ruth — 2,503
35. Carlton Fisk — 2,499
36. Billy Williams — 2,488
   D. Concepcion — 2,488
38. Nap Lajoie — 2,480
39. Max Carey — 2,476
40. Vada Pinson — 2,469
   Rod Carew — 2,469
42. Dave Parker — 2,466
43. Ted Simmons — 2,456
44. Bill Dahlen — 2,443
45. Ron Fairly — 2,442
46. H. Killebrew — 2,435
47. R. Clemente — 2,433
48. Andre Dawson — 2,431
49. Willie Davis — 2,429
50. Luke Appling — 2,422

RUNS

1. Ty Cobb — 2,246
2. Babe Ruth — 2,174
   Hank Aaron — 2,174
4. Pete Rose — 2,165
5. Willie Mays — 2,062
6. Cap Anson — 1,996
7. Stan Musial — 1,949
8. Lou Gehrig — 1,888
9. Tris Speaker — 1,882
10. Mel Ott — 1,859
11. Frank Robinson — 1,829
12. Eddie Collins — 1,821
13. Carl Yastrzemski — 1,816
14. Ted Williams — 1,798
15. C. Gehringer — 1,774
16. Jimmie Foxx — 1,751
17. Honus Wagner — 1,736
18. Jim O'Rourke — 1,732
19. Jesse Burkett — 1,720
20. Willie Keeler — 1,719
21. Billy Hamilton — 1,690
22. Bid McPhee — 1,678
23. Mickey Mantle — 1,677
24. Joe Morgan — 1,650
25. Jimmy Ryan — 1,642
26. G. VanHaltren — 1,639
27. Robin Yount — 1,632
28. Paul Waner — 1,627
29. Dave Winfield — 1,623
30. Al Kaline — 1,622
31. Roger Connor — 1,620
32. Fred Clarke — 1,619
33. Lou Brock — 1,610
34. Jake Beckley — 1,600
35. Ed Delahanty — 1,599
36. Bill Dahlen — 1,589
37. R. Henderson — 1,586
38. George Brett — 1,583
39. Rogers Hornsby — 1,579
40. Hugh Duffy — 1,552
41. Reggie Jackson — 1,551
42. Max Carey — 1,545
43. George Davis — 1,539
44. Frankie Frisch — 1,532
45. Dan Brouthers — 1,523
46. Tom Brown — 1,521
47. Sam Rice — 1,514
48. Eddie Mathews — 1,509
49. Al Simmons — 1,507
50. Mike Schmidt — 1,506

HITS

1. Pete Rose — 4,256
2. Ty Cobb — 4,189
3. Hank Aaron — 3,771
4. Stan Musial — 3,630
5. Tris Speaker — 3,514
6. Carl Yastrzemski — 3,419

7. Honus Wagner	3,415
Cap Anson	3,415
9. Eddie Collins	3,312
10. Willie Mays	3,283
11. Nap Lajoie	3,242
12. George Brett	3,154
13. Paul Waner	3,152
14. Robin Yount	3,142
15. Rod Carew	3,053
16. Lou Brock	3,023
17. Dave Winfield	3,014
18. Al Kaline	3,007
19. R. Clemente	3,000
20. Sam Rice	2,987
21. Sam Crawford	2,961
22. Frank Robinson	2,943
23. Willie Keeler	2,932
24. Rogers Hornsby	2,930
Jake Beckley	2,930
26. Al Simmons	2,927
27. Zack Wheat	2,884
28. Frankie Frisch	2,880
29. Mel Ott	2,876
30. Babe Ruth	2,873
31. Jesse Burkett	2,850
32. B. Robinson	2,848
33. C. Gehringer	2,839
34. Eddie Murray	2,820
35. George Sisler	2,812
36. Vada Pinson	2,757
37. Luke Appling	2,749
38. Al Oliver	2,743
39. Goose Goslin	2,735
40. Tony Perez	2,732
41. Lou Gehrig	2,721
42. Rusty Staub	2,716
43. Bill Buckner	2,715
44. Dave Parker	2,712
45. Billy Williams	2,711
46. Doc Cramer	2,705
47. Luis Aparicio	2,677
48. Fred Clarke	2,672
49. Max Carey	2,665
50. Nellie Fox	2,663

TOTAL BASES

1. Hank Aaron	6,856
2. Stan Musial	6,134
3. Willie Mays	6,066
4. Ty Cobb	5,854
5. Babe Ruth	5,793
6. Pete Rose	5,752
7. Carl Yastrzemski	5,539
8. Frank Robinson	5,373
9. Tris Speaker	5,101
10. Dave Winfield	5,063
11. Lou Gehrig	5,060
12. George Brett	5,044
13. Mel Ott	5,041
14. Jimmie Foxx	4,956
15. Ted Williams	4,884
16. Honus Wagner	4,862
17. Al Kaline	4,852
18. Reggie Jackson	4,834
19. Robin Yount	4,730
20. Rogers Hornsby	4,712
21. Ernie Banks	4,706
22. Eddie Murray	4,699
23. Al Simmons	4,685
24. Billy Williams	4,599
25. Cap Anson	4,577
26. Tony Perez	4,532
27. Andre Dawson	4,529
28. Mickey Mantle	4,511
29. R. Clemente	4,492
30. Paul Waner	4,478
31. Nap Lajoie	4,474
32. Dave Parker	4,405
33. Mike Schmidt	4,404
34. Eddie Mathews	4,349
35. Sam Crawford	4,328
36. Goose Goslin	4,325

37. B. Robinson	4,270
38. Vada Pinson	4,264
39. Eddie Collins	4,263
40. C. Gehringer	4,257
41. Lou Brock	4,238
42. Dwight Evans	4,230
43. Willie McCovey	4,219
44. Willie Stargell	4,190
45. Rusty Staub	4,185
46. Jake Beckley	4,147
47. H. Killebrew	4,143
48. Jim Rice	4,129
49. Zack Wheat	4,100
50. Al Oliver	4,083

DOUBLES

1. Tris Speaker	792
2. Pete Rose	746
3. Stan Musial	725
4. Ty Cobb	724
5. George Brett	665
6. Nap Lajoie	657
7. Carl Yastrzemski	646
8. Honus Wagner	640
9. Hank Aaron	624
10. Paul Waner	605
11. Robin Yount	583
12. Cap Anson	582
13. Charlie Gehringer	574
14. Harry Heilmann	542
15. Rogers Hornsby	541
16. Joe Medwick	540
17. Al Simmons	539
18. Lou Gehrig	534
19. Al Oliver	529
20. Frank Robinson	528
21. Dave Parker	526
22. Ted Williams	525
23. Willie Mays	523
24. Ed Delahanty	522
25. Dave Winfield	520

26. Joe Cronin	515	
27. Babe Ruth	506	
28. Tony Perez	505	
29. Goose Goslin	500	
30. Rusty Staub	499	
31. Sam Rice	498	
Al Kaline	498	
Bill Buckner	498	
34. Heinie Manush	491	
35. Mickey Vernon	490	
Eddie Murray	490	
37. Mel Ott	488	
38. Billy Herman	486	
Lou Brock	486	
40. Vada Pinson	485	
41. Hal McRae	484	
42. Ted Simmons	483	
Dwight Evans	483	
44. Brooks Robinson	482	
45. Zack Wheat	476	
46. Andre Dawson	473	
Jake Beckley	473	
48. Jim O'Rourke	467	
49. Frankie Frisch	466	
50. Jim Bottomley	465	

TRIPLES

1. Sam Crawford	309
2. Ty Cobb	295
3. Honus Wagner	252
4. Jake Beckley	243
5. Roger Connor	233
6. Tris Speaker	222
7. Fred Clarke	220
8. Dan Brouthers	205
9. Joe Kelley	194
10. Paul Waner	191
11. Bid McPhee	188
12. Eddie Collins	186
13. Ed Delahanty	185
14. Sam Rice	184

15. Edd Roush	182
Jesse Burkett	182
17. Ed Konetchy	181
18. Buck Ewing	178
19. Stan Musial	177
Rabbit Maranville	177
21. Harry Stovey	174
22. Goose Goslin	173
23. Zack Wheat	172
Tommy Leach	172
25. Rogers Hornsby	169
26. Joe Jackson	168
27. Sherry Magee	166
Roberto Clemente	166
29. Jake Daubert	165
30. Pie Traynor	164
George Sisler	164
Elmer Flick	164
33. Nap Lajoie	163
Lou Gehrig	163
George Davis	163
Bill Dahlen	163
37. Mike Tiernan	162
38. George VanHaltren	161
39. Sam Thompson	160
Heinie Manush	160
Harry Hooper	160
42. Joe Judge	159
Max Carey	159
44. Ed McKean	158
45. Jimmy Ryan	157
Kiki Cuyler	157
47. Tommy Corcoran	155
48. Earle Combs	154
49. Harry Heilmann	151
Jim Bottomley	151

HOME RUNS

1. Hank Aaron	755
2. Babe Ruth	714
3. Willie Mays	660

4. Frank Robinson	586
5. Harmon Killebrew	573
6. Reggie Jackson	563
7. Mike Schmidt	548
8. Mickey Mantle	536
9. Jimmie Foxx	534
10. Ted Williams	521
Willie McCovey	521
12. Eddie Mathews	512
Ernie Banks	512
14. Mel Ott	511
15. Lou Gehrig	493
16. Willie Stargell	475
Stan Musial	475
18. Dave Winfield	453
19. Carl Yastrzemski	452
20. Dave Kingman	442
21. Eddie Murray	441
22. Billy Williams	426
23. Darrell Evans	414
24. Andre Dawson	412
25. Duke Snider	407
26. Al Kaline	399
27. Dale Murphy	398
28. Graig Nettles	390
29. Johnny Bench	389
30. Dwight Evans	385
31. Jim Rice	382
Frank Howard	382
33. Tony Perez	379
Orlando Cepeda	379
35. Norm Cash	377
36. Carlton Fisk	376
37. Rocky Colavito	374
38. Gil Hodges	370
39. Ralph Kiner	369
40. Joe DiMaggio	361
41. Johnny Mize	359
42. Yogi Berra	358
43. Lee May	354
44. Dick Allen	351

45. George Foster	348
46. Ron Santo	342
47. Jack Clark	340
48. Boog Powell	339
Dave Parker	339
50. Don Baylor	338
51. Joe Adcock	336
52. Bobby Bonds	332
53. Hank Greenberg	331
54. Willie Horton	325
55. Gary Carter	324
56. Roy Sievers	318
57. Lance Parrish	317
George Brett	317
59. Ron Cey	316
60. Reggie Smith	314
61. Al Simmons	307
Greg Luzinski	307
63. Fred Lynn	306
64. Rogers Hornsby	301
65. Chuck Klein	300
66. Cal Ripken	297
67. Rusty Staub	292
68. Jim Wynn	291
69. Darryl Strawberry	290
70. Hank Sauer	288
Bob Johnson	288
Del Ennis	288
73. Frank Thomas	286
74. Kent Hrbek	283
75. Ken Boyer	282
76. Ted Kluszewski	279
77. Rudy York	277
78. Roger Maris	275
Brian Downing	275
Joe Carter	275
81. Steve Garvey	272
82. George Scott	271
83. Gorman Thomas	268
Brooks Robinson	268
Joe Morgan	268

86. George Hendrick	267
87. Vic Wertz	266
88. George Bell	265
89. Bobby Thomson	264
90. Tom Brunansky	261
Harold Baines	261
92. Vada Pinson	256
Larry Parrish	256
Bob Allison	256
95. John Mayberry	255
96. Andy Thornton	253
Joe Gordon	253
Larry Doby	253
99. Joe Torre	252
Bobby Murcer	252

RUNS BATTED IN

1. Hank Aaron	2,297
2. Babe Ruth	2,213
3. Lou Gehrig	1,995
4. Cap Anson	1,981
5. Stan Musial	1,951
6. Ty Cobb	1,937
7. Jimmie Foxx	1,922
8. Willie Mays	1,903
9. Mel Ott	1,860
10. Carl Yastrzemski	1,844
11. Ted Williams	1,839
12. Al Simmons	1,827
13. Frank Robinson	1,812
14. Dave Winfield	1,786
15. Honus Wagner	1,732
16. Reggie Jackson	1,702
17. Eddie Murray	1,662
18. Tony Perez	1,652
19. Ernie Banks	1,636
20. Goose Goslin	1,609
21. Nap Lajoie	1,599
22. Mike Schmidt	1,595
George Brett	1,595
24. H. Killebrew	1,584

Rogers Hornsby	1,584
26. Al Kaline	1,583
27. Jake Beckley	1,575
28. Willie McCovey	1,555
29. Willie Stargell	1,540
30. Harry Heilmann	1,539
31. Joe DiMaggio	1,537
32. Tris Speaker	1,529
33. Sam Crawford	1,525
34. Mickey Mantle	1,509
35. Dave Parker	1,493
36. Andre Dawson	1,492
37. Billy Williams	1,475
38. Rusty Staub	1,466
39. Ed Delahanty	1,464
40. Eddie Mathews	1,453
41. Jim Rice	1,451
42. George Davis	1,437
43. Yogi Berra	1,430
44. C. Gehringer	1,427
45. Joe Cronin	1,424
46. Jim Bottomley	1,422
47. Robin Yount	1,406
48. Ted Simmons	1,389
49. Dwight Evans	1,384
50. Joe Medwick	1,383
51. Johnny Bench	1,376
52. Orlando Cepeda	1,365
53. B. Robinson	1,357
54. Darrell Evans	1,354
55. Lave Cross	1,345
56. Johnny Mize	1,337
57. Duke Snider	1,333
58. Ron Santo	1,331
59. Carlton Fisk	1,330
60. Al Oliver	1,326
61. Roger Connor	1,322
62. Pete Rose	1,314
Graig Nettles	1,314
64. Mickey Vernon	1,311
65. Paul Waner	1,309

66. Steve Garvey	1,308
67. R. Clemente	1,305
68. Enos Slaughter	1,304
69. Hugh Duffy	1,302
70. Eddie Collins	1,300
71. Sam Thompson	1,299
72. Dan Brouthers	1,296
73. Del Ennis	1,284
74. Bob Johnson	1,283
75. Hank Greenberg	1,276
Don Baylor	1,276
77. Gil Hodges	1,274
78. Pie Traynor	1,273
79. Dale Murphy	1,266
80. Zack Wheat	1,248
81. Bobby Doerr	1,247
82. Lee May	1,244
Frankie Frisch	1,244
84. George Foster	1,239
85. Bill Dahlen	1,233
86. Gary Carter	1,225
87. Dave Kingman	1,210
88. Bill Dickey	1,209
89. Bill Buckner	1,208
90. Chuck Klein	1,201
91. Bob Elliott	1,195
92. Joe Kelley	1,194
93. Tony Lazzeri	1,191
94. Boog Powell	1,187
95. Joe Torre	1,185
96. Heinie Manush	1,183
97. Jack Clark	1,180
98. Gabby Hartnett	1,179
99. Vic Wertz	1,178
100. Sherry Magee	1,176

STOLEN BASES

1. Rickey Henderson	1,095
2. Lou Brock	938
3. Billy Hamilton	912
4. Ty Cobb	891
5. Tim Raines	751
6. Eddie Collins	744
7. Arlie Latham	739
8. Max Carey	738
9. Honus Wagner	722
10. Joe Morgan	689
11. Willie Wilson	667
12. Tom Brown	657
13. Bert Campaneris	649
14. Vince Coleman	648
15. George Davis	616
16. Dummy Hoy	594
17. Maury Wills	586
18. G. VanHaltren	583
19. Hugh Duffy	574
20. Bid McPhee	568
21. Ozzie Smith	563
22. Davey Lopes	557
23. Cesar Cedeno	550
24. Bill Dahlen	547
25. John Ward	540
26. Herman Long	534
27. Patsy Donovan	518
28. Jack Doyle	516
29. Harry Stovey	509
30. Fred Clarke	506
Luis Aparicio	506
32. Clyde Milan	495
Willie Keeler	495
34. Omar Moreno	487
35. Brett Butler	476
36. Mike Griffin	473
37. Tommy McCarthy	468
38. Jimmy Sheckard	465
39. Bobby Bonds	461
40. Ron LeFlore	455
Ed Delahanty	455
42. Curt Welch	453
43. Steve Sax	444
44. Joe Kelley	443
45. Sherry Magee	441
46. John McGraw	436
47. Tris Speaker	434
Paul Molitor	434
49. Mike Tiernan	428
50. Bob Bescher	427

WALKS

1. Babe Ruth	2,056
2. Ted Williams	2,019
3. Joe Morgan	1,865
4. Carl Yastrzemski	1,845
5. Mickey Mantle	1,733
6. Mel Ott	1,708
7. Eddie Yost	1,614
8. Darrell Evans	1,605
9. Stan Musial	1,599
10. Pete Rose	1,566
11. H. Killebrew	1,559
12. Lou Gehrig	1,508
13. Mike Schmidt	1,507
14. Eddie Collins	1,499
15. Willie Mays	1,464
16. Jimmie Foxx	1,452
17. Eddie Mathews	1,444
18. Frank Robinson	1,420
19. R. Henderson	1,406
20. Hank Aaron	1,402
21. Dwight Evans	1,391
22. Tris Speaker	1,381
23. Reggie Jackson	1,375
24. Willie McCovey	1,345
25. Luke Appling	1,302
26. Al Kaline	1,277
27. Ken Singleton	1,263
28. Jack Clark	1,262
29. Rusty Staub	1,255
30. Ty Cobb	1,249
31. Willie Randolph	1,243
32. Jim Wynn	1,224
33. Pee Wee Reese	1,210
34. Richie Ashburn	1,198

35. Brian Downing	1,197	
36. Eddie Murray	1,187	
Billy Hamilton	1,187	
38. C. Gehringer	1,186	
39. Dave Winfield	1,171	
40. Donie Bush	1,158	
41. Toby Harrah	1,153	
Max Bishop	1,153	
43. Harry Hooper	1,136	
44. Jimmy Sheckard	1,135	
45. Lou Whitaker	1,125	
46. Ron Santo	1,108	
47. George Brett	1,096	
48. Stan Hack	1,092	
Lu Blue	1,092	
50. Paul Waner	1,091	

STRIKEOUTS

1. Reggie Jackson	2,597
2. Willie Stargell	1,936
3. Mike Schmidt	1,883
4. Tony Perez	1,867
5. Dave Kingman	1,816
6. Bobby Bonds	1,757
7. Dale Murphy	1,748
8. Lou Brock	1,730
9. Mickey Mantle	1,710
10. H. Killebrew	1,699
11. Dwight Evans	1,697
12. Dave Winfield	1,609
13. Lee May	1,570
14. Dick Allen	1,556
15. Willie McCovey	1,550
16. Dave Parker	1,537
17. Frank Robinson	1,532
18. Willie Mays	1,526
19. Rick Monday	1,513
20. Greg Luzinski	1,495
21. Eddie Mathews	1,487
22. Frank Howard	1,460
23. Lance Parrish	1,447

24. Jack Clark	1,441
25. Jim Wynn	1,427
26. Jim Rice	1,423
27. George Foster	1,419
28. George Scott	1,418
29. Darrell Evans	1,410
30. Andre Dawson	1,398
31. Carl Yastrzemski	1,393
32. Carlton Fisk	1,386
33. Hank Aaron	1,383
34. Rob Deer	1,379
35. Larry Parrish	1,359
36. Robin Yount	1,350
37. Ron Santo	1,343
38. Gorman Thomas	1,339
39. Babe Ruth	1,330
40. Deron Johnson	1,318
41. Willie Horton	1,313
42. Jimmie Foxx	1,311
43. Eddie Murray	1,285
44. Bobby Grich	1,278
Johnny Bench	1,278
46. C. Washington	1,266
47. Juan Samuel	1,261
48. Ken Singleton	1,246
49. Duke Snider	1,237
50. Ernie Banks	1,236

BATTING AVERAGE

1. Ty Cobb	.366
2. Rogers Hornsby	.358
3. Joe Jackson	.356
4. Ed Delahanty	.346
5. Tris Speaker	.345
6. Ted Williams	.344
7. Billy Hamilton	.344
8. Dan Brouthers	.342
9. Babe Ruth	.342
10. Harry Heilmann	.342
11. Pete Browning	.341
12. Willie Keeler	.341

13. Bill Terry	.341
14. George Sisler	.340
15. Lou Gehrig	.340
16. Jesse Burkett	.338
17. Nap Lajoie	.338
18. R. Stephenson	.336
19. Wade Boggs	.335
20. Al Simmons	.334
21. John McGraw	.334
22. Paul Waner	.333
23. Eddie Collins	.333
24. Mike Donlin	.333
25. Cap Anson	.332
26. Stan Musial	.331
27. Sam Thompson	.331
28. Heinie Manush	.330
29. Tony Gwynn	.329
30. Rod Carew	.328
31. Honus Wagner	.327
32. Tip O'Neill	.326
33. Bob Fothergill	.325
34. Jimmie Foxx	.325
35. Earle Combs	.325
36. Joe DiMaggio	.325
37. Babe Herman	.324
38. Hugh Duffy	.324
39. Joe Medwick	.324
40. Edd Roush	.323
41. Sam Rice	.322
42. Ross Youngs	.322
43. Kiki Cuyler	.321
44. Charlie Gehringer	.320
45. Chuck Klein	.320
46. Pie Traynor	.320
47. Mickey Cochrane	.320
48. Ken Williams	.319
49. Kirby Puckett	.318
50. Earl Averill	.318

SLUGGING AVERAGE

1. Babe Ruth		.690
2. Ted Williams		.634
3. Lou Gehrig		.632
4. Jimmie Foxx		.609
5. Hank Greenberg		.605
6. Joe DiMaggio		.579
7. Rogers Hornsby		.577
8. Johnny Mize		.562
9. Stan Musial		.559
10. Willie Mays		.557
11. Mickey Mantle		.557
12. Hank Aaron		.555
13. Ralph Kiner		.548
14. Hack Wilson		.545
15. Chuck Klein		.543
16. Duke Snider		.540
17. Frank Robinson		.537
18. Al Simmons		.535
19. Dick Allen		.534
20. Earl Averill		.534
21. Mel Ott		.533
22. Babe Herman		.532
23. Fred McGriff		.531
24. Ken Williams		.530
25. Willie Stargell		.529
26. Mike Schmidt		.527
27. Barry Bonds		.526
28. Chick Hafey		.526
29. Hal Trosky		.522
30. Wally Berger		.522
31. Harry Heilmann		.520
32. Dan Brouthers		.519
33. Charlie Keller		.518
34. Joe Jackson		.517
35. Willie McCovey		.515
36. Ty Cobb		.512
37. Danny Tartabull		.510
38. Eddie Mathews		.509
39. Jeff Heath		.509
40. Harmon Killebrew		.509
41. Darryl Strawberry		.508
42. Jose Canseco		.507
43. Bob Johnson		.506
44. Bill Terry		.506
45. Ed Delahanty		.505
46. Sam Thompson		.505
47. Joe Medwick		.505
48. Jim Rice		.502
49. Tris Speaker		.500
50. Jim Bottomley		.500

ON-BASE AVERAGE

1. Ted Williams	.483
2. Babe Ruth	.474
3. John McGraw	.465
4. Billy Hamilton	.455
5. Lou Gehrig	.447
6. Rogers Hornsby	.434
7. Ty Cobb	.433
8. Jimmie Foxx	.428
9. Tris Speaker	.428
10. Wade Boggs	.428
11. Ferris Fain	.425
12. Eddie Collins	.424
13. Dan Brouthers	.423
14. Joe Jackson	.423
15. Max Bishop	.423
16. Mickey Mantle	.423
17. Mickey Cochrane	.419
18. Stan Musial	.418
19. Cupid Childs	.416
20. Jesse Burkett	.415
21. Mel Ott	.414
22. Roy Thomas	.414
23. Hank Greenberg	.412
24. Ed Delahanty	.412
25. Charlie Keller	.410
26. Eddie Stanky	.410
27. Jackie Robinson	.410
28. Harry Heilmann	.410
29. Roy Cullenbine	.408
30. Rickey Henderson	.408
31. Denny Lyons	.407
32. R. Stephenson	.407
33. Joe Cunningham	.406
34. Arky Vaughan	.406
35. Paul Waner	.404
36. Charlie Gehringer	.404
37. Pete Browning	.403
38. Lu Blue	.402
39. Joe Kelley	.401
40. John Kruk	.400
41. Mike Hargrove	.400
42. Luke Appling	.399
43. Elmer Valo	.399
44. Ross Youngs	.399
45. Ralph Kiner	.398
46. Joe DiMaggio	.398
47. Elmer Smith	.398
48. Richie Ashburn	.397
49. Johnny Mize	.397
50. Roger Connor	.397

ON-BASE PLUS SLUGGING

1. Babe Ruth	1.163
2. Ted Williams	1.116
3. Lou Gehrig	1.080
4. Jimmie Foxx	1.038
5. Hank Greenberg	1.017
6. Rogers Hornsby	1.010
7. Mickey Mantle	.979
8. Stan Musial	.977
9. Joe DiMaggio	.977
10. Johnny Mize	.959
11. Mel Ott	.947
12. Ralph Kiner	.946
13. Ty Cobb	.945
14. Willie Mays	.944
15. Dan Brouthers	.942
16. Joe Jackson	.940
17. Hack Wilson	.940
18. Hank Aaron	.932

19. Harry Heilmann	.930	8. Ty Cobb	1,136	49. Jim Rice	834
20. Frank Robinson	.929	9. Tris Speaker	1,131	50. Al Oliver	825
21. Earl Averill	.928	10. George Brett	1,119		
22. Tris Speaker	.928	11. Ted Williams	1,117	**GAMES PITCHED**	
23. Charlie Keller	.928	Jimmie Foxx	1,117	1. Hoyt Wilhelm	1,070
24. Ken Williams	.924	13. Reggie Jackson	1,075	2. Kent Tekulve	1,050
25. Fred McGriff	.923	14. Mel Ott	1,071	3. Lindy McDaniel	987
26. Chuck Klein	.922	15. Dave Winfield	1,058	4. Rich Gossage	966
27. Duke Snider	.921	16. Pete Rose	1,041	5. Rollie Fingers	944
28. Barry Bonds	.920	17. Mike Schmidt	1,015	6. Gene Garber	931
29. Ed Delahanty	.917	18. Rogers Hornsby	1,011	7. Cy Young	906
30. Babe Herman	.915	19. Ernie Banks	1,009	8. Sparky Lyle	899
31. Al Simmons	.915	20. Al Simmons	995	9. Jim Kaat	898
32. Dick Allen	.914	21. Honus Wagner	993	10. Don McMahon	874
33. Mike Schmidt	.912	22. Andre Dawson	980	11. Jeff Reardon	869
34. Bob Johnson	.899	23. Al Kaline	972	12. Phil Niekro	864
35. Bill Terry	.899	24. Eddie Murray	964	13. Lee Smith	850
36. Chick Hafey	.898	25. Tony Perez	963	14. Roy Face	848
37. Mickey Cochrane	.897	26. Robin Yount	960	15. Charlie Hough	837
38. Hal Trosky	.892	27. Willie Stargell	953	16. Tug McGraw	824
39. Willie McCovey	.892	28. Mickey Mantle	952	17. Nolan Ryan	807
40. Willie Stargell	.892	29. Billy Williams	948	18. Dennis Eckersley	804
41. Sam Thompson	.888	30. Dwight Evans	941	19. Walter Johnson	802
42. Eddie Mathews	.888	31. Dave Parker	940	20. Gaylord Perry	777
43. Danny Tartabull	.887	32. Eddie Mathews	938	21. Don Sutton	774
44. Billy Hamilton	.887	33. Goose Goslin	921	22. Darold Knowles	765
45. Harmon Killebrew	.887	34. Willie McCovey	920	23. Tommy John	760
46. Goose Goslin	.887	35. Paul Waner	909	24. Jack Quinn	756
47. Charlie Gehringer	.884	36. Charlie Gehringer	904	25. Ron Reed	751
48. Jackie Robinson	.883	37. Nap Lajoie	903	26. Warren Spahn	750
49. Roger Connor	.883	38. Harmon Killebrew	887	27. Gary Lavelle	**745**
50. Al Rosen	.882	39. Joe DiMaggio	881	Tom Burgmeier	745
		40. Harry Heilmann	876	29. Willie Hernandez	744
EXTRA BASE HITS		41. Vada Pinson	868	30. Steve Carlton	741
1. Hank Aaron	1,477	42. Sam Crawford	864	31. Ron Perranoski	737
2. Stan Musial	1,377	43. Joe Medwick	858	32. Ron Kline	736
3. Babe Ruth	1,356	44. Duke Snider	850	33. Clay Carroll	731
4. Willie Mays	1,323	45. Roberto Clemente	846	34. Jesse Orosco	714
5. Lou Gehrig	1,190	46. Carlton Fisk	844	35. Johnny Klippstein	711
6. Frank Robinson	1,186	47. Rusty Staub	838	36. Greg Minton	710
7. Carl Yastrzemski	1,157	48. Jim Bottomley	835	37. Jim Galvin	705

38. Stu Miller	704	
39. Joe Niekro	702	
40. Bill Campbell	700	
41. Bob McClure	698	
42. Pete Alexander	696	
43. Bob Miller	694	
44. Eppa Rixey	692	
Grant Jackson	692	
Bert Blyleven	692	
47. Early Wynn	691	
48. Eddie Fisher	690	
49. Dave Righetti	688	
50. Ted Abernathy	681	

GAMES STARTED

1. Cy Young	815
2. Nolan Ryan	773
3. Don Sutton	756
4. Phil Niekro	716
5. Steve Carlton	709
6. Tommy John	700
7. Gaylord Perry	690
8. Jim Galvin	689
9. Bert Blyleven	685
10. Walter Johnson	666
11. Warren Spahn	665
12. Tom Seaver	647
13. Jim Kaat	625
14. Frank Tanana	616
15. Early Wynn	612
16. Robin Roberts	609
17. Pete Alexander	599
18. Fergie Jenkins	594
19. Tim Keefe	593
20. Bobby Mathews	568
21. Kid Nichols	561
22. Eppa Rixey	552
23. C. Mathewson	551
24. Mickey Welch	549
25. Jerry Reuss	547
26. Red Ruffing	536

27. Rick Reuschel	529
Eddie Plank	529
29. Jerry Koosman	527
30. Jim Palmer	521
31. Jim Bunning	519
32. John Clarkson	518
33. Jack Powell	516
34. Tony Mullane	504
Jack Morris	504
36. Gus Weyhing	503
Charley Radbourn	503
38. Joe Niekro	500
39. Bob Friend	497
40. Mickey Lolich	496
41. Burleigh Grimes	495
42. Claude Osteen	488
43. Sam Jones	487
44. Jim McCormick	485
45. Luis Tiant	484
Ted Lyons	484
Bob Feller	484
48. Bobo Newsom	483
Red Faber	483
50. Bob Gibson	482

COMPLETE GAMES

1. Cy Young	749
2. Jim Galvin	646
3. Tim Keefe	554
4. Kid Nichols	531
Walter Johnson	531
6. Mickey Welch	525
Bobby Mathews	525
8. Charley Radbourn	489
9. John Clarkson	485
10. Tony Mullane	468
11. Jim McCormick	466
12. Gus Weyhing	448
13. Pete Alexander	437
14. C. Mathewson	434
15. Jack Powell	422

16. Eddie Plank	410
17. Will White	394
18. Amos Rusie	392
19. Vic Willis	388
20. Tommy Bond	386
21. Warren Spahn	382
22. Jim Whitney	377
23. Adonis Terry	367
24. Ted Lyons	356
25. George Mullin	353
26. Charlie Buffinton	351
27. Chick Fraser	342
28. Clark Griffith	337
29. Red Ruffing	335
30. Silver King	329
31. Al Orth	324
32. Bill Hutchison	321
33. Joe McGinnity	314
Burleigh Grimes	314
35. Red Donahue	313
36. Guy Hecker	310
37. Bill Dinneen	306
38. Robin Roberts	305
39. Gaylord Perry	303
40. George Bradley	302
41. Ted Breitenstein	300
42. Lefty Grove	298
Bob Caruthers	298
44. Ed Morris	297
Pink Hawley	297
46. Mark Baldwin	296
47. Brickyard Kennedy	293
48. Early Wynn	290
Eppa Rixey	290
50. Bill Donovan	289

SAVES

1. Lee Smith	401
2. Jeff Reardon	365
3. Rollie Fingers	341
4. Rich Gossage	309

5. Bruce Sutter	300	
6. Dennis Eckersley	275	
7. Tom Henke	260	
8. Dave Righetti	252	
9. Dan Quisenberry	244	
10. Sparky Lyle	238	
11. John Franco	236	
12. Hoyt Wilhelm	227	
13. Gene Garber	218	
14. Dave Smith	216	
15. Bobby Thigpen	201	
16. Roy Face	193	
17. Doug Jones	190	
18. Mike Marshall	188	
19. Mitch Williams	186	
20. Kent Tekulve	184	
Randy Myers	184	
Steve Bedrosian	184	
23. Tug McGraw	180	
24. Ron Perranoski	179	
25. Lindy McDaniel	172	
26. Bryan Harvey	171	
27. Gregg Olson	160	
Jeff Montgomery	160	
29. Rick Aguilera	156	
30. Stu Miller	154	
31. Don McMahon	153	
Jay Howell	153	
33. Roger McDowell	151	
34. Greg Minton	150	
35. Ted Abernathy	148	
36. Willie Hernandez	147	
37. Jeff Russell	146	
38. Dave Giusti	145	
39. Darold Knowles	143	
Clay Carroll	143	
41. Gary Lavelle	136	
42. Todd Worrell	134	
43. Dan Plesac	133	
44. Bob Stanley	132	
Jim Brewer	132	

46. Jesse Orosco	130
Ron Davis	130
48. Mike Henneman	128
Steve Farr	128
50. Terry Forster	127

SHUTOUTS

1. Walter Johnson	110
2. Pete Alexander	90
3. Christy Mathewson	79
4. Cy Young	76
5. Eddie Plank	69
6. Warren Spahn	63
7. Tom Seaver	61
Nolan Ryan	61
9. Bert Blyleven	60
10. Don Sutton	58
11. Ed Walsh	57
Jim Galvin	57
13. Bob Gibson	56
14. Steve Carlton	55
Mordecai Brown	55
16. Gaylord Perry	53
Jim Palmer	53
18. Juan Marichal	52
19. Vic Willis	50
Rube Waddell	50
21. Early Wynn	49
Luis Tiant	49
Fergie Jenkins	49
Don Drysdale	49
25. Kid Nichols	48
26. Jack Powell	46
Tommy John	46
28. Doc White	45
Red Ruffing	45
Robin Roberts	45
Phil Niekro	45
Addie Joss	45
Whitey Ford	45
34. Bob Feller	44

Babe Adams	44
36. Milt Pappas	43
37. Bucky Walters	42
Catfish Hunter	42
Tommy Bond	42
40. Mickey Welch	41
Hippo Vaughn	41
Mickey Lolich	41
43. Mel Stottlemyre	40
Ed Reulbach	40
Claude Osteen	40
Sandy Koufax	40
Larry French	40
Jim Bunning	40
Chief Bender	40
50. Jerry Reuss	39
Sam Leever	39
Tim Keefe	39

WINS

1. Cy Young	511
2. Walter Johnson	417
3. Christy Mathewson	373
Pete Alexander	373
5. Jim Galvin	364
6. Warren Spahn	363
7. Kid Nichols	361
8. Tim Keefe	342
9. Steve Carlton	329
10. John Clarkson	328
11. Eddie Plank	326
12. Don Sutton	324
Nolan Ryan	324
14. Phil Niekro	318
15. Gaylord Perry	314
16. Tom Seaver	311
17. Charley Radbourn	309
18. Mickey Welch	307
19. Early Wynn	300
Lefty Grove	300
21. Bobby Mathews	297

22. Tommy John	288	63. Jerry Koosman	222
23. Bert Blyleven	287	Hooks Dauss	222
24. Robin Roberts	286	65. Joe Niekro	221
25. Tony Mullane	284	66. Jerry Reuss	220
Fergie Jenkins	284	67. Earl Whitehill	218
27. Jim Kaat	283	Bob Caruthers	218
28. Red Ruffing	273	69. Mickey Lolich	217
29. Burleigh Grimes	270	F. Fitzsimmons	217
30. Jim Palmer	268	71. Wilbur Cooper	216
31. Eppa Rixey	266	72. Jim Perry	215
Bob Feller	266	Stan Coveleski	215
33. Jim McCormick	265	74. Rick Reuschel	214
34. Gus Weyhing	264	75. Chief Bender	212
35. Ted Lyons	260	76. Billy Pierce	211
36. Red Faber	254	Bobo Newsom	211
37. Al Spalding	253	Charlie Hough	211
Carl Hubbell	253	79. Jesse Haines	210
39. Bob Gibson	251	80. Milt Pappas	209
40. Vic Willis	249	Don Drysdale	209
41. Jack Quinn	247	Vida Blue	209
42. Joe McGinnity	246	83. Bob Welch	208
43. Amos Rusie	245	Dennis Martinez	208
Jack Powell	245	Eddie Cicotte	208
45. Jack Morris	244	86. Hal Newhouser	207
46. Juan Marichal	243	Carl Mays	207
47. Frank Tanana	240	Bob Lemon	207
Herb Pennock	240	89. Al Orth	204
49. Mordecai Brown	239	Silver King	204
50. Waite Hoyt	237	91. Jack Stivetts	203
Clark Griffith	237	Lew Burdette	203
52. Whitey Ford	236	93. Charlie Root	201
53. Tommy Bond	234	Rube Marquard	201
54. Charlie Buffinton	233	95. George Uhle	200
55. Will White	229	96. Bucky Walters	198
Luis Tiant	229	Jack Chesbro	198
Sam Jones	229	98. Dazzy Vance	197
58. George Mullin	228	Adonis Terry	197
59. Catfish Hunter	224	Jesse Tannehill	197
Jim Bunning	224	Bob Friend	197
61. Mel Harder	223	Larry French	197
Paul Derringer	223		

INNINGS

1. Cy Young	7,355.1
2. Jim Galvin	6,003.1
3. Walter Johnson	5,915.0
4. Phil Niekro	5,404.1
5. Nolan Ryan	5,386.0
6. Gaylord Perry	5,350.1
7. Don Sutton	5,282.1
8. Warren Spahn	5,243.2
9. Steve Carlton	5,217.1
10. Pete Alexander	5,190.0
11. Kid Nichols	5,056.1
12. Tim Keefe	5,047.1
13. Bert Blyleven	4,970.0
14. B. Mathews	4,956.1
15. Mickey Welch	4,802.0
16. Tom Seaver	4,782.2
17. C. Mathewson	4,780.2
18. Tommy John	4,710.1
19. Robin Roberts	4,688.2
20. Early Wynn	4,564.0
21. John Clarkson	4,536.1
22. C. Radbourn	4,535.1
23. Tony Mullane	4,531.1
24. Jim Kaat	4,530.1
25. Fergie Jenkins	4,500.2
26. Eddie Plank	4,495.2
27. Eppa Rixey	4,494.2
28. Jack Powell	4,389.0
29. Red Ruffing	4,344.0
30. Gus Weyhing	4,324.1
31. J. McCormick	4,275.2
32. Frank Tanana	4,188.1
33. B. Grimes	4,179.2
34. Ted Lyons	4,161.0
35. Red Faber	4,086.2
36. Vic Willis	3,996.0
37. Jim Palmer	3,948.0
38. Lefty Grove	3,940.2
39. Jack Quinn	3,920.1
40. Bob Gibson	3,884.1

41. Sam Jones	3,883.0
42. J. Koosman	3,839.1
43. Bob Feller	3,827.0
44. Amos Rusie	3,769.2
45. Waite Hoyt	3,762.1
46. Jim Bunning	3,760.1
47. Bobo Newsom	3,759.1
48. Charlie Hough	3,687.2
49. George Mullin	3,686.2
50. Jack Morris	3,682.2

STRIKEOUTS

1. Nolan Ryan	5,714
2. Steve Carlton	4,136
3. Bert Blyleven	3,701
4. Tom Seaver	3,640
5. Don Sutton	3,574
6. Gaylord Perry	3,534
7. Walter Johnson	3,509
8. Phil Niekro	3,342
9. Fergie Jenkins	3,192
10. Bob Gibson	3,117
11. Jim Bunning	2,855
12. Mickey Lolich	2,832
13. Cy Young	2,803
14. Frank Tanana	2,773
15. Warren Spahn	2,583
16. Bob Feller	2,581
17. Jerry Koosman	2,556
18. Tim Keefe	2,545
19. C. Mathewson	2,502
20. Don Drysdale	2,486
21. Jim Kaat	2,461
22. Sam McDowell	2,453
23. Luis Tiant	2,416
24. Sandy Koufax	2,396
25. Jack Morris	2,378
26. Robin Roberts	2,357
27. Early Wynn	2,334
28. Rube Waddell	2,316
29. Juan Marichal	2,303

30. Charlie Hough	2,297
31. Lefty Grove	2,266
32. Eddie Plank	2,246
33. Tommy John	2,245
34. Jim Palmer	2,212
35. D. Eckersley	2,198
Pete Alexander	2,198
37. Vida Blue	2,175
38. Camilo Pascual	2,167
39. Bobo Newsom	2,082
40. Dazzy Vance	2,045
41. Roger Clemens	2,033
42. Rick Reuschel	2,015
43. Catfish Hunter	2,012
44. Mark Langston	2,001
45. Billy Pierce	1,999
46. Red Ruffing	1,987
47. John Clarkson	1,978
48. Whitey Ford	1,956
49. Amos Rusie	1,934
50. Bob Welch	1,925

WINNING PERCENTAGE

1. Al Spalding	.796
2. Dave Foutz	.690
3. Whitey Ford	.690
4. Bob Caruthers	.688
5. Lefty Grove	.680
6. Vic Raschi	.667
7. Larry Corcoran	.665
8. Christy Mathewson	.665
9. Sam Leever	.660
10. Sal Maglie	.657
11. Dick McBride	.656
12. Dwight Gooden	.655
13. Sandy Koufax	.655
14. Roger Clemens	.655
15. Johnny Allen	.654
16. Ron Guidry	.651
17. Lefty Gomez	.649
18. John Clarkson	.648

19. Mordecai Brown	.648
20. Dizzy Dean	.644
21. Pete Alexander	.642
22. Jim Palmer	.638
23. Kid Nichols	.634
24. Deacon Phillippe	.634
25. Joe McGinnity	.634
26. Ed Reulbach	.632
27. Juan Marichal	.631
28. Mort Cooper	.631
29. Allie Reynolds	.630
30. Jesse Tannehill	.629
31. Ray Kremer	.627
32. Firpo Marberry	.627
33. Eddie Plank	.627
34. Chief Bender	.625
35. Don Newcombe	.623
36. Nig Cuppy	.623
37. Addie Joss	.623
38. Fred Goldsmith	.622
39. Doc Crandall	.622
40. Carl Mays	.622
41. Carl Hubbell	.622
42. Bob Feller	.621
43. Mel Parnell	.621
44. John Tudor	.619
45. Clark Griffith	.619
46. Bob Lemon	.618
47. Cy Young	.618
48. John Ward	.617
49. Urban Shocker	.615
50. Jeff Tesreau	.615

EARNED RUN AVERAGE

1. Ed Walsh	1.82
2. Addie Joss	1.89
3. Mordecai Brown	2.06
4. John Ward	2.10
5. Christy Mathewson	2.13
6. Al Spalding	2.14
7. Rube Waddell	2.16

8. Walter Johnson	2.17	49. Carl Weilman	2.67	38. Stump Weidman	1.78
9. Orval Overall	2.23	50. Nick Altrock	2.67	39. Pete Donohue	1.80
10. Will White	2.28			40. Jesse Barnes	1.80
11. Ed Reulbach	2.28	**FEWEST WALKS**		41. Carl Hubbell	1.82
12. Jim Scott	2.30	1. Al Spalding	0.49	42. Juan Marichal	1.82
13. Tommy Bond	2.31	2. Candy Cummings	0.49	43. Slim Sallee	1.83
14. Eddie Plank	2.35	3. Tommy Bond	0.49	44. Bill Bernhard	1.83
15. Larry Corcoran	2.36	4. George Bradley	0.60	45. Lew Burdette	1.84
16. George McQuillan	2.38	5. George Zettlein	0.61	46. Curt Davis	1.85
17. Eddie Cicotte	2.38	6. Terry Larkin	0.71	47. Ed Siever	1.86
18. Ed Killian	2.38	7. Dick McBride	0.74	48. Larry Corcoran	1.87
19. Doc White	2.39	8. John Ward	0.92	49. Ed Walsh	1.87
20. George Bradley	2.42	9. Fred Goldsmith	0.96	50. K. Raffensberger	1.88
21. Nap Rucker	2.42	10. Bobby Mathews	0.97		
22. Jeff Tesreau	2.43	11. Jim Whitney	1.06	**RATIO**	
23. Jim McCormick	2.43	12. Jim Galvin	1.12	1. Addie Joss	8.71
24. Terry Larkin	2.43	13. Deacon Phillippe	1.25	2. Ed Walsh	9.00
25. Chief Bender	2.46	14. Will White	1.26	3. John Ward	9.40
26. Hooks Wiltse	2.47	15. Babe Adams	1.29	4. Christy Mathewson	9.53
27. Sam Leever	2.47	16. Jack Lynch	1.38	5. Walter Johnson	9.55
28. Lefty Leifield	2.47	17. Addie Joss	1.41	6. Mordecai Brown	9.59
29. Hippo Vaughn	2.49	18. Cy Young	1.49	7. George Bradley	9.80
30. Candy Cummings	2.49	19. Guy Hecker	1.51	8. Babe Adams	9.83
31. Bob Ewing	2.49	20. Lee Richmond	1.53	9. Tommy Bond	9.83
32. Hoyt Wilhelm	2.52	21. Jesse Tannehill	1.56	10. Juan Marichal	9.91
33. Noodles Hahn	2.55	22. Jim McCormick	1.58	11. Rube Waddell	9.92
34. Pete Alexander	2.56	23. C. Mathewson	1.59	12. Larry Corcoran	9.94
35. Slim Sallee	2.56	24. Red Lucas	1.61	13. Deacon Phillippe	9.95
36. Deacon Phillippe	2.59	25. Nick Altrock	1.62	14. Sandy Koufax	9.96
37. Frank Smith	2.59	26. Pete Alexander	1.65	15. Ed Morris	9.97
38. Ed Siever	2.60	27. Jumbo McGinnis	1.65	16. Will White	10.00
39. Bob Rhoads	2.61	28. Tiny Bonham	1.67	17. Chief Bender	10.01
40. Tim Keefe	2.62	29. Ed Morris	1.67	18. Charlie Ferguson	10.05
41. Cy Young	2.63	30. Noodles Hahn	1.69	19. Sid Fernandez	10.05
42. Vic Willis	2.63	31. Charlie Ferguson	1.72	20. Terry Larkin	10.05
43. Red Ames	2.63	32. Fritz Peterson	1.73	21. Eddie Plank	10.07
44. Barney Pelty	2.63	33. Robin Roberts	1.73	22. Tom Seaver	10.09
45. Claude Hendrix	2.65	34. Charley Radbourn	1.74	23. Pete Alexander	10.09
46. Joe McGinnity	2.66	35. Dick Rudolph	1.77	24. Tim Keefe	10.09
47. Dick Rudolph	2.66	36. Al Orth	1.77	25. Doc White	10.10
48. Jack Taylor	2.66	37. Bret Saberhagen	1.78	26. Roger Clemens	10.11

27. Hoyt Wilhelm	10.12
28. Bret Saberhagen	10.16
29. Cy Young	10.17
30. G. McQuillan	10.18
31. Hooks Wiltse	10.18
32. Noodles Hahn	10.19
33. Jim McCormick	10.19
34. Catfish Hunter	10.21
35. Nick Altrock	10.27
36. Sam Leever	10.27
37. Fergie Jenkins	10.28
38. Don Sutton	10.28
39. A. Messersmith	10.29
40. Ed Reulbach	10.29
41. Jeff Tesreau	10.30
42. Gary Nolan	10.31
43. Jim Whitney	10.32
44. Don Drysdale	10.33
45. C. Radbourn	10.34
46. Jack Chesbro	10.35
47. Barney Pelty	10.35
48. Tiny Bonham	10.38
49. Fred Goldsmith	10.38
50. D. Eckersley	10.39

PITCHER PUTOUTS

1. Phil Niekro	386
2. Jack Morris	375
3. Fergie Jenkins	363
4. Gaylord Perry	349
5. Don Sutton	334
6. Tom Seaver	328
Rick Reuschel	328
Tony Mullane	328
9. Jim Galvin	324
10. Robin Roberts	316

PITCHER ASSISTS

1. Cy Young	2,014
2. C. Mathewson	1,503
3. Pete Alexander	1,419
4. Jim Galvin	1,382

5. Walter Johnson	1,351
6. Burleigh Grimes	1,252
7. George Mullin	1,244
8. Jack Quinn	1,240
9. Ed Walsh	1,208
10. Eppa Rixey	1,195

PITCHER CHANCES ACCEPTED

1. Cy Young	2,243
2. C. Mathewson	1,784
3. Jim Galvin	1,706
4. Walter Johnson	1,627
5. Pete Alexander	1,608
6. Burleigh Grimes	1,477
7. George Mullin	1,473
8. Ed Walsh	1,441
9. Vic Willis	1,395
10. Jack Quinn	1,379

PITCHER FIELDING AVERAGE

1. Don Mossi	.990
2. Gary Nolan	.990
3. Rick Rhoden	.989
4. Lon Warneke	.988
5. Jim Wilson	.988
6. Woodie Fryman	.988
7. Elmer Riddle	.987
8. Larry Gura	.986
9. Pete Alexander	.985
10. General Crowder	.984

CATCHER GAMES

1. Carlton Fisk	2,229
2. Bob Boone	2,225
3. Gary Carter	2,056
4. Jim Sundberg	1,927
5. Al Lopez	1,918
6. Rick Ferrell	1,806
7. Gabby Hartnett	1,793
8. Ted Simmons	1,771

9. Johnny Bench	1,742
10. Ray Schalk	1,727

CATCHER PUTOUTS

1. Gary Carter	11,785
2. Carlton Fisk	11,369
3. Bob Boone	11,260
4. Tony Pena	9,968
5. Bill Freehan	9,941
6. Jim Sundberg	9,767
7. Johnny Roseboro	9,291
8. Johnny Bench	9,249
9. Lance Parrish	9,076
10. Johnny Edwards	8,925

CATCHER ASSISTS

1. Deacon McGuire	1,859
2. Ray Schalk	1,811
3. Steve O'Neill	1,698
4. Red Dooin	1,590
5. Chief Zimmer	1,580
6. Johnny Kling	1,552
7. Ivey Wingo	1,487
8. Wilbert Robinson	1,454
9. Bill Bergen	1,444
10. Wally Schang	1,420

CATCHER CHANCES ACCEPTED

1. Gary Carter	12,988
2. Bob Boone	12,434
3. Carlton Fisk	12,417
4. Tony Pena	10,919
5. Jim Sundberg	10,774
6. Bill Freehan	10,662
7. Johnny Bench	10,099
8. Lance Parrish	10,000
9. Johnny Roseboro	9,966
10. Ted Simmons	9,821

CATCHER FIELDING AVERAGE

1. Bill Freehan .993
2. Elston Howard .993
3. Ron Hassey .993
4. Jim Sundberg .993
5. Joe Azcue .992
6. Mike LaValliere .992
7. Sherm Lollar .992
8. Dave Valle .992
9. Buddy Rosar .992
10. Tom Haller .992

FIRST BASE GAMES

1. Jake Beckley 2,377
2. Eddie Murray 2,368
3. Mickey Vernon 2,237
4. Lou Gehrig 2,137
5. Charlie Grimm 2,131
6. Joe Judge 2,084
7. Cap Anson 2,082
8. Ed Konetchy 2,073
9. Steve Garvey 2,059
10. Joe Kuhel 2,057

FIRST BASE PUTOUTS

1. Jake Beckley 23,709
2. Ed Konetchy 21,361
3. Eddie Murray 20,842
4. Cap Anson 20,794
5. Charlie Grimm 20,711
6. Stuffy McInnis 19,962
7. Mickey Vernon 19,808
8. Jake Daubert 19,634
9. Lou Gehrig 19,510
10. Joe Kuhel 19,386

FIRST BASE ASSISTS

1. Eddie Murray 1,828
2. Keith Hernandez 1,682
3. George Sisler 1,529
4. Mickey Vernon 1,448
5. Fred Tenney 1,363
6. Chris Chambliss 1,351
   Bill Buckner 1,351
8. Norm Cash 1,317
9. Jake Beckley 1,315
10. Joe Judge 1,301

FIRST BASE CHANCES ACCEPTED

1. Jake Beckley 25,024
2. Eddie Murray 22,670
3. Ed Konetchy 22,653
4. Charlie Grimm 21,925
5. Cap Anson 21,749
6. Mickey Vernon 21,256
7. Stuffy McInnis 21,200
8. Jake Daubert 20,762
9. Lou Gehrig 20,597
10. Joe Judge 20,565

FIRST BASE FIELDING AVERAGE

1. Steve Garvey .996
2. Don Mattingly .996
3. Wes Parker .996
4. Dan Driessen .995
5. Mark McGwire .995
6. Jim Spencer .995
7. Frank McCormick .995
8. Mark Grace .994
9. Keith Hernandez .994
10. Carl Yastrzemski .994

SECOND BASE GAMES

1. Eddie Collins 2,650
2. Joe Morgan 2,527
3. Nellie Fox 2,295
4. Charlie Gehringer 2,206
5. Lou Whitaker 2,162
6. Willie Randolph 2,152
7. Frank White 2,150
8. Bid McPhee 2,126

9. Bill Mazeroski 2,094
10. Nap Lajoie 2,035

SECOND BASE PUTOUTS

1. Bid McPhee 6,545
2. Eddie Collins 6,526
3. Nellie Fox 6,090
4. Joe Morgan 5,742
5. Nap Lajoie 5,496
6. Charlie Gehringer 5,369
7. Bill Mazeroski 4,974
8. Bobby Doerr 4,928
9. Willie Randolph 4,859
10. Billy Herman 4,780

SECOND BASE ASSISTS

1. Eddie Collins 7,630
2. Charlie Gehringer 7,068
3. Joe Morgan 6,967
4. Bid McPhee 6,905
5. Bill Mazeroski 6,685
6. Nellie Fox 6,373
7. Willie Randolph 6,336
8. Nap Lajoie 6,262
9. Frank White 6,250
10. Lou Whitaker 6,244

SECOND BASE CHANCES ACCEPTED

1. Eddie Collins 14,156
2. Bid McPhee 13,450
3. Joe Morgan 12,709
4. Nellie Fox 12,463
5. C. Gehringer 12,437
6. Nap Lajoie 11,758
7. Bill Mazeroski 11,659
8. Willie Randolph 11,195
9. Frank White 10,990
10. Lou Whitaker 10,771

SECOND BASE FIELDING AVERAGE

1. Ryne Sandberg	.990
2. Tom Herr	.989
3. Jose Lind	.988
4. Rich Dauer	.987
5. Doug Flynn	.986
6. Marty Barrett	.986
7. Jerry Adair	.985
8. Jim Gantner	.985
9. Lou Whitaker	.984
10. Frank White	.984

THIRD BASE GAMES

1. Brooks Robinson	2,870
2. Graig Nettles	2,412
3. Mike Schmidt	2,212
4. Buddy Bell	2,183
5. Eddie Mathews	2,181
6. Ron Santo	2,130
7. Eddie Yost	2,008
8. Ron Cey	1,989
9. Aurelio Rodriguez	1,983
10. Sal Bando	1,896

THIRD BASE PUTOUTS

1. Brooks Robinson	2,697
2. Jimmy Collins	2,372
3. Eddie Yost	2,356
4. Lave Cross	2,306
5. Pie Traynor	2,289
6. Billy Nash	2,219
7. Frank Baker	2,154
8. Willie Kamm	2,151
9. Eddie Mathews	2,049
10. Willie Jones	2,045

THIRD BASE ASSISTS

1. Brooks Robinson	6,205
2. Graig Nettles	5,279
3. Mike Schmidt	5,045
4. Buddy Bell	4,925
5. Ron Santo	4,581
6. Eddie Mathews	4,322
7. Aurelio Rodriguez	4,150
8. Ron Cey	4,018
9. Sal Bando	3,720
10. Lave Cross	3,706

THIRD BASE CHANCES ACCEPTED

1. Brooks Robinson	8,902
2. Graig Nettles	7,177
3. Buddy Bell	6,723
4. Mike Schmidt	6,636
5. Ron Santo	6,536
6. Eddie Mathews	6,371
7. Jimmy Collins	6,074
8. Eddie Yost	6,015
9. Lave Cross	6,012
10. Pie Traynor	5,810

THIRD BASE FIELDING AVERAGE

1. Brooks Robinson	.971
2. Rico Petrocelli	.970
3. Ken Reitz	.970
4. George Kell	.969
5. Steve Buechele	.968
6. Don Money	.968
7. Don Wert	.968
8. Hank Majeski	.968
9. Willie Kamm	.967
10. Heinie Groh	.967

SHORTSTOP GAMES

1. Luis Aparicio	2,581
2. Ozzie Smith	2,322
3. Larry Bowa	2,222
4. Luke Appling	2,218
5. Dave Concepcion	2,178
6. Rabbit Maranville	2,153
7. Bill Dahlen	2,132
8. Bert Campaneris	2,097

9. Tommy Corcoran	2,073
10. Roy McMillan	2,028

SHORTSTOP PUTOUTS

1. Rabbit Maranville	5,139
2. Bill Dahlen	4,850
3. Dave Bancroft	4,623
4. Honus Wagner	4,576
5. Tommy Corcoran	4,550
6. Luis Aparicio	4,548
7. Luke Appling	4,398
8. Herman Long	4,225
9. Bobby Wallace	4,142
10. Pee Wee Reese	4,040

SHORTSTOP ASSISTS

1. Luis Aparicio	8,016
2. Ozzie Smith	7,793
3. Bill Dahlen	7,500
4. Rabbit Maranville	7,354
5. Luke Appling	7,218
6. Tommy Corcoran	7,106
7. Larry Bowa	6,857
8. Dave Concepcion	6,594
9. Dave Bancroft	6,561
10. R. Peckinpaugh	6,337

SHORTSTOP CHANCES ACCEPTED

1. Luis Aparicio	12,564
2. R. Maranville	12,493
3. Bill Dahlen	12,350
4. Ozzie Smith	11,758
5. T. Corcoran	11,656
6. Luke Appling	11,616
7. Dave Bancroft	11,184
8. Honus Wagner	10,617
9. Bobby Wallace	10,445
10. Herman Long	10,361

All-Time Leaders

SHORTSTOP FIELDING AVERAGE

1. Tony Fernandez	.980
2. Larry Bowa	.980
3. Ozzie Smith	.979
4. Cal Ripken	.978
5. Frank Duffy	.977
6. Spike Owen	.977
7. Alan Trammell	.977
8. Mark Belanger	.977
9. Dick Schofield	.977
10. Bucky Dent	.976

OUTFIELD GAMES

1. Ty Cobb	2,935
2. Willie Mays	2,842
3. Hank Aaron	2,760
4. Tris Speaker	2,698
5. Lou Brock	2,507
6. Al Kaline	2,488
7. Dave Winfield	2,468
8. Max Carey	2,421
9. Vada Pinson	2,403
10. R. Clemente	2,370

OUTFIELD PUTOUTS

1. Willie Mays	7,095
2. Tris Speaker	6,788
3. Max Carey	6,363
4. Ty Cobb	6,361
5. Richie Ashburn	6,089
6. Hank Aaron	5,539
7. Willie Davis	5,449
8. Doc Cramer	5,412
9. Vada Pinson	5,097
10. Andre Dawson	5,077

OUTFIELD ASSISTS

1. Tris Speaker	449
2. Ty Cobb	392
3. Jimmy Ryan	375
4. George VanHaltren	348
Tom Brown	348
6. Harry Hooper	344
7. Max Carey	339
8. Jimmy Sheckard	307
9. Clyde Milan	294
10. Orator Shaffer	289

OUTFIELD CHANCES ACCEPTED

1. Willie Mays	7,290
2. Tris Speaker	7,237
3. Ty Cobb	6,753
4. Max Carey	6,702
5. Richie Ashburn	6,267
6. Hank Aaron	5,740
7. Willie Davis	5,592
8. Doc Cramer	5,584
9. Vada Pinson	5,269
10. Andre Dawson	5,231

OUTFIELD FIELDING AVERAGE

1. Brian Downing	.995
2. Terry Puhl	.993
3. Brett Butler	.992
4. Pete Rose	.991
5. Ted Uhlaender	.991
6. Amos Otis	.991
7. Joe Rudi	.991
8. Mickey Stanley	.991
9. Don Demeter	.990
10. Robin Yount	.990

MANAGER WINS

1. Connie Mack	3,731
2. John McGraw	2,763
3. Bucky Harris	2,157
4. Joe McCarthy	2,125
5. Sparky Anderson	2,081
6. Walter Alston	2,040
7. Leo Durocher	2,008
8. Casey Stengel	1,905
9. Gene Mauch	1,902
10. Bill McKechnie	1,896

MANAGER WINNING PERCENTAGE

1. Joe McCarthy	.615
2. Jim Mutrie	.611
3. Charlie Comiskey	.608
4. Frank Selee	.598
5. Billy Southworth	.597
6. Frank Chance	.593
7. John McGraw	.586
8. Al Lopez	.584
9. Earl Weaver	.583
10. Harry Wright	.581

TEAM WINNING PERCENTAGE

1. **New York-AL**	**.564**
2. **New York/San Francisco-NL**	**.541**
New York-NL	.553
San Francisco-NL	.517
3. **Brooklyn/ Los Angeles-NL**	**.523**
Brooklyn-NL	.514
Los Angeles-NL	.539
4. **Chicago-NL**	**.518**
5. **Detroit-AL**	**.518**
6. **Pittsburgh-NL**	**.518**
7. **Kansas City-AL**	**.517**
8. **Boston-AL**	**.510**
9. **Cincinnati-NL**	**.506**
10. **Cleveland-AL**	**.506**
11. **St.Louis-NL**	**.505**
12. **Chicago-AL**	**.504**
13. **Toronto-AL**	**.501**
14. **Montreal-NL**	**.489**
15. **Boston/Milwaukee-Atlanta-NL**	**.488**
Boston-NL	.478
Milwaukee-NL	.563

Atlanta-NL	.478	**Oakland-AL**	**.480**	Baltimore-AL	.533
16. Los Angeles/		Philadelphia-AL	.478	**22. Philadelphia-NL**	**.466**
California-AL	**.483**	Kansas City A's-AL	.404	**23. NY Mets-NL**	**.464**
Los Angeles-AL	.477	Oakland-AL	.521	**24. Washington/**	
California-AL	.484	**20. Washington/**		**Texas-AL**	**.457**
17. Houston-NL	**.483**	**Minnesota-AL**	**.479**	Washington-AL	.418
18. Seattle/		Washington-AL	.465	Texas-AL	.477
Milwaukee-AL	**.483**	Minnesota-AL	.505	**25. San Diego-NL**	**.447**
Seattle Pilots-AL	.395	**21. St.Louis/**		**26. Seattle-AL**	**.432**
Milwaukee-AL	.487	**Baltimore-AL**	**.478**	**27. Colorado-NL**	**.414**
19. Philadelphia/KC/		St.Louis-AL	.433	**28. Florida-NL**	**.395**

TEAM WINS

	W	L		W	L
1. New York/			**15. Philadelphia/Kansas City/**		
San Francisco-NL	**9,034**	**7,673**	**Oakland-AL**	**6,877**	**7,459**
New York-NL	6,067	4,898	Philadelphia-AL	3,886	4,248
San Francisco-NL	2,967	2,775	Kansas City A's-AL	829	1,224
2. Chicago-NL	**8,936**	**8,307**	Oakland-AL	2,162	1,987
3. Pittsburgh-NL	**8,426**	**7,852**	**16. St.Louis/Baltimore-AL**	**6,790**	**7,427**
4. Boston/Milwaukee-			St. Louis-AL	3,414	4,465
Atlanta-NL	**8,398**	**8,815**	Baltimore-AL	3,376	2,962
Boston-NL	5,118	5,598	**17. Los Angeles/**		
Milwaukee-NL	1,146	890	**California-AL**	**2,553**	**2,728**
Atlanta-NL	2,134	2,327	Los Angeles-AL	308	338
5. Brooklyn/			California-AL	2,245	2,390
Los Angeles-NL	**8,309**	**7,573**	**18. Houston-NL**	**2,473**	**2,648**
Brooklyn-NL	5,214	4,926	**19. Washington/Texas-AL**	**2,405**	**2,860**
Los Angeles-NL	3,095	2,647	Washington-AL	740	1,032
6. Cincinnati-NL	**8,043**	**7,857**	Texas-AL	1,665	1,828
7. New York-AL	**7,943**	**6,134**	**20. New York Mets-NL**	**2,372**	**2,740**
8. St. Louis-NL	**7,892**	**7,734**	**21. Kansas City-AL**	**2,059**	**1,921**
9. Philadelphia-NL	**7,778**	**8,902**	**22. Montreal-NL**	**1,948**	**2,034**
10. Detroit-AL	**7,456**	**6,938**	**23. Seattle/Milwaukee-AL**	**1,924**	**2,061**
11. Boston-AL	**7,321**	**7,043**	Seattle Pilots-AL	64	98
12. Cleveland-AL	**7,270**	**7,104**	Milwaukee-AL	1,860	1,963
13. Chicago-AL	**7,228**	**7,127**	**24. San Diego-NL**	**1,783**	**2,203**
14. Washington/			**25. Toronto-AL**	**1,351**	**1,344**
Minnesota-AL	**6,887**	**7,476**	**26. Seattle-AL**	**1,166**	**1,532**
Washington-AL	4,223	4,865	**27. Colorado-NL**	**67**	**95**
Minnesota-AL	2,664	2,611	**28. Florida-NL**	**64**	**98**

Index

Aaron, Hank, 202, 210, 235, 270, 271, 272, 273
Abbaticchio, Ed, 72
Abbott, Jim, 191, 349
Abernathy, Ted, 249, 250
Adams, Ace, 179, 181
Adams, Franklin P., 72
Adcock, Joe, 199, 202
Aguilera, Rick, 334
Aikens, Willie, 315
Alexander, Dale, 113, 143
Alexander, Doyle, 334
Alexander, Pete, 92, 97, 120, 125
Allen, Bob, 47
Allen, Dick, 244, 245, 283, 284, 285, 306
Allen, Johnny, 150, 157
Allen, Lee, 106, 113
Alomar, Sandy, 345
Alou, Felipe, 241
Alou, Jesus, 241
Alou, Matty, 240, 241
Alston, Walter, 227, 263, 303
Altrock, Nick, 74
Alvarez, Wilson, 339
American League Championship Series (ALCS), 297, 325, 339, 343, 345, 348, 350
Anderson, Harry, 211
Anderson, Sparky, 283
Andujar, Joaquin, 338, 340
Angell, Roger, 284
Anson, Cap, 14, 23, 26, 28
Antonelli, Johnny, 219, 220, 268
Aparicio, Luis, 245, 260, 305, 344
Appling, Luke, 145, 318
Arellanes, Frank, 68
Arlen, Harold, 135
Arlett, Buzz, 131, 147
Armas, Tony, 319
Arroyo, Luis, 257
Ashburn, Richie, 185, 207, 229, 231, 263
Ashford, Emmett, 264
Atlanta Braves, 36, 203, 241, 261, 263, 271, 272, 273, 276, 289, 296, 303, 313, 317, 332, 335, 338, 342, 346, 347, 349
Atz, Jake, 130
Averill, Earl, 123, 143
Avila, Bobby, 305

Baer, Bugs, 81
Bagby, Jim, 120, 122

Bagby, Jim Jr., 152
Bahnsen, Stan, 288
Bailey, Ed, 210
Bakely, Jersey, 17
Baker, Bock, 69
Baker, Dusty, 270
Baker, Frank "Home Run," 84, 103
Baldwin, Lady, 22
Baltimore Orioles, 10, 11, 20, 22, 23, 35, 37, 38, 42, 43, 45, 46, 48, 49, 57, 130, 131, 198, 209, 214, 215, 224, 227, 236, 239, 242, 245, 249, 251, 253, 258, 262, 268, 286, 294, 296, 297, 300, 308, 323, 326, 327, 334, 338, 342
Bancroft, Dave, 132
Bankhead, Tallulah, 201
Banks, Ernie, 169, 202, 206, 207, 242, 244, 316
Bannister, Floyd, 334
Barker, Len, 338
Barnes, Ross, 7, 27
Barney, Rex, 186
Barnie, Billy, 43
Barr, Jim, 289
Barrett, Red, 187
Barry, Jack, 103
Barzun, Jacques, 231
Bassler, Johnny, 110, 127
Bateman, John, 245
Bates, Frank, 41
Bates, Johnny, 60
Bauman, Joe, 226, 227
Baxes, Jim, 213
Baylor, Don, 303
Bearden, Gene, 187, 213, 290, 345
Beaumont, Gerald, 24
Beaumont, Ginger, 72
Beckley, Jake, 45, 47
Bedrosian, Steve, 332
Beisser, Arnold, 350
Belcher, Tim, 338
Bell, Buddy, 346
Bell, Cool Papa, 140, 162
Bell, George, 316
Bell, Gus, 210
Bell, Jay, 314
Bell, Les, 120
Bench, Johnny, 275, 280, 283, 300, 320
Bender, Charles "Chief," 65, 88, 89, 94, 95
Beniquez, Juan, 278
Bennett, Charlie, 24

Index

Index

Index

Index

Index

Index

Index